To Rose   from Ethne & Graham
    Christmas 1984

To Ethne & Graham.
greatly appreciated, but as I cannot
read now, I am going to let you
read it and give me the highlights when
we meet, soon I hope.
        Love,
        Aunt Rose.

WE WALKED VERY WARILY

A History of Women at McGill

The Donaldas' First Graduating Class, 1888
Back Row: Eliza Cross, Martha Murphy, Blanche Evans *Middle Row:* Octavia Grace
Ritchie, Jane Palmer *Front Row:* Alice Murray, Georgina Hunter, Donalda McFee

WE WALKED VERY WARILY

A History of Women at McGill

by

Margaret Gillett

EDEN PRESS
WOMEN'S PUBLICATIONS
Montréal Canada

WE WALKED VERY WARILY
A History of Women at McGill
Margaret Gillett

Credits:
This book has been published with the help of a grant from the Social Science
Federation of Canada, using funds provided by the Social Science and Humani-
ties Research Council of Canada. *Cover Illustration:* F. Earl Christy, "College
Girl" Postcard, Rare Books and Special Collections, McLennan Library,
Design: J.W. Stewart, *Typesetting:* Vicky Bach and Molly Pulver, Hamilton.

ISBN: 0-920792-08-1
First Edition

Printed in Canada at John Deyell Company
Dépôt légal - troisième trimestre 1981
Bibliothèque nationale du Québec

Canadian Cataloguing in Publication Data

Gillett, Margaret, 1930-
  We walked very warily

Includes index.
ISBN 0-920792-08-1

1. McGill University - History. 2. Education of women - Canada - History. 3. Education, Higher -
Canada - History. 4. Women - Canada - Social conditions. I. Title.

LE3.M22G54   378.714'281   C81-094583-5

To the Memory of
Janet Alene Vickers Gillett

Table of Contents

List of Illustrations

i

ACKNOWLEDGEMENTS

Many people have shown great kindness and co-operation in providing and preparing the illustrations. Their help is gratefully acknowledged. Special thanks are due to Mrs. Esther England Cushing, Dr. Stanley Frost and Ms Susan Button of the McGill History Project, Mrs. Florence Tracy of the Royal Victoria College, Professor Helen Neilson, Dr. Gladys Bean, Mr. Marcel Cäya, Mr. Stanley Triggs of the Notman Photographic Archives, Ms Betsy Hirst and Ms Cynthia Taylor of the McGill Public Relations Office, Ms Charlotte Hussey of *The McGill News*, Mrs. Elizabeth Lewis and Mr. Garry Tynski of Rare Books and Special Collections, Dr. James Darragh of the Royal College of Physicians and Surgeons, Canada, Mr. Rolf Selbach and Mr. Jack Goldsmith of the Instructional Communications Centre, and Mr. Sean Huxley of the Educational Media Centre.

I would like to record my particular appreciation to Ms Pamela Chichinskas for her dedication in producing this book, to Mr. John Stewart, designer, for his patience and skill, and to Ms Sherri Clarkson of Eden Press Women's Publications for her faith in this work and her generosity in allowing so many illustrations.

M.G.

Preface

There are already several books and many articles which deal in various ways with the story of McGill, but *We Walked Very Warily* is the first attempt to write a full-scale history of women at this University. During the years of its preparation, it raised a fair amount of interest and comment, including much welcome encouragement. However, one quipster remarked, "So you're writing a history of women at McGill! What are you doing in the afternoon?" And, in a letter to *The McGill News*, a Vice Principal challenged the project, accusing it of reverse sexism, recommending that all history writing effort be concentrated on the two-volume general work then being compiled by Dr. Stanley Frost. The latter defended the idea of a history of women at McGill on the principle of specialized studies. He recognized that like the particular account of a department, or individual scholar, or research activity, the record of a specific group such as women could have a legitimate place in the historiography of an institution as complex as a modern university.

Then the question was raised as to whether or not this would be a "feminist" history, with the implication that, if feminist, then not impartial, perhaps not quite scholarly. The quality of the scholarship is left for the critic to judge, but I would have no embarrassment in acknowledging that this work is honestly feminist in that it obviously focuses on women and that it takes into account issues, events, personalities and accomplishments previously overlooked in the annals of McGill. Thus, like good feminist history, it tries to complete the cultural record which has so often omitted "the other half" of humanity or failed to take it seriously. This book is also to an extent a "revisionist" history, as it reinterprets some of the already recorded events and personalities of the past. Whatever the adjective, *We Walked Very Warily* is no mere rehash of previous works, nor is it an exercise in institutional hagiography. It is an account and analysis of the events and ideas connected with the education and work of women at McGill, together with a respectful recognition of some individual accomplishments. Unfortunately, it has not been possible to chronicle the contributions of all the noteworthy women associated with the University, but material aplenty has been found for another volume at some other time.

This has been a fascinating project to research and data have come from many sources—from official records in the McGill University Secretariat, the McGill University Archives and the Public Archives of

Canada; from McGill annual reports, minutes of meetings, and official statistics of various kinds; from campus publications such as *The McGill News,* the *Reporter,* the *McGill Daily* and earlier student journals; from personal letters, scrapbooks and all manner of memorabilia; from interviews with present and former students, professors and administrators; from newspapers, periodicals and even from those other histories. The claim is therefore made that, though this is indeed a specialized history, it is not limited or parochial in its outlook; it is not a case of special pleading. The developments recorded often involved the entire McGill community, the significant participants were the men as well as the women of the University, and the issues frequently transcended the boundaries of our campus.

Throughout the preparation of the book, I had invaluable support from a great many people who gave freely of their time, recollections and scholarly expertise. It was a special joy for me to meet some of the oldest living alumnae and to have had conversations with Rae Christie Mowat, B.A. '06, her sister Edith Christie Mowat, B.A. '07, and Esther Ryan, B.A. '06. Scores of other people of many vintages answered my questions, offered suggestions, supplied information and gave pictures. These included distinguished persons such as A. Vibert Douglas, Ph.D. '26, H. Rocke Robertson, Robert E. Bell, and the late Elizabeth Monk, B.C.L. '23, as well as people who, quite erroneously, considered themselves as "ordinary." To all of them, my grateful thanks.

In particular, I wish to acknowledge the interest and generous help of Stanley B. Frost, Director of the McGill History Project, and his cheerful assistant, Susan Button. I also greatly appreciate the perceptive and candid reading of the manuscript given by E. Andrew Allen, former Director of Information at McGill. My thanks also go to the personnel of the McGill University Archives, especially Archivist Marcel Caya and Assistant Archivist Robert Michel who were wonderfully patient; to research assistants who helped at different stages—Andrea Vabalis, Susan Gottheil, Sally Weary, Faith Wallis, the late Jeanette Rudolph, Kathleen O'Connor and Céline Guilbert; to colleagues who read all or parts of the manuscript and offered useful criticisms—Gladys Bean, Mildred Burns, Edward H. Bensely, Geraldine Dubrule, Kyre Emo, Joan Gilchrist, Michael Herschorn, Keith Jobling, Victoria Lees, Maysie MacSporran, Helen Neilson, Eigil Pedersen, and Kay Sibbald; to friend and neighbour, Muriel Roberts, who kindly helped with the final preparation of the manuscript.

My thanks are also due to Esther England Cushing, daughter of Octavia Grace Ritchie England, who supplied a great deal of material from her mother's era; Muriel Roscoe, Helen Reynolds, Mary Robertson, Donna Runnalls, and Florence Tracy, past and present

Wardens of the Royal Victoria College; to Phebe Prowse, daughter of Rosalie McLea; to the alumnae whose own memories appear in Chapter 6 and to Jessie Boyd Scriver, M.D. '22, who—as indicated in Chapter 7 —inadvertently supplied the book's title. I also want to pay special tribute to Isobel L. Wright, whose unflagging support sustained the project through all its phases.

Finally, I wish to thank George Flower, Dean of McGill's Faculty of Education, for his confidence in my work, and the Faculty of Graduate Studies and Research, the Social Science and Humanities Research Council of Canada and the Social Science Federation, without whose financial support this publication would hardly have been possible. I gratefully acknowledge their help.

Margaret Gillett

McGill University

Introduction

"What Would You Have a Woman Know?"

Many years ago, the serious question, "What would you have a woman know?" was put to Mrs. Malaprop, one of the classic comic characters of English drama. It is a good question which many people more profound than she have attempted to answer. Some of their responses have certainly not been very amusing for, what any society would have a woman know depends on what that society believes a woman ought to know. Sadly, some societies have thought that precious little would suffice.

Upon scrutiny, the apparently straightforward question, "What would you have a woman know?" veils many a tantalizing complexity so that the search for answers only reaches back to still more questions. Inevitably it will raise considerations of why a woman would want to know anything, or what use she would make of it. These queries in turn will lead to others such as "What is woman's role in society?", "What is the degree of woman's educability?" and finally to the fundamental question, "What is Woman?"

Throughout human history, Woman has been regarded in a dazzling variety of ways. In some cultures she was deemed a god and, in the Christian tradition, the Mother of God. Often she has been regarded as "the other," the outsider, assumed to be included in "Man" unless matters of privilege or power made such an assumption inconvenient. In Western society, she has been revered, respected, accepted, ignored and scorned. She has consistently been seen as "the weaker sex," the bearer of children, in need of protection, fragile on her pedestal, emotional rather than intellectual. She was assigned to playing supportive roles as helpmate, domestic servant or companion rather than allowed to take on dominant or assertive functions. She was the evil temptress, Eve, the whore, the sex object, or she was the very guardian of morality. Her image seems to have wavered with the whims of Man.

The basic question, "What is Woman?" underlies the history of women in general and thus it underlies the history of women in any particular context, including McGill. This question can be discerned very clearly in the 19th century when women's admission to higher

1

education was hotly debated and often coldly denied. It can be found at McGill with two almost archetypically opposite answers provided by two very important men, Principal J. William Dawson and Professor of Philosophy, J. Clark Murray. Principal Dawson defined Woman as "Lady"—wife, mother, homemaker—and accordingly believed her education should be largely cultural and given separately from men. Professor Murray defined her as "Person"—independent being and potential worker—and thus considered she should have access to professional education in the natural company of men.

The ramifications of the Lady/Person debate are found in the early chapters of this book, especially Chapter 4 which considers some of the long-smouldering arguments between Dawson and Murray. They also underlie the later sections. The academic consequences of the "What is Woman?" issue were not settled with women's admission to college nor even with the acceptance of co-education. They can still be found in more recent controversies such as the validity of Women's Studies. Whether acknowledged or not, they affect the manner and matter of female education as well as the terms of women's employment in the university and the wider community.

The chivalrous view of the Lady is undeniably charming but while it was being espoused by courteous gentlemen, the legal status of women throughout much of the 19th century was hardly gallant. According to British common law, which also applied in North America, women were classified with children, criminals and idiots. Upon marriage, women underwent "civil death"—marriage meant a man and a woman became one, and he was the one. Married women lacked control over their own earnings, could not choose their domicile, could not legally sign papers, bear witness, manage property or vote. Their husbands owned their persons, their services and any income derived from their work outside the home. Clearly, the "Lady" had her limitations.

One of the most significant consequences of the "Lady" definition of Woman in the context of education is that it places a taboo on certain kinds of knowledge. Not only are there certain ways in which a Lady may and may not behave, there are also certain things which she may not know. As the obvious example, in the Victorian era it was not considered meet and proper that the Lady should know about sex. This meant more than just the intricacies of intercourse, but also the social extensions of sex such as prostitution, venereal diseases and sexual slavery. Ultimately, anything unpleasant—thus, a great many aspects of the real world— must be kept from reaching her delicate ears, shaded from her sensitive eyes. By definition, a Lady did not know about perversions, violence or even such vulgar things as money. If she admitted to knowing about them, she was damning herself, lowering her own social status, forfeiting respect. Her embarrassment, her blushes might not save her, they might just give her away.

Hence, the Lady's reality was limited. Her opinion was accordingly based on partial information. Her judgment was therefore necessarily inferior. She could not defend herself, she could not argue for nor claim intellectual equality because she could not know what it was that she did not know. She could not even be a party to deciding whether or not she ought to know. Thus, even though she was high on the pedestal, the politics of ignorance kept her in her subordinate place.

Since the conventions of ladyhood dictated that she must never learn *all*, they clearly limited the amount and kind of education she might receive. The protective patriarchal ethic required that she not be exposed to any situation where there was even a risk of intellectual contamination. She should thus be shielded from the crassness of college life where, ideally, any subject might be explored to its limit. Pushed to its extreme, this argument held that higher education was unnecessary, inappropriate and even dangerous for the Lady. She would not require training for a profession in order to earn a living because she would be provided for; she must not encounter ideas which are in the natural domain of men; she should not be expected to learn about events, practices or conditions that might threaten her health, her well-being and, by extension, the health and well-being of her family and the community. For their sake, she must not bother her pretty little head about things that are best left to men.

Overcoming the taboo on knowledge would require enormous strength and courage as well as careful judgment in order that some desirable elements of womanhood might be maintained and combined with the reality of personhood. If this were to be done, it would have to be done by people who recognized the need, who had some inkling of the existence of the world from which they were being excluded, who therefore had some peripheral acquaintance with ideas. In other words, they must be people of the educated classes—the upper class or the middle class. Those who were Ladies by birth, the traditional nobility, the undisputed ladies of the upper class, were not particularly anxious to try to promote change. For them to do so would mean both destroying their protected, privileged status and denying their assigned identity. So it was the women of the middle class who accepted the challenge, ran the risks and pushed for higher education for members of their sex.

In so far as "ladylikeness" still retains an element of the traditional taboo on knowledge, it may be that the Lady and the Academic are incompatible. Since the ideal of the Lady has not disappeared from our society, this may help to account for a reluctance on the part of women to become deeply involved in the world of ideas, and partly explain the fact that in 1980 only about 14% of the academic staff in Canadian universities were women. The development of a symbiosis between Lady and Academic is still in process.

Another fundamental issue related to the question of the nature of Woman concerns the power of a dominant idea, the way in which a strong *idée fixe* determines attitudes and behaviour, regardless of whatever contrary evidence may be produced. This is apparent in the early chapters of this book, but it is also very obvious in Chapter 7 which deals with the intense struggle for women to be accepted into the traditionally male professions. Proved intelligence, ability, strength and courage had little effect against entrenched beliefs. As a prominent Canadian biographer wrote at the dawn of the 20th century, "... the man must be obstinate in his prejudices who disdains to acknowledge the need of the good of the reforms in female education that have begun to atone for the long injustice of the past. Of course, in the woman (as in the man) of genius there is an innate force that impels her to the attainment of what is essential for the fulfilment of her destiny."[1] Many of our grandmothers found their paths to intellectual and professional careers blocked by those who clung obstinately to the past.

Yet another broad concept basic to this work has to do with the nature of the history of education. A study of the status of women in education and society does little to reinforce a commonly held view that social history is a long record of steady, if gradual, progress. Rather, it suggests that change is not linear but is erratic; it is cyclic or perhaps spiral in form, with periods of growth followed by stagnation and regression during which the battles thought to have been won have to be refought. There are many dead ends and constant new beginnings which show that things are not necessarily getting better and better.

Even a cursory glance through Rashdall's celebrated *The Universities of Europe in the Middle Ages* will reveal that there were a number of women scholars and professors in the earliest days of formal higher education—but they seemed to disappear by the 18th century; just a slight acquaintance with social history makes it clear that the "Women's Liberation Movement" of the 1960's and 70's is not the first attempt to demand women's rights or to demonstrate women's abilities. However, the impetus and impact of previous movements have tended to evaporate unless vigorous attempts were made to preserve them. Thus, isolated achievements or fragile token gestures should not be mistaken for solid, on-going improvements. For example, McGill's appointment of Carrie Derick in 1912 as the first female full Professor at any Canadian university did not herald a significant innovative trend in McGill's employment pattern nor a thoroughly egalitarian attitude toward women. Indeed, in matters of co-education and the admission of women to Medicine, McGill lagged far behind Toronto and other Canadian universities. Inconsistencies have been part of the story of women at McGill and of Woman's progression through history.

Throughout the ages, the notion of what Woman is, has had a direct effect on what kind of education, if any, would be appropriate for girls and women. An astounding number of treatises has been produced on the subject, a few have become part of our common cultural heritage, most have lapsed into the limbo reserved for quaint ideas. As far back as the Golden Age of Greece, Socrates pointed out that to the extent that women were to participate in society, they should have the same up-bringing as men for, just as there was no difference in the training of dogs and bitches, so there should be no distinction between the education of male and female humans. This extraordinary idea did not survive into the Christian era. More typical was St. Jerome's advice recommending that a young girl should be taught the scriptures, reading, writing and domestic skills but "boys with their wanton thoughts" should be kept from her. The convents of the Middle Ages continued this tradition of segregated piety and literacy but in the homes of the wealthy, girls were sometimes schooled with their brothers though they were usually instructed in the gentle "maidenly" arts such as embroidery, painting and singing. Renaissance Humanists such as Erasmus and Thomas More envisaged utopias where education was equal for all and More even put some of his theory into practice in the advanced intellectual training he gave his daughter. Poullain de la Barre showed in *De l'Egalité de deux sexes* (1673) why she was convinced that an education identical in all respects would eliminate the inequalities between men and women, differences which were mostly caused by Society not Nature. Alas, Jean-Jacques Rousseau in *Emile* (1763) epitomized the prevailing view:

> A woman's education must be planned in relation to man. To be pleasing in his sight, to win his respect and love, to train him in childhood, to tend him in manhood, to counsel and console, to make his life pleasant and happy, these are the duties of woman for all time, and this is what she should be taught while she is young. (Book V)

Influential though he undoubtedly was, Jean-Jacques did not convince everyone. People like Mary Wollstonecraft held the other idea. In *The Vindication of the Rights of Women* (1792) she wrote:

To improve both sexes they ought, not only in private families, but in public schools, be educated together. If marriage be the cement of society, mankind should all be educated after the same model, or the intercourse of the sexes will never deserve the name of fellowship, nor will women ever fulfill the peculiar duties of their sex, till they become enlightened citizens, till they become free by being enabled to earn their own subsistence, independent of men. . . .

While Rousseau sentimentally exclaimed, "O how lovely is her ignorance!" Wollstonecraft scornfully questioned, "Why should they [women] be kept in ignorance under the specious name of innocence?"

In the approaching 19th century, Wollstonecraft's words were to gather more and more weight. That age of industrialization brought with it revolutions in ideas pertaining to both science and society. Darwin's theory of biological evolution was echoed in the social theory of Herbert Spencer and others. Thus, laws of nature and conditions of humanity previously deemed to have been eternally fixed by God were seen by new thinkers as evolving. They were both changing and changeable by human effort. Throughout that age, the growing demands for the democratization of social institutions meant cries for the abolition of slavery and child labour, the unionization of workers, universal suffrage including votes for women, and free, secular education for all children. Towards the end of that revolutionary century, Freudian psychology appeared on the intellectual scene and new non-theistic philosophies such as Pragmatism and Existentialism cast doubt on many old certainties. Insistence on higher education for women took root amid all this intellectual flux and social turmoil; it grew on a varied mixture of idealism and expediency.

In England, a Governesses' Benevolent Institution was formed in 1841 as an effort to provide some instruction for the numerous unfortunate young women of relatively "gentle birth" but straitened circumstances who had to earn their livings by tutoring the children of the well-to-do. This was not only intended to improve the quality of their work, but also their status and pay. The series of lectures thus began by the Rev. Frederick D. Maurice of King's College, London, developed into Queen's College in 1848 and in the following year Bedford College for Women was opened. Though these institutions accepted girls as young as twelve years of age as well as mature women, and did not attempt to vie for recognition as the equivalent of the colleges for men, they were at least a start. Further developments in London came in 1850 when the Mechanics' Institute opened two courses to women, while elsewhere Anne Jemima Clough and Josephine Butler promoted the North of England Council for the Higher Education of Women. This was another organization to provide academic and general lectures and, through its efforts, Cambridge University agreed in 1869 to provide a matriculation level examination for women. Five years later, when the examination was opened to men, it became the Higher Local Examination, and the informal lectures promoted by the Council merged into the Cambridge University Extension Scheme.

Relatively advanced cultural classes were thus available to some women in England, but that was not enough for reformers like Florence Nightingale, who asked, "Why have women passion, intellect and moral activity—these three—and place in society where no one of the three can be exercised?" Nor did second best satisfy Emily Davies who in 1864 had harassed the Taunton Commission, a government inquiry into the national state of education, until it agreed to include girls in its study. Davies' treatise on *The Higher Education of Women* (1866) scoffed at the different male and female occupations and "peculiarities," concluding that they were raised arbitrarily and demanding equal professional education for women. In 1869, an experiment in higher education for women proved successful when six young women rented a house in Hitchin, near Cambridge, and some of the foremost university professors gave their time and knowledge to prepare them for the Cambridge examinations. By 1873, thanks in part to Emily Davies, the venture had moved to Cambridge and was incorporated as Girton College. But it remained unofficial and peripheral, even though the professors were authentic Cambridge, the curricula identical, and the results often splendid. Indeed, during the 1880's the examination grades were spectacular, with women ranking very high in Classics and Mathematics, both considered male preserves. In 1890, Philippa Fawcett, a student of Newnham, another women's college, headed the Mathematics honours list, or in Cambridge parlance, "she placed above the Senior Wrangler." This indiscretion was sometimes blamed for Cambridge's reluctance to bestow its degrees on women and it was not until 1948— after the Second World War—that it relented and granted degrees to women on equal terms with men.

Meanwhile at Oxford, the wives and sisters of some of the dons tried to organize classes for women during the 1860's.[2] Though they had the help of some of the University men, the support was not sufficient to overcome centuries of tradition. Thus John Ruskin, who wrote so loftily about women as "queens," when asked to admit women to his lecture on Art sniffed, "I cannot let the bonnets in, on any condition this term." So that movement died, but a series of "Lectures for Ladies" was established in 1873 through the efforts of Mary Humphry Ward and other women, again with the encouragement of some prominent professors. Five years later, Dr. Edward Talbot and some friends established "a small hall in connection with the Church of England" for the reception of women desirous of availing themselves of the special privilege which Oxford offered for higher education. This became Lady Margaret Hall, named in honour of the pious and learned mother of Henry VIII. The following year (1879), Dr. John Percival opened the non-denominational Somerville College, named for Mary Somerville, an informally educated astronomer of great distinction whose paper on "Magnetic Properties of Violet Rays of the Solar System" had been read to the Royal Society back in 1826.

Both Lady Margaret Hall and Somerville were initially little more than residences but they gathered academic respectability and their students garnered the reputation of scholarship. They were supervised by the Association for the Education of Women (A.E.W.), which arranged lectures and tutorials, collected the academic fees and, until 1893, provided chaperones for the occasions when women were admitted to the regular lectures with the male students. For the most part, the women students took their classes in the A.E.W. hall (modest rooms over a baker's shop) and lectures were a repetition of instruction given to the male students by the same professors. Like the women of Cambridge, those of Oxford were "unofficially present." They too were denied the degree—though by 1894 all examinations including those in Medicine were opened to them. As the Chancellor, Lord Curzon, put it, "Oxford may be said to yield the reality while withholding the name."[3]

The issue of degrees for women was debated hotly over the years by members of the Oxford Congregation. One of the participants in that debate was the celebrated creator of "Alice"—Mathematics don, Charles L. Dodgson, alias Lewis Carroll. He showed some sympathy for those who deprecated the introduction into the ancient university of that "modern social monster, the He-Woman" and he thought the real way out from the "perplexity" would be for Oxford, Cambridge and Dublin to petition the Crown to grant a charter for a Women's University— whether the women wanted it or not.[4] Such a solution was never to be for, after due deliberation and in the aftermath of World War I, Oxford voted to admit women to its degrees. The decision was retroactive so that any woman who had ever qualified for an Oxford degree could now be eligible to receive one. Thus on October 14, 1920, at the first convocation admitting women, there were 549 of them to receive B.A.'s, M.A.'s or B.C.L.'s. At the women's first appearance, and again when they stood before the Vice-Chancellor, spontaneous cheers burst forth in the ancient Sheldonian Theatre and many long-deferred dreams were at last fulfilled. As for the other English universities—London had fully accepted women since 1878 and the institutions of the 20th century generally did so from the times of their foundation.

In the United States, higher education for women began a little earlier and ran a rather different course. It is generally acknowledged that the pioneer of female education in that country was Emma Willard, a Vermont teacher and dentist's wife. In 1819 she boldly presented to the New York State Legislature ''A Plan for Improving Female Education'' in which she claimed that women's education had been left to the mercy of private adventurers and so she sought government patronage for a superior female seminary. Though financial support proved limited, Willard opened her Female Seminary at Troy, N.Y. in 1821—the year in which McGill College was chartered. Her view of Woman's role was basically traditional—woman's true place was in the home. However, she believed that ''housewifery might be greatly improved by being taught not only in practice, but in theory'' and that it was important for the mothers of America to be educated since they would have the responsibility for the upbringing of future citizens. Furthermore, she thought that women should have ''real'' education for their own intellectual satisfaction. Following Willard's inspiration, Female Seminaries flourished, especially in the East, and by the end of the century about two hundred had been established. Though often derided as frivolous or intellectually inconsequential, the best of them, such as Mary Lyon's Mount Holyoke, provided rigorous instruction in academic subjects as well as ''finishing'' graces.

Other reformers, for example, Catherine Beecher, believed that women should have a professional as well as a domestic education. Her Female Seminary at Hartford, Conn., emphasized the preparation of teachers. Beecher saw that there was a national need for women as teachers in the common schools and that these teachers must be trained. Public ''Normal Schools'' for the training of teachers also began to appear from 1839 and they, too, took hold. Women were more readily accepted in teaching because it was an extension of domestic child-care, they received a fraction of the wages paid to men and, in any event, there were not enough men available for the amount of work to be done. But Normal Schools were not really colleges, either.

True higher education for women came a little closer when Oberlin College, Ohio, admitted four women to its degree course in 1837. However, even in that small, raw institution they were second-class citizens and were required as part of their ''education'' to perform some domestic work, tasks not demanded of the male students. Later, a diluted and abridged ''Ladies' Course'' was made available as an alternative to the degree programme. In the East, a few private institutions—

for example, Cornell in 1870—also admitted women on a co-educational basis, as did the State universities when they developed in the Mid-West during the 60's. Iowa, Wisconsin, Michigan and Utah were among the earliest of these. They tended to accept women, not just because of the free, frontier mentality and the democratic principles involved, but also because they needed the additional revenues women's fees would produce. As will be noted repeatedly in this study, economic factors have been crucial to the history of women's higher education generally and, specifically, co-education was often conceded in the Western States because the Legislatures could not afford to establish separate male and female institutions. It was pointed out that, granted higher learning should be made available to women, the only alternative to co-education for most institutions was poverty, and co-education was the lesser evil.

In 1861, with the founding of Vassar at Poughkeepsie, N.Y., academic education in a prestigious separate college became a possibility for women in the Eastern United States. Vassar, which actually began its classes in 1865, provided the model of intellectual quality to compare with the established men's colleges and it was soon followed by Swarthmore, Smith, Wellesley, Radcliffe, Barnard, Bryn Mawr and others. Though they were not always headed by women,[5] they did offer opportunities for women to achieve secure, high status positions in academe. For example, M. Carey Thomas, who had found Emma Willard's Seminary unstimulating and had passed through "the fiery ordeal" of co-education at Cornell, was President of Bryn Mawr from 1894 to 1922. Some of the élite women's colleges were located near "Ivy League" men's colleges, so that social contact with men was possible, but the administration and the instruction generally remained separate until the 1960's. These "co-ordinate" colleges provided a third alternative to co-education or completely separate higher education for women. This was true in other places as well and rarely was co-education fought and won on its pedagogic merits. On at least one occasion, co-education was recommended as a measure to reduce the incidence of masturbation and homosexuality among an all-male student body. That particular argument does not seem to have been raised at McGill, but the question of co-education was a major issue for several decades.

During the second half of the 19th century, the movement for women's education was apparent in most parts of the world—in Tzarist Russia, in the kingdoms of Europe and as far afield as colonial Australia. However, though widespread, it was by no means all-embracing and uniform. Some countries which appeared to place high value on formal education were still unwilling to extend the privilege to women, and a member of the Prussian House of Deputies disdainfully dismissed the matter with, "The world will not go to wrack and ruin if the women have to wait a little longer." On the other hand, some countries such as Switzerland, which retain conservative policies toward women even in the 20th century, made higher education available relatively early. The University of Zurich offered co-education at both the undergraduate and graduate levels in the 19th century and M. Carey Thomas received her Ph.D. from it in 1882. Philosophers, educators, writers, even poets continued to hold divergent views on the higher education of women. Thus, while Alfred Lord Tennyson envisioned an all-female university "with prudes for proctors, dowagers for dons and sweet girl graduates,"[6] Charles Kingsley counselled, "Be good, sweet maid, and let who can be clever. . . ."[7]

In Canada, colleges gradually began to open their doors to women for partial studies during the 1860's. Some of the country's most prominent educators, such as Egerton Ryerson, Chief Superintendent of Schools in Upper Canada, approved the sentimentalized tradition of grace and polish as the real education of ladies and opposed co-education, even at the grammar school level; others, such as George Ross, who became the Minister of Education in Upper Canada, believed young men and women should be educated together. Inevitably, there were lively debates. The first Canadian college to grant women degrees was Mt. Allison, Sackville, N.B. In 1875 it bestowed upon Grace Annie Lockhart a B.Sc. This degree was then the product of a three-year programme and was therefore less prestigious than the four-year B.A. Nevertheless, it gave Lockhart the distinction of being the first woman to earn a degree in the British Empire. Seven years later (1882), Mt. Allison conferred the first female B.A. in Canada upon Harriet Starr Stewart. The next year, it awarded Miss Stewart the first M.A.[8] In 1883, Victoria College (Cobourg, Ontario) became the first Canadian institution to award a medical degree to a woman when it graduated Augusta Stowe, M.D., C.M. Other institutions began to follow the lead and, one by one, the barriers fell. In 1884, Acadia awarded one female B.A. and Queen's two;[9] the next year, Dalhousie gave one and Toronto five; Trinity (Toronto) granted the first Mus.Bac. in 1886; and Manitoba and New Brunswick each bestowed one B.A. in 1889.[10]

McGill, which had watched with particular interest the unfolding developments elsewhere, graduated its first class of women in 1888. Though McGill was not the first in Canada, it was the first university in the Province of Quebec to accept women. The senior French-language universities waited until the 20th century to admit members of *la deuxième sexe*—Laval accepted them in 1910, l'Université de Montréal in 1915.

* * *

On the surface, it would appear that the higher education of women advanced inexorably once the movement got under way. However, the fundamental issues of the nature of Woman and Society remained as stumbling blocks and many other barriers, both flimsy and formidable, were erected in its path. Still, toward the end of the 19th century it was possible for an optimist to imagine that the crucial problems were solved. Thus, in his commencement address to Smith College in 1880, Daniel Coit Gilman, the President of Johns Hopkins University, pronounced:

> I am glad to believe that there are some points respecting the education of women which may be considered as settled in this age of Victoria. Nobody now questions,
> 1. Whether the male or the female mind is superior;
> 2. Whether women are to be allowed to have college education;
> 3. Whether women can earn their livelihood by congenial intellectual pursuits;
> 4. Whether women can control their own acquisitions; and finally, allow me to add,
> 5. Whether women are to assume the duties of men before men assume the duties of women.
>   The one question now most debated is this: What is the best education for women, and how shall that education be secured; or in other words, what shall our daughters study?[11]

If Gilman were guilty of the hyperbole commencement orations often produce, he had nevertheless identified some of the basic issues in women's education. Unhappily they were not as settled as he suggested, for, at best, society as a whole was still uncomfortably ambivalent about them. And his question, "What shall our daughters study?" has not found a definitive answer, even yet, though it has been raised time and again.

One clear-cut opinion on this perennial issue had been given in 1775 when Richard Brindley Sheridan's Mrs. Malaprop was asked, "What would you have a woman know?" and she confidently replied:

> . . . I would by no means wish a daughter of mine to be a progeny of learning; I don't think so much learning becomes a young woman; for instance—I would never let her meddle with Greek, or Hebrew, or Algebra, or Simony, or Fluxions, or Paradoxes, or such inflammatory branches of learning—neither would it be necessary for her to handle any of your mathematical, astronomical, diabolical instruments:—but . . . I would send her, at nine years old, to a boarding school, in order to learn a little ingenuity and artifice. Then, Sir, she

should have a supercilious knowledge in accounts; and as she grew up, I would have her instructed in geometry, that she might know something of the contagious countries;—but above all . . . she should be mistress of orthodoxy, that she might not misspell, and mispronounce words so shamefully as girls usually do; and likewise that she might reprehend the true meaning of what she is saying. This . . . is what I would have a woman know;—and I don't think there is superstitious article in it.[12]

Mrs. Malaprop's recipe is an almost perfect parody of the advice of Jean-Jacques Rousseau quoted above, and it serves not only to mock the frivolous nature of much of traditional female learning, but also to point to one of the sharpest weapons used against the serious education of women—humour.

In the 17th century, Molière had laughed at "Les précieuses ridicules" and "Les femmes savantes," for they were "bien loin de ces moeurs"; in the 18th century, Dr. Johnson compared the woman preacher and the dancing dog, thus creating one of his most quoted jests; and it was in this tradition of wit that in the 19th century Honoré Daumier established the classic caricature of the earnest, learned woman. His lampoons of those curious female creatures who filled their heads with inappropriate knowledge and garbed their legs with atrocious blue stockings turned into stereotype. "Blue Stocking"[13] became synonymous with the educated, independent woman and it was a term charged with negative overtones. The Blue Stocking was an object of scorn, derision, even pity. Mothers would teach their sons to avoid her, their daughters to fear her. She would be doomed to a sterile, lonely existence, unmarried and unmarriageable, for who would want an opinionated, strong-minded woman? Nothing could be worse. It was utterly unnatural. The sobriquet retained currency throughout the 19th century and was sometimes applied to the women of McGill. Just as one can now hear on campus the disclaimer, "I'm not a Women's Libber, but . . . ," so the early female students were usually at pains to deny they were Blue Stockings—Octavia Grace Ritchie, a member of the first class of women at McGill, did so in her Valedictory Address in 1888. The joke inevitably made educated women defensive.

Some inkling of what it was like to be a pioneer of higher education for women was provided by M. Carey Thomas (B.A. Cornell '75, Ph.D. Zurich '82) in an address to an alumnae group at Bryn Mawr in 1907. She recalled:

The passionate desire of the women of my generation for higher education was accompanied through its course by the awful doubt, felt by the women themselves as well as the men, as to whether women as a sex were physically and mentally fit for it. . . . I was always wondering whether it could be really true, as everyone thought, that boys were cleverer than girls. Indeed, I cared so much that I never dared to ask any grown up person the direct question, not even my father or mother, because I feared to hear the reply. I remember often praying about it and begging God if it were true that, because I was girl, I could not successfully master Greek and go to college and understand things, to kill me at once, as I could not bear to live in such an unjust world. It was not to be wondered at that we were uncertain in those old days as to the ultimate result of women's education. Before I myself went to college I had seen only one college woman. I had heard that such a woman was staying at the house of an acquaintance. I went to see her with fear. Even if she had appeared in hoofs and horns I was determined to go to college all the same. But it was a relief to find this Vassar graduate tall and handsome and dressed like other women. When, five years later, I went to Leipzig to study after I had been graduated from Cornell, my mother used to write me that my name was never mentioned to her by the women of her acquaintance. I was thought by them to be as much of a disgrace to my family as if I had eloped with the coachman. . . . [14]

Almost any woman who stepped out of the traditional domestic sphere was exposing herself to comment and criticism that ranged from good-natured "teasing" to cruel sneers of derision. Thus, a news item in the Albany, N.Y. *Register* in 1854 reporting on "the feminine proganda-nists of women's rights" noted that "the people were disposed to be amused by them, as they are by the wit of the clown in the circus, or the performance of Punch and Judy on fair days, or the minstrelsy of gentle-men with blackened faces, on banjos, the tambourine and the bones. But the joke is becoming stale. . . . " Stale or not, the joke seemed good for endless repetition. The Cologne *Gazette* in 1888 described how "in Berlin a great number of weary, grey, old women of scarcely thirty years creep about in the attempt at acquiring a man's education; all vivacity of feeling, all womanly emotions, and physical health besides has left them. Truly educated and cultured men avoid them, uneducated ones flee them, and the healthy natural women shun their society. Thus these girls stand like hermaphrodites between the two sexes."[15] Even England's humorist weekly, *Punch,* which often commented favourably on the educated "New Woman," also played the game with this "Nursery Rhyme for the Times," published in 1875:

Sally was a pretty girl
Fanny was her sister;
Sally read all night and day
Fanny sighed and kissed her.

Sally won some school degrees
Fanny won a lover;
Sally soundly rated her,
And thought herself above her.

Fanny had a happy home,
And urged that plea only;
Sally she was learned — and
Also she was lonely.

In Canada as well, the educated woman was too good a target for the humorist to ignore. McGill's famous Stephen Leacock often took a shot at her, even in the 20th century. In his essay on "Oxford as I See It," for example, he confessed that he found the presence of young women "flittering up and down the streets of Oxford" to be "very distressing" and he openly averred that "in all that goes with physical and mathematical science, women, on the average, are far below the standard of men. There are, of course exceptions. But they prove nothing. It is no use to quote to me the case of some brilliant girl who stood first in physics at Cornell. There is an elephant in the zoo that can count up to ten, yet I refuse to reckon myself his inferior." In "We are Teaching Women All Wrong," he said: "At McGill the girls of our first year have wept over their failures in elementary physics these twenty-five years. It is time that some one dried their tears and took away the subject."

For Leacock, the singular woman who did prove to be a scholar was, indeed, single. Inevitably she would be loveless, husbandless, childless. There was nothing new about this view. The lonely, learned spinster has constantly recurred in literature, debate and conversation about the higher education of women. In the late 19th century, the fear of educated unmarriageability was real and pervasive. It was taken out of the realm of folklore and placed firmly in the domain of science when Dr. Edward H. Clarke, with all the authority of his M.D. and a connection with Harvard at his command, published a book called *Sex in Education or A Fair Chance for the Girls.* It was an immediate best-seller, demanding a second edition in little more than a week after its original publication in 1873. Its widespread influence lasted for years. Clarke asserted that "The problem of Woman's sphere . . . is not to be solved by applying to it abstract principles of right and wrong. Its solution must be obtained from physiology, not from ethics or metaphysics.'' He concluded that women's physiology was simply not organized for the strain of ''brain work.'' Women were prone to overexcitement, they should be cautious about physical exercise and they should not be placed in competition with men. Co-education would be extremely harmful and could enduce neuralgia, uterine disease and hysteria—possibly to such an extent that the children of co-educated women might be born deformed. In short, the higher education of women, especially with co-education, would lead to a drastic national dilemma, it would lead to racial suicide.

No wonder Dr. Clarke's book was eagerly accepted or heartily condemned wherever it was read. Those who opposed Clarke's view could cite from their observation with counter-evidence of the many healthy young women who could be seen in schools and colleges in Europe and North America. At McGill in the 90's, the Director of Physical Education even showed that there was a positive correlation between high academic results and high athletic achievement among women students. Still, Clarke's extraordinarily popular book gave comfort and support to those who wanted to believe him.

Among these was G. Stanley Hall, the prominent American psychologist, whose works were also widely read and frequently used as texts in colleges and teacher training institutions. Hall cited the testimony of physicians and educators as he tried to show that girls' health, especially during menstruation, was adversely affected by education. He condemned current attempts to make women's higher education identical with men's because it ran counter ''to the proper supposition of motherhood'' and he encouraged every effort ''to keep the mental back and every method to bring the intuitions to the front.'' Other practitioners of the newly emerging Social Sciences found the health and marriageability of educated women a fertile area of inquiry. They compiled statistics comparing the marriage rates of college graduates and other women and showed, not only that the graduates' marriage rate fell far below the 80-90% national average for non-college women, but also those who did marry did so later and had far fewer children.

While an observer from France noted that in U.S. women's colleges, ''Flirtation decreases in proportion to the increase in culture,''16 researchers ''proved'' that colleges had the effect of separating out and attracting the ''non-productive type of woman who is more or less lacking in the normal sex instincts.''

Robert J. Sprague, a frequent contributor to the *Journal of Heredity*, showed that of the 959 Vassar graduates of the classes of 1867-1892 only 53% were married in 1915, and on average they had produced only

1.91 children each. The other élite Eastern women's colleges had similar records, though Wellesley's marriage rate was as low as 31%. Comparisons with male counterparts showed that approximately 76% of Harvard and Yale graduates married, while at co-educational Stanford, 73% of the men and 49% of the women who graduated between 1892 and 1900 were married within ten years. The marital record for the early women at McGill was consistent with this general picture. Supporters of higher education for women warned against the gross acceptance of such statistics, pointing out that social class, financial status and other factors must also be considered. However, such warnings were not necessarily noticed by parents in the often-emotional debates about the advisability of letting their daughters go to college; there appeared to be plenty of "scientific proof" to discourage the higher education of women.

In 1884—the year in which women were admitted to McGill's Faculty of Arts—*Punch* neatly summarized the principal anti-education arguments with these lines:

> O pedants of these later days, who go on undis-
> cerning,
> To overload a woman's brain and cram our girls
> with learning,
> You'll make a woman half a man, the souls of
> parents vexing,
> To find that all the gentle sex this process
> is unsexing.
> Leave one or two nice girls before the sex your
> system smothers,
> Or what on earth will poor men do for sweet-
> hearts, wives and mothers?

We may smile at gentle "Punch"—after all, it was just meant as a joke—but almost a century later we still need to be wary of his arguments. Even though college marriage (and divorce) rates have certainly climbed in the interval, some women are still not quite sure that their heads really should be "crammed with learning." Contemporary social scientists, building upon the work of Martena Horner, have identified among many of the "nice girls" in North American colleges a diffidence that amounts to a fear of success. The motive to avoid success is not confined to women but it does seem to occur more frequently among them, just as general expectations for female success in certain spheres remain lower. The patronizing phrase, "You do very well, for a woman . . ." can still be heard on campus. Lower expectations give women a perfect "out" if they choose to take it. Those who do so and those who have qualms about succeeding are probably still victims of the fear of the old Blue Stocking. Deep down, they believe that it is just "not right" for a woman to triumph over a man; they still see Woman as the subordinate member of humanity; in the extreme, they may be among those whom an Australian poet identified as—

> Talented girls who found the disgrace
> Of being a woman made genius a crime.[17]

Other women have managed to escape this major curse and have learned to ignore the many subtle "put downs" they encounter and to overcome grossly discriminatory rules, regulations and practices. Many of the women of McGill, both pioneers and moderns, have been women of this kind, women who had the determination (without apology) to achieve their full intellectual potential, or, at least, to give it the good old college try. In that process, few felt any special need or urgency to be hostile to men. Indeed, they appreciated the essential help and encouragement some men gave them. They satisfied themselves that it was not, after all, impossible or aberrant or evil that they should read Greek, or study Medicine, or solve some of the problems of Nature. They knew there was an extremely fine line between their firm insistence on their own intellectual competencies and the gentle social behaviour with which they felt more comfortable. They knew the line was there and they walked it very warily.

Part I

ADMISSION

Chapter ONE

The Principal and the Paradox

McGill College received its royal charter in 1821, just a couple of years after the publication in New York of Emma Willard's "A Plan for Improving Female Education." Of course, these two events had no connection with each other. For one thing, in the early 19th century education influences reached Lower Canada chiefly from the east—from Nova Scotia and across the Atlantic rather than from the south; and for another, there was absolutely no concern on the part of the founders of McGill for the higher education of women. These gentlemen had plenty of other problems with which to grapple, as the story of the origins of the institution shows.

James McGill was a wealthy Montreal fur trader and businessman of Scottish origins who died in 1813 at the age of sixty-nine, a "venerable and respectable citizen who had long and deservedly filled the most elevated stations in his community."[1] He had left a will in which he bequeathed his farm of forty-six acres known as Burnside and the sum of £10,000, a part of his fortune, for the establishment of a college to bear his name. There was at least one significant condition attached to this bequest, namely that the college should be built within ten years of his death. Though it revealed a canny understanding of contemporary political and social realities and the proclivity toward procrastination, this proviso was to be the cause of considerable pressure, frustration and, eventually, litigation. The will stipulated that if the conditions were not met, the property would revert to the benefactor's heirs.

Ten years may seem to be an adequate span of time just to begin a college, especially given the prospect of property and funds, but it was not excessive in this case. Indeed, there was a very real possibility that the bequest might be lost; since the heirs considered they had sufficiently strong grounds to challenge the claim of the college they took their complaints as far as the supreme legal authority, the Privy Council in London. This serves to highlight the fact that part of the difficulty in getting the college started, and certainly a contributing factor to the delay in its effective operation, was the fact that the Canadas were still very much colonies, so that sanction for all significant actions had to be obtained from England. This complicated an already complex specific situation and delayed educational development in general.

Up to the time when James McGill died there was no institution of higher learning for English-speaking people in Lower Canada. There were a number of French language seminaries throughout the province but some of these had belonged to the Jesuits and were closed when the Society of Jesus was suppressed by the Pope (Clement XIV) in 1791. Their property was confiscated by the colonial government and moneys from the Jesuit Estates were used for a variety of purposes, including some support for schools. However, in James McGill's day, there were even relatively few lower schools. Those that did exist were either private enterprises or were run by religious groups and the general lack of education was a matter of serious concern. Both officials and socially aware English-speaking citizens such as James McGill saw the need for education as a means to help amalgamate the English and the French peoples, to spread Protestantism, and to prevent young men from seeking collegiate education elsewhere—especially in the United States where they might be exposed to subversive republican ideas. Over the years, a number of attempts were made to establish government supported schools, committees were struck, reports were written. But both enthusiasm and purpose came to naught until Bishop Jacob Mountain's forceful intervention. Mountain summed up the situation as he saw it in 1796:

> It is well known that the lower orders of the people in this Province are for the most part deplorably ignorant; that the very slender portion of instruction which their children obtain is almost entirely confined, amongst those who do not live in the Towns, to the girls alone; and more especially, it is notorious that they have hitherto made no progress towards the attainment of the language of the country under which government they have the happiness to live. This total ignorance of the English language on the part of the Canadians draws a distinct line of demarcation between them and his Majesty's British subjects in this Province, injurious to the welfare and happiness of both; and continues to divide into separate peoples those, who by their situation, their common interests and their equal participation of the same laws and the same form of Government, should naturally form but one. If the evils are confessedly great which arise from this want of a community language, it should seem expedient to endeavour to provide an immediate remedy for the defect, and it should also seem that this can only be done by facilitating as much as possible the means of acquiring the English language to the children of the Canadians. The plan which I would beg leave to submit for this purpose is simple and I trust practi-

cable. . . . It is briefly this: That a certain number of English School Masters, to be hereafter determined, should be employed and paid by the Government; that one of these should be placed in each of the cities and towns, and in the most considerable villages for the purposes and under the express obligation of teaching the English language gratis when required, at an easy rate; that Trustees or Commissioners should be appointed to manage the fund which the Government in its bounty may see fit to appropriate to this end, to determine the number of masters that may be required, the respective salaries, and the number of children that they shall respectively teach gratis, to fix the rate at which Writing and Arithmetic shall be taught on, and to have the power of removing the Masters for incapacity or neglect of Duty, and of promoting them successively to the more lucrative situations for able and meritorious conduct.[2]

Mountain's forthright ideas on language and education make interesting reading in the light of the late 20th century socio-political happenings in Quebec. In their own day they were very powerful and led almost directly to the passage in 1801 of an Act to Establish the Royal Institution for the Advancement of Learning. The Royal Institution was to be the administrative body for a rationalized, province-wide network of schools, from elementary to post-secondary. These schools were to be set up in every parish where the local people requested them, but authority for them rested not with the local people but with the Governor who appointed members to the Institution, nominated teachers, and approved the location of schools. It should be noted that this system, though highly centralized, was voluntary and also allowed existing private and religious schools to continue. While it met increasing opposition from the Roman Catholic hierarchy, at its peak in 1829 the Royal Institution controlled 84 schools where the language of instruction might be either French or English and the profession of faith either Catholic or Protestant. However, the importance of the Royal Institution in this context is not that it offered a partly-realized opportunity for a democratic, state-supported school system; the significance here is that it was to be the body entrusted to set up a college under the terms of James McGill's will. Indeed, the legislation providing for the Royal Institution had encountered general dissatisfaction and had languished from 1801 until 1818 when it was implemented specifically so that McGill's generous bequest would not be lost. Yet five years had then passed since the benefactor s death; the college had to be established in the next five or the money and the Burnside Estate would revert to the heirs and remain forever out of reach.

Delays continued. The Board of the Royal Institution for the Advancement of Learning was to be appointed from London. That required time. Thus, the Royal Institution did not really begin to function until 1820 and the charter it drew up for the college did not receive royal approval until 31st March, 1821—a date now recognised as McGill University's official birthday. This charter provided for the establishment of a University or College "for the Education of Youth in the principles of true religion and for their instruction in the different branches of science and literature." The governing body was to be composed of the Governor and the Lieut.-Governor of Lower Canada, the Lieut.-Governor of Upper Canada, the Bishop of Quebec, the Chief Justice of Upper Canada and the Principal of the College; and had the authority to make all the rules governing the College, to make appointments and to determine salaries; there were to be four Professors and "such Fellows, Tutors and Scholars as the Statutes of the College may provide for"; the Principal and the Professors were to be elected by the Governors but the Crown reserved the right of approval; the Governors, Principal and Fellows constituted a body politic and corporate in deed and in law which might sue and be sued as well as receive such benefactions and donations as might be given to it. The provision concerning the ability to sue and be sued was put into effect long before any of the professors were appointed or the first students enrolled.

In 1820, James McGill's heir, François Desrivières (who was Mrs. McGill's son by a former marriage), had refused to hand over the Burnside estate to the Royal Institution. And so began a series of protracted and expensive lawsuits which taxed the energies and persistence of the Trustees and the Governors for years to come and which were not finally decided until 1835. Meanwhile, on June 24, 1829, McGill College was officially inaugurated even though it was not ready to begin to function as an institution of higher learning. At that time it had no students at all and the appointment of its four professors was only a paper formality. Life was brought to this most theoretical of colleges by "engrafting" the Montreal Medical Institution which was an organization set up in 1822 as the teaching wing of the new Montreal General Hospital. However, it found that it was unable to obtain a charter to grant degrees, and thus existed a situation in which the Medical Institution had four professors, some students but no charter, and McGill College had a charter, legal authority to appoint four professors, but no students. The mutual benefits of amalgamation were obvious, the practical difficulties were overcome and the Montreal Medical Institution became the McGill Faculty of Medicine. It continued as McGill's only Faculty until 1843 when Arts at last came into being.

Anyone who believes that life was simpler in "the old days" might consider the wheelings and dealings, the court cases against the heirs, the institutional wranglings with Bethune, the second Principal, who would not vacate Burnside House, the politics of language and religion, the pressures of time, the difficulties of communications, the financial worries and the brushes with bankruptcy during McGill's first forty years. A full and fascinating account of all this may be found in Stanley Frost's *McGill University*.[3] Only the barest outlines have been sketched here, but these should be sufficient to show that McGill University did not have a quick and easy birth and that the people involved in the project had a great many problems with which to contend. Higher education for women, a relatively rare and dubious innovation, was not among them. It was not even contemplated.

Around mid-century, after this contentious, shaky if well-endowed beginning—the College began to flourish under an amended charter and the robust guidance of its fifth Principal, John William Dawson. It was during Dawson's regime of almost forty years that women were admitted to McGill, and it is therefore important to know something about this man and his ideas.

Dawson, the son of Scottish immigrants, was born at Pictou, Nova Scotia in 1811. He was brought up in a pious family atmosphere and grew to share his father's deep religious convictions, his keen love of

McGill College (c. 1860)

nature and his attraction to books. Young William's interest in rocks and fossils was encouraged at Pictou Academy by the pioneering educator, Thomas McCulloch, and his knowledge of natural sciences was later extended by lectures at the University of Edinburgh. His first job was in his father's bookselling business in Pictou, but he maintained his scientific interests which led to the publication in 1855 of *An Acadian Geology.* This, the first of many works, brought some of the new scientific thinking of Europe to bear upon the geology of Nova Scotia and received a good measure of international acclaim. Meanwhile, Dawson had accepted Joseph Howe's invitation to become the first Superintendent of Education for his province. This very demanding position, in his own words, required that he "act rather as an educational missionary than in a merely official capacity," convincing the population at large of the virtues and necessity of education. He toured the province, examined the inadequate state of the schools and drew up a master plan for a thorough-going instructional system. His "grand plan" included ideas on curriculum reform, the efficient management of schools, and the establishment of a normal school for the preparation of teachers. Though he was not yet thirty and very strong, the strain of this work proved great and, after suffering a severe fever, he resigned.

However, it was not long before he was again involved in educational matters, this time as a member of the New Brunswick Commission examining the future of King's College, Fredericton. This assignment gave him an opportunity to consider seriously the nature of higher education and the place of the college in society. The experience was to prove of fundamental value when, in the summer of 1855, he was appointed Principal of McGill.

His educational views can fairly be called enlightened for their time. He believed in the advantages of a classical education yet he was convinced that the curriculum should be adjusted to accommodate new scientific knowledge as well as the North American environment. A good deal of his thinking was conventional, yet there was clearly a progressive, even romantic, element in it. He saw nature as both a source of scientific law and a source of wonder and awe. He believed that the benefits of higher education might be spread more widely and considered that there was no necessity for the imposition of religious tests for admission—a tradition to which the ancient universities in England still clung. And he held that women had a capacity for education. Such opinions were enlightened, but not revolutionary—perhaps they could best be classified as "orthodox liberal." Dawson did not have to wage a lonely campaign in attempting to implement them. They were consonant with the positions taken by leading educators of the mid-nineteenth

Principal J. William Dawson, 1859

century—for example, Egerton Ryerson in Canada, Frederich Froebel, Johann Herbart, Emily Davies, Matthew Arnold in Europe, or Henry Barnard and Francis Parker in the United States. Most importantly, Dawson's views were compatible with those of the public-spirited men who comprised the Board of Governors of McGill. This basic harmony of view on many of the fundamental educational issues contributed very positively to Dawson's career at McGill and enabled him to exercise leadership without fear of administrative friction.

In addition to the Principalship, John William Dawson was given the Chair of Natural History and Chemistry and such was his energy and ability he was able to continue his productive scholarship. The range of his interests and level of productivity may be deduced from the titles of some of his publications: *Arachaia, or Studies on the Cosmogony and Natural History of the Hebrew Scriptures* (1858), *Breathers of the Coal Period* (1863), *Handbook of Canadian Zoology* (1870), *Report on Silurian and Devonian Flora of Canada* (1871), *Report on the Geological Structure of Prince Edward Island* (1871), *Science and the Bible* (1874), *The Dawn of Life* (1875), *Origin of the World* (1880), *Fossil Men* (1881), and *Links in the Chain of Life* (1882). It is clear from these how Dawson's interest in science and religion converged, but if the titles suggest he had an evolutionary approach to the universe, they mislead. With steady conviction Dawson maintained a staunch belief in the Biblical explanation of the origin of life and he rejected Darwinism. This philosophical orientation inevitably had far-reaching consequences, especially, as we shall see, for his attitude toward women.

Dawson's preoccupations with scientific research and administrative duties consumed most of his waking hours so that in his Nova Scotia days he complained that he "had no time to keep up acquaintances with anyone." He liked people and while he was studying in Edinburgh he had met a young woman with whom he was very much impressed. Margaret Mercer was then seventeen. On his return home, he began a long and increasingly personal correspondence with her.

William Dawson's letters to Margaret Mercer reveal a strong but considerate person who wanted to share his vigorous interests with a sympathetic companion. He wrote frequently and fully, giving her accounts of his daily life in Nova Scotia, discussing some of his ideas, revealing his values. He sent her gifts—in September 1841, "a few curios from Nova Scotia," including a rocking chair, a box, a basket with porcupine quills; on another occasion, magazines, preserved strawberries and cherries, plus moccasins which she pronounced "too gaudy for everyday wear!" "I prefer to keep them," she said, "for a drawing room curiosity and as an additional remembrance of the donor."[4] His letters were warm, more ardent than hers. In July, 1841, he wrote:

I have not, as you see, sufficient Patience to wait for an answer to one letter, before writing another. . . . Yet I have nothing of importance to tell you, even about my constant subject—myself, except that I have been so busily employed in my old occupations that I have scarcely any time even for a week. . . . Perhaps if you were here I should make a greater effort—But this is what you used to call flirtatious. . . . If you were here now you might have loads of flowers and fruit and bright blue skies such as you seldom see. . . . When you write, be sure and do not let the distance which separates us cause you to be more distant in your written than in your spoken conversations. It has, at least, no such effect on me. . . . [5]

His "written conversations" with her were serious, respectful, romantic and sometimes didactic. On one occasion he sent her *Alcott's Young Woman's Guide,* not because he thought she required anything of the kind, "but as a specimen of a class of books, even more abundant in America than they are in Britain, and whose object, that of improving society by raising the character of women, is a good one, whether the mode which they adopt be the best or not. Alcott is one of the most popular of this kind of writer in the U. States, and I believe most of his opinions on matters of health and education are correct though some 'ornaments' for example may be extreme. Let me know what you think of it. . . . If I had time I would perhaps write more, but it would only be sentimental, philosophical or sheer nonsense, so it is no great loss."[6]

On another occasion he wrote:

I have now the pleasure of sending you a few stuffed birds,[7]—which I hope you will accept as tokens of my remembrance and gratitude. . . .

He then gave her detailed instructions as to how to unpack them and set them up so that their tails and beaks would be properly mounted but, he conceded, "the butterflies and moths may be placed anywhere you choose." He then proceeded to give her a few hints respecting the habits and character of her "guests" and identified No. 1 as "the hummingbird, with its ruby throat and emerald back. . . ." After a poetic description of the bird and its habitat, he confessed that he shot it himself and "when I saw the poor fellow lie bleeding among the grass, I felt as if I had been guilty of a very bad action." After he had commented on each specimen in turn, he took the opportunity to note that:

My birds may afford one more lesson, pleasing at least to me that, as birds of passage return each year to their native lands, so absent friends may meet again. . . ."[8]

William Dawson and Margaret Mercer did meet again because, as he told her, "It has, as you know, been a dream of mine that our fates might be connected."[9] He said that he knew the fulfilment of this dream "was improbable and that I had much to do before it could even be possible, and therefore scarcely dare to hope much with regard to it." But his dream took him back to Edinburgh, he wooed her once more in person, and they were married in 1847.

Mrs. Dawson was probably with him in October 1855 when the new Principal first saw McGill. He doubtless needed her reassurances as he surveyed that discouraging scene described in his autobiography:

> Materially it was represented by two blocks of unfurnished and partly ruined buildings, standing amidst a wilderness of excavators' and masons' rubbish, overgrown with weeds and bushes. The grounds were unfenced, and pastured at will by herds of cattle, which not only browsed on the shrubs, leaving unhurt only one great elm, which still stands as "the founder's tree." . . . The only access from town was a circuitous and ungraded cart-track, almost impassable at night. The buildings had been abandoned by the new Board and the classes of the Faculty of Arts were held in the upper storey of a brick building, the lower part of which was occupied by the High School.[10]

Elsewhere he described the little brook which ran through the campus and to which the McGill estate owed the name "Burnside," noting that along the brook there was a certain amount of coppice of thorn, young birch and alder, but so cropped by cattle and broken by "juvenile ramblers" that it presented a very unsightly appearance. But he added, "To me and my wife the improvement of the grounds was a congenial task."[11]

If physically McGill College was unprepossessing, academically it was not much better. There were three Faculties—Medicine, Arts and Law—with a total of about seventy students and a teaching staff of twenty-two, "only one of whom was exclusively devoted to the work of his professorate."[12] From this inauspicious beginning, Dawson worked to build an institution of international reputation.

Until his retirement in 1893, John William Dawson strove to secure the financial foundations of the college, to beautify the grounds, to expand the building programme, to appoint professors of merit, to govern wisely, to improve methods of teaching, to attract students. Withal, he taught Natural Science himself, studied, wrote and published. His family life appears to have been solidly happy, his five children a source of satisfaction, and his church a continuing inspiration. In brief, he grew to be the patriarch of both home and college, the

Margaret Mercer Dawson, 1866

eminent Victorian whose prodigious energy and many accomplishments commanded the respect of his colleagues and the love of his family, and whose contributions to science and education were recognised with a knighthood in 1884. Indeed, Sir William Dawson was honoured many times, perhaps none more movingly than in 1892, shortly before his retirement, when his portrait painted by Wyatt Eaton was formally presented to McGill. For that occasion, a laudatory ode was composed by Mrs. Wyatt Eaton. It was read, not by the lady herself, but by Professor Henry Bovey, and its sentiments must have been echoed by many in the audience:

Sir William Dawson

Kind face, and voice that hath a sound so true
That from the first all confidence can win,
High forehead, many-lined, and firm, strong chin,
And eyes of pale and tender Scottish blue—
That mildly, sweetly, subtly look you through,
As if all flesh and raiment were too thin
To veil from them that secret casque within,
Or turn the calm directness of their view.
    I saw thee standing in the vestibule,
One day in April, when the sprouting land
Was loud with bird-joys—as we came away
Oh, that I, too—thought I—could sing to-day,
For I was happier that I clasped thy hand,
Oh, noble master of a noble school.

* * *

Included in the ''noble master's'' multifarious interests was the matter of the education of women. This was an enduring concern, but by no means was it a championing of sexual equality. Rather, Dawson believed that male and female intellectual capacities were different and that male and female social roles were distinct, divinely assigned, eternal and without much conflict or even overlap. From his Scottish heritage he was undoubtedly exposed to John Knox's view that ''Woman in her greatest perfection was made to serve and obey man, not to rule and command him. . . . After her fall and rebellion committed against God . . . she was made subject to men by the irrevocable sentence of God.'' Though he clothed it with kindness and gentility, Dawson's social philosophy was consistent with that traditional view of Woman. Woman's nature was different from Man's. Woman should therefore have a different upbringing, one that was "suitable to the cultivation or development of the powers inherent"[13] in their beings.

Ideally, so Dawson believed, all education should provide for symmetrical growth, "the various capacities inherent in the pupil must be developed . . . in such a manner as to produce a perfect and harmonious form." It follows logically then, that if women and men are basically different, the symmetrical development of their inherent capacities would require different treatment. "The constitution and physiological habitudes of woman—her excitable nervous temperament, and special liability to be unduly stimulated by emulation, love of approbation, and shall I say ambition, to undue exertion—should be taken into account in every system of education for women."[14] Likewise, there should be a "difference in the manner of teaching suited to the differences in the mind and character between the sexes, and to the different spheres of society and professional action open to women."[15]

In the Nature vs. Nurture debate, one of the great intellectual controversies of his time, Dawson stood firmly on the side of Nature. Scientist though he was, he rejected the Darwinian theory of evolution and its social consequences. This had very significant implications for his attitude toward the education of women, as did the fact that his world view was based on his literalist approach to Christianity.

In a fairly extensive and generally favourable commentary on Dawson when he was host to the British Association for the Advancement of Science in 1884, a contemporary reporter noted, "He still clings to the pre-Darwinian philosophy, and stands in the fore-front of the opponents of the new school. Many of his fellow workers are impatient with him for this, but among the people his fame has become greater on this very account, not a few regarding him as the champion of their faith against what they believe the most gigantic and rampant heresy that has exercised the world since the time of Moses."[16] For Dawson, the basic rules of nature were laid down by God and therefore a truly Christian society must respect the divinely accorded needs and functions of men and women. Women had an important place in the scheme of things, even if "the world has yet to see the full blessings of the ministry of Christian women,'[17] and he believed the "highest possible culture for women is necessary if we would be more than half civilized."[18] This need for general culture did not mean they should have professional training. From Dawson's point of view, "if women must be prepared for permanent professions it is because the world is out of joint." He conceded that the Christian system allowed "women to engage in useful avocations" but ordinarily they were to be "sustained in the privileges of domestic life by their male relations."

Dawson would claim that his insistence on "difference" would not necessarily mean that women were inferior. Quite the contrary. Women were special creatures who had to be protected by men. His argument was essentially the kind of benign patronizing so many women through-out the ages have found difficult to detect and impossible to dispel. The appeal lies in the compliment. The effect of this approach can be seen quite clearly with respect to education.

Dawson thought that every educated person, man or woman, should have acquaintance with mathematics, chemistry and logic "which alone can support any sound knowledge of nature, or adequate culture of the powers we must employ in order to gain the mastery of the world around us, and occupy our place therein as the image of God." He said the "great practical difficulty is the right teaching and proportioning of these studies" and he would not "bespeak for women precisely the same education in these pursuits accorded to our young men in our exist-ing colleges, but something better." [19] The idea of "something better" may appear very attractive, even flattering, to the intended benefici-aries. However, the practical difficulties associated with "something better" were bound to be so great and the delay in waiting until "the time was right" was sure to be so long that the "something better" might never even be attempted. Thus it might well become an empty illusion, lip service, hypocrisy, an ideal always deferred, always out of reach.

Similarly, Dawson said that woman's profession was "the highest in the world—that of wife and mother—the high priestess of the family, earth's holiest shrine—the rule of the well-regulated household, which is the sole possible basis of any sound morality and true prosperity—the wise and thoughtful regulator of all those social reunions, charities and benevolences which make life so agreeable." [20] This idealistic concept of women's work may have had some relevance for the ladies of the upper classes but it completely ignored the working women of the "lower orders." [21] How unrealistic for a pragmatic man of action like John William Dawson. Yet this position was very typical of the liberal Victorian patriarch and its acceptance was a fundamental requirement for the women in his family and social environment. Dawson was, according to his lights, a kindly person, but he was not a radical social reformer; he was a thinker, but not a profound philosopher; he was a doer, as his many real accomplishments show. He did not question the received values of his church and so he rejected some of the most creative scientific thinking of his day; he did not seriously question the class system which kept the lower orders in their place nor the caste system which kept women in theirs.

John William Dawson was clearly not a misogynist, in many ways he was a humanitarian; he was in fact a formidable representative of the respectable, conservative element of his times and his liberal opinions were always tempered by that. His views were shared by many of his contemporaries, including two influential Canadian educators— Egerton Ryerson, Ontario Superintendent of Schools and Daniel Wilson of University College, Toronto. Both these gentlemen were Dawson's friends, and if they did not help form his point of view they certainly must have reinforced it.

Principal Dawson spoke and wrote a great deal about the education of women—probably more than any other principal of McGill, before him or since. He was sensitive to the fact that this was one of the significant social and pedagogic issues of the 19th century. However, it is noticeable that he said very little about the education of his wife or of his three daughters. Yet it is known that both Margaret Mercer Dawson and Anna Dawson Harrington served as his amanuensis or secretary, in a sense subsidizing his work, providing an invaluable domestic milieu that made his professional accomplishments possible. Lady Dawson, fondly called ''my dear partner'' on public occasions, was also frequently mentioned in McGill publications as receiving guests, presiding at teas, or helping to host the ''At Homes'' which Sir William gave for his students. She was also a founding and active member of the Montreal Ladies Educational Assocation.

The Dawson women were intelligent, literate people and like the male members of the family they took real interest in the important issues of the day, including the question of female education. None of them attended college, nor were they entirely convinced that formal higher education was a good thing for women. However, while they basically accepted the conventional mores that assigned them inevitably to supporting roles, they sometimes chafed at the restrictions of their lot. Like her husband, Margaret Mercer Dawson was a believer in the traditional family and her sense of duty to her own kin had at least partly contributed to the length of their epistolatory courtship. Still, she was a woman of spirit who had married despite her family's lack of enthusiasm. A flash of that spirit showed during the correspondence with William Dawson. Her letter of August 1842 read in part:

> Dear friend:
>   . . . I must allude to a sentence in one of your letters, you say that my letters are beautifully written, is this intended as a compliment? recall to your recollection a remark you have made to me when you were here—that good writing was the sign of a little mind. I am not given to carping and criticizing much, but I could not help smiling when I read it, I knew you did not apply it in such a sense to me although had you been honest you would. . . .
>
>   Adieu for the present
>   Margt. A.Y. Mercer [22]

Dawson was probably rationalizing when he made the connection between good writing and a little mind—his own hand was often all but indecipherable—and her neat letters do not disguise her ability to think. In another example, she not only gave a clear portrayal of her everyday existence but also called into question her part in it:

My dear friend

Whitewashing season has again returned with all its accompaniments of rubbing & scrubbing & moving & polishing, as graphically described by Chambers in one of his papers.—& "all desolate & lonely" have I worked till the very points of my fingers are aching. Painters and paperhangers have been my most frequent companions for the last week. We have got the diningroom papered & have removed our sittingroom to the sunny side of the house, also the nursery, alias my room, which is a decided improvement.—Well, after all, you lords of the creations are rather enviable as otherwise: you adopt a business or profession, & by giving due attention to it you become professionals. But woman! hurries from one occupation to another seldom gets above mediocrity even in the commonplace routine of ordinary duties.—I know that it is not intended we should ever enjoy that extent of capacity or strength of judgment which you do, but still by better training we might surely be made more fit companions for you. If in anything we excel it is surely in the quickness of our perceptions, & in conversation; for this last we get little credit—it proves too frequently a source of annoyance. "I cannot help thinking that those who make a display of their own imperfections, are only angling for praise"; says Gray—You must not think this my motive when I say, judging from my own mind & observation of others, I believe nearly half of woman's existence is spent in a sort of dreary consciousness—ideas floating across her mind, without one being definitely arranged or followed out. But what was my starting point?—Whitewashing! & how has it led me into such a train of thought as to make a comparison between the mind of man & woman? I had better leave off, before dipping too deep in a subject too abstract for me to follow out. . . .

Yours very sincerely
Margaret A.Y. Mercer 23

And it is interesting to see how modestly, or how cleverly, she couched her complaint about the lack of education accorded her and other women: "I know that it is not intended we should ever enjoy that extent of capacity or strength of judgment which you do, but *still by better training we might surely be made more fit companions for you.*" Given her feelings on this matter and her husband's professed interest in women's education, it seems incredible that their daughters should have to voice similar complaints about lack of training. Many years later, Anna wrote to her brother, Rankine:

> What is your opinion of college education for girls? I am clear it is not well as a universal application, but I have always myself felt very inferior to you boys in mixed groups, with accurate working knowledge, & recognise the secure powers in the able women who have had the college course. Now, I think my mind is just as good in quality as most & has a clearness & an easy perception ahead of most & yet it has been of comparatively little use, because of lack of training.[24]

The problem of lack of intellectual training which bothered both Margaret and Anna Dawson might so easily have been overcome by Sir William if his belief in education for women had been as strong as his faith in the divinely ordained family, or perhaps if his public educational credo had been fully applied to his private life. But his views on female education were clearly tempered by those on the feminine social role, and since this was always to be helpmate and dependent, formal intellectual development for women was not absolutely necessary. Neither his wife nor his daughters were apparently able to break through the barriers of convention and his formidable will. Margaret Mercer must have anticipated this, for in one of the most perceptive of her early letters to him she said:

> My dear friend,
>   . . . each time I sit down to write to you I have to wage war against my extreme timidity or want of self-confidence. I am its unwilling bondslave, having a strong desire to be free but without the moral courage necessary for striking off its fetters. . . . Many thanks for the sketch of your everyday existence which comfort[s] me a little & brings you nearer the capacity of a social companion instead of the esteemed but unapproachable philosopher whose image . . . reigns over instead of participates in my pleasures. . . . [25]

It would appear that even as a young man, even before his public prominence, William Dawson was able to inspire awe. As the highly respected Sir William he must, indeed, have been imposing.

However, this "esteemed but unapproachable philosopher" was to be approached in the spring of 1884 by a small band of undaunted graduates of the Montreal High School for Girls. They were boldly seeking admission to McGill. Although they were well qualified academically, they were debarred from higher education because they were female. They knew this and they knew Principal Dawson's august reputation. They must also have known that Dawson had given support to the idea of education for women, so their supplication was well worth a try. There was a chance of success, for who could say whether the Principal's advocacy of education for women or his belief in their traditional role would win the day. Would it be the liberal reformer or the conservative Dawson who would hear their plea? They were to come face to face with the paradox of John William Dawson, the Principal who held some of the most profoundly conservative beliefs but who was instrumental in facilitating some of the most forward-looking changes at McGill.

Chapter TWO

The First Steps

The *Prospectus* of McGill College for 1884-85 came back from the printer in July 1884. There was nothing unusual about it, not a word to indicate that 1884 would be a historic year at McGill, no hint that women were about to be admitted to the student body. Yet, what was unanticipated in July was a reality in October. By then, women had been accepted as undergraduate students in the Faculty of Arts. This happened quite dramatically and suddenly, but not without preliminary manoeuvering. There were at least ten clearly distinguishable steps which preceded women's acceptance as McGill students. One of the first and most far-reaching of these preliminary events can be traced to the early years of Dawson's principalship. This was the founding of the McGill Normal School, which took place just two years after Dawson arrived in Montreal.

It will be remembered that as Superintendent of Education in Nova Scotia, Dawson had recommended the establishment of a Normal School in that province. He genuinely believed in the necessity for teacher preparation if the general standard of education were to be raised. This kind of thinking was shared by educators in Montreal and elsewhere. Indeed, the founding of teacher training institutions was one of the significant trends of 19th century education and was related to the democratization of society and the spread of mass public instruction. This occurred in Europe, the United States, Canada and other parts of the "civilized world." In this country the earliest training institutions were set up in Nova Scotia and Canada West (Ontario) and the movement had the support of influential people such as Governor General, Sir Edmund Head and Pierre-Joseph Chauveau, Superintendent of Schools in Canada East (Quebec). Education in Canada West was at that time undergoing basic transformation and modernization, thanks to the energy and vision of the renowned Superintendent of Schools, Egerton Ryerson. William Dawson visited Ryerson during the Christmas vacation of 1855 and found him more than willing to give advice on educational policies and procedures.[1] So it happened that Dawson's concern for teacher training was shared by leaders outside McGill and also found support from the Board of Governors and others within the College.

In January 1857, an order-in-council called for the establishment in Lower Canada of two French-Catholic and one English-Protestant Normal Schools. Dawson hardly expected to have the principalship of the latter added to his growing responsibilities but, when the McGill Normal School opened in March that year, Dawson not only had to direct the new establishment, he also had to teach Natural Science there. The Normal School was operated by McGill on behalf of the Province and was not an integral part of the College's academic programme. Its association with McGill was intended "to enable the pupil-teachers to derive such benefits from the university as its large means of education allow it to offer."[2] The purpose of the Normal School was to "give a thorough training to male and female teachers."

The entering class totalled 52, of whom 44 were young women of about 16 years of age, who held certificates of character and conduct, knew the rudiments of grammar and arithmetic "as far as the rule of three" and had some knowledge of geography. In his opening address, Principal Dawson expressed his satisfaction with the quality of the students. He said he had hoped more men would have enrolled, but he attributed the initial paucity of males to the fact that there was hardly sufficient time to recruit them, especially since there were "so many avenues of more lucrative employment" than teaching. He seemed unembarrassed to acknowledge that the McGill Normal School was "practically a professional college for Women" and he approved regulations that with some minor exceptions applied equally to both sexes. The rules said: "There shall be no intercourse between male and female pupil-teachers while in school, or when going to, or returning from it." However, since there were so few men, joint classes of men and women were acceptable.

The work of the Normal School, a major contribution to the historical development of education in the Province, proceeded without particular complication. By 1870, when Dawson handed over the direction of the School to William Henry Hicks, he had had more than a dozen years of satisfactory work in the instruction of young women and equally lengthy experience in the administration of a programme with predominantly female students. There is no evidence that he found the students wanting or that he had any problems with mixed classes. This is important to note, in view of his later objections to co-education in the Faculty of Arts. The acceptability of co-education at the Normal School was probably more related to the low social status of teachers generally than to any liberality of viewpoint on his part. The Victorian ethic which Dawson upheld was clearly class-related. It placed women of the upper echelons on pedestals while it consigned lower class women to factories and mines—and schools.

Despite the prevalence of honeyed words about the importance of teachers, teaching has historically been an occupation of low wages and low prestige. During the 19th century it became "feminized" in much the same way factories and shops did—by employing "working women" and paying them less than their male counterparts.[3] When Dawson and other Victorians wrote about the higher education of women or about the nature of Woman, they did not have in mind these working women who fended for themselves in a male-dominated world; they were thinking of "ladies" who had to be protected in the sanctity of the home. The basic dichotomy of their thinking tends to absolve them of the charge of intentional hypocrisy, but it does not alter the inconsistency of their behaviour toward persons of the female gender. This helps explain why there was a gap of 27 years between the establishment of the Normal School and the admission of women to the Faculty of Arts, and the even longer wait before co-education was fully accepted at McGill.

McGill Normal School, Belmont St., Montreal

* * *

The history of the Normal School indicates that Dawson was not unwilling to teach young women. Indeed, there is some evidence he even enjoyed it. This was shown again in a second step toward higher education for women. In the early 1860's an arrangement was made for the pupils of a private girls' school to attend Professor Dawson's McGill lectures in Natural Science. The school was headed by Hannah Willard Lyman, a person of both intelligence and enterprise and who later was appointed first Lady Principal of Vassar College, N.Y. There is some confusion as to whether Miss Lyman made the request to the Principal or whether he himself took the initiative and invited the girls to come to his afternoon lectures.[4] In any event, he welcomed these new students, the first females to attend actual McGill College classes, though they were not, of course, formally enrolled. They might fairly be considered Dawson's guests. There was plenty of room for them, and since his regular class numbers were small and the lecture room was relatively large, propriety could easily be maintained by having the young ladies sit in a separate part of the hall. Any unseemly conduct would have been discouraged by the fact that Miss Lyman or other teachers always accompanied the girls.

It appears that the whole arrangement was successful, but there is also some confusion about how long it lasted. Dawson said ''one session''[5] but in a letter from Côté House dated April 2, 1863 which accompanied a gift of some ornaments of Canadian gold, Miss Lyman thanked him on behalf of ''the young ladies, teachers and pupils who have had the delight and profit of your instructions the last two years. . . .''[6] It seems that Dawson's memory may have been at fault here and perhaps also when he accounted for the termination of the arrangement with the explanation that, ''No difficulty, so far as I know, arose, but the experiment was in some respects unsatisfactory, so after the experience of one session, it was tacitly dropped by mutual consent.''[7] The girls' attendance at his classes might have been merely inconvenient for the school or it might simply have ceased because Miss Lyman went off to Vassar. In any event, the episode showed that Dawson was willing to lecture to young ladies and that they could sit in the same classroom as young gentlemen with no particularly disastrous consequences.

Indirectly, Hanna Willard Lyman was to make yet another contribution to the cause of higher education for women in Montreal. After her death in 1871, a number of her former students decided to establish in her memory a fund for the promotion of education of young ladies. They apparently appealed to Principal Dawson for advice on the best way to proceed and he drafted a memorandum suggesting (1) a lectureship for ladies, with the lecturer to be approved by the Board of Governors of McGill College, (2) a money prize or bursary to be awarded annually by

Hannah Willard Lyman

the McGill Corporation[8] or the Protestant School Commissioner to the best pupil in, say, English and History or Natural and Physical Sciences, (3) a gold or silver medal for the best pupil. Dawson noted, ''Either of the above would not only be a proper tribute to Miss Lyman, but of great service in the promotion of the higher education of young ladies. It might encourage the promotion of ladies' classes and would in any case stimulate the preparation of the higher classes in the ladies' schools and introduce a system of examinations for young women similar to that now so useful in England.''[9]

Dawson indicated that he preferred the idea of a Lectureship, but the final decision was to establish a scholarship or prize for ''students of any non-denominational College for Ladies in Montreal, affiliated to the McGill University or approved as of sufficient standing.''[10] The fund was to be held in trust by the McGill Board of Governors until such a college was established. Meanwhile, the interest was to be used as prizes (''books, properly inscribed'') in connection with the Montreal Ladies' Educational Association (M.L.E.A.).

The establishment of the Hannah Willard Lyman Prize, which is still offered by McGill, was a third aspect of growing interest in female education. A fourth was the founding of the Trafalgar Institute. This was frequently mentioned by Dawson as one of the preliminary steps toward the admission of women to McGill, but it was probably more by way of a detour than a direct path.

In 1867, Donald Ross, a wealthy Montrealer of Scottish extraction, drew up a will which included elaborate plans for a residential school for girls. His intention was ''to do the greatest amount of good possible in educating the female sex, or young girls.''[11] His school, the Ross Institute, was to serve a hitherto neglected segment of the population, girls from 14 to 18 years of age, people who had very little with which to occupy their minds between elementary school and marriage. Its purpose was ''to qualify young persons for discharging in the best possible manner such duties as ordinarily devolve to the female sex.''[12] There were clearly specified class and religious restrictions on the ''young persons,'' however, for Ross stipulated that ''pupils shall belong, not to the lower ranks, but to the families of the respectable and middle ranks,'' while preference in scholarships would be given to the daughters of Presbyterian ministers.

The lady principal, who was to receive a salary of £400, was to be ''not only the head of the house, but the prudent, loving and anxious mother of the girls.'' It was thought best if she were ''a married lady . . . free from the encumbrances of a young family,'' but all the teachers were to be ''unmarried ladies or widows and have their homes in the Institute over and above their salaries,''[13] which ranged from £150-200.

The school as a whole was to provide an atmosphere that was "an imitation of a well-governed house or household, where ladylike behaviour, unselfish consideration of others, quiet, gentle courtesy are made the prevailing influences." In short, this was to be a highly conventional institution to prepare girls for their traditional roles. Any connection with higher education was tangential rather than direct, general rather than specific, for the Ross Institute was not designed to break new ground nor to lead its graduates on to college.

The school was inaugurated in 1871, not as the Ross Institute but as the Trafalgar Institute. The name was altered to maintain the historical association of the "Trafalgar" property on which the school was to have been situated.[14] The Trustees included, along with Donald Ross and seven clergymen or representatives of Protestant churches, "J. William Dawson, LL.D., Principal of McGill College and his successors in office." However, six months later, before the Institute was yet functioning, Donald Ross died. Since his estate did not amount to the $400,000 Ross had deemed necessary for the project and, despite the fact that the Trustees published the will in an attempt to solicit additional funds, it seemed as if the elaborate plan would die with its originator.

Rescue came in 1883 when James Barclay, the new minister of St. Paul's Presbyterian Church, prevailed upon a wealthy businessman, Donald A. Smith, to donate $30,000 to the cause. Donald Smith's intervention was both timely and crucial here as it was to be later at McGill. His contribution, together with a handsome bequest of $16,000 by Miss Ann Scott,[15] "a maiden lady of this city," made it possible for the Trafalgar Institute to begin its work in 1887 in "a commodious residence on the mountainside" surrounded by one and a half acres of lawns and gardens. The "highest talent available in Montreal" was to be employed as teachers but, in accordance with the prevailing tradition of 19th century Canadian education, the important posts were filled by people from Britain—Miss Woollan, the first acting Principal, had taught German in a "large ladies' school" and in "high families in England," while Miss Grace Fairley, the first Principal, hailed from Edinburgh. Miss Fairley admitted to being "a Scot bristling all over with prejudices," but a contemporary newspaper found much to praise in her and the way she ran the school. The reporter noted, "Her soft brown eyes, and her smile which haunts you not because it claims a self-attracted homage, but because it centres its homage in you, indicates that the prejudices are as firm as the granite of her native land for all that is good, and as solid against the un-good as are the oaks of her adopted land."[16]

At first, the enrolment at the Trafalgar Institute was small—only three boarders—but by the second year there were 20 as well as several day girls. In those early years, Trafalgar did not aspire to provide young women with preparation for university entrance. In the words of its prospectus, it aimed at "the higher intellectual culture" but did not want "the ordinary duties of home life" to be overlooked. Its focus was to maintain the role of woman as chatelaine, not scholar. It may be conceded that through its general concern for female education and its slight connection with Dawson, it provided a frail link in the chain of events that brought women to McGill.

*　*　*

The Trafalgar Institute was a private school. Its public counterpart was the Montreal High School for Girls, a sixth and very significant development. If higher education for women was to be something more than a curiosity or a privilege of the élite, it would need to have the strong foundations provided by quality secondary education accessible to all girls.

The Montreal High School for boys had been established in 1843, incorporated with the University a decade later. By 1871, the idea for a parallel girls' school was discussed by the School commissioners. The usual "practical difficulties" kept it from serious consideration until February, 1874 when Dawson, as a member of the Protestant Board of School Commissioners, raised the matter again. It then received such a favourable hearing that a committee of three, including Dawson himself, was appointed to recommend a site and a plan of operation for a girls' high school. The committee was swift and positive in its work, presenting its report in a few weeks but, again, delays occurred. Finally, a decision was made to set up temporary classes in rented rooms and to hire a lady principal, Miss L.H. Scott, and four teachers, all graduates of the McGill Normal School. This decision was made in May, 1875[17] and the Montreal High School for Girls began its work in the fall with an attendance of 149. This was a very creditable enrolment for such an innovative scheme, especially considering that at the boys' High School, which had then been operating for 32 years, there were only 188 pupils. A comparison between the first year enrolment at the public High School for Girls and the private Trafalgar Institute (149:3) is also instructive as an indicator of the way in which questions of cost deferred or depressed educational opportunities for women. It seems obvious that many young women were merely waiting for schooling they could afford.

The new school was an undoubted success. In just two years it had prepared seven young women, including Dawson's daughter Eva, for

School Examinations of McGill University.

Senior Certificate for Women.

The Governors, Principal, and Fellows of McGill College hereby certify that

Mina Douglas

from *The High School Montreal.*

has passed the Examination prescribed by the University for Candidates for the title of Associate in Arts, in English Grammar, Reading, Dictation, Arithmetic, British History, Geography,

With creditable answering in Latin French, German, Geometry, Algebra, History, Advanced Geography, English Literature,

And is thereby entitled to receive a

Senior School Certificate

of this University.

In witness whereof, the undersigned have hereto set their hands and the Seal of the University, at Montreal, this *eighth* day of *June* in the year of our Lord one thousand eight hundred and seventy seven.

C. D. Day. L.L.D. B.C.L. Chancellor

J.W. Dawson, LL.D. F.R.S. Principal

William T. Leach D.C.L. LL.D

Geo: Cornish L.L.D. Ex. in Classics

T. Darey M.A. B.C.L. Ex. in French.

C.H. McLeod Markgraf M.A. Ex. in German

Alex'd Johnson M.A. Ex. in Mathematics.

Robert Laing M.A. Ex. in English

Wm Craig Baynes. B.A. Registrar.

The First Diploma Ever Awarded to a Woman by McGill, 1877

the University School Certificate Examination. Not only did they do well academically, but their conduct was excellent and Miss Scott was able to testify to "their uniformly lady-like demeanour."[18] Ladylike or not, they were Montreal High girls who, in 1884, were bold enough to beard Principal Dawson in his office and ask for admission to McGill. Over the years the school was to supply the university with a great many excellent students. The quality of teaching and learning at the Montreal High School for Girls proved quite clearly that women were capable of intellectual effort, yet this was a proof that had to be demonstrated again and again. Eight years after the school's opening, a Montrealer named Thomas Dirling presented the City Council with a petition complaining about the severity of the competition which was "causing excessive pressure on the brains of both teachers and pupils" and steps were thereupon taken to make honours courses optional and to "remove all strain, mental or bodily, that might be supposed to arise from overwork."[19] Perhaps such measures were justified—as they might also have been at the boys' High School—but they suggest the reservations many parents still felt in exposing their daughters to "hard" learning.

Undoubtedly, there was considerable stress associated with the university entrance examinations. Established by Dawson in 1875 and administered jointly by McGill and Bishop's College, Lennoxville, these exams were intended to serve as Province-wide admission standards. Boys who passed in Latin, Greek, Algebra and Geometry were regarded as matriculated in the Faculty of Arts and those who took Senior Certificates became "Associates in Arts of the University" (A.A.). After two years of being open exclusively to males, the exams were opened to "Boys or Girls, under 18 years of age, from any Canadian School." Now young women were able to take the tests, but they were still denied admission to college. This did not appear to affect their performance and they soon proved that they were as scholastically competent as their brothers.

In the 1877 examinations (the first which girls were permitted to take), there were ten successful female candidates and fifteen male. The results were ranked in order of their aggregate score and, while boys filled the first three places (and the last two), Mina Douglas, a graduate of the Montreal High School for Girls, came fourth. Other girls, all pupils from Montreal High or the Collegiate Institute, Hamilton, did well. Nine of them got "creditable mentions" in French, Geometry, Geography, and English Literature; in addition, half or more received "creditable mentions" in Latin, German, Algebra, and Scripture. Mina Douglas had "creditable mentions" in all nine subjects—but what became of her? In 1877 she was not admissable to McGill or Bishop's and, though she would have been accepted at the Normal School, her

name does not appear in those records. Miss Douglas had the distinction
of being recognised by Principal Dawson as the first member of her sex
to receive a formal certificate from McGill University, but this apparently did not help her further an academic career—at least, not in the
Montreal area.

Being permitted to take the examinations was a seventh step in the
progress of women toward higher education, but it must have seemed a
grudging, "cat and mouse" kind of concession. Women were now
tantalizingly close to McGill, but they were still not inside. We have a
glimpse of what it felt like to be in that situation in a memoir by one of
those early high school graduates. Some fifty years later, Octavia Grace
Ritchie wrote of those days:

> For five consecutive years, a small group of school girls had passed
> from grade to grade, and, in the autumn of 1883, had entered
> the final class and were being prepared for the ordeal of the A.A.
> examinations the following June. Their record had been high
> throughout, and they looked forward to ranking well in the final
> tests. There was a rude awakening. The disconcerting discovery was
> made that in the curriculum, as arranged for the girls, Greek had
> been entirely omitted and German provided as an optional substitute
> for another subject. Thus they saw themselves deprived of the
> chance of 1500 marks, which was open to the boys of the sixth form,
> and there seemed no hope of surmounting such a handicap.[20]

Simply by the way that the rules were structured, the girls could never
equal the boys.

The situation seemed impossible, yet the girls from Montreal High
were still willing to try. Octavia Ritchie had spent two years at school in
Germany and so she found it relatively easy to brush up on her German
and to take the examination course in that subject. The Head Girl of the
school, Rosalie McLea, who was obviously as brilliant as she was determined, undertook to study Greek. She was tutored by George Murray,
the Classics master of the boys' school, in the formidable task of
covering three years of Greek in one—and that one, the year of the final
school examinations.

When the results appeared in June, 1884, even Principal Dawson
was impressed. He called them "an event unexampled in our previous
connection with the school examinations of the universities." Rosalie
McLea's and Octavia Ritchie's names were at the top of the list and the
other girls did well. Even more astounding, Rosalie had come first in the
Province in Latin and Greek and had the highest total marks on record!
Yet, if all this effort, enthusiasm, and dazzling proof of women's intel-

50

STANDING IN THE EXAMINATIONS, 1884.

No.   ASSOCIATES IN ARTS.

4.	Rosalie McD. McLea (Girls' High School, Montreal),	1300	Marks.
8.	Octavia G. Ritchie (Girls' High School, Montreal),	1179	"
15.	John L. Day (High School, Montreal),	1111	"
44.	Charles R. Hamilton (Bishop's College School, Lennoxville),	1028	"
46.	Henri G. Joly (Bishop's College School, Lennoxville),	987	"
29.	James E. Le Rossignol (High School, Montreal),	976	"
27.	Charles B. Gordon (High School, Montreal),	943	"
23.	Charles J. F. Martin (High School, Montreal),	939	"
7.	Hellen R. Y. Reid (Girls' High School, Montreal),	907	"
45.	Wm. C. G. Heneker (Bishop's College School, Lennoxville),	903	"
47.	Edward A. Robertson (Bishop's College School, Lennoxville),	839	"
55.	Mary E. E. Hunt (Waterloo Academy),	802	"
48.	Charles C. Smith (Bishop's College School, Lennoxville),	781	"
5.	Alice J. Murray (Girls' High School, Montreal),	770	"
9.	Jessie W. Stewart (Girls' High School, Montreal),	768	"
41.	F. H. Pickel (Cowansville Graded School),	760	"
53.	George R. Kinloch (Lincoln College, Sorel),	754	"
2.	Emily C. Forbes (Girls' High School, Montreal),	749	"
20.	W. Archibald H. Kerr (High School, Montreal),	703	"
54.	George Lyman (Lincoln College, Sorel),	696	"
19.	Alexander M. Jeffrey (High School, Montreal),	690	"
6.	Lillias S. Molson (Girls' High School, Montreal),	641	"
1.	Hattie W. Bennett (Girls' High School, Montreal),	631	"
31.	John Paterson (High School, Montreal),	627	"
32.	Robert H. Reid (High School, Montreal),	625	"
43.	Edmund H. Duval (Bishop's College School, Lennoxville),	614	"
18.	Walter L. Jamieson (High School, Montreal),	610	"
36.	Reginald D. Dyer (High School, Montreal),	538	"

JUNIOR CERTIFICATES.

3.	Frances H. Hadley (Girls' High School, Montreal),	701	"
52.	Arthur L. Crawford (Lincoln College, Sorel),	622	"
30.	Alexander F. Mitchell (High School, Montreal),	526	"
49.	Frederick A. Stabb (Bishop's College School, Lennoxville),	466	"
51.	Minnie M. Howe (Hatley Academy),	458	"

The "Unexampled" Results of 1884

lectual capacities was a matter for wonder, it was still not quite enough. Women had been permitted to study for the examinations, even encouraged, but they were still prohibited by virtue of their sex from going any further.

* * *

In a summary of the moves made toward the acceptance of women as members of the McGill community, Principal Dawson noted, "It is inevitable that our progress should be by fits and starts and somewhat unequal, thus lacking that majestic uniformity which we see in Nature. . . ."[21] An example of this lurching toward the inevitable is found in what came to be called "Dr. Wilkes' resolution," though credit should have gone to the Chancellor Judge C.D. Day and Mr. John Dougall. It was a promising, but ultimately abortive, effort to admit women to McGill.

Early in 1870, the Board of Governors, having, as Chancellor Day put it, "long felt the inadequacy of the pecuniary means of the University,"[22] made a public appeal for endowment money. As a result, a meeting attended by friends of the College was held in the library in February to discuss the development and funding of McGill. Judge Day mentioned the idea of higher education for women. Mr. Dougall, a McGill graduate (B.A. '60, M.A. '67) and editor-owner of the liberal newspaper, *The Witness*, later elaborated on this. He resolved that a committee be appointed to "consider the propriety of making provision for higher female education, in connection with McGill University, in order to supply a great and much felt want in the community and to aid the present subscription for a permanent endowment."[23] He said that he had attended the Vassar College commencement the previous summer and had seen a class of ladies graduate with as high attainments as those of the regular universities, and he grieved that Canada offered no such advantages. He further noted that the existing facilities at McGill could "be used for both sexes with little or no increase of expense," adding persuasively that "they were as far as concerned one sex, running to waste." He thought that McGill could maintain its reputation by throwing open its doors to women, as the University of Michigan had done. He was convinced that the public mind was "ripe for this change" and its popularity would greatly aid the fund drive. The Rev. Dr. Henry Wilkes, Principal of the Congregational College, a member of the McGill Corporation, and son-in-law of Chancellor Day, said he was prepared to second Dougall's resolution, provided it was referred directly to McGill, rather than to a committee. So it happened that, after some procedural niceties, Dr. Wilkes resolved and Mr. Dougall seconded the following motion:

> This meeting rejoices in the arrangements made in the Mother
> Country and on this Continent, to afford young women the opportu-
> nities of a regular College course; and being persuaded of the vital
> importance of this matter to the cause of Higher Education and to the
> well-being of the community, respectfully commends the subject to
> the consideration of the Corporation of the University for such action
> as the expected addition to the Endowment may enable them to
> take.[24]

The time certainly seemed propitious for this resolution. It passed
unanimously and the fund drive raised almost $58,000.[25] Some of this
money was earmarked for special purposes—for example, Jane
Redpath's gift of $1,667 was specifically for an exhibition in Arts, and
Peter Redpath's $20,000 was to endow the Chair of Natural Philosophy.
Even though Dawson was correct when he said "no part of these sums
was . . . specially devoted to the education of women,"[26] there still
should have been some money to take initial steps toward implementing
the "Wilkes' resolution." Chancellor Day must honestly have expected
this to happen, for at an entertainment in honour of the donors he made
a speech in which he devoted more time and emphasis to higher education for women than to any other issue, and it was clear that this was
specifically one of the purposes of the fund-raising campaign. He said in
closing:

> There is no surer evidence of the degree of . . . education, which is an
> essential part of the Christian civilization of a people, than the social
> position of its women. And it is for the enlargement of the means of
> furthering this great objective, of vital importance to both sexes and
> all classes, that the University has made its appeal for sympathy and
> succour.[27]

Nothing could be clearer than that last sentence. But despite this and
despite the Chancellor's recognition that McGill was "woefully behind
the age," nothing happened. Why? Was there a breach of faith?

From an objective 20th century viewpoint, categorically, Yes. A
clear resolution concerning a new path for the University was passed
unanimously; funds were sought to implement that resolution; money
was raised; no effort was made even to try to implement the resolution;
the money was all spent for other ends. That such a misappropriation of
funds could occur without risk of protest was only possible because the
intended benefactors of the new programme, women, were powerless
and therefore could safely be ignored.

From a 19th century patriarchal viewpoint, no serious wrong was
committed. A resolution was passed, funds raised, and then the money

was used for the real purposes of the University—the academic and professional education of young men. The resolution about women was not a serious or binding one and no harm could possibly be done by ignoring it. Indeed, it was a far better thing to have attempted to develop the University proper, than to dissipate scarce funds on peripheral matters such as the education of women. If women were to have higher education, this would happen all in good time. The time was not ripe, the money was needed for other ends, and the public were not ready for it.

Pragmatically, as Dawson claimed later, there may have been no female applicants to McGill at that time. But what a very lame excuse! There might well have been applicants if the University had given them any sign of encouragement, if arrangements had been made to admit women—just as the 149 pupils appeared almost over night when the Montreal High School for Girls was opened only five years later. It seems incredible, given the evidence of public and corporate support, a mandate which virtually necessitated action, and Dawson's professed interest in higher education for women, that the Principal did not push for it. Why did he miss such an excellent opportunity?

There is no evidence that the "Wilkes' resolution" was brought to the Corporation to which it had been directed—at least, there is no record of it in the Minutes. When the results of the endowment drive were reported at some length in January, 1871, members thought that if the sum raised had been $150,000, "the Governors would probably have been enabled to sustain a school for practical science"[28] —but not a word about women. They also said that more money would have provided scholarships to help "young men of good natural parts but limited means find . . . openings to the highest success in life"—but not a word about women. Even though all members of Corporation received copies of Chancellor Day's speech and even though Day, Dawson and Wilkes attended Corporation meetings all year, not the slightest effort seems to have been made to do anything about admitting women. Why? One can only assume that no one really wanted to. It would appear that the Governors had used the idea as a means to get money, that it was not a case of equity but of economics. The result was that McGill missed a promising chance to lead the way in Canada, leaving to Mt. Allison the honour of graduating the first woman in 1875.

The "Wilkes' resolution" represented an eighth aspect of interest in women's education. The ninth followed directly from it. In the summer of 1870, Principal Dawson and his wife visited England. As an aftermath of the Wilkes affair, he agreed "to collect information respecting the movements in progress in the mother country" concerning women's education. Accordingly, he visited the nascent women's colleges at London and Cambridge and learned about the "lectures for ladies'' which had been organized in several centres. Upon his return to Montreal, Dawson drafted a proposal for classes for the Higher Education of Women based largely on the Ladies' Educational Association of Edinburgh. His proposal called for the establishment of ''The Ladies' Educational Association of Montreal'' and was similar to a scheme begun two years earlier in Toronto by his friend Dr. Daniel Wilson, President of the University College. The aim of the new organization was ''to be the provision of lectures on literary, scientific and historical subjects for the higher education of women, and eventually if possible, the establishment of a College for ladies in connection with the University.''[29] Dawson devised both operational details and curriculum. Members, who were to pay a fee of $12, were to be ladies—but a gentleman, not a member of the Association, was to be Treasurer. Since he felt that the university had a moral obligation to do something for the higher education of women, he discussed the scheme with several of the professors at McGill, and then took it to some of Montreal's most socially prominent women.

As a result, a meeting was held at Belmont Hall, the residence of Mrs. Anne Molson. Dawson's proposal and McGill's cooperation were accepted, the Montreal Ladies' Educational Association (M.L.E.A.) was duly established and, in its first year, attracted a membership of 167 women. The membership list was a veritable ''who's who'' of middle and upper class English-speaking Montrealers. Names such as Molson, Redpath, Atwater, Greene and Dawson could be found among the ordinary members and on the committees. The President was Mrs. Anne Molson, the Honorary Secretary was Mrs. Lucy Simpson, whom Dawson called ''one of our most experienced educationists,''[30] and the first Patroness was Her Exellency, the Countess of Dufferin. The Honorary Treasurer was Mrs. Molson's husband, John.

The question of male membership was considered by a special subcommittee which sent inquiries to a number of similar organizations in Canada and abroad to see how they handled this matter—whether men were permitted to be members, to attend classes as auditors, or to take part in the administration. This survey revealed an interesting variety of procedures: in Toronto, gentlemen were absolutely excluded from all classes except the introductory lectures but the organization was managed by a small joint committee of ladies and gentlemen; from Boston came advice for the ''ladies to keep the *management* of the society in their *own* hands''; from Dublin they learned that there were gentlemen among the life-governors, life-members and ordinary members; from Birmingham came the comment that the ladies would ''be happy to have gentlemen as life-members, or otherwise, but we do not wish to have them work with us . . . ''; from Edinburgh, the telling remark that when

Ladies' Educational Association.

Patroness:

HER EXCELLENCY THE COUNTESS OF DUFFERIN.

General Committee:

MRS. MOLSON, *President.*

MRS. T. B. ANDERSON,
" SIMPSON. } *Vice-Presidents.*

MISS LUNN, *Honorary Secretary.*

JOHN MOLSON, Esquire, *Honorary Treasurer.*

MRS. ANDREW ALLAN,	MRS. LAY,
" ALBERT ATWATER,	" LEWIS,
" BALDWIN,	" LOVELL,
" CHAMPION BROWN,	" HENRY LYMAN,
" BRYDGES,	MISS MACINTOSH,
MISS ADELAIDE CAMPBELL,	MRS. MERCER,
MRS. CRAMP,	" GEORGE MOFFATT,
" DAWSON,	" OXENDEN,
" DURNFORD,	" L. J. A. PAPINEAU,
" G. H. FROTHINGHAM,	" REDPATH,
LADY GALT,	MISS RIMMER,
MRS. GIBSON,	MRS. H. SCOTT,
MISS GORDON,	MISS SYMMERS,
MRS. E. K. GREENE,	MRS. JOSEPH TIFFIN, JR.
" GREENSHIELDS,	" VANNECK,
MISS HERVEY,	" THOS. WORKMAN.
MRS. GAVIN LANG,	

Executive Committee:

MRS. CHAMPION BROWN,	MRS. PAPINEAU,
" DAWSON,	" THOS. WORKMAN,
" LOVELL,	

Honorary Members;

HON. CHARLES DEWEY DAY, D.C.L., LL.D.

PRINCIPAL DAWSON, LL.D., F.R.S., F.G.S.

VEN. ARCHDEACON LEACH, D.C.L., LL.D.

HON. J. J. C. ABBOTT, D.C.L., Q.C.

G. W. CAMPBELL, Esq., M.A., M.D.

PROFESSOR P. J. DAREY, M.A., B.C.L.

REV. PROFESSOR CORNISH, LL.D.

T. STERRY HUNT, Esq., LL.D., F.R.S.

PROFESSOR GOLDWIN SMITH, M.A.

Members of the M.L.E.A.: The English-Language Elite

the Association was first contemplated, the names of eighty distinguished men were obtained "to give it a sort of social stability"; the
Cambridge Association said that no gentlemen were admitted to the
lectures, but the executive contained both ladies and gentlemen; and
Rugby recommended an executive composed of equal numbers of men
and women. Having taken all this advice into consideration, the
M.L.E.A. decided to invite the Chancellor, Vice-Chancellor and Deans
of Faculty of McGill College to become honorary members, along with
the four professors who so kindly consented to deliver the lectures of the
first session. They also made it known that while their executive would
be women only, they would seek advice from the men when the need
arose.[31]

In the fall of 1871, a public announcement was circulated stating
that the M.L.E.A. would offer four courses of College Lectures during
the winter. The general plan of lectures indicated that it would not be
possible to "take up drilling on elementary subjects" but the programme would deal with subjects not usually taught in schools and
which afford valuable information as well as training. Each course was
intended to be complete in itself, yet efforts were to be made to provide
continuity. Examinations were optional. The subjects to be taught were
to include Literature, History, Philosophy, and Natural Sciences.

The members of M.L.E.A. considered the question of curriculum
very carefully. They were determined to do more than supply mere
entertainment or popular lectures. This venture was not intended to be a
dilettante affair but was to supply solid intellectual fare for "students,
who, having received ordinary school instruction, are now prepared to
take an active part in their own education."[32] The women recognised
that their difficulties included limited scholarly experience and lack of
academic preparation. The establishment of the Montreal High School
for Girls four years after the M.L.E.A. was to help solve the problem to
some extent, but right from the outset the M.L.E.A. was determined
that serious work would be done. A carefully conceived report on educational aims drafted by Anne Molson and Lucy Simpson specified that the
certificates awarded at the end of the courses should be "*real* pledges
for *real* attainment," preparing the way for academic degrees.[33] This
goal was partly realized in 1883 when McGill agreed to award the
"Associate in Arts" diploma to successful candidates . . . but this still
did not mean they were admissable to the University.

Fittingly enough, Principal Dawson delivered the opening address
for the first (1871-72) session of the M.L.E.A. His topic was also appropriately entitled "Thoughts on the Higher Education of Women."

This was a long and important speech, illustrating that Dawson was
quite cognisant of developments elsewhere. Indeed, it gives a clear and

useful account of the status of higher education for women as a whole. It also shows Dawson knew that the several concessions to women made by McGill were not at all unique, yet he considered them sources of satisfaction. He said:

> We cannot as yet boast of a Ladies' College; but our classes for the present session will provide for substantial instruction in the structure and literature of the two most important languages in this country, and for an introduction to that great department of science which relates to inorganic nature. I think we have reason to congratulate ourselves on the nature of the course and to be hopeful of the results. . . .
>
> Several features of the present movement afford, I think, especial reasons for congratulation. One is that this is an Association of Ladies for educational purposes—originating with ladies, carried on by them, supported by their contributions. Another is that the movement is self-supporting, and not sustained by extraneous aid. It will, I hope, attract to itself endowments which may give it a stronger and higher character, but its present position of independence is the best guarantee for this, as well as for all other kinds of success. Another is that the Association embraces nearly all that is elevated in social and educational standing in our city, and thus has the broadest and highest basis that can be attained among us for any effort whatever. Still another is that we are not alone, nor are we indeed in the van of this great work. I need not speak of the United States, where the magnificent Vassar College, with which the name of one of our excellent and learned women [Hannah Willard Lyman] was connected so usefully, and the admission of ladies to Cornell University, the University of Michigan and others, have marked strongly the popular sentiments as to the education of women. In Canada itself, Toronto, and even Quebec and Kingston, have preceded us, though I think in the magnitude of our success we may hope to excel them all. In the mother country, the Edinburgh Association has afforded us the model for our own; and the North of England Educational Council, the Bedford College in London, the Hitchin College, the Cambridge Lectures for Ladies, the admission of ladies to the middle-class examinations of the Alexandra College in Dublin, are all indications of the intensity and direction of the current. On the continent of Europe, Sweden has a state college for women. The Victoria Lyceum at Berlin has the patronage of the Princess Royal; the University of Paris has established classes for ladies, and St. Petersburgh has its university for women. All these movements have originated not only in our own time but within a few years, and they are evidence of the dawn of a new educational era, which, in my judgment, will see as great an advance in the education of our race as that which was inaugurated by the revival of learning and the

establishment of universities for men in a previous age. It implies not
only the higher education of women, but the elevation, extension and
refinement of the higher education of men. . . . 34

Dawson concluded with exhortations to the women to take the work
seriously, reminded them of their responsibility as pioneers, called upon
men to cooperate, and, in a quote from Dr. Wilson of Toronto, stoutly
averred that in spite of ''prejudices inherited from a dead past'' higher
education for women was inevitable and could not be prevented.

This was fine rhetoric, but it did not entirely coincide with Dawson's
subsequent behaviour. He still seemed to be struggling with personal
reservations. While he undeniably gave impetus and support to the
M.L.E.A., he did not rush to make the ''inevitable'' college education
for women a reality. Perhaps he was confidently waiting for events to
take care of themselves, but he did not bring any formal resolutions
before the McGill Corporation or Governors nor did he take any other
official action to see that the ''Wilkes' resolution'' was ultimately
implemented.

Though it was something less than a true college for women, the
M.L.E.A. was an undoubted success. The women managed their own
affairs very competently, charging moderate fees, yet remaining self-
sustaining and paying their lecturers ''handsomely.'' The Association
lasted 14 years, usually offering four, but sometimes more, courses
annually. Throughout that time, the McGill professors who gave the
lectures found that its members took the work seriously and were intelligent, devoted students. These lecturers included Prof. T. Sterry Hunt
on Natural Philosophy, Dr. William Osler on ''The Structure and Habits
of the Lower Forms of Life,'' Rev. Dr. J. Clark Murray on Logic, Rhetoric, and Political Economy, Prof. Theo Lafleur on French Literature,
Prof. Charles E. Moyse on Shakespeare, Dr. T.G. Roddick on Domestic
Hygiene, Prof. D.P. Penhallow on Structural and Systematic Botany,
Ven. Archdeacon Leach on English Literature, Prof. Goldwin Smith on
British History, and Dawson himself on Natural Sciences. Dawson
refused to accept payment for his lectures and the M.L.E.A. members
were grateful to him for his liberality. Their annual reports also made
frequent references to his varied contributions to their work. The 1882-
83 volume, for example, noted:

On Thursday, January 11th, Dr. Dawson gave the opening lecture of
his course on ''Invertebrate Animals,'' the first attended by ladies in
the Peter Redpath Museum, an era in the history of the Ladies'
Educational Association. As this important advantage is due to Dr.
Dawson's influence and interest in the Association, its members beg

to thank him again for his continued kindness as well as for his most interesting course of lectures. It is unnecessary to say that with Dr. Dawson as a lecturer, and on one of his favourite subjects, the lectures were most attractive.[35]

None of these middle class, well-mannered women of the Montreal Ladies' Educational Association doubted Dawson was doing as much as he possibly could to further higher education for members of their sex. His contribution to the slowness of their progress seems to have gone entirely unchallenged, undetected, unsuspected.

If the members of the M.L.E.A. were fairly satisfied with the way things were going, the professors who gave the courses were well pleased with their students. Each year they commented on their courses and each year there were three recurrent themes: the enthusiasm of the students; the high quality of their work; but the disappointingly few examination candidates. For example, Dr. Robert Craik wrote about his Chemistry course:

> The attendance throughout the Course was large and uniform, consisting of between fifty and sixty students and a still larger number of lady auditors. Their attention, order and punctuality were deserving of the highest praise. . . . At the final examination, eleven students presented themselves, all of whom passed in a satisfactory manner, many of the papers being of a degree of excellence for which I was by no means prepared. I can only regret that a larger number of students did not present themselves at this examination. . . .[36]

J. Clark Murray noted that, in general, a good number of exercises in Logic were ''perfectly faultless'' and ''considering the limited time during which the subject was studied, I have been agreeably surprised at the thorough acquaintance with the fundamental principles of Logic evinced in many of the examination papers and other exercises.''[37] Dr. Wright regretted that only 15 out of 150 sat for the examination in Physiology but he concluded:

> My report would be incomplete were it to end without an expression of surprise from me at the high degree of excellence exhibited in many of the answers. Several of them were so perfect as to receive the full number of marks, and others so close to those as to fall short by a very small deficiency.[38]

Professor John Campbell went even further. In his report on the 1876 examination in Ancient History and Literature he explained the very high grade he had awarded:

The marked excellence of one of the answers of the Lady who stands at the head of the First Class called for more than the maximum allotted to it, so superior was it to any answer that I had anticipated receiving. As the other answers were perfect, this will account for the papers of that student being marked a little above the maximum.[39]

Perhaps Archdeacon Leach showed the highest degree of appreciation, since M.L.E.A. member, Louisa Swilt, who had a record of perfect exam papers, became his third wife. Principal Dawson, too, was impressed. In summing up his course on Useful and Ornamental Stones, he said:

On the whole I had every reason to be pleased with the attention and intelligence of the class and the answering in the examination was quite equal to that of any class of college students having similar opportunities. I only regret that a larger number of the students did not come up for examination, as I have reason to believe that many others could have given as creditable answers as those who actually appeared.[40]

If there was some unwitting condescension in the "surprise" that so many of the professors felt at the excellence of the results, the women of the M.L.E.A. did not appear to notice. They were gratified by the praise and by the confidence the professors had in them. They recognised that some of their success might be attributed to "the novelty of the movement" to promote higher education for women, but they also gave due credit to those who had "a true love of knowledge." They regretted that more members did not avail themselves of "the valuable test which the examinations afford" and, to induce more to take the exams, in 1874 reduced the number of lectures per session from 80 to 60 and ultimately to 40. Yet they defended the auditors. At the end of M.L.E.A.'s third year, a committee composed of Louisa G.F. Molson and Mary Mercer reported:

These lectures need not give only desultory information to non-students, for auditors also can carry away many precious grains of knowledge, to be pondered over later, during some of the few quiet moments that occur in busy households. The lecture room may prove itself a freshener during every day cares, bringing recollections of a time that was freer for mental effort, reviving associations and memories, and while daughters are studying, mothers can keep their interest fresh in the work, and not fall quite behind in the race for knowledge.[41]

Given the women's enthusiasm, it is not quite clear why so many did not take the examinations. Neither the intrinsic satisfaction nor the possibility of receiving a Hannah Willard Lyman prize seemed sufficient for some to overcome their reticence. Probably their reasons were similar to those of some contemporary students in Continuing Education —dislike of the inevitable stress of exams, lack of time, fear of failure, and low value attached to the certificates—compounded, in many cases, by a strong sense of culturally induced insecurity. Even if the certificates were not enough to entice all M.L.E.A. members to take the exams, more than 1,000 were issued during the life of the Association; striking evidence of the efforts made by these women emerging from the home.

The leadership constantly stressed the academic nature of courses and resisted popularization, in spite of the financial temptation to offer more domestic fare. However, when in 1878 their new Patroness, Princess Louise, suggested it would be well to offer courses in Domestic Economy, "which properly lies at the root of the highest life of every true woman,"[42] they modified their policy. Lectures in Domestic Economy and Cookery, Household Surgery, Domestic Medicine, and Nursing and Hygiene met with considerable success and helped subsidize the academic work. One of the cookery classes proved embarassing when, "due to an unfortunate inadvertance," a number of "respectable servants" appeared. One commentator noted, "There is a distinct hint that their presence resulted in the loss to the course of its academic flavour, but in gain to the dining tables of many citizens."[43]

Another method to raise money was to offer associate membership at the reduced annual fee of $3. Ninety-five new members were recruited in this way and so the Association was able to continue until 1885. The fact that the M.L.E.A. survived for 14 years in the face of financial difficulties and the possibility, ever-present in voluntary organizations, of factionalism and personality conflict, bears testimony to the strength and dedication of the women who began it. These same women—Anne Molson, Margaret Murray, Jane Redpath, Mary A.N. Mercer, Margaret Dawson, Lucy Simpson, Bessie Symmers, Sarah Smith and others—had continued to support it enthusiastically and intelligently. With the help of McGill, they made a real contribution to the education of their sisters and daughters. Nevertheless, some of them were not fully satisfied and still hoped for regular college education for women. Indeed, one of their last annual reports noted that they had "good ground for trusting that means will be found for the carrying on of classes in connection with the Association in regular rotation, as preparation for a college course."[44]

In summary, there could be little doubt of the M.L.E.A.'s success. From the point of view of the many lecturers who set the three-hour long

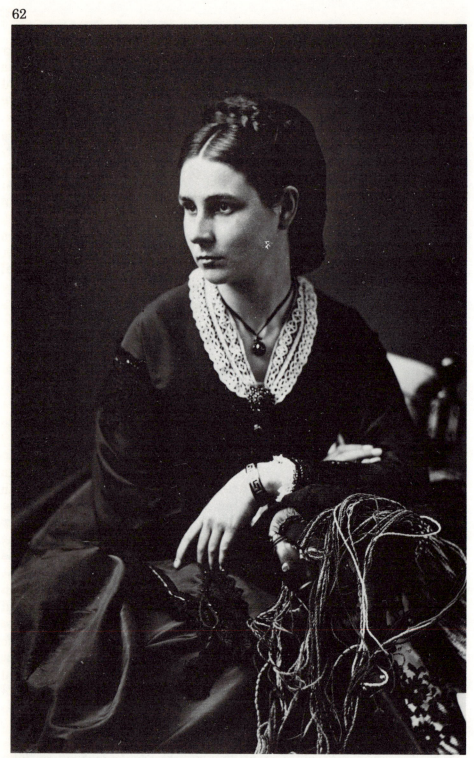

Anna Dawson, 1871

formal examinations, the M.L.E.A. work was "gratifying," the standards achieved "excellent," the attendance, punctuality and attention
"exceedingly good" or even "everything that could be desired," and
the note-taking "careful and accurate." For the English-speaking
women of Montreal, the M.L.E.A. offered access to the world of ideas,
contact and colleagueship with other women, opportunities to be active
in their own improvement and a glimpse of academic life. In Dawson's
view, the Association was "doing good educational work and preparing
the public mind for something more systematic"[45] and he stated that it
had "done very much to elevate the whole educational tone of the
city."[46] Dr. Roddick considered it a "success" and Professor J. Clark
Murray thought its very existence a recognition of women's rights to a
higher culture, but it was only a partial, and therefore an unsatisfactory,
measure. He could see no permanent solution to the problem of
women's higher education "until the stronger sex abandon the selfish-
ness with which they have ungallantly persisted in jostling their sisters
out of all the avenues which lead into the Temple of Knowledge."[47]
Murray decided to take a firm step himself to clear the path for women,
the tenth on the way to college admission.

* * *

In October, 1882, J. Clark Murray presented a motion to the McGill
Corporation that "the time has come when educational advantages of
the Faculty of Arts should be thrown open to all persons without distinction of sex." The question was discussed and then referred to an
eight-man committee for investigation. This Committee of Corporation
upon the Higher Education of Women included Principal Dawson,
Professor Murray, Mr. J.R. Dougall (the original mover of the "Wilkes'
resolution") and others who held varying views on the matter. They
proceeded to send out questionnaires to institutions in Canada, the
United States, Britain and Europe and hoped to make a report by the
January 24th, 1883 meeting of Corporation. This committee/question-
naire technique might have been an obvious and legitimate procedure,
but given the professed on-going interest in women's education held by
Dawson, Murray, Dougall and some of the others, it might also have
been a delaying tactic. In the many speeches Dawson made over the
years on this subject, he always made references to the practice in other
countries—see for example, his opening address to the M.L.E.A.,
quoted above. In view of all his apparent concern, the concessions
McGill had already made and the success with female students in the
M.L.E.A., the question could have been decided locally on the basis of
the principle that women could and should have access to higher educa-

Helen R.Y. Reid

tion. Dawson's hesitancy suggests a colonial type of mentality that was unwilling to make changes unless the innovations had been tried and proven elsewhere.

Be that as it may, the questionnaires were sent out to other countries and, not surprisingly, the responses were slow in coming in. It was therefore necessary to postpone full consideration of the Committee's findings until the meeting of 6th June. By then it was becoming clear that the issue was not whether women should have higher education but whether it should be separate or co-educational. The inquiry found respondents in favour of both of these possibilities, and those which had opted for co-education reported no ill effects to the institution or to male or female students. The "separate" option involved either separate classes within an existing college or completely separate colleges. There were models for both. Dr. Murray, who favoured co-education, proposed that "in the opinion of Corporation as soon as arrangements can be made, this University should admit Women to the Faculty of Arts, on substantially the same terms as men."[48]

At the same meeting, a letter was read from the Graduates' Society with the Resolution that, "This Society will hail with satisfaction any steps that the authorities may take leading to the admission of women to the privileges of the University." These two motions were amended by Dr. Alexander Johnson, Dean of Arts, to read:

> *Resolved,* that this Corporation approves the admission of Women to all the examinations in Arts, and will hail with pleasure the establishment of a separate Women's College, to be affiliated to the University, for the purpose of specially preparing female students for the examinations.

The discussion became heated, the matter postponed until the following week, and then, since consensus was still not reached, postponed for more than a year. On a motion by septuagenarian, Sir Francis Hincks, and by the slim margin of 10 to 9, the June 13, 1883 meeting resolved that "further consideration and discussion be postponed until the regular meeting of the Corporation to be held in October, 1884." Corporation obviously felt no sense of urgency, no strong pressures to effect what Dawson, in 1871, had held to be inevitable. The Hincks' resolution noted that by the support and encouragement it had given the Ladies' Educational Association of Montreal, the University had given proof of its intention to advance the interests of higher education for women and that it "would preserve so far and in such direction as may be found expedient." Their consciences were clear, though expediency may not be the noblest of principles to guide a university!

Rosalie McDonald McLea

Meanwhile, Principal and Mrs. Dawson were again planning to visit Britain and again undertook to survey the status of higher education for women and to take particular note of the methods by which it was implemented. In November 1883, Dawson wrote to his daughter, Anna (now Mrs. Harrington):

> I have been getting quite a quantity of information about ladies' colleges, which I am writing out and sending in instalments to Mr. Ferrier [The Chancellor] for general information, and am making notes for a more full report when I return. There has within the past few years been quite an energetic debate all over England in reference to this and to technical schools: and many and most contradictory experiments are being tried. [49]

And in April the following year, Margaret Dawson wrote home:

> Today Papa has gone to Oxford to be present at the final discussion as to whether ladies are to be admitted to go up for examination for the higher degrees. It is expected to be hotly contested. [50]

This correspondence shows that Dawson did indeed carry out his promise to investigate further and it also suggests the ongoing family interest in the topic. Unfortunately, there does not appear to be any letter extant recording Dawson's reaction to the Oxford vote, which went in favour of women.[51] A Montreal newspaper did note:

> One of the objects of his journey to England . . . was to examine into the subject of the higher education of women and of co-education. It is reported that he has become favourable to the latter idea, and, as soon as a class of matriculants can be prepared, will throw open the doors of McGill to ladies.[52]

Such was Sir William Dawson's prestige and standing, both in the community and the university that, had he wished to do so, he could have "thrown open the doors to the ladies." But the newspaper report proved to be only a rumour. A ready-made class of matriculants, those four doughty Associates in Arts from the Montreal High School for Girls, had presented themselves to him shortly after his return to Canada. These four - Rosalie McLea, Octavia Ritchie, Alice Murray and Helen Reid—were exhilarated by their success in the examinations. They had previously met at Helen Reid's home to talk about their future with Helen's mother, an intelligent and supportive woman. Someone speculated, "What about asking for admission to McGill?" It was a bold idea, but Mrs. Reid urged them to approach Principal Dawson himself. Rosalie McLea and Helen Reid were chosen to present their demands to McGill's imposing Principal. Helen Reid, who was "only fourteen and

. . . scared,'[53] said Rosalie did most of the talking. Though Dawson recognised that they had claims to higher education and realized they were "an expression of popular demand that had hitherto been missing," he "was obliged to point out that the university did not have the funds that this movement would entail."[54] Lack of money and the inappropriateness of the moment—those indisputable excuses of the administrator—turned them away.

Octavia Ritchie later described how Principal Dawson conceded that since "an active demand had come from those 'who had the greatest claim to consideration,' perhaps some means might be found to provide classes to prepare them for the Senior Associate in Arts Examination."[55] In other words, he promised to consider the possibility of their taking the McGill examinations without attending McGill classes. He also suggested that the prospects might be brighter if there were more applicants. Still, Ritchie was not optimistic about the chances for real progress for she knew that the Principal was particularly busy just then and she thought he dismissed the matter of the admission of women from his mind.

Though the names of eight female applicants were soon submitted, nothing appeared to be changed. However, the Principal had not entirely "dismissed the matter from his mind." He contacted Rev. Canon Norman, Vice-Chancellor of Bishop's College and together they put out a circular appealing for funds. This circular noted that the two universities had jointly offered to women who had passed the Associate in Arts (A.A.) examination the opportunity to take the Senior A.A. (approximately equivalent to the "Intermediate" examinations held at both universities), but that the universities "hitherto provided no means of instruction to fit candidates for these examinations." It further noted tht eight young women had applied and therefore it was proposed to establish first year college classes in cooperation with the Ladies' Educational Association, hoping that one or other of the universities could make arrangements for anyone who desired to continue to the final examinations to do so.

The estimated cost of this scheme was $1,000 to $2,000 per annum in addition to student fees, and the purpose of the circular was "to ascertain if there are friends of education sufficiently interested in this important matter to furnish the necessary amount."[56] Here, then, was another public appeal for funds for higher education for women, one which might have led to more action than the "Wilkes" appeal. However, it was far short of a full recognition of the need or the justice of the demand. If money were the real problem, why did Dawson at that point not appeal for money to conduct classes at McGill for women—for the students who had headed the A.A. examinations lists? At every turn the

Donald Alexander Smith

solid wall of his value system, benignly disguised, seemed to block progress. The circular appeal was just one more in the series of small concessions and fine words—no wonder Octavia Ritchie and the others were disappointed. But then suddenly, the pattern was broken by a dramatic and quite unexpected intervention. A *deus ex machina* arrived on the scene and prodded Principal Dawson into action.

Sir William Dawson was very busy that summer. It was the summer that McGill and Montreal hosted the meetings of the prestigious British Association for the Advancement of Science. Dawson took the honour very seriously, as honour it was, for this was the first time the British Association had convened in Canada. So it would only have been on a matter of considerable importance that he consented to leave one of the meetings. This was in order to speak with the Honourable Donald A. Smith. The Principal recalled that the wealthy businessman asked him "if it was desired to establish collegiate classes for women, and stated that, if so, he was prepared to give the sum of $50,000 on conditions to be settled by him."[57]

This sudden offer took Dawson completely by surprise. He had not approached Mr. Smith and had no idea that he was interested in higher education for women, nor even in McGill for that matter. But he found the "coincidence of the demand for higher education" and "the offer of so liberal a benefaction" to be "one of those rare opportunities for good, which occur but seldom to any man, and which are to be accepted with thankfulness, and followed up with earnest effort."[58] He could hardly have done otherwise. He called a meeting of the Board of Governors on 13th September, 1884 and laid before them the letter Donald Smith had written to confirm his offer:

> 1157 Dorchester Street
> Montreal
> 11th September, 1884.

My Dear Sir William Dawson:

In carrying out the intention given expression to when I had the pleasure of speaking to you on the subject of a College for the Education of Women a few days back, I beg to hand you herewith my Cheque, No. 0465, of this date, on the Bank of Montreal, for Fifty Thousand Dollars, $50,000, to your own order.

This sum of fifty thousand dollars is to be invested by the Board of Royal Institution, Governors of McGill College, and the income thereof to be employed in sustaining a College for Women, with Classes for their education in Collegiate Studies; the same to be wholly under the management and control of the Corporation of McGill University.

It is my desire, that in connection with this endowment, the seat

M'GILL UNIVERSITY.

—:o:—

Higher Education of Women.

—:o:—

Classes on the subjects of the first year in Arts, under the "Donald A Smith Endowment," will be opened on MONDAY, OCTOBER 6th by professors and lecturers of the University.

Details as to hours and places of meeting will be announced as soon as possible.

The entrance examination for regular students, except in the case of those who have already passed as associates in arts, will consist of Latin, Algebra, Geometry, English and History, as in the University Calendar, with Greek optional, as stated below. Candidates not prepared to pass in all of the above subjects, but qualified to take three or more of the courses of study, may be admitted as Partial Students ; and in consideration of the shortness of notice every possible allowance will be made for special cases. The course of study will include Latin, Greek, French or German, English, Mathematics and Chemistry. In case of Greek an option is allowed in favour of a second modern language. A limited number of ladies, members or students of the "Ladies' Educational Association," will be admitted as occasional students to particular courses of lectures on obtaining special tickets from the "Ladies' Association" and satisfying the professors of their fitness to go on with the work.

Fee for the session, $20. Matriculation, $4 (in the year of entrance only). Library, (optional), $4. Ladies' Association ticket, admitting to one course of lectures, $4.

Candidates for entrance are requested to present themselves in the Lecture Room of the "Peter Redpath Museum" on SATURDAY, the 27th SEPTEMBER at THREE p.m., to enter their names and make arrangements respecting examinations and subjects.

Copies of the calendar and announcements of the special course for women, so soon as printed, may be obtained on application to the undersigned.

W. C. BAYNES, B.A.

Secretary.

McGILL COLLEGE OFFICE, ⎰
24th Sept., 1884. ⎱

230

now held by the Rev. Canon Norman, D.C.L., in the Corporation of the University, should be rendered permanent by his election as a Governors' Fellow on the expiry of his present tenure of office as Chairman of the Protestant Board of School Commissioners, and also that the Rev. James Barclay, B.A., should be appointed and continued as a Governors' Fellow.

It is further my wish that there should be two Lady Visitors of the College, to be called respectively the Patroness and Vice-Patroness, these, should I so desire it, to be nominated by myself.

Believe me, very faithfully yours,

(Signed) DONALD A. SMITH [59]

Principal Dawson presented this letter to the Board of Governors on September 13 when the cheque and the conditions attached to it were accepted. The resolution of acceptance included a statement that "the thanks of the Board be conveyed to the Honorable Mr. Smith on behalf of the University and of all interested in higher education of women." [60] A week later, the whole matter was reported to a special meeting of Corporation and it now appeared that the major difficulties were resolved. All that remained to be settled were the practical matters relating to space allocation, curriculum, schedules, and instructors.

Things moved quickly. Since the McGill *Prospectus* for 1884-85 was already published, special announcements were placed in the newspapers informing the public of what had happened and calling for applications. At last there was a public and official invitation for women to come to McGill. After all the preliminary measures, the temporizing, the waiting, the efforts and the frustration, the Faculty of Arts was finally opening to women.

Chapter THREE

The Donaldas

Up the avenue, one Monday early in October, a little group of girls hastened with high hopes and fast beating hearts. Turning to the left, they mounted the broad steps of the Peter Redpath Museum and entered its wide portal. It had been arranged that *separate* classes for them should be conducted in this building. Octavia Ritchie, who was one of the "little group," recalled that, "To mark the dignity of our new status, we had lengthened our skirts and put up our hair, coiled smoothly at the nape of the neck."[1]

It would be unrealistic to think that once women were admitted to the Faculty of Arts the basic story of women at McGill was complete or that it could be summed up with some academic equivalent of ". . . and so they lived happily ever after." In fact, much remained to be done: the University had to cope very quickly with some tricky logistical problems; the new students had to prove themselves to themselves as well as to others; ideological battles still had to be fought; more principles had to be established, and more practical gains had to be made. These were matters both for the Fall of 1884 and for many years to come.

The immediate problems with which the University had to grapple were complicated by the prevailing Dawsonian/Victorian ideology. Since women were regarded as such very different creatures—superior or inferior, feebler or more fragile, more sensitive or less hardy, depending on the interpretation—they could not be simply incorporated into the student body without quite special arrangements. Thus, there must have been a great flurry of activity in the administrative offices of McGill in September 1884 for, once the decision to admit women was taken, Principal Dawson, Dean of Arts Johnson, and Registrar Baynes all seemed to move with extraordinary speed, efficiency and even flexibility. Though we in the 20th century with our computer technology may tend to think that administrative procedures have been streamlined, we might marvel at the way in which these Victorians quickly settled the myriad practical problems in order that women's classes could begin at once. There was no trace of procrastination at this point. The responsibility for this was indubitably Dawson's. Though announcements were

73

issued under other names, his hand can be seen in the drafting of all the significant regulations. It is an illustration of both the autocracy and effectiveness of his administration; it is also much to his credit that he did not dally further. Perhaps a cynic might comment that to have done so would have been to risk the endowment but still, Dawson might reasonably have tried to beg off for another year to have time to put the machinery in order. However, he did not do so and everything was arranged in good time.

Corporation accepted the Donald A. Smith endowment on September 20 and within four days public announcements were made of the particular admission requirements for women.[2] These indicated that women who had Associate in Arts certificates with passes in Latin, Algebra and Geometry were now to be accepted as fully matriculated and would be accepted as undergraduates in the Donalda Special Course for Women; others would be required to pass the entrance examinations in Latin, Algebra, Geometry, English, and History as set forth for male students. Greek was optional for women. Candidates who qualified in at least three subjects could be admitted as Partial students and, "in consideration of the shortness of notice, every possible allowance will be made for special cases." A limited number of members of the M.L.E.A. were to be accepted as Occasional students, provided they obtained special tickets from the M.L.E.A. and the permission of the professors concerned. Later, it was specified that Occasionals were not "liable to examination except voluntarily" but, if they took the tests and if they were successful, they were eligible for certificates. Given the preference that the members of the M.L.E.A. had shown for not taking examinations, this arrangement must have pleased many of the part-time students.

The regulations set up a prestige-linked hierarchy among the students of "Undergraduates," "Partials," and "Occasionals" that persisted for years, but they did permit women with a variety of backgrounds and interests to apply. So, when classes began on October 6, there were seven undergraduates, seven partials, and fourteen occasionals, giving a total of twenty-eight women.[3] This was a very satisfactory number, under all the circumstances, and since there were only 163 men in the Faculty of Arts in 1884, it constituted almost 15% of the total enrolment. Every woman student, whether a regular undergraduate or a mere occasional, was soon called a "Donalda," a name obviously derived from that of the donor of the endowment which had made their entry to McGill possible. This name applied particularly to the women of the 1880's and 90's, but it did survive into the 20th century. It was one of the things that set women apart from the other students.

The full course of study open to women of the first year was a fixed

Jane Palmer
Martha Murphy

Georgina Hunter
Octavia Ritchie

programme of Latin, French or German, English, Greek or a second modern language, Mathematics or Chemistry. Fees were to be the same as for men except, curiously, the library fee was optional and the gym fee was not required, since gym instruction for women was not immediately available. Since only the exceptional young woman like Rosalie McLea had studied Greek in her pre-college education, there was a tendency for the Donaldas to eschew the Classics programme of studies in favour of the Scientific. This preference continued for many years and accounts for the somewhat unexpected fact that some of the earliest graduate degrees earned by women at McGill were also in the Sciences. (See Appendix A.)

* * *

The basic terms of admission for women were fairly straight-forward. Complications arose because of the perceived necessity for separate instruction. This involved providing separate rooms, not only classrooms but also waiting rooms, so that the women would not be forced to mingle with or even encounter men should they wish to avoid them. Even this detail of organization did not escape the Principal's intervention and among his papers a rough sketch has been found of the reallocation of space in the East Wing of the Arts Building which was to become the women's headquarters. The Redpath Museum with its convenient separate entrances had already been used for M.L.E.A. classes and was used for the Donaldas until the renovations were completed. New furniture was quickly purchased. Later, in the Arts Building, certain entrances and stairways were designated for the use of women and three classrooms, a waiting room and a lobby had to be suitably arranged and furnished. The rent for these rooms ($250 per year) plus the extra expenses for the janitor, light and heat were charged to the Donalda Endowment, but the additional furniture was to be paid for out of student fees. The intention was that the higher education of women, like all other McGill ventures, should be self-financing.

As might be expected, new arrangements for staffing had to be made. In some cases, the professors agreed to repeat their lectures to the female students for additional remuneration; in other cases, additional tutors were engaged. One of the most necessary of the new appointments was that of chaperone, and here Dawson took the advice of the Honorary Secretary of the M.L.E.A. (Lucy Simpson) and the Secretary (Helen L. Gairdner). Miss Gairdner, who had been with the M.L.E.A. since 1881, now became "Lady Superintendent" of the Donaldas to be responsible for their day-to-day welfare. She had to attend classes with them and the Donaldas recalled how "the beloved

Donalda McFee
Blanche Evans

Alice Murray
Eliza Cross

Lady Superintendent . . . sat with her knitting in the tiny laboratory, where a young but circumspect lecturer directed the chemical experiments of unsophisticated freshwomen.''[4] Miss Gairdner's and the other additional salaries were paid from the Endowment.

The Endowment was a generous one but it was not sufficient to meet large scale expenses over a long period. Rather, it was intended to cover the cost of the first two of the four years of the Arts programme. The question of the two senior years had to be faced quite soon. Fortunately, help was now close at hand. On October 4, 1884—just two days before the first class for women met—the Hon. Donald A. Smith was appointed a Trustee of the Royal Institution for the Advancement of Learning and a member of the Board of Governors of McGill. Less than five years later he was to become Chancellor. As a Governor, he was in a good position to monitor and maintain the programme which he had helped begin. Thus, on October 6, 1886, Sir Donald—as he now was—increased his endowment by $70,000 making a total of $120,000. The additional funds were to cover the costs of the courses in the third and fourth years and he also added a cheque for another $1,600, the amount of interest on the new endowment from the previous May and which was

Redpath Museum Where the Donaldas Had Their First Classes

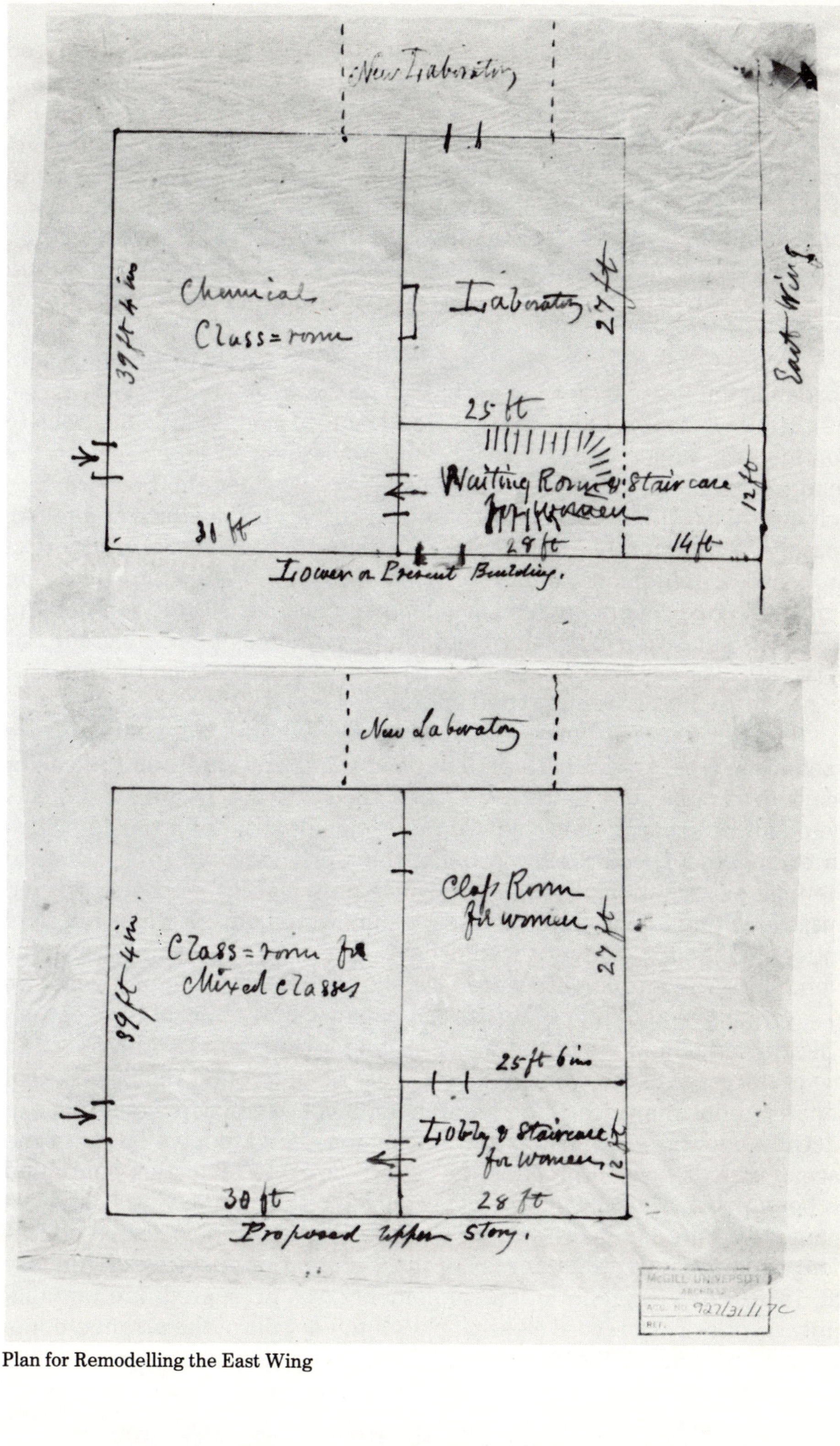

Plan for Remodelling the East Wing

intended to meet the current expenses until further revenue was derived from the capital. Smith's gift, constituted the greatest endowment McGill had yet received and was naturally much appreciated by his colleagues on the Board. A formal notarial deed, "The Donalda Endowment for the Higher Education of Women," was executed in the autumn of 1886. At that time, Sir Donald Smith in acknowledging the Governors' thanks said that "it gave him the greatest pleasure . . . to have executed a Deed that was not only the commencement of this important work, and which he trusted might grow, at an early date, into a College for Women."[5]

Apart from the financial considerations, there were practical and academic implications for the extension of the Donalda Special Course. As early as October, 1884, Corporation resolved that it was "desirous to continue the education of Women who have entered its classes to the final examinations."[6] It therefore wished to consider the best ways to achieve this, "either in separate or mixed classes for the third and fourth years." Consequently, the Faculty of Arts prepared a detailed report of proposed arrangements and submitted it to Corporation the following January.[7] This report noted that it had to consider "three methods in which the education of the third and fourth years may be conducted. 1st. Separate Classes. 2nd. Mixed Classes. 3rd. A Combination of both." It leaned in favour of the combined approach.

For the first two years of the Arts programme the courses were fixed. Since there were both optional and required courses in the senior years, a complicated pattern was designed so that required subjects would all be separate but some of the optionals would be mixed.[8] Such an arrangement would allow women the "privilege" of proceeding to the final examinations by taking only separate classes if they so wished but, "if willing to join mixed classes," they would have a wider range of options. Honours students would have to attend the same classes as men, since the enrolments were already very small—ranging from two to seven men—and did not justify the expense and effort of duplication. These arrangements had the virtue of minimizing costs and respecting the preferences of the women, but it must be noted that the principle of separate education, which had long been invoked to keep women out of McGill, now was sacrificed. How quickly it seemed to have fallen in the face of expediency. In practice, however, separate education continued to be supported as the norm, especially for the junior years, and remained the predominant pattern despite strong support for co-education. Unfortunately, the minutes of the Corporation meeting of January 28, 1885, when the report on arrangements was presented, are tantalizingly cryptic. They record clearly enough the details of the arrangements but give no hint of the discussion. That there was on that occasion a

Helen L. Gairdner, Lady Superintendent

lively debate on the issue of separate vs. co-education is virtually certain from the last prosaic sentence: "Rev. Dr. Murray, Hon. Donald A. Smith and others having spoken upon the subject, the Corporation adjourned. . . ." Murray was the champion of co-education, Smith the supporter of separate education, and a confrontation most probably took place at that meeting.

Smith's support for separate education was a critical matter for the lives of all women at McGill. His was the money, he was the piper and McGill had to dance to his tune — at least to some extent. Dr. Murray, for one, clung staunchly to his own convictions and separate vs. co-education remained a live issue and a continuing source of controversy, bitterness and bad feeling both on campus and in the newspapers. It was clearly an emotional question which the actual advent of women had not completely resolved. It is also hard to avoid the impression that as his connection with McGill increased, Donald Smith's insistence on separate education grew. Initially, it did not seem to be an extremely important component of his approach to women's education. For instance, it is not spelled out as one of the conditions of the original gift. Perhaps he made it clear orally to Dawson, but he did not emphasize it in his letter of September 11, 1884 when he sent the first cheque. (See Chapter 2.) There is really nothing in that letter that categorically specifies separate education. The special conditions deal with quite different matters. There is a striking difference between this letter and the Deed of Gift of 1886.

If Donald Smith's position became firmer or more conservative, was it because Murray irritated him at the meeting of January 28, 1885 or was it because he found Dawson's views more persuasive? Did the more genteel members of the M.L.E.A. have something to do with it, or was it simply a matter of personal conviction? Was it, as has been suggested,[9] an attempt to appear super-respectable in polite Montreal society to offset the fact that, when Smith was in the wilderness working for the Hudson's Bay Company, he had married himself to his wife with dubious legality? Was he taking on the trappings of gentility to disguise the fact that his fortune had its foundation in trapping? Or was he, as more cynical commentators might hypothesize, making an effort to please Her Majesty, Queen Victoria, and to win civic honours? Whatever the reason, or combination of reasons, the fact remained that Smith's alleged concern for separate education and Dawson's implementation of this policy soon became a matter for public debate and newspaper controversy.

The first newspaper comments on the advent of women to McGill were favourable. In late September, 1884 the *Witness* had rejoiced in "the most timely and liberal gift of Mr. Smith," noting that "the time had fully come for our university to enter into that movement for collegiate education for women which has advanced with so rapid strides in the Mother Country and in the United States.''[10] It opined that there would probably be little difficulty in continuing the course through the third and fourth years, even if in some of the classes women students might have to attend in the company of men. It evinced no horror at the thought of possible co-education, not even mild disapproval.

In October, shortly after the classes for women had actually commenced, Sir William Dawson submitted to Corporation the *Report on the Higher Education of Women* which he had prepared ostensibly on behalf of the beleaguered Committee set up two years earlier, following J. Clark Murray's motion that ''the doors be thrown open'' to women. Technically, though women were now at McGill owing to the special circumstances of Donald Smith's gift, Corporation still had not made a basic policy decision on college education for women. The special committee on this question had been circumvented and had not formally discharged its function. In his report, Dawson drew but little from the Committee's work, rather he relied upon his own more recent observations in Britain. This fourteen-page printed document [11] gives an overview of existing practices, some enrolment statistics and an account of arrangements. It shows that Dawson found a variety of procedures, including the successful use of mixed classes at London and Bristol and ''did not hear of any serious practical difficulties.'' However, he did not agree with the argument of its supporters, namely that mixed education fitted women better for the real struggle of life in competition with men. Dawson did not approve of this ''hardening process'' and believed it did not commend itself to women generally and thus it showed signs of diminishing. He noted for example, that co-education had been abandoned at Owens College, Manchester. On the other hand, he found separate education flourishing at Bedford College and Cheltenham, where there appeared an ''air of refinement and Christian influence quite different from that in ordinary colleges for men.'' And he found an eclectic pattern at Oxford and Cambridge where separate colleges for women were established but members of both sexes attended intercollegiate or university lectures. After all this, he considered McGill.

His recommendations showed quite clearly how expediency, not principle, governed the issue. ''As to our own action in this matter,'' he said, ''I have felt this must be practically regulated, not so much by the theoretical views which we might be inclined to favour, as by the demand on the part of women for a higher education . . . and by the means placed at our disposal to establish classes for the purpose.''[12] He then briefly described the events of the summer, Smith's endowment, and the establishment of the special classes for women, commenting optimistically on the prospect of these continuing, or the possible erection of a building "which need not be large or expensive," for a women's college. "On the whole," he commented, "I think the Corporation of the University has reason to congratulate itself on having already attained a safe and progressive position in this important matter."[13]

It would seem that by the action of Donald Smith, McGill had been spared the painful necessity of taking a firm decision on the principle of college education for women and was now feeling comfortably "safe and progressive." Apparently it had stumbled into a satisfactory situation which Dawson took to be more or less ongoing. Not everyone greeted such a prospect with equanimity, and not everyone seemed to realize that the separate classes were to be permanent.

Somewhat ironically, Dr. J. Clark Murray, in response to a critical letter to the Editor of *The Witness,* defended McGill, asserting:

> . . . it appears that an erroneous impression prevails with regard to the action of McGill University in opening certain classes for women. It is true that a temporary arrangement has been made to meet the emergency of a request on the part of some young ladies to be admitted to the advantages of the University, but the corporation has explicitly refused to commit itself to the institution of a separate college or a separate course of lectures for women and, in accepting the munificent gift of the Hon. Donald A. Smith, stipulated only that it should be applied to the general purpose of "the higher education of women."[14]

Murray, who was a member of Corporation and presumably, therefore, in a position to know, obviously expected some deliberate decision to be taken. The confusion and the University's failure to take a clear policy stand was seized upon by the *Montreal Star.* After some preliminary skirmishing in which the newspaper asserted and the Principal denied that the University was divided against itself on the higher education for women, and that it had no definite policy on separate or co-education, the *Star* sent reporters to interview the individual members of Corporation. (Corporation, which was an antecedent to the McGill Senate, included the Principal, the Governors and elected Fellows.) The reporters posed three questions:

> I. At the date of the special meeting of the Corporation called to consider the Donald A. Smith Donation in September last, was there not in the orders of the day for the October meeting of Corporation a resolution proposing to open the Arts Faculty to women on the same terms as men?

II. When the resolution accepting the Smith Donation was submitted to the Corporation, was it not opposed by several members on the ground that it might be interpreted as committing the Corporation to a particular policy with regard to the subject of co-education, and was it not amended in deference to such opposition in order to avoid that interpretation?

III. When the said resolution was allowed to pass, was it not on a specific assurance given by Sir William Dawson that it should not in any manner affect the discussion upon the question of the policy of the University in the matter? [15]

Those members of Corporation who had not been present at the September meeting were asked to state their "views as to the wisdom of instituting separate classes, taking into consideration the financial condition of the University."

The questions were obviously based on some knowledge of what had been happening at McGill, even though the meetings of the Corporation and the Board of Governors were closed to reporters and to the public. They were submitted to half (22 out of 44) of the members of Corporation and the individual responses were published. Twelve had little to say—some because they felt ill-informed about or indifferent to the issue, some because they thought the transactions of Corporation were confidential and should not be discussed with the press, Murray because he said his views were well known, and Dawson, who did not care to see the questions.

A majority of those who responded directly to the questions answered affirmatively to all three; others could not remember; no one categorically denied them. In other words, they were convinced that the question of the admission of women on equal terms to men still had to be debated and decided by Corporation. From the respondents as a whole, there was some support for co-education, mainly on the ground that it would involve the University in less expense, but Mr. John Dougall had no fear of evil consequences and believed it could result in a higher moral tone. However, a marked overall preference for separate education emerged, both for pragmatic reasons such as respecting the wishes of the donor (and where there was one gift, others might follow) and on the assumption that "the institution of mixed classes would be a remarkably hazardous experiment." The Rev. Dr. Douglas stated that "if he had a daughter who wished to matriculate, he would hesitate very gravely about allowing her to join any mixed classes."

Dawson's reaction to the *Star's* survey was immediate. By the following day, he issued as a twelve-page printed pamphlet a series of public "letters" which he had previously published in the *Gazette*.

These were written in order to explain McGill's position on the admission of women and to refute the *Star's* earlier criticism. In the preface to his pamphlet, Dawson called the *Star's* questions "leading (or more properly misleading)" and complained that a new and important work, one with a "very delicate nature" and which was "liable to misapprehension," was being threatened by the newspaper. In the "letters," Dawson acknowledged that in accepting Donald Smith's money and passing regulations for the Special Course for Women, the University did agree to separate education at least for the junior years, otherwise, he believed the administration would have been guilty of behaving fraudulently and with the intent to deceive. He noted, also, that the University did not bind itself to spend on women's education one extra penny from other sources, nor to commit itself to any particular method for the senior years. He denied that there was anything subversive in having the Faculty of Arts consider what method should be used, since this matter properly fell within the jurisdiction of that Faculty. He noted, as he had in a previous report, that if there were no additional endowment it would be necessary to open some of the advanced classes to women, but it was hoped to provide a choice of separate or co-education. He made the point very strongly: "Should we be unable to give any choice in the matter, I should dread the responsibility involved" and in "case of any *faux pas* or *mésalliance,* such as we sometimes hear of in connection with mixed education, I should in the case of *compulsory* co-education, feel myself morally disgraced, and that is a risk which I do not propose to incur on any consideration whatever."[16]

Dawson's sense of responsibility toward the women students can well be appreciated and it must have been warmly applauded by many of his contemporaries. However, the general problem throughout his regime—and beyond—was the blurring of any distinction between the prevailing *in loco parentis* philosophy, which succoured all students, and a patriarchal approach, which gave special attention to women and in the process denied them certain freedoms. The line of demarcation may be difficult to see, especially when it is obscured by clichés such as the special fragility and refinement of female sensibilities or the innately noble and moral nature of women. It is also difficult to follow Dawson's reasoning, given in the "letters" and elsewhere as a rationale for separate education, namely that women would exert a refining influence on education if instructed in all-female classes. How could their influence permeate through the barriers of separation? However, Dawson's account of the current official actions seemed eminently reasonable and his claims to have acted in good faith essentially convincing. Yet something was amiss. Just what this was can be found in the "letters" that dealt with the history of the McGill situation. In

"Retrospect of Proceedings up to 1884," there is an interesting statement which reveals the basic source of the controversy with the *Star*.

> Since 1870, when the higher education of women was brought under
> the notice of the friends of the university by the Rev. Dr. Wilkes
> [sic], the subject has never been altogether absent from our minds,
> and all those concerned in the management of the university have
> earnestly desired to share in this great work. But we felt that, except
> in so far as we would act in connection with the Ladies' Educational
> Association or by opening our examinations to women, we were
> unable to do much good. So cautious did we feel it necessary to be in
> the matter, that, unlike our sister university in Ontario, we did not
> style our examinations for women matriculation examinations, but
> gave them a special title, lest they might be supposed, as in Ontario,
> to give a legal right to force an entrance into our classes. [17]

There, in the last sentence, is the reason why the girls from
Montreal High technically could be denied admission and why Rosalie
McLea had to do three years of Greek in one in order to fulfill all the
requirements—their curriculum had been purposely designed to make
them inadmissable. But the most significant word in that statement is
"cautious." It was caution in the guise of high moral principle (unless
and until money was forthcoming) that stifled action and that underlay
the inconsistency in Dawson's position on higher education for women.
This caution, in turn, derived from the concept of Woman based on an
idealistic reverence and even fear. Because of this caution, the abstract
principle of whether or not women could and should have higher education was never really confronted and the actions that would follow
logically from it were left in abeyance. That is why the *Star* could, and
did, accuse McGill of drifting into higher education for women.

The *Star* was not convinced by Dawson's explanations. In lengthy
editorials on December 6 and 20, it dismissed his latest pamphlet as
worthless and partisan. It defended its own actions as well as the validity
of its questions to members of Corporation and, for the first time,
attacked the Principal directly. It implied he had brought extraordinary
pressure to bear on the committee investigating the question of women's
admission, causing the long delay in reaching a decision, and it accused
him of manipulating the dealings with the Smith endowment in order to
make separate education the ongoing practice at McGill. It demanded to
know what had really happened at the September, 1884 meeting of
Corporation, what were the exact terms of the correspondence with the
Hon. Donald Smith, and what was the wording of the original motion of
thanks. The *Star* was convinced that the donation was not accepted by

Corporation in the sense maintained by Dawson and it quoted Sir Francis Hincks to the effect that "there is nothing in the condition of the Smith endowment that committed the college to any line of action and the mode of carrying on the higher education of women at McGill is still an open question."[18] It also criticized Dawson for the secrecy in which he conducted the university's affairs and called for open meetings of Corporation.

The editorial writer was obviously a supporter of co-education, noting that while "there are difficulties connected with co-education as with any other," no member of Corporation, not even Dawson, had brought any valid objection against it. Furthermore, there could be no objection to co-education in the first two years that would not also apply to the two senior years. In short, the *Star* was convinced that McGill would spend its money more wisely on enlarging classrooms and improving equipment—which would have to happen in any event—than on separate education when the whole university needed improving. It called upon McGill to "open its doors to all alike, without regard to sex or creed."[19]

Dawson must have been embarrassed to discover that the *Star's* position was explicitly endorsed by the McGill *University Gazette,* the student publication. A December editorial said:

> . . . it appears the height of folly to divert large sums of money, that might be applied to the general improvement of the college, for the purpose of maintaining separate classes. It must be patent to all that this is the real state of the case, for the last benefactor of the University is not an educationist, and the conditions of his gift have probably been determined upon the advice of some one in authority, presumably the Principal. Whoever is the Hon. Mr. Smith's adviser in this matter is certainly not acting in the best interests of the University, and should Mr. Smith insist that this gift be applied to the maintenance of separate classes, the Corporation will be perfectly justified in refusing his benefaction. It is unfortunate that one, whose wisdom has done so much towards building up the University, should have so firmly taken the rather peculiar and inconsistent stand of wishing to weaken an old established faculty, for the sake of founding a new.[20]

This editorial concluded by hoping that Sir William would modify his position. However, when a new editorial board came into office a couple of months later it decided, out of loyalty to its *alma mater* and its esteemed Principal, not to discuss the co-education matter any further. The *Star,* believing it had served some useful purpose in bringing the matter to the attention of the public, also withdrew from the debate. And so the affair died down, leaving the arrangements for separate education in the Donalda Special Course just about where they had been.

* * *

One of the outcomes of all the strife in the papers and on campus was undoubtedly that the legal terms of Donald Smith's second gift were very specific. A Deed of Donation was not drawn up until 1886, and in contrast to the simple, personal letter containing the original $50,000, this was a very formal document. It applied to the total gift of $120,000 for the higher education of women and contained conditions "Without which the grant would not have been made." These called for "a distinct special class in the Faculty of Arts; but as soon as possible the classes shall be erected into a separate College of McGill University for the higher education of women, with a separate building. . . ." They also specified that "the conduct and management of classes for women [shall be] entirely separate from the classes for men, and that no portion of the endowment . . . shall at any time be applied either directly or indirectly to sustain mixed classes of the two sexes."[21]

The terms of this deed would seem to leave no doubt about separate education and also seem to have been designed to protect the man who had borne the brunt of the *Star's* attacks. It is reasonable to believe that Principal Sir William Dawson attempted to make sure that the issue of separate and co-education would be settled once and for all when the University gratefully accepted Sir Donald Smith's generous gift. As the years went by, the benefactor's wishes on separate education were invoked whenever controversy on the point arose. But suspicions still linger that the idea was Dawson's not Smith's. Smith was no educator, no social philosopher. He was a very involved, very successful businessman who learned how to delegate authority to trusted officials and how to take advice. He was open to suggestions, incorporating them into his public credo and taking credit for them where appropriate. A parallel can be drawn to the Strathcona Trust for the instruction of school children in physical drill. In a recent paper in the *Canadian Journal of History of Sport and Physical Education*, Lorne V. Sawula showed that "Historians have all too easily honoured Lord Strathcona [Donald Smith] as the founder of military physical training in Canadian schools. . . . For it was Sir F.W. Borden, Minister of Militia and Defence for Canada, who actually was the initiator of the concept behind the internal and external policies of the Trust. However, it was Strathcona's money which enabled the ideas of Borden to become a working reality."[22] Borden gave Strathcona the idea, Strathcona supported it and, once the project proved successful, became enthusiastic, increasing his monetary contribution and lending his name to the programme. The same basic process might well have taken place with regard to separate education for women at McGill. Just as Borden's ideas became known as Strathcona's, so might have Dawson's.

Meanwhile, the business of the University continued and the practical problems associated with having women on campus awaited solution. Before returning to these, however, it might be noted in passing that in all the debate over the specific use of the Smith endowment for separate education, the argument was never put forward that the restriction would indeed ensure education for women since it would stop the money from being absorbed into general revenues and used for other purposes.[23]

The supporters of separation—at least as reported in the *Star*—seemed to take it on faith that separate education was a moral issue and that ladies must be protected, even from gentlemen scholars. Had they examined their position more closely they would have realized that it was very unfair to the men of McGill, whom they must have assumed to be sex maniacs. The Rev. Dr. Douglas, for example, is reported to have said that, "It was very well to say that the presence of ladies in the classes would put restraint on the young men, but the old proverb said that familiarity breeds contempt, and it was certain that the continued presence of ladies would do away with the restraining effect."[24] This somehow conjures up the curious vision of overwrought young men attempting to storm the barricades erected by Helen Gairdner's knitting wool!

* * *

An indication of the nature of the problems to be faced by the University can be seen from the fact that the members of the Corporation were not certain what they should do about degrees for women. They noted that some other universities awarded women only licentiates, certificates of attendance, or statements of examination results and they considered these as viable alternative possibilities. They hesitated particularly at the thought of granting females the B.A., assuming the Donaldas would proceed that far, and earn the degree, for the word "bachelor" seemed highly inappropriate. To avoid this difficulty, it was suggested that "the degrees conferred on women shall be indicated by the same initial letters as those for men, and that the titles of the degrees shall be chosen to correspond to the initials both in Latin and English."[25] Accordingly, after due consideration of the etymology, the titles of "Baccalaureate," "Magistra" and "Doctrix" were proposed. However, by 1886 Corporation had decided in favour of awarding to women the same B.A. as to men and granting them all the privileges of advancing to the same higher degrees.[26] This welcome decision refer-red only to the Faculty of Arts and entirely ignored the possibility of women's participation in the professional faculties. That was to be a fight for the future.

The question of prizes, scholarships, and medals for women was not so contentious as the matter of degrees. In the first year, Corporation recommended that, provided the donors had no objections, awards should be open to members of both sexes, at least until separate endow-ments such as the Hannah Willard Lyman Fund for women could be established. Members of Corporation considered endowments of that kind were desirable "because of the small number available for either sex, and also because one of the chief dangers to be dreaded in classes for Women, is too severe competition, causing injury to health, and because the conditions of competition between Women and Men, are necessarily different from those of competition between students of one sex."[27] Belief in this last difference must have been partly a question of blind faith in received sex stereotypes, but was not necessarily only that. A considerable body of "respectable" academic opinion held then — and possibly still does — that the intellectual functions of men and women are inherently different so that direct competition between them is academi-cally invalid, if not somehow immoral.

Regardless of all these arguments, the essential fact remained in the Fall of 1884 that women were at McGill. The first class of Donaldas and those in the next few testing years seemed to be very aware of their responsibilities to their supporters and to all members of their sex. According to one of them, each was conscious that "she bore the weight of formulated womanhood upon her shoulders, although men, even then, were not expected to live to the ideal man."[28] Yet, despite the necessity of being "womanly" while proving themselves intellectually competent, despite their apprehensions, their separatedness from the other students, the stuffiness of the rooms in the East Wing and the skepticism of some of the professors, they loved McGill and had a wonderful time. Certainly they were serious students, eager to prove they could cope with the work but, as Octavia Ritchie said, "We were not at all typical 'blue stockings'; on the contrary we were full of life, fun-loving, and at times even irrepressible."[29] These earnest pioneers were sentimental as well as studious, as Ritchie confessed. "Some of us indulged in hero-worship, common to the youth of both sexes. The special object of our romantic adoration was a certain sad, pale-faced instructor [George H. Chandler]. To win a quiet word of approbation from him, we spent long weary hours in solving some intricate mathe-matical problem, or we walked many blocks out of our way on the mere

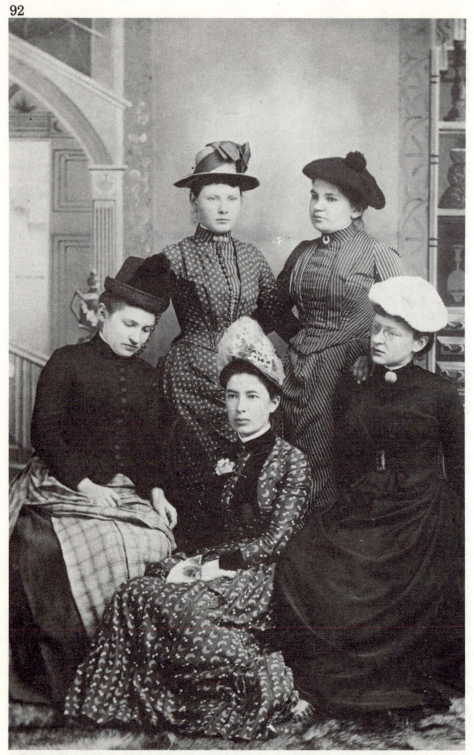

A Group of Donaldas, including Maude Abbott, Grace Ritchie and Blanche Evans

chance of meeting him and receiving a bow and smile of recognition.''

These were the days when ''Montreal was a great sleepy old town, free from noise and bustle, with wood sidewalks, dimly lighted at night by flickering gas jets.''[30]

Though the Donaldas found such an environment to have ''few distracting interruptions and much leisure'' and to be ''well suited to meditation and intellectual concentration,'' they also saw both its romantic and its funny side. Their English instructor [Theodore ''Polly'' Lafleur] was young, eloquent and always ready to enlarge on the beauties of the language. Perhaps it was not surprising that they soon observed that one of their number developed an extraordinary interest in English together with a habit of detaining the intructor by lengthy questions. When mild hints failed to make her change her ways, the other Donaldas decided on drastic measures. ''One evening several of us resolved on a deed of darkness. Like guilty conspirators, a deadly vow of secrecy upon our lips, we crept down the basement stairs, and joining hand to hand, with a sudden pull we turned off the gas! Then through the ensuing blackness we fled to the sound of the professor's irate voice, summoning a bewildered janitor to throw light on the situation. This hint proved effective, but for many days the perpetrators went trembling in fear of discovery, which never came.''[31]

The Donaldas had their separate classes, but they did not go unnoticed on campus and the sheltered existence the Victorian ethos tried to impose upon them inevitably created personal problems. Sometimes the other students stared at them quite blatantly or stood in lines waiting for them to go past. Elizabeth Irwin recalled that ''it required courage in those days to walk from the East Wing to Molson Hall, or the old Library below the Hall. It meant . . . running the gauntlet of the men students who, not yet accustomed to the intrusion of the feminine element, greeted our appearance with the strains, long since forgotten, of 'Hop Along, Sister Mary,' . . . .''[32] Reference to this song recurs, both in the contemporary accounts of the Donaldas and in their reminiscences. In February 1885, one of them complained anonymously, ''We rather do object to being told in so elder-brotherly a style to 'Hop a-long, Sister Mary'. . . . Indeed some of our most strong-minded ladies have wept bitter tears over this insult. Please understand, once and for all, we don't hop!''[33] Octavia Ritchie said that the Donaldas were ''at first blushingly self-conscious,'' but that they ''soon grew indifferent to the refrain'' even though ''for many years the performance was a source of great diversion to the men.'' Apparently, the men had a number of songs they sang *at,* rather than *to,* the women students. Another favourite was ''She Walks Abroad a Dandy with the Buttons Off her Boots,'' which they were likely to sing if they discerned any untidiness in a Donalda's appearance.

This experience of these pioneer women of McGill was strikingly similar to that of Madelon Stockwell, the first female student at the University of Michigan. As this lone woman left the campus after her first day in class in 1870, she found herself running a gauntlet of young men students lined up in force on either side of the path to the gate, "hoping to stare her out of countenance."[34] At least the Donaldas had the comfort of each other's company and, naturally, they kept together. Even with this mutual support, the Donaldas must have needed moral stamina to overcome their fellow students' jibes, whether or not they were intended to be "good-natured." This was essentially the same kind of "guts" that the first black students had to have in more recent years when they integrated all-white schools. The Donaldas were not as militant as the Blacks, of course. Indeed, Elizabeth Irwin commented that "they were thankful to be tolerated."[35] Yet they were not always self-effacing and in 1887 they fought for and won the right to wear academic dress to class like the other students. This must have been an important symbolic victory, one which enhanced their self-recognition as legitimate students. They could draw some self-confidence from the robes of academia but there were many others who still had to be convinced they could be scholars.

For the Donaldas, going to McGill, entering the male domain, demanded considerable determination in order to overcome the misgivings of some of their friends and even of their mothers. Not all the women of Montreal would have wanted their daughters to go to college. Many must have respected the values of "the lady" which kept the fear of the blue stocking very much alive. This antipathy toward the "strong-minded woman" persisted. As a case in point, Alice Lighthall, who was a great-granddaughter of the Rev. Dr. Wilkes and whose father, W.D. Lighthall, an historian and poet, encouraged her to enter McGill in 1911, recalls that her mother would permit her only to register as an Occasional not as a regular undergraduate.[36] Mrs. Lighthall apparently did not care how many courses her daughter took, as long as she did not get a degree and risk the opprobrium of being considered an intellectual. Many mothers were certain that a degree would mean the end of all hopes of marriage, a home and true womanly fulfilment. This is doubtless one of the explanations for the greater number of Occasional than Undergraduate women students in those early years at McGill. And it may be that "motherly intuition" was right, as far as it went. Though comparative statistics are not available for the marriage rates of the Occasionals and the Undergraduates, it seems probable that the Occasionals married more. A survey by Lady Superintendent Helen Gairdner in September 1898 noted that of the 108 Donaldas who had then graduated, only 16 had married.[37] This figure is well below the

My dear Octavia

    I am addressing you by the old name which we all called you in the beloved College days. Your charming article in the McGill News brought back vividly the pleasure of those four happy years. I have always thought that the first class of women students had, particularly during its first year in the

Peter Redpath Museum, a unique and exceptionally delightful experience which no subsequent classes even in their pleasant surroundings which the magnificent Royal Victoria College now offers them can equal, and it pleased me to read in your reminiscences that that had been Miss McFee's opinion. The paper you so kindly sent me I shall place among my most treasured belongings.

With gratitude, and many thanks. Believe me.
Affectionately yours.
    Adaline Van Horne.
      Per J. S. h.
January. 13th 1935.

Letter from an Original Donalda

national average, but it is statistically inexact and does not reveal, for example, whether the graduates married later or whether they never married at all. However, it is known that, of the first graduating class of eight women, four did not ever marry. This proportion is not surprising for graduates of Vassar and the other Eastern U.S. women's colleges at that period also had marriage rates of around 50%.

The odds did not change rapidly. Other statistics compiled in 1920 showed that by 1919, a total of 533 women had graduated from McGill and of these, 194 or about 36.4% had married.[38] In order to give the graduates time to find a husband, it might be fairer to consider these same statistics only from 1888 to 1914. Over that period, there was a total of 184 women graduates, of whom just over 45% had married by 1920 (i.e. at least six years after graduation).

There are no parallel statistics for McGill alumni, for there has been little interest in the question of male matrimony. It has been assumed that higher education presents no special hazard for men's marriageability, that men will marry or not as they choose, and that any correlation between their degrees and marriage rates would be frivolous or irrelevant. These same arguments have gradually been applied to women. That is probably one reason why no more recent statistics on McGill alumnae marriage rates have been compiled. Both the more general acceptance of college education for women and the passage of time help obscure appreciation of the pressures to which the Donaldas were subjected and the dreadful opprobrium of spinsterhood. In spite of the quite real risks of dying "old maids," those early women seemed to have been happy at McGill.

Somehow, they managed to balance their own intellectual ambitions and prevailing social expectations. They apparently avoided raising the strong and bitter hostilities that greeted women on some other campuses (Queen's and Cornell, for example) and yet they were not completely meek. On occasion, they would even challenge Sir William Dawson. They seemed to have admired and respected him, though they were not overawed and they called him "Sir Billy" behind his back. It will be recalled that Dawson held a literalist view of the origin of the universe and so it is not surprising to learn from Carrie Derick that in the 80's, evolution was not yet taught at McGill except by inference in Botany and Geology and then without a Darwinian label.[39] However, after a visit to the caves in the south of France, Dawson gave a vivid lecture on the rich relics of pre-historic human beings to be found there. His "sincere and simple orthodoxy" made the Donaldas curious as to how he managed to reconcile his geology and theology. One of them wondered whether he thought that Adam and Eve, after their expulsion from the Garden of Eden, became the first cavemen and another had the temerity to ask the

Carrie M. Derick, B.A. '90

Principal if that, indeed, was what he thought. Dawson replied gravely, "I suppose we must think so." Later, they laughed at his prediction that airships were an impossibility since muscle was the only motor power of sufficiently light weight for aerial flight.[40] However, they knew he was a scientist of repute and that all his predictions were not so far awry. They must have known that at the meeting of the British Association in 1884, he had predicted an earthquake and that, before the scientists had disbanded, the earthquake had occurred.

Dawson maintained a fatherly interest in the women students and, like the other professors, often invited them to tea at his home. He was a hero to many of them. Seventy years after her graduation in 1894, Isobel Brittain still recalled classes with the Principal. She remembered well how,

> Whenever he could, he took us out of doors and one of the most memorable lessons we had is still vividly with me. It was a Saturday and Sir William took us to St. Helen's island on the first ferry of the day. He seated himself on a huge boulder and we students sat around on the grass and he told us all about rocks and rock formations. His language was beautifully chosen, his personality and teaching ability unsurpassed. He kept his students spellbound. . . .

Excursions such as these were, of course, single-sex affairs. The usual practice was for one professor to take the young men up Mount Royal in search of, say, botanical specimens, while another mentor would lead the women off in the other direction. Even the social gatherings at the Dawsons tended to be separate or, as one Donalda put it, they "precluded dangerous contact with men students" and "every girl was sent home by herself in a cab."[41] The Donaldas fondly believed that it was they who were being protected until one day Carrie Derick had a conversation with Lady Dawson. The latter feared that love affairs, possibly serious ones, might occur between men and women listening to the same lectures. When Derick, a natural science honours student, tried to allay her fears by assuring her that there was little risk of romance since females mature earlier than males and they would be unlikely to fall in love with students of their own age, she received the crushing retort, "I was not thinking of the young women, but of our sons."[42]

* * *

Perhaps any worried matron of Montreal had some cause for concern, for the Donaldas could be very enterprising. In their second year on campus, they established their own tennis club, a somewhat aggressive and "modern" move for it was just a decade since tennis had arrived in North America and only one year after women's matches were begun at Wimbledon.

The Donaldas also set up their literary and debating group named for their benefactor, the Delta Sigma Society. They met each fortnight when they read essays and participated in both prepared and extemporaneous debates. They often discussed Canadian topics. They claimed this was "the only expression of special interest in our country's welfare, and her history past and present, that can be found in connection with either the men's or women's departments. There are in use no text-books on Canadian history,—no lectures are given on the government and administration of the country and the entrance examination seems to require no knowledge of the same."[43] Their debates were at once lively and serious. The very first was on the gentle theme, "Art versus Music as an Influence on the Human Race," but later topics were not so innocuous. They included current and perennial issues such as "Free Trade," "Women's Suffrage," "Capital and Labour," "Equal Pay for Equal Work" and "Co-operative Housekeeping." One report of Delta Sigma indicates that on December 8, 1887, "the members of this society repaired to the house of one of their honorary members, Mrs. J. Clark Murray, whither they had been invited to meet Sir Donald A. Smith, and to initiate him in the proceedings of the society which bears his initials. After the ladies had been presented to Sir Donald, the meeting was opened with a well-written paper by Miss Murphy, entitled: 'Vice Versa; or a society girl as viewed by a college girl.' The subject for debate was then given out: 'Are we better than our grandmothers?' The question was an interesting one, referring as it did, to the recent stand taken by women with regard to the study of Arts and Medicine in the Universities."[44]

Principal Dawson monitored the activities of the Delta Sigma Society and generally gave his approval. However, when a really contentious local issue appeared, he could and did invoke censorship. Early in 1888, the expressly forbidden topic of "Co-education" happened to come up spontaneously and was debated by Delta Sigma. The *Montreal Star* reported that there was a large attendance at this event and "the whole question was carefully discussed." According to the newspaper, the vote on the debate "must have come as a surprise to some, when only the smallest minority—2 we believe—were found in favor [sic] of separate education, the system it has been tried to set in motion at McGill."[45]

Perhaps if the vote had gone the other way, Principal Dawson would not have been so angry. As it was, he was most upset that his orders had been disobeyed and that "Co-Education" had been debated. He apparently also thought that the publicity might deter Sir Donald Smith from giving McGill more money to support a women's college, something he was then contemplating doing. Therefore, the officers of the Delta Sigma Society were called upon to explain their actions to Sir William. Their "unmitigated joy for having asserted a right to freedom of speech"[46] faded during the "bad half hour" they spent with the Principal. Yet, while they promised not to do it again, they seemed unconvinced by the censor's motives "and left his presence wondering whether their opinions really were of such importance as to deter, in all probability, 'their generous and noble benefactor' from doing something almost royally magnificent for future Donaldas." Carrie Derick suggested that they privately questioned Dawson's right of censorship and she said that "they also discussed the ethics of establishing an institution and trying to fix its policy for all time."[47] The Donaldas might have been able to see more clearly than Dawson that social change would sooner or later challenge and undermine the efforts to maintain separate education.

In all fairness, however, this incident with its display of paternalism should be related to the context of the McGill of the time. Most students were very young, females were required to be at least sixteen years of age, but males might be less, so that Dawson and the other professors often treated male students, too, like children. In a memoir of the period, Sir Andrew Macphail wrote,

> . . . one or two of the ordinary courses differed little from a grammar school, save that certain of the classes were lacking in discipline. One professor sent a troublesome boy to see the Principal. The boy returned not appreciably chastened. "Did you see the Principal?" "Yes, Sir." "What did he say to you?" "Nothing; you only told me to see him." "Well, go and speak to him." The boy returned. "What did you say to the Principal?" "I said 'Good morning, sir.' " "What did he say to you?" "He was very polite; he lifted his hat, and said, 'Good morning.' "[48]

By comparison, the Donaldas probably seemed quite mature! And if the first women at McGill were not always meek and demure, their male contemporaries were not always churlish or childish. Indeed, they were quite gracious in their acceptance of the innovation of having women in their midst. In their first issue for 1884, which was published about a month after the Donaldas appeared on campus, the editors of the McGill *University Gazette* extended their "heartiest welcome to the ladies who have taken the initiative in applying for admission to our College halls." They further assured the women that they were glad to have them there and that "we shall watch your success, not with jealous and spiteful eyes, but with appreciative and delighted attention."[49] In a similarily supportive vein, a senior student laughed at the freshmen who, according to rumour, had petitioned the Faculty of Arts to have their Christmas examinations separately from the women. "What a shame it is," he scoffed, "that the Faculty should ask them to compete with the girls, and be ranked in the same class-lists with them."[50] In the event, the Faculty of Arts did announce that the Donaldas would not be ranked with the other students, but it seems to have forgotten to put this into practice for, while the examinations were held separately and the results revealed at different times and in different rooms, men and women were ranked together. The Donaldas did very well, and again, the *University Gazette* applauded warmly. Under the heading, "Ladies First," it said, "We heartily congratulate the ladies upon the success which has attended their first examination in McGill. That success was not wholly unexpected, it is only another evidence of the effect of concentration and industry." Then it spoiled the effect by going on to imply that the men had not really been trying and urged them on to greater effort. "Our lazy Freshmen may well take a lesson from their rivals. No longer will it be safe for them to divide their energies between hockey, football, the regular course, and the private lines of reading which most first year students lay out for themselves. Steady application must now be the rule if the men are to hold their own."[51]

The Donaldas obviously appreciated the support they received from the men of McGill and one of them wrote:

> I should like to express our sincere gratitude for the kindly welcome we received from the gentlemen undergraduates, they have shown kindly feeling on every possible occasion. In the *Gazette* we have been wished every manner of success in our studies, and all kinds of nice little speeches have been made about us. [52]

Then, with a relaxed touch of humour, she added, "Especially have we been gratified by your showing us so plainly that we belong to your numbers by your cordial and overpowering invitation to join in the thick of the scrimmage in your football-matches. Which invitation, out of consideration of the other side, we thought best to refuse."

* * *

The *University Gazette* and, later, other campus publications maintained an ongoing interest in the whole question of higher education for women—so much so that, one of the Donaldas commented during the *Star* controversy that "lately murders, suicides, and even liquid hints at the doings of Carnival week have sunk into shadow and comparative oblivion besides the all-absorbing topic of 'The Higher Education of Women.' " She appeared to be tired of the quarrel over separate or co-education and urged the men involved to "say all the bitter things you have to say now, and then fill up the space formerly occupied by these words with poetry, essays, or even sensational stories!"[53] This the *University Gazette* proceeded to do, but even then it published a great deal of material on "the all-absorbing topic." Its "College News" column frequently included items on women in other universities; "Societies" gave space to Delta Sigma, the Ladies Missionary Society, and the Theo Dora Society; "Between Lectures," which was a miscellaneous section, contained numerous brief reports on the women of McGill; and then there were many jokes about female students and an occasional poem. "Feathers From the East Wing" was the Donaldas' own regular column, edited by Blanche Evans. In 1892, the *McGill Fortnightly* began publishing as a "Journal of Literature, University Thought and Event" and it had women on its Editorial and Business Boards from the beginning. After five years, the *Fortnightly* gave way to the weekly *Outlook*. Lucy E. Potter was the first general editor of the *Outlook* and, indeed, she was the first woman to hold that position on any McGill student publication. It is perhaps surprising to find that in the 19th century, women were both the material for copy and active participants in college journalism.

In the earliest Donalda years, the *University Gazette* was the only student publication. Fortunately, its tone was generally sympathetic to the general question of higher education for women. For example, it included a note on "Unfortunate Vassar," which reportedly had become the butt of jokes simply because it was the pioneer North American college for women;[54] and, apropos of women in Belgian universities, came the comment that, "It is difficult enough for men to achieve even moderate success as lawyers or doctors; and the task of women even when it is not illegal for them to practise medicine or jurisprudence, is even harder."[55] Less enthusiastic was a report on foreign students at the University of Geneva where, "it is not an uncommon sight for a Russian student (female) to be found working away in 'Anatomie' with a lighted cigarette in her mouth."[56]

The campus paper seemed to have accepted women as students, but not as smokers. It observed in 1887, "The Principal has allowed the ladies to assume the students' gown at lectures: but he has kicked strongly, and, we think, justly, against their wearing plug hats and cigarettes in the streets."[57] The following year, it published the following poetic aversion to "The Cigarette Smoker," who was clearly the symbol of the fast and loose woman:

I

Mark her, as she stands,
Match alight,
Eyes as bright,
Shielding with her hands
The tender flame;
Holding in her lips,
Where the bee, Love, sips,
Joy of Leisure
Beyond measure,
Cigarette by name.

II

There! it makes her cough.
If she smoke
Must she choke
When the fumes come off?
Now she denies
Cigarette her lips
Holds it burning,
To ash turning
Till at last it dies.

III

Thus she lit my heart,
Lit it well
With the spell
Of love's magic art;
And just as I
Burned with all love's fire,
Shrank from my desire,
Let my yearning
And heart burning
Into ashes die.[58]

It may well be that, in these later days of anti-smoking campaigns, the sentiments of the 19th century student poet will find renewed support.

The *University Gazette* also commented with surprise on a report that at the University of Geneva, co-education was "against the wishes of nearly all the parties concerned." In the autumn of 1884, one of its editorials had discussed the report presented to Corporation by Sir William Dawson and had queried the notion that co-education was not gaining ground and that in one instance had been abandoned. To the editors of the *University Gazette*, "this state of things seems strange." They argued reasonably: "We are allowed, and the plan works alright,

[sic] to attend church with the ladies; and it is difficult to understand why we cannot with equal pleasure sit together and listen to the lectures of a professor, especially in the department of Arts.''[59]

* * *

While McGill had made special provision for classrooms for the women students, not until the turn of the century was it able to provide residential accommodation. Until then, students lived at home or in approved boarding houses. A concerned graduate noted that of the 43 undergraduates in 1893, more than a third came from outside Montreal —from Saint John N.B., Hamilton, Huntingdon, Ottawa, Quebec, and Trois Rivières—and she saw both a residence and dining hall as crying needs.[60] The physical welfare of the students, however, was not over-looked. Both Miss Gairdner and Miss Barnjum, who was appointed as an instructor in gymnastics in 1888, had responsibility in this area. Miss Barnjum was the sister of Frederick S. Barnjum, who had been asso-ciated with gymnastics at McGill since 1867. She came to instruct the Donaldas following a resolution by the Faculty of Arts:

> That if a number of students in the Donalda Department, not less than 12, be willing to form a class in Gymnastics on the same terms of payment as men, the Faculty will recommend to the Governors that the necessary arrangements be made.[61]

Miss Barnjum and her assistants [62] appeared to endorse the view that exercise would relieve the stress of intellectual activities. The question of the incompatibility of study and the female brain was still a live issue, and the journalist who wrote that college girls suffer from ''a morbid self-consciousness, and a tense excitability which causes a pro-portionate loss of mental power,''[63] still found a sympathetic reader-ship. Furthermore, Harvard professor Edward Clarke's *Sex in Education —A Fair Chance for the Girls,* though published in 1873, still exerted strong influence throughout North America. It predicted that concen-trated study, examinations and the stress of competition with men would permanently disable women—their biological functions would be so affected that if higher education for women persisted for 50 years, wives would have to be imported. Mabel Norton Evans, writing in the *McGill Fortnightly,* was unafraid that gymnastics would cripple the Donaldas in this way; rather she saw more danger in the traditional female up-bringing and fashionable clothing. In a statement that could almost be mistaken for a 1970's consciousness raiser, she said:

When girls are young they join their brothers in many games, and nothing contributes more towards their healthy development; but as time goes on they must gradually withdraw themselves from this active fun, even a good romp among themselves being looked upon as unbecoming. The gradual lengthening of the skirt and the lengthening of the dress make such exercise difficult if not impossible, and the girl soon finds that walking is now almost the only exercise within her reach, and one which is very difficult to keep up unless a special object demand it. The inevitable results follow, the color leaves the cheek and the brightness the eye; headaches, the proof of indigestion, are too frequently present; the muscles become soft and flabby for want of exercise, and the circulation is impaired. Under such condition the brain cannot be properly fitted to carry on the heavy mental work which forms such a large part of the occupation of this time of life.[64]

McGill's Director of Physical Education, R. Tait McKenzie, concurred. The man who was to become famous as a sports physiology artist, welcomed women to the gym programme, even though the facilities were only a cold shower in a dark corner, the heating by two wood stoves was totally inadequate, the ceiling was in such a condition that falling plaster was a hazard and the roof was so leaky that on rainy days the floor was covered with pools of water. Undeterred by all this, some of the women enjoyed the gym work and it was reported of one Donalda that, "although she endangered the lives of those around her by the wild swinging of clubs at first, she now manages them so skillfully as to inspire wonder instead of dread."[65] The active women also encouraged each other, urging more to turn out for tennis because its "imperative demand for a quick eye, steady hand and swift foot precludes the possibility of deep thought."[66] As a result of efforts such as these, Tait McKenzie was able to report on the favourable relationship between the Donaldas' scholastic and athletic achievements:

. . . the gymnasts not only make a good showing at examinations but are much less exhausted than the others. A senior and junior prize has been given by Sir Donald Smith and the standing of the winners for the last three years is significant. In 1889-90 the winner of the senior prize took first rank honours and the philosophy medal. The junior prize was captured by a young lady who came out first in the ordinary course.

In 1890-91, the holder of the first prize took a good stand in her B.A. examinations and the junior winner has first rank honours and the philosophy prize to her credit.

In the session 1891-92, the medal prize and first rank honours in philosophy were won by the best gymnast, and the junior winner, besides six other prizes, took a higher stand than has ever been taken by a lady undergraduate before. Three out of four of the medalists in the Donalda course were gymnasium girls, as one of their number writes, "The girls who come through their examinations with the fewest headaches and backaches and with the brightest faces are those who give the hour or two weekly to the delightful work of Miss Barnjum."[67]

The Donaldas' achievements were the more creditable considering that the women were assigned the gym during the very inconvenient early morning hours and they received minimal financial support for their tennis club—a total of $25 in 1898, for example, while the men received $750. These are the kinds of inequities which nowadays might call for "affirmative action" but they did not generate much protest in the 80's and 90's.

* * *

While the health of the Donaldas was a matter of concern, Corporation was assured that "the daily walk to and from classes, though involving some fatigue and exposure, has been advantageous."[68] However, in 1886 one of the most brilliant of the original women undergraduates withdrew. Rosalie McLea left McGill after two highly successful years. She did not withdraw because her health was strained; she stepped aside so that her brother, Ernest, might have the opportunity to study Applied Science at McGill. It was by no means an unusual occurrence that, if necessary, a young woman's education should be sacrificed for her brother's, but Rosalie McLea must have been heartbroken.

It was no wonder that the little group of Donaldas was distressed when Rosie dropped out. Described by one of her friends as "handsome brilliant, magnetic,"[69] she scored the highest marks ever in the Associate of Arts examination. She had been the one to speak to Dawson on the "momentous mission" seeking entry to McGill. She was a leader of her group and the first President of Delta Sigma. Her departure was a blow. Though she never returned to McGill, she stayed in touch with the women students and helped them in their efforts to gain admission to the medical faculty. She is reported to have helped raise at least $12,000 for that purpose.[70] In 1935, shortly after her death, Rosalie McLea's memory was honoured when a presentation of her portrait was made to the Delta Sigma Society. Her friends were convinced that though she did not become a graduate of McGill, Rosalie McLea had contributed a great deal to the success of the Donalda experiment and that later generations of women at McGill had reason to thank her.

Before the third year was over, two more left the ranks of the Donaldas—Mary Simpson to be married and Helen Reid because of serious illness. The latter, another of the little group that had called on Dawson, now found herself separated from her classmates. Disappointed and disheartened, she almost gave up. However, she was persuaded to return, repeated the year, and graduated in 1889 with the second group of women, winning first class honours in Modern Languages as well as the Governor General's Gold Medal. This fine academic performance was followed by a dedicated career of public service. Her activities with the Canadian Patriotic Fund during World War I in particular, earned her national and international recognition, numerous medals and distinctions. Withal, she maintained strong links with McGill. She was an important force in the early days of the School of Social Work, where she lectured in Public Health, and was also instrumental in the development of the School of Graduate Nursing. In 1918 she was selected by the Board of Governors as one of its nominees on the Corporation of the University. She was the first woman graduate to be so chosen.[71] How fortunate that Helen R. Y. Reid, one of the intrepid pioneers of women's education at McGill, returned to finish her course.

While the original class lost three members, it gained two along the way. Jane V. Palmer, who had received her preparatory training in England and at the McGill Normal School, joined the class of '88 in the third year. So did Georgina Hunter. Miss Hunter had been a teacher at the Montreal High School for Girls and had actually taught some of the Donaldas there. She was to graduate with highest standing in the honours course in English Language and Literature and as winner of the Shakespeare Gold Medal. Later, she became Lady Principal of the Girls' High School, served as teachers' representative on the Protestant Committee of the Council of Public Instruction of Quebec, and worked indefatigably for the Canadian Patriotic Fund during the War. She, too, kept her ties with McGill, helping establish the Alumnae Society and becoming its first president.

Donalda McFee was another of the first class of women with an outstanding academic record. After graduation, she took Dr. J. Clark Murray's advice to study Philosophy at Cornell, then she moved on to Leipzig where she worked under Wilhelm Wundt. She became the first McGill alumna to earn a Ph.D., which was awarded *cum laude* by the University of Zurich in 1895. It should be noted that the interests of these original Donaldas were not confined to the Humanities. Blanche Evans was to graduate with First Class Honours in Science—though she was also a talented painter who felt herself privileged to draw the fossil leaves for one of Sir William Dawson's publications, and for four years she was the editor of the "Feathers From the East Wing" column in the *University Gazette*. Until her marriage she taught drawing and natural science then, as she recorded, "her married life was mainly spent in furthering the career of a brilliant husband who died just when his success as an ear specialist was established."[72] Alice Murray, who also became a teacher, Martha Murphy, who went on to graduate work at Cornell, and Eliza Cross, who was remembered as a "sweet, serene, good looking girl who did not allow her early engagement to interfere with her studies," all succeeded at McGill and formed part of the first graduating class. Eliza Cross married the Rev. Dugald Currie, also a McGill graduate and their son, George, was to become not only the first McGill student whose parents were both alumni of the University, but also a lecturer in Accounting, President of the Graduates' Society, and member of the Board of Governors.

The final member of that special class of '88 was Octavia Grace Ritchie. She had been prominent in the struggle for admission, had played a leadership role throughout the four years in the Faculty of Arts, and had graduated with first class honours in Natural Science. She was

Donalda Reunion, May 1938 (*Standing, l. to r.*) Esther England, Martha Murphy Breithaupt, Susan Cameron Vaughan, Marion Taber Byers (*Sitting, l. to r.*) Georgina Hunter, Grace Ritchie England, Donalda McFee, Maude Abbott

chosen to give the Valedictory Address on behalf of her class on the historic occasion when women first received B.A.'s from McGill. [73]

For many years, McGill students had participated actively in their graduation ceremony with an address by the most distinguished of their number. In 1888, with a class of Donaldas about to graduate, it was decided to have two valedictorian addresses—one representing the women, one the men. The addresses were duly prepared and submitted to the Principal. Unfortunately, Sir William Dawson did not altogether approve of what Octavia Ritchie intended to say and he exercised his powers of censorship. He also stipulated that her speech, as amended by him, was not to be delivered from the same rostrum that the men used.

What aplomb it must have taken for a young woman of 20 to rise before a packed audience that included not only the distinguished Principal and all the begowned dignitaries of McGill, but also Governor-General Lord Lansdowne who was Visitor of the University. What confidence it must have taken for her to read, without benefit of microphone, her address to that imposing audience. What spirit it must have taken to approach the prohibited rostrum, as she did, and to deliver her speech as originally prepared. The spokeswoman for the first Donaldas was quite unintimidated as she acknowledged her responsibility to the cause of higher education for women.

In her valedictory on April 30, 1888 "Tavie" Ritchie recounted the history of the admission of women to McGill and spoke of the progress made during the four years in the Faculty of Arts; she thanked Sir Donald Smith for his generous help; and noted, to laughter from the audience, that the first club formed by the Donaldas was the lawn tennis club "so might be dispelled the prevailing idea that the members of the Donalda course, with but few exceptions, are blue stockings."[74] Then boldly she assailed the forbidden section. "The doors of the Faculty of Arts were opened four years ago; those of Medicine still remain closed. When will they be opened?" Voices from the audience could be heard to exclaim, "Never!" "That's so!" "Shame!" Someone clapped. Ritchie continued, emphasizing the need for medical women in the missionary fields and asked if it were right for the University to deprive women of doing good. She concluded strongly with "A medical course should be provided for women in this city and in this Province. Sometime it must be done; the only question is when?"

As she sat down amid the applause and the presentation of a bouquet of flowers from the gentlemen students, a kindly neighbour asked solicitiously, "Are you not very tired?" "Tavie" Ritchie was anything but wilted. She was triumphant.

In his response, Principal Dawson recounted his version of the admission of women to McGill, agreed that "eminent success" had

Universitas McGill,

Monte Regio, in Provincia Canadensi. Omnibus ad quos hae Literae pervenerint Salutem.

NOS REGENTES, PRIMARIUS ET SOCII COLLEGII McGILL, TESTAMUR;

Octaviam Grahiam Ritchie

per illud tempus quo apud nos commorata est, omnes disciplinas quae ad Artium Facultatem hujus Universitatis pertinent, diligenter ac feliciter navasse et, praestitis rite omnibus exercitiis ad hoc constitutis, Gradum

Baccalaureatus in Artibus

adeptam esse.

In cujus rei Testimonium, Sigillum Universitatis Literis hisce more usitato subscriptis apponi fecimus.

Datae in Comitiis solennibus die Tricesimo Mensis Aprilis
Anno Domini MDCCCLXXXVIII

J. Ferrier. Cancellarius.
J. Gulielmus Dawson, LL.D. Primarius.
Carolus F. A. Markgraf, A.M. Litt. Germ. Prof.
Joannes Clark Murray, LL.D. Log. et Eth. Prof.
B. J. Harrington, B.A. Ph.D. Chem. et Min. Prof.

The Degree of the First Woman Valedictorian, 1888

attended the enterprise, saying that he could not have wished for better students than this first class. He touched but lightly on the matter of professional education for women, all but dismissing it as a simple matter of supply and demand. He ended on a note of good will: ". . . we shall always take a special interest in our first graduating class of women, and . . . you leave us now with our sincere good wishes."[75] Lord Lansdowne, too, was impressed, offering his congratulations "in the name of a Sovereign who by her own bright example has shown that the sex is no disqualification for the discharge of the highest duties of the State." He was so enthusiastic he suggested that henceforth the office of Visitor "should be held conjointly by the Governor-General and his wife"—an idea no one took very seriously.

But in that Spring of 1888, the eight new Bachelors of Arts left the hall in triumph. According to the *Montreal Gazette,* "In their flowing gowns and black silk hoods lined with red and white, they gave the impression of seriousness and grace, and looked anything but the conventional bluestocking."[76] These eight were the first of an ever-increasing stream of successful women students; they were admired, scorned, respected, loved; they were the prototypes of McGill's version of the "Sweet Girl Graduate," soon to be celebrated by an unknown poet in *Old McGill:*

The Sweet Girl Graduate

"You're a modern production," the young man said,
"And a skirt it is true that you wear—
Yet in the exams you all come out ahead!
Do you think, with your sex, it is fair?"

"Long ago," said the girl, "I was under your thumb,
And was thought not to have any brain:
But now that I'm perfectly sure I have *some*—
It's amusing the prizes to gain!"

"You're a girl," said the youth, "and you used to look sweet
When knitting or cooking the dinner:
But now on the steps of McGill when we meet,
You look worried—and certainly thinner!"

"Long ago," said the girl, "we were given as wives,
To be fooled by such creatures as you!
But now we're enlightened and give our young lives
To colour our stockings with blue."

"You're a girl," said the youth, "and you put great reliance
On Men when you're frightened by Mice—
But to take up the study of Medical Science!
Do you think, for a girl, it is nice?"

"Long ago," said the girl, with a toss of her head,
"You kept us in ignorance drear:
But now we know everything written or said,—
And there's nothing on earth that we fear!"

"You are mad," said the youth, who was looking most glum,
"On things such as Hydrostatics!
For you surely must know that you'll never become
A mother by Mathematics."

"I know all the sciences, that is enough,"
Said the girl, as she put on her glasses;
"Do you think I want *Love* or such finicking stuff?
Be off!—I must go to my classes." [77]

Chapter FOUR

"...All This Hubbub"

Monday, April 30, 1888 was an important day with historic overtones. Eight Donaldas had just become part of a very select group of women in Canada, or for that matter, in the entire world, who could rightfully add the revered letters "B.A." to their names. Perhaps some of the people who had been present at the graduation ceremony might have been embarrassed by Octavia Ritchie's boldness, but the Donaldas must have been enormously proud of her and her valedictory address. Tuesday, May 1, 1888 was also an important day with far-reaching consequences. After the ceremonies at the university, the Delta Sigma Society met once more to congratulate the graduates and to consider some questions of intellectual interest. Since this was a very special occasion, written invitation cards were issued. These invitations requested members of Delta Sigma and their friends to gather at the home of Mrs. Jessie Ritchie, Octavia's mother, to hear an "Essay, Debate, and Address by Dr. Murray."

The meeting began with the reading of a prize-winning essay by former Donalda, Rosalie McLea. This was followed by a debate on "Co-operative Housekeeping," an avant-garde topic, especially considering this was more than a decade before the publication of Charlotte Perkins Gilman's radical work on the subject. Georgina Hunter and Helen Reid took the affirmative side, which called for a thorough rethinking of the traditional domestic role of women, while Carrie Derick and Alice Murray spoke for the negative. Dr. J. Clark Murray was then asked to fulfill his promise to say something about the visit he had made to Vassar College at Christmas.

Dr. Murray began by describing the buildings and their management by the first Lady Principal, Hannah Willard Lyman, and commenting upon the fact that Vassar was one of the first institutions to provide collegiate education for women. As he proceeded, Murray suggested that, had Matthew Vassar, the founder, lived longer he probably would have left his money in a different way. According to Murray, Mr. Vassar was genuinely interested in developing higher education for women and would have endowed a college to form an annex to some other college

113

where women would have their separate residence and so forth, but would attend classes with men.[1] Murray was aware that this view was not universally held, but he himself was in favour of co-education.

Indeed, Murray had quite openly declared his position the previous evening at the annual University Dinner held at the Windsor Hotel. Principal Dawson had not been present. He apologized in advance that "some important considerations prevent us from leaving our own buildings on an occasion so important. . . ."[2] Unfortunately, he could not have known just how important that evening was to be, or how its aftermath would haunt him for the rest of his life. Had he been present and heard the speeches, he might have revised his opinion about current attitudes toward co-education. He might then have had more sympathy with the tone of Dr. Murray's later pronouncements on the subject and his relationship with that gentleman might have been different. He might have been spared a very long and unpleasant argument.

The University Dinner which Dawson missed was generally a happy celebration at the end of the academic year. On this occasion, a goodly number of learned professors from McGill were in attendance, as well as educators from other parts of Canada and the United States. The guests included some who had just received McGill honorary degrees. The Rev. Dr. J. Clark Murray, who was a witty, forceful after-dinner speaker, had been called upon to talk, and according to the account in the Montreal *Daily Witness* the following day, he was greeted with tremendous applause. He commented favourably on recent developments in some of the Scottish universities where students could elect their own Rector and, as he spoke of the education of women, "he was cheered to the echo." There were some "rights," he is reported to have said, which the best women did not care much about; but there was one which all must acknowledge—their right to the highest culture of which they were capable. Those who had most at heart the importance and sacredness of the family as the centre of all that was best in humanity felt most strongly that no education was too high for her whose influence was most potent. However, the advantages of higher education had been denied women, not through any fault of theirs, but by the power of tradition. The old universities originated in monasteries and traces of their monastic character still existed. For example, in a college of St. Andrew's University, Scotland, there was a rule that no woman must enter except the washerwoman—and she must be over sixty!

Murray said that the whole spirit of the modern world was against separation and that social morality would not be promoted, but hindered, by keeping the sexes apart. Keeping the sexes separate was not God's order of life, but an artificial order of our own manufacture. In academic life, the intermingling of men and women would have the same good results as in outside society. This was greeted by "great cheering" and supported by another strong speech by Dr. Anderson, one of McGill's new LL.D.'s, who told how "the men and women get on together in Prince Edward Island."[3] A contemporary commentator noted:

> Judging from the speeches delivered at the Windsor Hotel on Monday Evening by Principals MacVicar, Henderson, Dr. Heneker, Dr. Anderson, Hon. W.W. Lynch and others, the question of co-education of the sexes seems to be the popular cry. And McGill college, which has ever sought to be in the front, must see to it that she is not left behind in the race to provide higher education for women.[4]

The discussion of co-education was open, free and genial so that Murray must have felt no hesitation in expressing his support for it the following day at the Delta Sigma Society meeting. He said he saw no reason why both men and women should not receive lectures together, though they might have separate entrances to each class-room, if desired, and occupy different sides of the room. Or, he added (most probably with a smile and tongue in cheek), they could be railed off if necessary! Murray also commented upon the fact that the members of the Delta Sigma Society had already debated the question of co-education. The outcome of that debate must have surprised him somewhat because he added that until he heard about how the motion in favour had been approved by all but two votes, he had had no idea the Donaldas supported co-education so strongly. From this it must be assumed that he had not previously raised the matter with his students in class and this was the first time he had broached the subject directly with the Donaldas. Now, however, he reportedly urged the students present "to make their voices heard as an important body in the university."[5]

Dr. Murray's talk was probably as popular at the Delta Sigma meeting as his speech had been at the University Dinner. But someone found it offensive. Someone reported it immediately to Principal Dawson. He was not amused. Apparently in haste and anger and with no consultation whatsoever, he wrote to his Professor of Philosophy the very next day:

May 2, 1888

Rev Dr. Murray:

Dear Sir:

Reports having reached me from credible sources that at a meeting called by officers of the Delta Sigma Society, and held yesterday, and at which many students of the classes for women were present, an address was delivered by you tending to influence the minds of students against the regulations of the University for their separate education in accordance with the obligations entered into with the founder of the Donalda College for Women; and as such action on your part would be directly subversive of good discipline, and contrary to the Statutes and Regulations, it becomes my duty as Principal to ask that you will give me such statement as may enable me to inform the Board of Governors respecting your said action; or if you prefer this, that you will communicate such information directly to the Chancellor. [The Hon. James Ferrier]

I regret to have to make such a request, and trust that you may be able to assure me that I have been misinformed.

You will kindly observe that I make no reference to the apparent infringement of the rules of the Faculty by a discussion held in a private house and of the subject of which no previous notification was given as required by the rules. This is for the Faculty to deal with as it may deem proper.

Nor does this communication call for any historical account of the agitation of subjects connected with the education of women or arguments respecting separate education, but simply asks for facts as to any tendency in the address above mentioned to appeal to the students as judges in a matter already determined by the University, or to cause them to be dissatisfied with the arrangements for their education under Chap. IV, Section 1, Sub-sec. 8 of the Regulations. In case of any such tendency I would further ask what course you propose to take in the matter and with reference to your personal obligations under chapter X, Section 1 of the Statutes.

I write to you promptly, in hope that any public discussion of the circumstances referred to may be averted in the interests of the University, which in view of the new endowments and legislation proposed, may be very seriously damaged thereby.

I beg to remain

Yours truly,

(Signed) J Wm Dawson
Principal

Dawson's reaction seems extraordinarily heavy-handed. Under the circumstances—the lightheartedness of spring, the triumph of the Donaldas' graduation, the end of the academic year, the positive and public newspaper reports on the speeches on co-education at the University Dinner, and the fact that the Delta Sigma meeting took place at a private house off-campus—Dawson might easily have ignored the whole thing. Later, he must have wished that he had. Alternatively, he could simply have asked Murray (or anyone else who had been present) what had happened at Mrs. Ritchie's or he might have sent Murray a brief note requesting a report on the evening. Incredible as it seems, he did not even check with Miss Gairdner, the Lady Superintendent, who was there to safeguard the morals of the young ladies. Not until December 1893, five and a half years later, did he ask her for a written account of Murray's presentation. It seems strange that on the basis of hearsay alone the Principal should have written such a stern, serious letter to one of his senior professors, and it is almost ludicrous that he should have cited chapter and verse of the University Regulations dealing with the provisions for the separate education of women and the Statutes referring to moral conduct and discipline.[6] It might be assumed that upon first hearing of Murray's alleged misdemeanor, he was furious and dashed off his accusation impulsively. However, three days later (May 5th), he was still so upset he did not wait for a reply but submitted his complaint to a special meeting of the Board of Governors.

The Governors presumably were at something of a loss and needed more information. They instructed Dawson to ask for an early reply from Dr. Murray and to advise him of the necessity for "cordial co-operation on the part of all connected with the university in the work of women's education."[7] They expected that Murray's answer would be "final and satisfactory." So, as instructed, Principal Dawson wrote once more to Professor Murray on 7th May, advising that he had "communicated a copy of the letter to the Chancellor and Board of Governors" and requesting a reply by May 12th.

But on the very day of the Governors' meeting, J. Clark Murray had begun a carefully considered, eleven-page reply to Dawson's first letter, which, after all, had been written only three days earlier. Murray was incensed, as Dawson must have known he would be. In subjecting Dawson's accusations to detailed scrutiny, he denied any responsibility for the Delta Sigma debate on co-education, resented the presence of an informer at the recent meeting, chided Dawson for "receiving the secret report of an officious talebearer," and utterly rejected the allegation that he was attempting to subvert the morals of the students. He denied Dawson's requests for facts "as to any tendency in the address to appeal to the students as judges or to cause them to be dissatisfied," noting: "I

Sir William Dawson, 1892

am surely justified by such a request in inferring that you yourself feel that, though determined to prosecute me before the Board of Governors, you have no ground to go upon and are therefore obliged to apply to me for the facts upon which to base your prosecution.''[8] Then he continued, with some sarcasm, ''It is not usual, I believe, even under very rudimentary forms of justice, to ask the accused to incriminate themselves; but I should have been perfectly willing to help you out of your difficulty, if I had the vaguest idea of what it is that you really want. My address was certainly one of the most unpretentious that I have ever delivered to any audience; and even though you are attempting to make a mountain of the little molehill, I adhere to the belief that it was little likely to exercise any influence worth speaking of upon my hearers. I fear I must also acknowledge that it was a very rambling affair; and among the various topics that I skimmed over, it is impossible to say what it was that your informer considered so suitable for your purposes. I regret therefore that I must refer you to your informer for the facts which you ask me to supply.'' As he continued, Murray took the opportunity to criticize the Principal and the Board of Governors for forcing separate education upon the University in opposition to the ''overwhelming majority of graduates and professors, as well as of students.'' In conclusion, he summarized the situation, spelling out his strong indignation at the complaint Dawson had made against him, ''respectfully but firmly'' requesting that the Principal's letter be ''frankly and fully'' withdrawn.

On 7th May, before he had mailed this response, Murray received Dawson's second missive and learned that the accusation had been laid before the Board of Governors. Murray regretted this serious step and added a P.S. ''. . . There can now be no doubt as to the legal aspect of your action; by your own admission you have made a deliberate attempt to damage my social and professional standing. In the event, therefore, of your refusing my request, there can of course be no alternative left for me, but that of placing the matter in the hands of my lawyers.''

Murray was correct in expecting Dawson to refuse his request to withdraw the accusation—matters had now gone too far for the Principal to retract gracefully. And well might Murray have wondered what to make of the whole thing. Why should a secure, respected person, so successful an administrator, so eminent a patriarch as Sir William Dawson, rush into an attack on a man he must have known would not be intimidated? Though Murray was 25 years his junior, they were well-matched adversaries who had been involved in several previous contretemps. Dawson must have been extremely angry at this apparent incidence of insubordination, yet it was not characteristic of him to be so rash as to make a serious written charge without some corroborating evidence. The identity of his informer was never revealed but perhaps his source had been more than one person, so that the complaint appeared to have the weight of substantiated information. Or perhaps his source had been a person so trustworthy, so credible, he had not hesitated for a moment to believe the report he received.

It is more than likely that Lady Dawson had been present at Mrs. Ritchie's on the evening of the Delta Sigma debate. It is well within the bounds of reason to think that it was she who told the Principal what Dr. Murray had said. In that case, Dawson would not feel that he needed to ask others for their version of what had happened. He would know he had been told the truth—though perhaps it was the truth out of context. The Lady Dawson theory would also account for the time factor— Dawson could have received the news on the very evening of the event. It could also account for some of the emotion in Dawson's response to Murray. Lady Dawson, who appears not to have had a lively sense of humour, might not have found Dr. Murray very entertaining. Her discomfort might well have caused her husband to leap into the fray on her account as well as for his own professional reasons.

Or, if Dawson simply felt that his prestige and authority as Principal were being undermined, he might have "over-reacted" just because he was so particularly sensitive about this matter of separate education. From a 20th century point of view it seems incredible that he could seriously have thought that the morals of the students and the good order of the university were threatened; from a Victorian prespective, this might have seemed a real possibility. It is also conceivable that, had Sir William attended the University Dinner and experienced the jovial ambiance and general approval expressed for co-education, he might not have reacted so strongly. In any event, a full-fledged controversy over the issue of separate vs. co-education was now launched between two men of comparable intelligence, stature, conviction and stubbornness. They kept it up for years and, in order to appreciate the debate, it is necessary to know more about Murray.

* * *

J. Clark Murray was another of the Scottish intellectuals who made such a substantial contribution to Canadian education in the 19th century. He was born in 1836 in Paisley, Scotland where he attended grammar school. After graduating from the University of Glasgow in 1854, he spent two years at the University of Edinburgh, another at Heidelberg and Gottingen, then returned to Edinburgh for a further three years studying theology. At Edinburgh he was in the heart of the "Scottish Enlightenment," coming under the influence of Francis

Hutcheson, its central figure, through another prominent Scottish thinker, Sir William Hamilton.[9] Hutcheson was a committed humanist, an educational reformer, and a proponent of adult education; Hamilton shared his intellectual interest in the mind, the nature of moral experience and the belief that human beings contain the seeds of goodness which can be developed and improved. Though he modified the ideas of Hamilton and Hutcheson in fashioning his own world view, Murray brought a good deal of the Scottish Enlightenment with him when he crossed the Atlantic.

In 1862 he was installed in the chair of Moral and Mental Philosophy at Queen's College, Kingston and then, ten years later, was appointed, presumably on William Dawson's recommendation, Professor of Logic and Mental and Moral Philosophy at McGill. Murray was energetic, outgoing, articulate. During his career he published more than 70 articles and a number of books, including *Outlines of Sir William Hamilton's Philosophy* (1870), *Ballads and Songs of Scotland in View of Their Influence on the Character of the People* (1874), *An Introduction to Ethics* (1891), *A Handbook of Christian Ethics* (1906), and *A Handbook of Psychology* (1884), rewritten as an *Introduction to Psychology* 20 years later and widely used as a text until displaced by the more experimentally oriented works of William James and his followers. Murray's interests were eclectic. His articles, essays or letters to editors touched on such varied topics as "The Problem of Alcohol," "Can Canada be Coerced Into the Union?" "Education in the Province of Quebec," "Gambling," "Industrial Legislation," "Helen Keller," "Religion and Morality," "Higher Education for Women," "Spelling Reform," "Senility," "University Reform in Canada," and "Co-education." He was a philosopher, not a sociologist, but he was a humanist deeply concerned about social issues and considered that the position of women was one of the greatest social problems of the day. While he was at Queen's he had lectured to the "Ladies' Classes," in 1870 he delivered the University address on "The Higher Education of Women," and, soon after his appointment to McGill, he spoke to the Ladies' Education Association on "The Rights of Women."

Murray defined Woman, not as an adjunct to Man, but as a "person with the right to freedom of action which is the inalienable right of every person who does not forfeit it by intruding upon the rights of others."[10] In his view, the first and most fundamental right of all human beings was the right of sheer physical existence, and women were often forced by physical or economic necessity into the "torturing" alternatives of marriage, or a life as a dependent upon relatives, or a life of "sadly unremitting and sadly unremunerative toil." Women learned to feel disgraced if they worked outside the home and thus they stayed at home,

Professor J. Clark Murray

becoming unnaturally confined, segregated. The Rev. Dr. Murray believed true Christianity required that "our social institutions shall draw no invidious distinctions between one sex and the other." However, this ideal had not been realized and, as far as education was concerned, colleges were "constituted and managed on the obvious supposition that their educational advantages shall be enjoyed by the male sex alone." But the reasons for women's exclusion were not good reasons. "Woman has not been considered in past arrangements for higher education because she has been assigned or permitted only a very limited range of duties or occupations." This limitation "conflicts with the natural right of every human being" and was "without foundation in natural justice." Every woman had a right "to be something more than a mere ornament of human life."

Murray's position could almost be described as "feminist," yet he too was a product of his time and he was no modern extremist. Like Dawson, he supported the home as an ideal and he also believed in sex-linked mental differences. In a speech given at Queen's convocation in 1871, the year before he came to McGill, Murray is reported to have said that "no one in his senses" could deny that there is "a difference between the mental condition of women and that of men." However, on the basis of his experience with the ladies' classes, he "wholly opposed" the very common supposition that young women were less competent than young men for the sustained intellectual discipline of university studies. He appreciated that the great difficulty with which young women had to contend was the want of preparatory training which boys received in high school. In 1877, when as an Old Boy he was present at the prize giving at Paisley Grammar School, he noted with gratification that the first prize for mathematics had been taken by a girl. This confirmed his opinion that if the same facilities for higher education which had hitherto been reserved for men were made available to women on equal terms, then the unexamined prejudice that women were intellectually inferior would disappear. He added that, "In the New World, whenever the universities had been thrown open to women, nothing but good results had followed; the work of the young women had received a more earnest tone, and the young men had had a good deal of their roughness softened down."[11]

In the Nature vs. Nurture controversy, Murray could see the importance of Nurture, and explained women's subject position in terms of tradition and limited opportunity rather than divine ordinance. His ideas were in harmony with John Stuart Mill's opinion that ". . . what is called the nature of Woman is an eminently artificial thing, the result of forced repression in some directions, unnatural stimulation in others."[12] Murray saw education as a means for fulfilling women's potential, just as it was for man's. While he still revered the ideal of the home, he could with genuine indignation see through the Victorian ethos that made middle-class women "plumes for the vanity of man."—This was a far cry from Dawson's concept of woman as the "ornament of the home." The educational tenets that follow from Murray's view of Woman and her role in society include the idea that women should study a much wider range of subjects than those traditionally allowed; women should have equal educational opportunities with men; women should be educated with men.

Murray seemed to live fairly consistently by his philosophy. His wife and daughters were educated and active. Coincidentally, his family life resembled Dawson's at several points. Murray's wife, like Dawson's, was named Margaret and was also a Scot; like the Dawsons, the Murrays had five children and, again like the Dawsons, their marital relations appear to have been harmonious. Murray may have been more public in his affections than Dawson. On one occasion, he expressed his husbandly feelings in an ode published in *Cassell's Magazine*. His poem, entitled "To My Wife on Her Birthday," began with an eulogy to summer and concluded with:

> But not for this alone the day is dear,
> That ushers in the joy of summer's prime;
> I love it more because the kindly year
>   seeking among his days the happiest time
> To lead thee, Wife, into this earthly sphere,
> Found none could with his purpose sweetlier chime.

The wives of Principal Dawson and Professor Murray have a bearing on the debate. Their personalities and the roles they played must have had some influence on their husbands' opinion of women, their place in society and their need for education. Both Margaret Mercer Dawson and Margaret Polson Murray appear to have been model wives: both helped their husbands with their work, serving as unofficial secretaries and helping entertain students;[13] both belonged to the M.L.E.A. and took part in church and charitable organizations in Montreal. Though they may have been alike in many ways, they were also rather different: Margaret Dawson was the more private person, Margaret Murray the more public. They may also be seen as representing two different streams of Victorian womanhood. Lady Dawson became the archetype of the eternal consort, Mrs. Murray the epitome of the female activist of her era.

Margaret Polson Murray was one of an emerging group of middle-class women who, in the last three decades of the 19th century, became

Dr. and Mrs. J. Clark Murray, 1865

increasingly involved in Canadian social issues. In what seemed a natural extension of their nurturing roles in the domestic sphere, these women created for themselves a mission to bring about reform in such fields as temperance, child labour laws, public health, and the female franchise. Their activities were based on a belief in their unique capacities and responsibilites as women and as mothers, but they were more organized and systematic than the traditional feminine workers of charity. Within this context, Margaret Murray represented a special aspect of a renascent imperialism which sought to strengthen Canadian ties with Britain, especially in the face of an influx of non-Anglo-Saxon immigrant groups. She was more important than merely the wife of a prominent professor; she was to become well-known and influential in her own right. Margaret Polson Murray was to be the founder of the Imperial Order Daughters of the Empire (I.O.D.E.).

Toward the end of the century, while on a trip to Britain, Margaret Murray was distressed to discover how little the women there knew of Canadian women. Her contacts with people from other parts of the Empire confirmed that such ignorance was widespread and it was mutual. With the outbreak of the Boer War (1899-1902), she considered the problem of lack of communication to be even more serious because it hindered women from co-operating in the noble war effort. She dreamed of ''a body of women banded together for the fundamental purpose of service to the Empire and the strengthening and preservation of Canada's connection with the Motherland.''14 Such an organization would engage in ''constructive educational and humanitarian effort,'' including ''special Canadianization work among the foreign-born, the care of soldiers and their dependents, tending the graves of those who fell on the field of battle, and perpetuating the memory of heroic deeds.'' In support of her cause, Margaret Murray travelled across Canada and in 1900 she sent telegrams to the mayors of all the provincial capitals, urging them to persuade prominent women to join this new venture. Response was slow and Mrs. Murray was on the point of giving up when word came that a chapter had been formed at Fredericton, N.B. Thus was born the I.O.D.E., with its motto ''One Flag, One Throne, One Empire.'' Despite the fact that some husbands claimed that I.O.D.E. stood for ''I Often Don't Eat,'' within a year it had spread across the country and was to be very active during both World Wars. It also took on international dimensions, developing ties with the Victoria League in Australia, New Zealand, the United Kingdom and other parts of the Empire. Though times have changed and the sun has set on the British Empire, Margaret Polson Murray's I.O.D.E. long continued as a viable, philanthropic, service organization with thousands of members in all ten Canadian provinces.

Margaret Polson Murray, Founder of the I.O.D.E.

Another of Margaret Murray's activities was journalism. She was editor of a magazine called *Young Canada,* contributed articles to serious journals such as *Nineteenth Century* and *Contemporary Review* and was Ottawa, Washington and Montreal correspondent for the Toronto-based paper, *The Week.* This publication has been described by a modern scholar as "the least tarnished mirror of Central Canadian culture"[15] of its time. Its editor was Goldwin Smith, who was against co-education. Still, it published many "intellectual and aggressively controversial" letters and articles on women, including some on the argument over co-education between John William Dawson and John Clark Murray. What was Margaret Polson Murray's part in this is left to conjecture, but it can hardly have been coincidental that some of the strongest criticism of Dawson was published in *The Week.*

* * *

Even before the outbreak of the Dawson-Murray hostilities in May, 1888, neither man was a stranger to controversy nor to publicity. They had already had academic, administrative and ideological differences of opinion. Reportedly, it was a constant source of surprise to Murray that a student of natural science like Sir William Dawson should spend his energies attempting to construct a cosmology in which the books of Genesis and Daniel figured prominently. For his part, Dawson thought that Murray made too heavy demands on his students. When Professor Murray asked what books might be left off his Honours reading list, Dawson suggested Spinoza's *Ethic* and Spencer's *First Principles.* Dawson, the fundamentalist, viewed these with suspicion but Rev. Dr. Murray, who believed that the Bible was an historical document but not infallible, kept the contentious works on his list.[16] (It might be noted that Dawson, who was to be called an autocrat, did not interfere with this.)

There had also been a problem relating to money, a lengthy disagreement about Murray's claim for a salary increase. This quarrel lasted for two years and ended with Murray's withdrawal of the claim. While that long hassle was tapering off, another was beginning. The issue in this case was also related to money but was directly connected with the question of separate education for women.

In February, 1888, there had appeared a newspaper report that a small institution in Ohio, Adelbert College, had abandoned co-education. Some people had interpreted this as a deliberate and general verdict against co-education, prompting Murray to write a lengthy letter to the Montreal *Daily Witness.* He averred that the Adelbert decision was an individual one only, based on expediency and local conditions not on general principle, and that the experience there, as elsewhere, had shown "not a single instance in which the system of co-education had been attended with undesirable results."[17] Further, Murray considered that what happened at Adelbert was no defence for the course taken by McGill College, where separate education required the same professors to do twice as much work and he concluded with a strong denunciation of the McGill arrangement:

> Nearly every professor in McGill College was already doing work which, in a properly equipped university, would have been distributed among two or three men; and yet, in spite of this—in spite of the success which has attended co-education wherever it has been tried,—the College has inflicted on its professors the cruel injustice of requiring them to go through this needless farce—to bear the intolerable burden—of repeating their lectures every day.

What a furore this created! Professor Moyse, Professor of English and future Dean of Arts, supported Murray and joined with his complaint about overwork. Sir Donald Smith received a note from Dawson drawing his attention to Murray's letter, and in response indicated that he felt that it was to be regretted, both for Dr. Murray's sake and in the interest of the College, that one of the professors "should place himself so markedly before the public in opposition to the policy adopted by the governing body of the university."[18] The Toronto *Educational Journal* took the opportunity to support higher education for women in separate colleges, but the Montreal *Witness* editorialized that it supported separate education only if co-education were impossible, suggesting that time would show it was futile for an institution to pledge itself against joint classes. The *Witness* also reported that Sir William Dawson professed himself surprised at the complaint, since no hint of the alleged inequities had been brought directly to him and the working arrangements for the separate classes had been established in consultation with the professors when women were first admitted more than three years earlier. However, this report was later retracted by the newspaper with a note that Sir William preferred to give information to the public in his own words in his own time. The Principal obviously took umbrage at the last paragraph of Murray's letter, especially the references to "a properly equipped university," "cruel injustice," "needless farce," and "intolerable burden"—these are all underlined on his copy of the newspaper clipping.

Dawson prepared a confidential memorandum which he took the trouble to have printed and circulated to the Governors before their meeting on May 25. In this statement he reviewed the history of the terms of women's admission, citing the deed of endowment, that, pending the establishment of a separate college for women, no part of the endowment income was to be used, "either directly or indirectly for the support of mixed classes of the two sexes"; noting that the professors had been asked to recommend methods of teaching separate classes which would not involve them in "any additional labour unless voluntarily undertaken and for special remuneration"; pointing out that all professors had accepted in writing the arrangements made and that none was required to give separate lectures to the honour work of the third and fourth years; remarking that repetition of lectures was not uncommon at any university, where the size of the classes warrant it, as was the case at McGill. He went on to give his own opinion that the "preference of the founder of the classes of separate education for women has been fully vindicated," the appointment of professorial assistants had been successful and when a separate college for women was established, it would have, at least in part, its own staff. He concluded strongly that it was his conviction that, given the endowment and the staffing situation, if McGill had "entered on the work of 'co-education,' it would scarcely have been possible to avoid a complete breakdown of its success and usefulness, whether for men or women." He "would certainly have declined to risk his educational reputation on the success of such an experiment" because even under the best of circumstances, the institution of classes for the higher education of women required a great amount of care, labour and responsibility.[19]

Meanwhile, Murray had written to Dawson specifically about two extra lectures he had delivered without remuneration in the Donalda course. Dawson read this letter to the Board of Governors who resolved immediately that the Principal be authorized "to settle with Dr. Murray"[20] for these extra classes. In quite a friendly letter (in which he referred to the *Witness'* account of his own reaction to Murray's letter as "a stupid paragraph"), Dawson advised Murray of the Governors' decision and hoped to meet him the next week to arrange payment. And so the affair ended—for the moment, for it was really a prelude to the long Dawson/Murray controversy that began in May. It is also relevant for an understanding of Dawson's anger at the Delta Sigma Society debate on co-education.

This *Witness* incident also had wider significance and is worth further examination. Dawson's memorandum to the Governors shows how seriously he took the slightest threat of co-education. His statement is a spirited defence of the separate education system as established at McGill, both in its *modus operandi* and its ideology. Dawson surely exaggerated when he claimed that a complete breakdown would have occurred if the first and second year women had been admitted to the same classrooms as the men. In 1884 there were 28 women students—

including regular, occasionals and partials—and they represented about 15% of the total Arts students. This was certainly a significant proportion, but surely not one to create complete chaos or breakdown. From a practical point of view, it ought to have been easier to integrate the newcomers into existing classes rather than to provide special sessions for them. Furthermore, Dawson's concern over the amount of "care, labour and responsibility involved in the institution of classes for the higher education of women" can be appreciated only in the light of his Victorian values. And this is the point. For Dawson, women were different and his view of them as delicate creatures needing protection and requiring special treatment caused the extra work. Dawson's memo to the Governors is, in reality, a defence of a particular view of Woman—his own view, though he continued to refer to it as that of the founder of the Donalda Special Course.

For his part, Sir Donald Smith did not appear to be outraged by Murray's letter to the *Witness* in terms of its attack on separate education. He objected to it, not so much on the grounds of substance but as a breach of protocol. He deemed it improper procedure for a professor to criticize publicly accepted university policy. Though Sir Donald said he had noticed Murray's letter, he did not rush to raise the issue with Dawson, but merely responded when the Principal brought it to his attention. He did not appear to be nearly so enthusiastic about defending separate education as did Dawson. He was not even agitated or concerned enough to attend the meeting of the Board of Governors. So the feeling persists that Smith's support for separate education, while genuine enough, was essentially secondhand. The driving force behind it was Dawson's and the mainspring of Dawson's defence of the system was his idealistic, traditional concept of Woman.

* * *

It must have been because of the strength of his beliefs and because of the history of trouble with the Rev. Dr. Murray, what he called "a long series of aggressions," that Principal Dawson took such precipitous action two days after the first Donaldas' graduation and the day following Murray's talk at Mrs. Ritchie's "At Home." It will be recalled that on the matter of Dawson's charge that Murray had "delivered an address tending to influence the minds of the students against the regulations of the University for separate education," Murray had been requested by the Governors to give a "final and satisfactory" reply. Murray responded promptly. He challenged the "production of a single word spoken as a statement" made during the speech in question that would substantiate the accusations against him, maintained that he had always abided by the regulations of the University, both in spirit and letter, claimed that the work in his classes for women could sustain the most searching scrutiny, and expressed pain that he should be charged without proper consultation on the part of the Principal.[21] This letter was transmitted to the Governors via Principal Dawson (who made a copy of it in his own hand). Dawson had also written an angry statement to Chancellor Ferrier, outlining his side of the question and defending his actions. He said he believed that Murray had been behind continuing attempts in the press and elsewhere to discredit separate education, and, while he admitted that he might have, as he had on former occasions, "taken no notice of the tendency of Dr. Murray's address," he now believed that "the circumstances in this case seemed to be fraught with danger to the University" and required immediate action. From the "testimony of several auditors," he considered that the address was a public protest to impress the community with the idea of antagonism between the students and the University, that it would discourage the students from attending classes and, above all, that it tended to "discredit as useless and even harmful" the liberality of the founder of the course for women. In a draft of his letter, he used Murray's phrase "evil influence" but finally thought better of it, merely accusing him of "one of the most serious offences that can be committed by a Professor, namely exciting agitations among students against the regulations and methods of the University."[22] However, on reading Murray's letter, Dawson added a P.S. to his own, noting his surprise that Murray continued to deny any wrongdoing, actual or intended, which "seems to have been so evident to his hearers" and acknowledged that it might have been possible that Murray's feelings "carried him further than he was aware or even remembers." Dawson conceded that if Dr. Murray could be induced to adhere closely to the regulations in the future, he would be willing to forego his complaint about the past.

The Governors considered these submissions and appointed two of their members, J.H.R. Molson and George Hague, to meet with Murray. They were authorized to "impress on him the obligations of the University in the matter of separate education of women and the necessity of cordial co-operation in carrying out the same and absence of agitation of questions already decided by the University except in the university bodies to which such questions belong."[23] Dawson wrote to Messrs. Molson and Hague explaining that he had not intended to offend or injure Murray but had acted in the name of "discipline and good academical morals. It was not an accusation . . . but the regulations of the University must not be held up to public ridicule."[24] The meeting with Murray took place, a report was prepared and was to be presented to the Governors on June 1, but the death of Chancellor Ferrier delayed this for four days. Then the Board resolved unanimously that in view of the terms of Sir Donald A. Smith's endowment, it must hold all officers of the University strictly bound to uphold the regulations for separate education, to support the Principal, and to abstain from public complaints or agitations before the students; that it trusted Dr. Murray would acquiesce to this, but if he wished to relinquish his teaching in the special classes for women and the remuneration attached, he might do so while undertaking to co-operate with those appointed "to discharge such duties in due fulfilment of the obligations of the University to provide separate education for women in all respects equal to that for men."[25] At the same meeting, the Principal sought and obtained permission to publish for the first time the full text of Sir Donald Smith's Deed of Endowment.

This might well have been the end of the incident, but Murray was not satisfied. He wrote again to the Board requesting an official minute formally acquitting him of the charge alleged to have been brought against his professional character. The Governors replied that the minutes contained no such charge and, while the Board was desirous to avoid all reference to the past and while it regretted any dissatisfaction on the part of Dr. Murray, it reminded him of the recent resolution and his obligations to the University.

Meanwhile, news of the affair had reached the press and some of the journalistic commentary almost reads as if it referred to the university in the 1960's during the period of student revolution. Editorials and letters, anonymous and signed, began to appear. Murray assured Molson and Hague that "none had emanated from him except under his own signature"[26] and both he and Dawson refused to be interviewed by reporters. Because the meetings of the Board of Governors and the Corporation were closed, there was much conjecture, but the *Montreal Star* managed to piece the story together. With increasingly large headlines, it reported on "The Co-Education Difficulty" and forecast possible dire consequences, maybe Murray's resignation or maybe a libel action against the Principal. The newspaper appeared to favour Murray, noting that he considered the matter a violation of his academic freedom, and it also took the opportunity to criticize the Governors for not making their meetings open and for not having representatives of the graduates on the Board. According to the *Star,* public opinion was strongly in favour of higher education for women and this had helped overcome the obstructionists who kept putting obstacles in the paths of "the young lady aspirant to academical fame."[27] By implication, Dawson was one of the obstructionists.

Some of the anonymous letter writers wondered what had happened to Dr. Murray's resolution of 1882 (the one calling for the Faculty of Arts to be open to women, and lost sight of when the Smith endowment was forthcoming).

Professor Hutchinson, at the graduates' annual meeting, demanded that the press be present at meetings of the Corporation. Another interested citizen wrote:

> The world moves. If McGill will *not* move, then McGill must stand to one side and let the living current of humanity flow and let earnest women go where obstacles are not thrown in their path, but where all the halls of learning, yes, even those of medicine, are heartily thrown open to them; and able, conscientious men will seek broader platforms where they can speak the thought that inspires them without suffering an underhand persecution which will not allow itself to be "met with and fought outright."[28]

Dawson, who had an undeniable record of contributing to the higher education of women, could hardly be accused of outright opposition to the cause. All the same, "Algonquin," writing in *The Week,* detected "disguised hesitation" in the original admission of women to Arts. This hesitation, he or she claimed, stemmed from a small minority of the Governors and their "feeling of deference to the Principal, who was known to be keenly opposed to the movement."[29] This writer pointed out how Dawson had jumped upon Donald Smith's money, ignored the Murray resolution that "classes be thrown open to women," said not a word about the long inquiry into co-education, and had simply taken separate education for granted even though the interest on the endowment would not be nearly sufficient for the conduct of a full separate course in Arts, so that, in spite of the generous intentions of the benefactor, the efficiency of the University was not increased but diminished. He or she accused McGill of keeping a watchful eye and a suspicious ear on Murray who, since he attracted more honours students than any other professor including Dawson, was "the first and most popular educator the College possesses."

Principal Dawson must have been very distressed at this attack. He drafted, but did not publish, a seventeen-point rebuttal, beginning with the comment that "Murray's original resolution in favour of co-education was entirely gratuitous and uncalled for at the time."[30] Governor George Hague did reply publicly in defence of the Board and, he claimed, on behalf of "another class who are sometimes entirely ignored . . . viz, the parents and guardians":

> The care of mothers for their daughters is a responsibility that cannot be set aside. Whatever may be the opinion of the nineteenth century

on the subject, the settled opinion of a good many previous centuries, and of the law of God, makes it incumbent upon parents to think
carefully of these things. . . . When the question was first discussed
in the college there was very considerable difference of opinion on
the subject. Not only was the Principal against co-education, but the
whole of the governors, many of them heads of families, and a considerable number of Professors and Fellows. . . . Those who have
had the most experience of the world, and whose observation
embraces the widest circle of the affairs of life, were almost wholly
against it. [31]

He objected to "Algonquin's" sneering style, denied a charge that
Montreal had failed to take an interest in McGill and, after a passing
allusion to Murray's letter to the *Witness* concerning the "farce" and
"intolerable burden" of separate education, praised the Principal for
responding to his high sense of duty and responsibility and taking
appropriate action. "Hence," he said, "all this hubbub."

The hubbub continued with a letter from as far afield as Winnipeg.
W.H. Turner, a former McGill student, began his correspondence with
the proposition that to understand McGill, one must know the Principal.
He knew him to be an entertaining lecturer, a pleasant host, a man of
unusual ability, great ambition and unyielding will who was able to call
to his aid resources of tact and craft that would be the making of any
politician. *But . . .*

> For forty years this man, who has had the moulding of the great
> University he presides over, has swayed it as completely as any
> despot ever ruled a people. Most of what he has done for it, he has
> done wisely. Such a man could not do otherwise. But now new ideas
> of education are crystallizing into methods, and he clings to the old
> with the same intense conservatism that made him conspicuous in
> natural sciences as the defender of threadbare theories. The man
> who broke up a united congregation, because the majority proposed
> the innovation of an organ, will not readily accept any reform so
> fraught, in his eyes, with risk as co-education. [32]

Turner also accused the Governors of having no opinion without
Dawson. In this he seems to be quite justified, for it is striking to review
the "behind the scenes" documents and to see how pervasive was
Dawson's influence. Almost every resolution of the Board of Governors
dealing with the Murray case is either drafted by Dawson or amended by
his hand. Clearly, the Principal did not feel constrained to disqualify
himself from participating in decision-making in a situation where he
himself was personally involved.

Citing the *Montreal Star's* survey of 1884, Turner also denied that public opinion in Montreal was against co-education and he accused Hague of *suppressio veri* and *suggestio falsi* for implying that the opinion of parents, which had never been sought, would have favoured separate education. He concluded with a tribute to Murray, "an honest and loyal gentleman, the most popular of professors whose lectures did more than those of any of the others to stimulate the students to thought and study."

In an even stronger letter, "Truth Seeker" endorsed Turner's dismissal of Hague's arguments and continued the criticism of the attempts to restrain Murray's freedom of speech. Hague had said Murray should not criticize university policy on separate education while he was receiving "emoluments" for the additional classes it entailed. "Truth Seeker" scoffed, "We find that the emolument (!) is at the rate of one hundred dollars a year for one lecture a week, including examinations, essays and other class work, not to talk of the breaking up of time and the irksome repetition. Roughly speaking *two dollars a week!* Emoluments!! Most of us pay much higher emoluments to have our coal shovelled in." [33]

This writer's scrutiny was very searching and he or she questioned whether the Board was justified in accepting Donald Smith's money for such a "superfluous scheme" as separate and repetitive classes and doubted that "the keen and successful financier whose name is attached to his endowment is responsible for the restriction accompanying it." With heavy irony, he or she hoped Mr. Hague might establish separate entrances, tellers and accountants for the lady patrons in his bank and angrily considered that the separate idea was an insult to the young men and women of Montreal and their parents. He or she also wondered why the Governors had not, in all that time, attempted to obtain objective testimony and suggested that the problem was now "to prevent what the Principal has done from recoiling on his own head." In conclusion, he or she demanded that the Graduates' Society call a public meeting and request Dr. Murray "to put all the correspondence which has passed regarding 'this hubbub' into their hands."

At the end of a summer of publicity and debate, the Montreal *Herald,* in an article entitled "Trouble at McGill" (which Dawson classified as a "specimen of notices inspired by Murray's friends"), declared that a crisis had now been reached. It predicted that if the calamity of Dr. Murray's resignation should occur, his friends, "and they are legion," would institute a law suit. [34]

Throughout the Fall, action continued both in the papers and on campus. George Hague defended the Governors in *The Week* and found that he had new attackers to contend with—now "Medicus," "A Friend of McGill," and "A Donalda Student." It is good to note that the Donaldas did not ignore this "hubbub" that raged around them. As the following letter shows, they supported their "beloved" Professor Murray against "Sir Billy" and the Board. It is also evident that they were not deceived by the patronizing, "ladies' school" approach to education for women.

> . . . We think, of course that it is a pity that the Principal did not withdraw his charges immediately, as he was in honour bound when he saw he had made ever so little a blunder, and I am sure we would all have admired him the more for it.
>
> I think it would be difficult for the Principal or Mr. Hague to find either in or out of the College a man who has been so conspicuously reticent about his opinions on co-education as Professor Murray. Indeed the general feeling is one of surprise at his falling in and doing the work of the separate classes as if it had been one of his pet schemes.
>
> . . . We are thankful to have the separate classes, even at the expense of the Professors, as they are better than nothing. The men flatter themselves very much if they fancy we care whether they are present or not. But if our separate classes are intended to develop into a separate college, a high-class ladies' school, we have enough of them already. What those of us who are in earnest want is a *University Education*, and nothing short it. . . . [35]

Murray must have been gratified by this defence as he himself tried to stay out of the debate in the papers. However, in response to some insistence from one of his "unknown friends," he indicated that he would be willing to agree to the publication of his side of the correspondence with the Governors. This infuriated Sir William Dawson, who by this time was feeling besieged. He complained to a Board member about the newspaper barrage as well as Murray's "insolent and untruthful" letter of May 1888 and his "hypocritical utterance" in *The Week* in November, 1889. Murray's conduct in this whole matter, he said, was beyond anything in his previous experience. However, he made it a rule to say nothing about Dr. Murray except when confronted by his statements directly and he felt "only sorrow that such a man should have the power of influencing students." [36]

But if journalistic reaction tended to favour Murray, the Board of Governors was clearly on Dawson's side. From the beginning of this affair to the end, the Governors had enormous confidence in the Principal and relied heavily on his judgment. In September, Murray had written to them again requesting absolute withdrawal of the charge of subverting morals or he "would seek vindication before another tribunal." Dawson considered this a threat and believed that Murray had waited since June to respond to the last resolution of the Board so that it would be too late to replace him for the new academic year. In response, the Board, acting again on a resolution drafted by Dawson, issued an ultimatum that Murray should either withdraw his letter or resign. Further, Murray must abide by the regulations of the University or the Board would "with utmost reluctance . . . take steps toward his emotion from his professorship."[37] The letter was withdrawn (according to Dawson, "very ungraciously" but according to Murray "fully and frankly" because it had been written under a misapprehension).

However, Murray did not let the issue rest. He wanted to know what was the current situation concerning women students at other colleges and wrote to the Registrar of the University of Toronto for information about the number of lady undergraduates, both regular and partial, and how many were non-residents of Toronto. The Registrar referred the inquiry to the President of University College, Dr. Daniel Wilson, a friend of Sir William Dawson's. Wilson informed Dawson of Murray's request with the notation, "As this may be meant for evil uses, I shall withhold my reply till I hear from you."[38] Not surprisingly, nothing came of this inquiry.

* * *

In April, 1889, after a lull in the hubbub, J. Clark Murray wrote once more to Sir William Dawson referring to a decision of the Board of Governors to act toward him "as one who is not even accused of having violated any Statute or Regulation of the University" and requesting all references to him in the minutes of four Board meetings be expunged. He pointed out, "It is an obvious principle of justice regulating all such minutes, that they shall admit no record that could possibly be interpreted as reflecting on the character of an innocent man. Their retention can do no conceivable good to any human being; their only effect is to fix a stigma on my memory as long as the University endures, by connecting my name with offences with which there is no more reason to associate with me than any other man."[39] He believed that the proposal would come most appropriately from Dawson and that, coming from him, "it would of course be at once adopted by the Board." Dawson refused. He said it would be better not to open the matter again, but Murray could put it before the Governors himself, if he wished. So Murray put it to the Governors, disappointed that Dawson had not "eagerly snatched the opportunity . . . of making a slight reparation of the wrong"[40] done to him the previous May. Dawson replied that he was unaware of any "wrong done" to Murray by him and that his action in

Dr Murray
Dawson

McGill College
Montreal   Sep 16. 1891

Dear Dr Murray,

I beg to acknowledge your favour of 10th inst and enclosed Memorandum which I return herewith.

I can only express my deep regret that you have not accepted the friendly suggestion made in my Reply to yours and that you make it the occasion to revive an accusation against myself which I had believed to have been made in haste

[...] unable to attend meeting [...] illness absence or [...] public affairs and when others as well as myself are overtaxed with details of additional requirements or financial matters of the utmost importance to the University and all connected with it [...]

and practically withdrawn by you, and which I must deny, being conscious of no other motives than a sense of duty to the University and a desire to consult your interests and feelings rather than my own. In these circumstances and after your direct appeals to the Board of Governors, and then [...]

just and considerate action — therein as well as in view of their resolutions declining to reopen the matter, I trust you will excuse me. [...] such action as that contemplated in your Memorandum.

Allow me to add [...] members of the Board are

A Fragment of the Dawson/Murray Correspondence

May was "prompted solely by a concern for the interests of the University, but was intended to guard . . . [Murray's] interests as well." [41]

Murray did not comment on this until October when he subjected Dawson's brief note to a rigorous eight-page analysis, one of the clearest letters of the whole canon of this controversy. Here was the Professor of Logic and Moral and Mental Philosophy showing his intellectual agility as he turned the argument against the busy administrator. He asked Dawson to "guard his interests" by writing him an official letter stating frankly that the report of the affair at Mrs. Ritchie's was without foundation, and therefore also to withdraw the complaint from the Board and to expunge the record. Dawson replied negatively, though in a tone that was much more conciliatory than heretofore, that the matter was now in the hands of the Governors. Indeed, a summary of the relevant minutes was prepared and circulated confidentially to the Governors—but, again, the draft of this document is in Dawson's hand.

The Governors were getting anxious. They were afraid that Murray was "building a record" and preparing to publish the whole correspondence, which he had not yet done. Dawson was advised to look over carefully all the letters to and from Murray and, if there was nothing that could be seen to his disadvantage, to close the correspondence or, "if you should find anything . . . continue to restate the whole matter so as to put your position in its proper light and . . . then close it." [42] Dawson followed this advice, writing to Murray that no further good would come from continuing the correspondence and emphasizing that he could find "nothing in his previous statement that either truth or friendship would require him to withdraw." [43] Furthermore, the Governors passed a resolution in December to the effect that "the Board declines to reopen the subject or to have any further correspondence" with Rev. Dr. Murray on this matter. [44]

It might be remembered that, while all this was going on, the regular work of the University continued. As was customary, the Principal was invited to address various campus and civic groups. His topic for the Delta Sigma Society that year was "Educated Women." He articulated his view of Woman as "the high priestess of the family" and took advantage of the occasion to remind the Donaldas that:

> The method introduced here, by the liberality of Sir Donald Smith while still imperfect, enables us to secure equal instruction for the sexes in separate classes with identical examinations and degrees and bids fair in its full development to place the Canadian ladies of the coming time in a position to be envied by their sisters abroad, while its influence on our school systems and on our colleges for men cannot fail to be in the highest degree beneficial. [45]

Montreal, 18th Feb. 1891

My dear Sir William,

I have to acknowledge your letter of the 4th inst, and I am pleased to know that you have read through the correspondence.

I regret, however, that you make no reference to the essential feature and origin of the correspondence,— the baseless slander with which you took the responsibility of staining my good name. It cannot be, that you are resolved neither to clear me from that slander yourself, nor to let me obtain from the Board any official evidence to show that the slander was proved to be absolutely destitute of foundation. I must assume that it is your wish to repair, as far as you can, the injury done to me by that slander. I trust, therefore, that at the first meeting of the Board you will be ready to make an official statement in the line which I suggested in my last letter; and I beg to submit a minute which, I think, should meet the views of all parties, as it is a bare statement of facts, and there is of course no one who wishes the truth suppressed.

It should not be difficult for you and the Board to go a great deal further in the way of generous language, after all the suffering you have inflicted upon me; but I should accept this record as closing the affair.

I shall be glad to wait upon you at any convenient hour.

Very truly yours,

J. Clark Murray

Sir W. Dawson,

Memo writes alleged false accusations and challenge to answer & no opportunity given and full exemption for ... ... all & ground of complaint!

A Fragment of the Murray/Dawson Correspondence

But while campus life went on, all was not quite as before. A row of such proportions was bound to have repercussions, a controversy so widely publicized was sure to have partisans, and the social life of the protagonists and their families was certain to be dislocated. Since the entire faculty of McGill during the 1880's was somewhere between 50 and 60 persons, and since social and cultural affairs were limited to a relatively small circle in Montreal, life must have been very awkward for the women in the Dawson and Murray households. Some indication of this is given in a letter in which Margaret Polson Murray refused an invitation from Margaret Mercer Dawson. She did so with considerable sorrow, explaining that,

> as a wife sometimes feels an injustice more keenly for her husband's sake, I have been compelled to seek my peace of mind in detaching myself from everything which can recall memories that have rendered my connection with the College a source of regret.
>
> I trust, however, that you will believe me when I say that it is the personal admiration we had for the Principal and the complete confidence we had in him which induced us to suffer the insult for a single day, and that not the least-regretted consequence of the whole matter is the interruption of the intercourse with him and with yourself which we had hoped to enjoy. [46]

The use of the past tense in that last paragraph is sadly significant and one can imagine how, as a result of their husbands' disagreement, the ladies must have been at pains to avoid each other.

* * *

The great co-education debate might now have been considered over. The correspondence was closed, the Board had simply required Murray to respect the University regulations, he had not resigned, there were no legal proceedings, the Principal had had his way, the endowment was safe and plans were in progress for an entirely separate college for women. Yet Murray was not satisfied. He still firmly believed that his reputation had been besmirched, that he had suffered an injury, that he had been singled out for gratuitous innuendo. He commented that it would be as inexcusable for the minutes of the Board to record that the University Treasurer must not embezzle the funds as it was to state that he should not subvert the morals of the students. Part of the difficulty might have arisen from his own sensibilities, or from his antagonism to Dawson, or from a number of other sources, but it was certainly aggravated by the fact that he still did not *know* what was in the minutes or what "slanderous report" Dawson had originally presented to the Governors. There had never been an open inquiry or a questioning of witnesses. None of the documents involved had been published. Murray considered himself innocent and was uneasy in his ignorance of what had happened at the Governors' meetings. He still wanted Dawson to withdraw his accusation in the same official manner as he had introduced it so that he [Murray] would be "completely exculpated" from the charge against him. He raised the matter again in October 1890, January, February, and April, 1891. Dawson's response was that it was in Murray's interest and duty to accept the position of the Board of Governors, which was both conciliatory and final. Dawson, who was now about seventy years of age, not very well, and hoping to retire, declined to be a party to a re-opening of the discussion. In a letter of October 1891, John Clark Murray appeared reluctantly to accept this decision and pressed his request no further.

But the matter was opened again early in 1893—this time by Dawson. About five years after Murray's famous "subversive" address, Dawson presented to the University Corporation a remarkable statement, part confession, part apology, part request for absolution:

> Being desirous to retire from my office in the University with the awareness that I have done all in my power to remove anything in my actions as Principal which may have been distasteful to any of my colleagues I beg leave to state that if in the differences of opinion which have arisen between Dr. Clark Murray and myself in regard to the education of women there has been anything on my part which appeared to him or this body in any way unjust or disagreeable to him I desire fully to withdraw the same and also to express my belief that Dr. Murray has endeavoured loyally to carry out the desires of the University in that matter even when they were not in accordance with his own views, I would also desire to say that if in the urgency of work or the difficulties which have beset my path I have at any time been impatient or thoughtless of the feelings or welfare of any member of the University I sincerely regret this and trust I may be forgiven, as having done what seemed at the moment in the interests of the University and its students. . . . 47

This was prompted both by his own impending retirement and the fact that Murray was considering an offer from abroad because he was still unhappy about this old grievance. Dawson wanted to leave things in good order and from his Little Métis retreat wrote to Murray in July, informing him of the general "apology" he had made in Corporation. Murray, who now had hope that his long-delayed request for the withdrawal was at last to be granted, responded warmly to the "kindly spirit" of Dawson's letter and said that after his many efforts to induce

Dawson and the Board to meet him on a friendly basis, they would not find him lagging behind in the earnestness of his "endeavours to obliterate every cause of unpleasantness."[48] He wondered what further specific action Dawson now contemplated. But Dawson had not intended anything more. On July 31, 1893 the "last day of his official life," he wrote once more to Murray to explain at a more personal level his side of the quarrel.

Dawson wrote that his actions of 1888 had been taken in good faith in what seemed to him at the time "an imminent danger" to Murray and to the University and that Murray's response had rendered *him* the accused party. He claimed that the proceedings of the Board were primarily based on Murray's letters of complaint about him, not on his complaints about Murray. He averred:

> The several resolutions of the Board, all of which were communicated to you but to no other person, were thus founded upon your own statements, without any interference on my part; but I am sure from the character of the gentlemen who prepared them were intended to be respectful and conciliatory.[49]

This paragraph does not entirely coincide with the record. Since Dawson drafted the Board's resolutions, including one calling for Murray's resignation unless he withdrew a certain letter, it hardly seems fair to say there was no "interference" on his part. What is more, as Dawson was to reveal later, Murray's letter of May 5, 1888, his first, longest and most complete defence, was not submitted to the Board. And the next paragraph seems to have been written with a lapse of memory or the rosy glow of retirement:

> I have made no accusation or defence, public or private, and have taken every opportunity to express my satisfaction with the manner in which you have discharged the duties committed to you by the Board of Governors.

He ended rather touchingly:

> I do not therefore feel that now on the last day of my official life I can do anything farther than express to you my sincere good wishes and the hope that you may not be stricken down as I have been but may long be enabled to retain your useful and honourable position in connection with the University.

Murray was not touched by this last, but profoundly regretted that Dawson had "relapsed into his unrelenting resolution to perpetuate the injury" he had done. He wrote:

> It is not necessary to dwell upon the explanations given in your letter, as they have nothing essentially to do with the injury which you have been asked again and again to repair. If you are satisfied with your conduct in taking this matter before the Board, I have repeatedly told you that I do not wish to interfere with your satisfaction, though I must once more draw your attention to the fact that your letter of May 7, 1888, begins with the statement that you had taken that step, not on account of any letter you had received from me, but *because you had received none.*[50]

Murray reiterated his protest that he had been falsely charged, that the resolutions of the Governors contained hurtful innuendos, and that only Dawson who had started the whole thing could clear his name—it would be easy for him to do and so much better for him than leaving an incubus hanging over the University.

Dawson, in his turn, was unmoved. So Murray again approached the Governors. In response to their request for information, Principal Emeritus Dawson drew up a confidential point-by-point record of events from the beginning of 1888, attaching copies of early correspondence, including Murray's reply to Dawson's first letter of complaint in May, 1888. Incredibly, Dawson indicated quite clearly that he had never before submitted that letter to the Board, but did so now "as justifying the Principal in holding that Dr. Murray had by its terms taken the matter out of the Principal's hands."[51] In other words, he did not submit that vital piece of evidence in the interests of justice but in his own defence, and his withholding it throughout all the previous inquiries and discussions must have affected the understanding and probably their sympathies. His summary was also misleading when he said that "As a meeting of the Board of Governors was called before a reply [to his letter of May 2, 1888] was received, the Principal reported his action to the Chancellor . . . ," implying that it was a regular meeting of the Board when, in fact, it was a special meeting called *after* Dawson had reported to Ferrier. Dawson concluded his statement with the contentious claim that "the Principal's interference though it has led to much trouble to himself and to the Board, had had the effect of arresting, for a time, the more public opposition to our work for Women, and to limit it to private and indirect methods, which will no doubt more or less continue till the Donalda Special Course shall be organised as a distinct College of the University."

Poor Sir William Dawson, who was widely and legitimately recognized as the maker of McGill, much honoured, respected, admired and loved, found himself in his old age and retirement defending his actions and his reputation. Now, for the first time, he called for a written report

47 Victoria Road
Dec. 23rd 1893.

Dear Sir William

The enclosed notes are the only memoranda I have of the meeting you refer to; and I am afraid that I cannot recal any thing further. I am sorry to hear that the matter is being brought up again. There has always been an undercurrent of dissatisfaction, and lately owing to the carrying out of some regulations in regard to societies of college students, it is a little more prominent than usual — You would perhaps see some expression of this in a letter in the last Fortnightly, though that contained many inaccuracies —

Thank you very much indeed for the copy of your book, which I shall value very highly — I am enjoying the possession of a nice set of Chamber's Encyclopedia to which the amount you so kindly gave me for my summer's work enabled me to purchase.

Wishing you and Lady Dawson a very happy Christmas I am yours sincerely
Helen Gairdner

Helen Gairdner's Belated Report

on the evening of May 1, 1888 from Miss Helen Gairdner, the Donaldas' chaperone who had heard Dr. Murray's address. Her recollections were remarkably clear after five and a half years and they coincided with the newspaper accounts of the University Dinner and Mrs. Ritchie's "At Home." Sir William also contacted Sir Donald Smith, now the Chancellor of McGill, and gave him additional documents, in case, he said, Dr. Murray is "determined to give further trouble" to the Board in respect to the course for women. Further, he requested permission to state his own case but claimed that he felt exonerated from having to show Dr. Murray further forebearance.[52]

In February, 1894, the Board of Governors of McGill University examined the entire controversy which had long since ceased to centre on the issue of co-education per se, but still had as its foundation a difference in basic philosophical orientation toward Woman. After the meeting, the Chancellor, Sir Donald A. Smith, benefactor of the Donalda Special Course for Women, wrote to the Principal Emeritus that the Board had referred Dr. Murray to "letters formerly sent out to him which gave him in half a dozen words the assurance that there was nothing in the minutes militating against his professional standing or his character and honour. . . . The matter is *finally* disposed of as far as the Board is concerned. We all feel that it cannot be reopened."[53] The Secretary returned the documents fowarded by Sir William and the matter was closed.

*   *   *

Who won?

Imbroglios of this kind rarely have clear winners. Both J. William Dawson and J. Clark Murray must have suffered personally during the long course of the co-education "hubbub" and it is extremely doubtful whether either shifted his opinion as a result of all the argument. As far as can be ascertained, Dawson continued to hold his idealistic view of women until his death in December, 1899 and Murray to hold his more realistic approach long after his retirement in 1903. There was some justification for both their positions and some irritation in their modes of debate—a measure of sanctimoniousness in Dawson's and a touch of sophistry in Murray's. However, since the next major development in the history of women at McGill was the establishment of the Royal Victoria College, a separate college for women, it would appear that Principal Dawson was actually the victor. Royal Victoria College was to set the tone for women's higher education for many years to come. Furthermore, even though conditions, mores and values have now changed quite radically, a Dawsonian ambiance may still be detected at

McGill: its corporate personality still reflects the solid, respectable burghers who helped build it to greatness.

On the other hand, co-education became a reality in the small honours classes almost as soon as women were admitted to the University and mixed classes in science subjects were not far behind. Throughout the 20th century, McGill has become increasingly co-educational so that, since World War II, co-education has simply been taken for granted as the unchallenged norm. Ultimately, then, the victory could be considered Murray's.

But, somewhat surprisingly, the issue is still alive. The argument is now embedded in questions such as the academic validity of separate Women's Studies. Ironically, contemporary feminists at McGill, who would have endorsed Murray's view of Woman rather than Dawson's, are now making a case for a kind of separateness in the form of women's courses, a Woman's Studies minor, a Senate Committee on Women, a Centre for Teaching and Research on Women, and a History of Women at McGill. These demands stem from a view of history which sees women as powerless and inarticulate so that, advisedly or inadvertently, the human record has been left incomplete. Areas of concern culturally assigned to women have been omitted from the record; they are also the areas omitted from systematic and serious study. Thus, the feminist seeks—at least temporarily—a period of *rattrapage* in which women may be studied, data amassed, role models established and female confidence encouraged. Ideally, of course, there should be no differences in the treatment of the sexes on campus, but since there are, these differences must be acknowledged, analyzed and any inequities corrected. Hence the need for separate arrangements.

A further irony of the situation is that the feminists of McGill are essentially Dawsonian—genteel, middle-class, reasonable. But, if they had a hero, it would be J. Clark Murray who was remembered by Octavia Ritchie as "the ardent champion of our rights and our revered teacher and friend. His gentle voice and fine face were the outer evidence of a beautiful personality where peace, goodness and spirituality dwelt. He ever directed our thoughts to high and noble ends, and was an abiding influence on our lives." [54]

Part II

ROYAL VICTORIA COLLEGE
AND
STUDENT LIFE

Chapter FIVE

R.V.C.:
The Founder and the Wardens

Throughout all the "hubbub," the Donaldas continued to do well at McGill and their academic success must have heartened their supporters and also must have encouraged Donald Smith to fulfill his promise to set up a college for the higher education of women. In the interval between 1884 and 1899, that is, from the admission of women to the Faculty of Arts to the establishment of the Royal Victoria College, Donald Smith had become an increasingly prominent figure in Canadian public life. His benefactions had grown and his interest in McGill had multiplied. During this period, he switched roles, moving from the *deus ex machina,* who had unexpectedly appeared and precipitated women's entry into degree work at McGill, to centre stage hero, the Chancellor of the University, who provided a complete women's college. Yet, even in the full view of the spotlight, Donald Smith retained an elusive aura of mystery, leaving obscure his reasons for the inclusion of higher education for women in his benefactions. Yet the fact is, that he gave land, a fully equipped building, and an endowment for operating expenses for the college. Ultimately, his individual contribution amounted to an unequalled one million dollars for the education of women at McGill. There was little in his background to have made this predictable.

Donald Alexander Smith was born of humble parents at Forres in the Scottish highlands not far from the "blasted heath" where Macbeth encountered the three witches. Those "weird sisters" probably had little to do with it, but Donald Smith had an almost magically successful career. At eighteen, he came to Canada with a letter of introduction declaring him to be "of good character, studious, painstaking and enterprising." This obtained him a job with the Hudson's Bay Company at "twenty pounds a year, all found" and he was sent to the fur room of the Company's Lachine office to be instructed "in the art of counting rat skins." After learning the rudiments of the trade, young Smith was sent to Tadoussac, then to Esquimaux Bay, Labrador where his persistence, energy and initiative led him into building roads and diversifying the activities of the trading post. In 1851, after thirteen long and difficult years, he was promoted to a chief trader, later to chief factor, and moved to the North West. There, as in Labrador, he not only gained the respect of his associates, but also the confidence of the native peoples. He worked closely with the latter, teaching them business habits, caring for them when they were sick. He was known to them as "Manitoupee-wanisque" or "Spirit of Iron."

In 1869, Sir John A. Macdonald sent Donald Smith to Fort Garry as commissioner to inquire into Louis Riel's rebellion. This was a danger-ous diplomatic mission which Smith effected with patience, insight and skill. He was now a public figure. Meanwhile, his personal wealth was mounting and he continued his connection with the Hudson's Bay Company. He was a commissioner of the Company for four years from 1870 and represented Selkirk in the House of Commons from 1871 to 1880. During part of that period he also represented Winnipeg in the Provincial Legislature. His fortunes were on the rise as he joined his cousin, George Stephen (later Lord Mount Stephen) in buying bonds of the St. Paul Minneapolis and Manitoba Railway. Then, at considerable financial risk, he helped rescue the Canadian Pacific Railway syndicate from near collapse. He also brought to the company much of the con-fidence that overcame the doubters who scoffed that the line would "never pay for its axle grease" and the detractors who decried the C.P.R. as the greatest fraud since the "South Sea Bubble." As a result of his crucial intervention in the C.P.R. it was he who had the honour in 1885 of driving in the last spike of the great east-west rail link that forged Canada together.

His life inevitably enclosed much struggle and controversy. One of the serious checks to his public career occurred in 1887 when he was unseated for irregular election practices and he failed to regain the seat for Selkirk. Nevertheless, he continued to flourish and to hold public positions of increasing importance. He was President of the Bank of Montreal in 1882 and 1887, Federal member for Montreal West from 1882 to 1896, Canadian High Commissioner in London from the latter year to 1913, as well as Governor of the Hudson's Bay Company, 1899-1913. He became Chancellor of McGill in 1889 and Chancellor of the University of Aberdeen in 1893.

In the course of his extraordinary career, he received many honours. He was knighted in 1886 and raised to the peerage in 1897, taking as his title "Baron Strathcona and Mount Royal." At his death in 1914, the barony passed to his only daughter, Margaret. Donald Smith had married Isabella Hardistry in 1853 when he was in Labrador. Her father was one of the Hudson Bay's trusted agents and her mother was the daughter of an Indian Trader. There was no priest or church for a

Lord Strathcona, Founder of R.V.C.

thousand miles and so the marriage was a simple contract without religious ceremony, a practical and not unusual custom under the circumstances. However, when Donald Smith became Lord Strathcona, a remarriage took place in the British Embassy in Paris and was ratified by a special Act of Parliament. Regardless of the formalities, the couple shared a lifetime companionship and devotion. Upon Lady Strathcona's death in November 1913, just a few weeks before that of her husband, the *Times* of London wrote:

> More than sixty years of singularly happy married life are ended. She was a woman who was beloved and trusted by a wide circle of friends and was conspicuous for her charitable nature.[1]

The *Daily Mail* noted that, though of retiring disposition, Lady Strathcona "worked quietly with her husband in those great imperial schemes which have done so much to strengthen the bonds between Canada and the mother country." The Montreal *Gazette* paid tribute to the "lady who is said to have exercised a quiet but profound influence on her husband in both his private and his public life." Strathcona's many long-term business and political associates echoed these sentiments. Charles Tupper, for example, wrote:

> No poor words that I can command can express the sorrow I feel at learning that the beloved partner of all your joys has been called away. From the first hour of our acquaintance, my lamented wife and I were indebted to her for her unremitting kindness and attention . . . .[2]

On Strathcona's own death early in 1914, the papers around the world were full of praise for his achievements and his benefactions. Like any public figure, Lord Strathcona had his critics but also many admirers. One writer believed "he has been invincible because he has so often been gentle; it was gentleness concealing strength;" another said, "nothing pleased Lord Strathcona more than to see his friends made happy;" yet another, "He was a constant and sure subscriber to every good public work in the Dominion."[3] His grand benefactions totalled in the millions and included gifts of £200,000 to King Edward's Hospital (London); with Lord Mount Stephen, a million dollars to the Royal Victoria Hospital (Montreal) plus $800,000 for maintenance; $200,000 for Lord Strathcona's Horse, a mounted rifle unit raised in 1899 for the war in South Africa; hundreds of thousands to McGill for a wide variety of purposes, including a medical building; as well as substantial amounts to Yale, Aberdeen and Queen's (Kingston) Universities. Even today, these are impressive sums; a century ago their purchasing power was enormous.

Though he was such a public man, Donald Smith's private world was not much in view. One of his biographers commented on "the web of mystery that has so long enveloped Lord Strathcona's personal antecedents and many of his notable actions. . . . Self-revelation was not one of his talents: he did not wear his heart on his sleeve. If he permitted legends to accumulate which a timely disavowal would have shattered, it may be that their currency appealed to his sense of humour."[4] He probably also liked to create his own legends and to do things that appealed to his sense of the dramatic—things like driving the last spike or suddenly appearing on the McGill campus, unannounced, with an offer of $50,000 for the higher education of women. The reasons for his original gift to McGill remain matters for conjecture. He left no clear personal statement about his interest in developing women's education nor account of why he particularly wanted to provide a college. The closest explanation is his response to a question from his brother John: "You are quite right," he wrote, "in thinking that, in the matter of this college, the memory of our sister Margaret was present in my mind. You well remember her gifts and her ambition to become a scholar."[5]

Margaret was one of his two sisters, neither of whom, according to the custom of the day, had much opportunity for higher education. Both died in 1841—Margaret at age twenty-seven, Marianne at sixteen. There do not appear to be any other references to either of them in connection with the cause of higher education, no dedication, no citation in the records of Lord Strathcona's speeches, no mention in the recollections of people associated with him at McGill. As a result, one cannot escape the feeling that, when it was put to him in so many words, Strathcona would agree that the thought of Margaret was an idea behind his gift of a woman's college. Undoubtedly it was a compatible and sympathetic motive but, on his own initiative, Strathcona did not mention it. He never publicly put forward the frustrated hopes of his long dead sister as the driving force behind one of his greatest benefactions, his gift of a million dollars for the Royal Victoria College. He never attempted to use Margaret as a source of inspiration for the women of McGill.

While brotherly affection and homage should not be entirely discounted, they do not seem to be sufficient reasons for Strathcona's interest in higher education for women. Consideration must also be given to other factors. Since Donald Smith was a man of keen perceptions, with many business and social contacts, it is likely that he was well aware of the general debate about higher education for women and also that he specifically knew about the benefactions of other wealthy men like Matthew Vassar, Ezra Cornell and Thomas Holloway (who founded Royal Holloway College for Women in England in 1886). It is not hard to believe that an enterprising, ambitious and liberal-minded man would recognize that the higher education of women was a good thing and a timely cause to support.[6] There were models in both the United States and England and this could well have been the kind of benefaction that would earn approval from the Queen. And because his initial gifts for the education of women at McGill produced satisfactory results, Smith was undoubtedly encouraged to continue offering them.

The real mystery lies in the reasons for the unexpected first offer of $50,000 in the summer of 1884. Did the Honourable Donald Smith suddenly decide out of personal conviction to support the higher education of women or was he persuaded to do so by someone else? Since, at that point, he was not influenced by Dawson,[7] it is a matter of conjecture as to whether there was someone else and, if so, who might he be? It will be remembered that in 1883, upon the urging of Rev. James Barclay, Smith had given $30,000 to the Trafalgar Institute for the post-primary instruction of girls. There is no evidence that Barclay pushed for the admission of women to McGill, and he was probably not responsible. Yet it is hard to believe that Smith, an outsider from McGill, would suddenly appear the following year on his own initiative and make such a generous offer. It is quite credible that he would do so if the matter of the admission of women to McGill were brought to his attention sympathetically by someone he knew and respected. That someone could have been Lucy Simpson.

Lucy Stanynought Simpson had been active in the Montreal Ladies' Educational Association since its establishment. According to Dawson, it was she who had originally seconded his proposal that such an association be formed.[8] She was its first Honorary Secretary, became a Vice-President and was always a steady supporter. She was an educator, operated her own school and was particularly interested in the higher education of women. Born in England in 1827, she married George William Simpson when she was sixteen and came with him to Canada. Her husband was a kinsman of Sir George Simpson, Governor of the Hudson's Bay Company and a gentleman of some means. Soon after their arrival in this country, George Simpson lost heavily in the stock market so that the young couple found themselves in serious financial difficulties. To help solve the problem, Sir George Simpson persuaded Lucy Simpson to open in Montreal a boarding school for the children of Hudson's Bay employees who were scattered across the Canadian wilderness in Company trading posts. At that time, the sons of Hudson's Bay officials were generally sent "home" to Scotland or England for their schooling but no provision at all was made for the daughters.

Lucy Stanynought Simpson

Somewhat reluctantly, Lucy Simpson opened a school for girls on Inkerman Terrace. She found she enjoyed the work. Her enterprise flourished and soon she had to move into larger quarters on Mansfield Street.

Mrs. Simpson's school developed into much more than a means for overcoming her family's financial crisis or a convenient hostel for Hudson's Bay Employees. Under her guidance it became one of the most prestigious private schools in Montreal. She thought seriously about the aims of education and exhorted her students to continue learning throughout their lives. In an end-of-year address in 1863 she charged them: "Let no consideration of pleasure or change induce you to leave off for a moment the work of self-education."[9] Her ideas on women's education were both realistic and idealistic and, on another occasion, she said:

> I have owned to a certain amount of sympathy with those who fear that much learning may spoil our daughters. But I should be sorry to have it thought that I prefer ignorance and believe in it. . . . We know that real scholars amongst men are refined and unassuming, and it will certainly be found that real scholars among women will be modest and reasonable. They will not be less womanly because they are well informed, nor less interesting because they are sensible and accomplished. Rightly accepted, I see in higher education that which will give brightness to a dull life. I see in it a check upon the aimlessness which too often comes in the years between school-time and marriage. . . . You need not keep your women ignorant in order that they may learn to cook. The best educated women I have known, were also the best housekeepers. It is the habit of learning which is wanted; and the power of self-help. . . .[10]

It was through her connection with the Hudson's Bay Company that, shortly after her arrival in Canada, Lucy Simpson had met a young clerk, Donald A. Smith. They became good friends, meeting frequently until he was appointed to a post at Mingen on the Lower St. Lawrence. While he made his fortune in the fur trade, she was engrossed in her school and the M.L.E.A. They met again in 1882 in Montreal and renewed their friendship. He must have appreciated her work and, as a tribute to all she had done for the education of girls, wished to endow her school. But just at that time, the school was being taken over by Bessie Symmers and Sarah Smith. It was self-supporting and was not in great need. From Lucy Simpson's point of view, funds were more urgently needed to permit women to continue with their collegiate education. The M.L.E.A. was fine, but it was a dead-end. There was nowhere in the

Province for young women to continue their education. And so, according to one of the earliest women graduates of McGill, "at the instigation of Mrs. Simpson, Donald Smith called upon the Principal whom he had not hitherto met, and offered him the Donalda Endowment with the result that the financial obstacles were removed."[11]

It cannot be proved, but it is entirely feasible that Lucy Simpson encouraged Donald Smith at just the right time and helped produce his lasting interest in the education of women at McGill, the interest which finally led to the endowment of the Royal Victoria College.

* * *

At his installation as Chancellor of McGill (1889), Sir Donald said briefly, "Something is required to be done for the department for women. Some of us had hoped that by this time there would have been such a college in existence, but from certain causes it has not been brought about. However, I think we may feel assured that before the lady undergraduates who join us this year are ready to leave the college, they will have a habitat of their own." Though that class of "lady undergraduates" had departed even before construction on their college had started, the idea was not abandoned. For one thing, Sir William Dawson would not let it drop, not even after his retirement. In 1894, in his last address to the Delta Sigma Society, Principal Emeritus Dawson noted that the college to be endowed by Sir Donald Smith was to be "a model college, honourable to Montreal and giving to students all that can be desired in home and social life, and with facilities for study not heretofore enjoyed in this country—a college the pride of all the friends of education, worthy of the patronage of our Visitor, as the representative of her most gracious majesty, and deserving the proud title of Royal Victoria."[12]

In making this ideal a reality, Lord Strathcona at last arranged for the purchase of land on Sherbrooke and University Streets. He employed an architect and engineers, mainly from C.P.R., to draw up plans and proceed with the building and furnishing of the college, for a total cost of $400,000. During the construction period, he himself was High Commissioner in London and apparently did not heed the warnings of the new Principal, William Peterson, that the architect did not seem to know much about the requirements of educational buildings. He was to discover later that only about thirty, rather than the desired one hundred, students could be accommodated.

Principal Peterson, who was supportive of women's education and extremely interested in the R.V.C. project, was the executive on hand to see to the academic and physical arrangements. He kept Lord

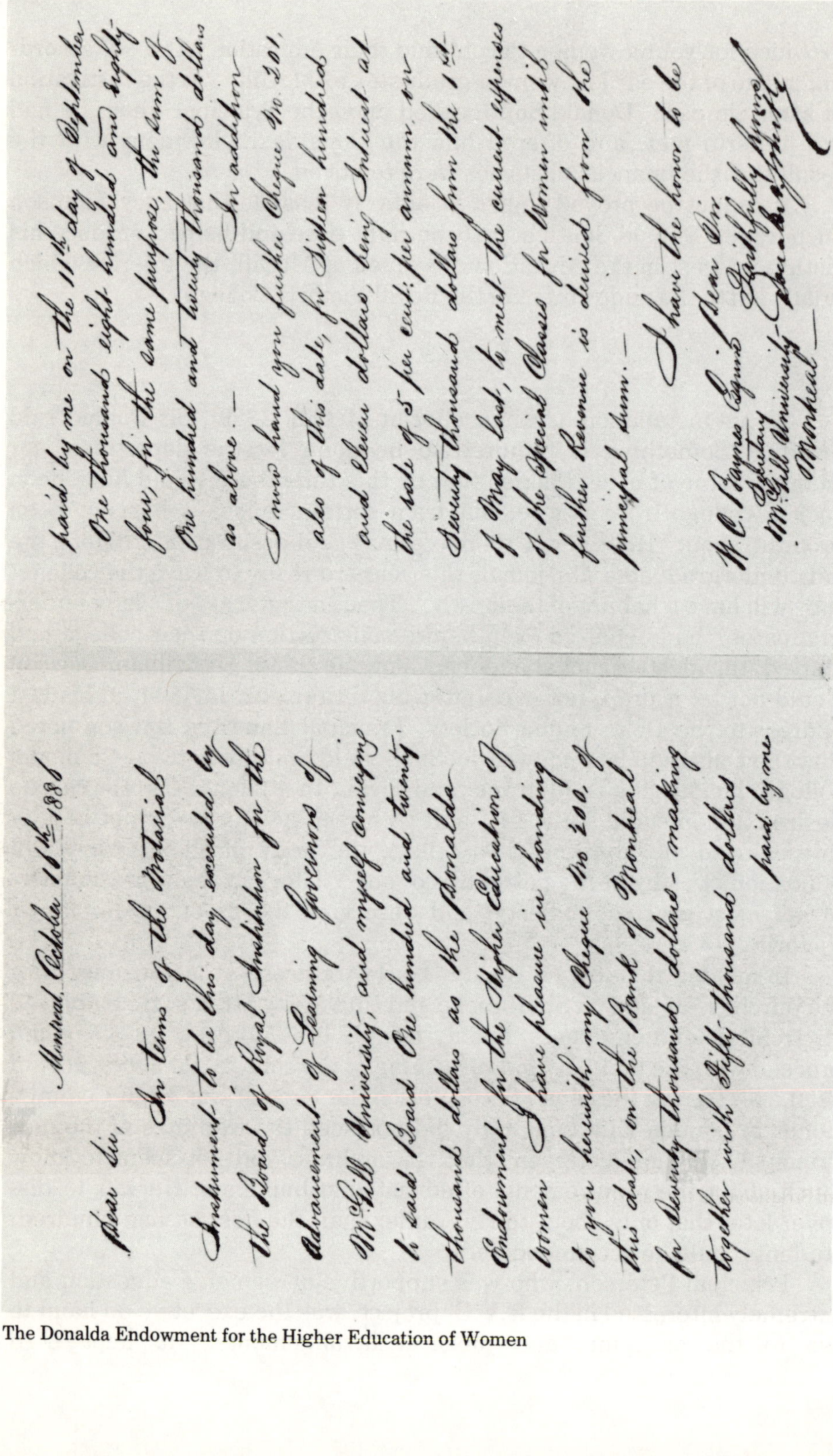

Montreal October 11th 1886

Dear Sir,

In terms of the Notarial Instrument to be this day executed by the Board of Royal Institution for the Advancement of Learning Governors of McGill University, and myself conveying to said Board One hundred and twenty thousand dollars as the Donalda Endowment for the Higher Education of Women I have pleasure in handing to you herewith my Cheque No 200 of this date, on the Bank of Montreal for Twenty thousand dollars - making together with Fifty-thousand dollars paid by me

paid by me on the 11th day of September One thousand eight hundred and eighty-four, for the same purpose, the sum of One hundred and twenty thousand dollars as above. -

In addition I now hand you further Cheque No 201, also of this date, for Eleven hundred and eleven dollars, being Interest at the rate of 5 pr cent: per annum, on Twenty thousand dollars from the 1st of May last, to meet the current expenses of the Special Classes for Women until further Revenue is derived from the principal sum. -

I have the honor to be

Dear Sir,

Faithfully yours
Donald A Smith

W.C. Baynes Esqre
Secretary
McGill University
Montreal -

The Donalda Endowment for the Higher Education of Women

Lord Strathcona in his Later Years

Strathcona informed through lengthy memoranda in which he outlined the new curricula being fashioned in the Faculty of Arts for the women's college and analyzed the college's implications for the University and its effects on staffing, maintenance and finance. The Principal had the advice of Sir William Dawson who still "strenuously advocated separate education" but Peterson could see that this system would significantly increase costs. He also knew that Lord Strathcona insisted on separate education but he demurred at the benefactor's suggestion that, in order to save money, women's options in the third and fourth years should be restricted. Peterson pointed out that such a move would be contrary to the original Donalda Endowment which guaranteed that "there should be identical education for both sexes."[13] He proposed instead that some co-education be accepted and "a certain latitude" be allowed the administration. He pointed out: "Under the new curriculum, the classes in the Third and Fourth Years will be doing work of a distinctly advanced character, — such as might justly claim rank with those Honour-Courses which, for twelve years past, have been taken in common (with excellent results) by men and women students *even during the first two years of the McGill course.*"[14] [Emphasis in the original] He also believed that if women wanted to take an unusual second year subject, such as Hebrew, where separate classes would clearly be uneconomic, the University would have no right to rule them out by any such decree as "Thou shalt *not* study Hebrew!"[15]

Meanwhile, the construction proceeded on a grand scale and, though the Governors were pleased and impressed with such elegance, they became increasingly concerned that the new building would be a "white elephant," nothing but a handsome financial burden. On December 13, 1898, William McDonald,[16] another of McGill's great benefactors, pointed out at the Governors' meeting that the annual deficit likely to be incurred by the Royal Victoria College was $10,000. This was an alarming amount.

There was some "friendly" rivalry between McGill's two great patrons. Earlier that year rumours had circulated that McDonald had indicated his willingness to give a million dollars to the Faculty of Arts if Strathcona would do the same for the Donaldas.[17] However, nothing happened until the very meeting at which McDonald complained of the impending deficit. Then Lord Strathcona advised the admiring Governors that his total endowment for the higher education of women (including the earlier $120,000) would indeed amount to one million dollars. He reassured them that "the income of this sum should prove sufficient to maintain the College and to relieve the University finances to such an extent as would materially assist in reducing the deficit pointed out by Mr. W. McDonald."[18] Strathcona must have enjoyed the effect his announcement caused as he triumphantly solved the problem of the potential deficit and "one-upped" McDonald at a single stroke.

The Montreal press hailed the news with excited headlines, such as "Floreat McGill"[19] and, at the next meeting of the Governors, Principal Peterson moved a formal vote of thanks, placing on permanent record an expression of the Board's "admiration of such munificence, displayed in a cause which he has so greatly benefited," conveying to His Lordship "the assurance of this Board's readiness to co-operate with him to the full extent of its ability in accomplishing the objects which he desires to promote."[20] Thus, the Royal Victoria College seemed to have an assured future and was to be ready for occupancy for the autumn of 1899.

* * *

The early prospectuses described the College in glowing terms, making clear that the imposing building was to provide an academic, administrative and recreational centre for resident and non-resident women students. On the ground floor were the administrative offices, including the living quarters of the Warden and the Secretary, the

R.V.C.—The Original Building

faculty room, students' common room, dining hall and three lecture rooms. On the first floor there were more lecture rooms, the library, a reading room, and a handsome assembly hall which came to be used for many special events of the University. On the second and third floors were the students' study-bedrooms. Each woman was to have a room of her own, while sitting rooms were available on either a shared or individual basis. A special announcement describing the new college left little doubt that the facilities were to be first class and assured prospective occupants that: "The rooms are completely furnished. No lamps, towels, table napkins, sheets or other necessary supplies need be brought by the student. No part whatever need be taken by the student in the care of her own room. The students' washing will be done in the College laundry at a fixed charge per dozen."[21] This brochure also mentioned the well-equipped gymnasium in the basement, which was to be in charge of competent instructors. Special attention would be "devoted to the application of exercise in cases of physical weakness." There was also an extensive lawn at the back and tennis courts nearby for recreation. The intention was that the building should be aesthetically pleasing and harmonious while the College was to be a gracious and comfortable home for both students and staff.

Lord Strathcona took a personal interest in the selection of the staff for Royal Victoria College. He was guided in this by the Principal of McGill and, on Dr. William Peterson's recommendation, he interviewed in London and subsequently appointed Hilda Diana Oakeley as the first head of the college. Miss Oakeley, following the model of Somerville College, Oxford, chose to be called the "Warden" rather than the "Lady Principal" and was somewhat amused to find that North Americans associated her title with prisons.

Miss Oakeley, who was a student of Philosophy, was born in 1867 in Durham in the north of England. Her father was one of Her Majesty's Inspectors of Schools and Miss Oakeley was raised in an upper middle-class atmosphere of learning, gentle manners and public service. She did not aspire to higher learning immediately upon succeeding in the Higher Local School Examinations, but tried for a literary career in London. Her hope to become a writer was put aside when the "peculiar thrill" of some University of London extension lectures turned her thoughts in other directions and to Oxford. In 1894, at the age of twenty-seven, she entered Somerville College to take "Greats" and to discover the enormous intellectual stimulation of Philosophy. Women were still not members of the University but were there "unofficially," almost on sufferance. They could not be awarded degrees, but they could take classes in their own colleges and, properly chaperoned, could attend University lectures with the men. For Hilda Oakeley, Oxford was both an

Hilda Oakeley

intellectual and an emotional experience. She wrote that because of "generous interest in the women's cause, we were extraordinarily fortunate in the tutors who spared time to supervise our work"[22] and she felt herself to be part of the ancient institution:

> To be *in* the University of Oxford, not merely as a visitor to a superior world, of so many men past and present who had helped towards the greatness of England, and provided the thoughts and knowledge which penetrated outside the shrine to the Court of the Gentiles and beyond! To be admitted to a share in the intellectual discipline, and the atmosphere which hung about those enchanted towers, spires, and halls! To wander along Queen's Walk, The High, The Turtle, or enter Oriel and Christ Church Halls, not as a stranger, but as an Oxford student, who came to learn what lay behind that ancient and modern austere sanctity, and visible pre-eminence of the intellectual life, in the wisdom of the past and the advancing search of the present! We trod those grey stones between grey walls, in the steps of thousands before us since the Grey Friars' days, and felt ourselves to be intimately children of Oxford, though unknown to the constitution.[23]

Oakeley's deep respect and feeling for intellectual tradition are obvious. They must have been pre-eminent among the reasons why Strathcona and Peterson selected her.

The appointment of the first head of Royal Victoria College was one of some consequence, to be greeted with a good deal of general interest in Canada. Miss Oakeley discovered this, rather to her embarrassment, on the voyage out when Sir Charles Tupper, who happened to be on board her ship, made unexpected references to her in a speech at the ship's concert. Some public reaction in Montreal was unfavourable because the appointee was not a Canadian; other opinion was favourable for precisely that reason, holding that English methods and standards would enrich local education. Oakeley herself sensitively recognized that any fresh ideas she could bring would only take root if she could enable people to see them from their own perspective.[24] In approving Hilda Oakeley, Lord Strathcona had appointed a woman of intelligence and sensibility; in accepting the appointment, Hilda Oakeley understood that Lord Strathcona had entrusted her with a great responsibility. He had told her:

> I need not say to you what a deep interest I take in the success of the Royal Victoria College, the Lady Principalship of which you have accepted as its first occupant, and I feel every confidence that your supervision of it will be of the most beneficial character—not alone in

teaching its pupils to become clever or even learned women, but also in instilling into their minds those principles and sentiments without which they cannot be true gentlewomen.[25]

On her arrival in Montreal, Hilda Oakeley was met by Principal Peterson, accompanied by Mrs. Caroline Cox, who was "a member of an English family well known for its progressive ideas on women's education" and wife of the professor of Physics. Later, Oakeley was to be welcomed by other members of the faculty, the Governors and their families, and members of the Montreal community as well as McGill students, alumnae and the people who were to work with her at Royal Victoria College. She found a fine staff had already been selected: Miss Helen Gairdner, formerly Secretary of the Montreal Ladies' Educational Association, Lady Superintendent of the Donaldas, and one-time Secretary to Principal Dawson, was now to be Secretary of the College. The Chief House-keeper was to be Mrs. A.L. Jarvis, late of the Wilkes Barre Hospital, Pa. and under her, a staff of eight women and three men. A local newspaper commented upon the importance of the domestic staff, noting that they had the responsibility for serving sensibly chosen diets, maintaining spotless cleanliness throughout the building, doing "irreproachable" laundry, and generally keeping the young ladies in good humour. Mrs. Jarvis' job was seen to require a most unusual union of tact, force and knowledge of household affairs.[26]

The academic staff consisted of five women, three resident and two non-resident. Hilda Oakeley considered herself fortunate to have, as Resident Tutor in English, Susan E. Cameron, B.A., M.A. (McGill), who had distinguished herself by winning the Gold Medal for English Language and Literature in 1895; Annie MacLean, a young Nova Scotian, graduate of Acadia who had earned her Ph.D. in Sociology at the University of Chicago, as Resident Tutor in Economics and History; Clara Lichtenstein, a brilliant Hungarian musician, who was brought out from Edinburgh as Resident Instructor in Music (Vocal and Instrumental); Vendla M. Holstrom, a native of Sweden and a graduate of Baron Nils Posse's gymnasium in Boston, as Non-Resident Instructor in Gymnastics; and Harriet Brooks, B.A. (McGill), 1898, winner of the Anne Molson Gold Medal in Mathematics and Natural Philsophy (Physics), as non-resident Tutor in Mathematics. Susan Cameron and Harriet Brooks were obviously excellent students. Their appointments symbolized the quality of instruction that was to be given at the Royal Victoria College and, in their persons, they provided a close link between the old Donalda Department and the new College. Kindly, good-humored Helen Gairdner, too, strengthened the connections between the past and future forms of education for women at McGill.

Hilda Oakeley remained as Warden from 1899 to 1905, when she returned to England to tutor in Philosophy at the University of Manchester. Later she became a senior administrator at King's College, London. While at McGill, she not only had the distinction of being the first head of the Royal Victoria College, but also the first woman to receive an honorary degree from the University, the first woman to give the annual University Lecture, and the first woman to be admitted as a member of the Faculty of Arts.27 Though she had done brilliantly at Oxford, because she was a woman, she had not been awarded a degree. Greatly to its credit, McGill made some amends by admitting her to the degrees of B.A. and M.A. a few months after her arrival. She thus had the dignity of a degree all the while she was working in the McGill academic milieu. After Oxford relented in 1920 and granted its degrees to women, Oakeley received her M.A. (Oxon.) retroactively and was later awarded a D.Litt. from the University of London. Her McGill University Lecture was on "History and Progress" and was, she said, "quintessential Oxford Greats." Given in 1900 at the invitation of Dr. Peterson, it was extremely well received and one professor commented that he had not previously heard such "sincere and lofty idealism" on a McGill dais.28

With the establishment of the Royal Victoria College, the old Donalda Department was closed, or as the prospectus put it, "students in attendance in what has hitherto been known as the 'Donalda Special Course for Women' will hereafter be received as students of the Royal Victoria College, whether resident or non-resident." Since, at the time of Miss Oakeley's arrival, the fine furnishings had not yet been installed and the newspapers were laughing at the fact that the College was equipped with nothing but seventy-seven mirrors, it was fortunate that the initial number of resident students was small. The very first one was Carolyn Louise Hitchcock, (B.A.'02) a tall young woman with red-gold hair, who was soon joined by four other residents and by the end of the year there were ten or eleven. However, all women students at McGill now technically belonged to R.V.C. and all R.V.C. students were required to register as students of McGill. Thus, in its first year (1899-1900), there were approximately a hundred women of R.V.C., including residents, non-residents and partials.

The women students, or Donaldas as they were still called, generally took their first and second year classes separately at the College, but had most of their senior and laboratory classes on the McGill campus proper. Though the College had its own tutors, regular McGill staff continued to teach the women. This was in accordance with the terms Lord Strathcona had indicated when he announced the endowment to the Board of Governors. The minutes show:

The Chancellor intimated his wish that the teaching in the Royal Victoria College should be undertaken by the present Professors and Lecturers of the University, with such additions to their number as the circumstances may require; with the condition that the main feature of the existing Donalda Endowment, viz. that the teaching given to women in lecture classes should be essentially separate education, not co-education, should be maintained in the new College with certain reservations and modifications. [29]

It cannot be denied that these conditions are quite clear—whether old instructors were involved, or new—separate, not co-education, was to be the norm for women at McGill. It is therefore curious that Hilda Oakeley should write in her autobiography, "I do not know what were Lord Strathcona's views on co-education." [30] She conceded that she imagined "they must have been rather cautious," but she really did not *know*. It would appear, therefore, that the question of co-education or separate education was not one of the topics that she and Lord Strathcona discussed at any great length, nor does it occur in any of the letters he wrote her—all but two of which she passed on to her successor and they now repose in the McGill Archives. Separate education cannot have been anything the Chancellor emphasized to the Warden of the Royal Victoria College. Strathcona's name was invoked often enough in support of it, particularly by conservatives like Dean Alexander Johnson, but zealots might have distorted the preferences of the founder. This is unfortunate because it has left an impression of R.V.C. in the early days as very cloistered and the Warden as very "straight-laced."

However, Hilda Oakeley was no prim, stern Victorian "dragon." She had been quite comfortable with co-education at Oxford and was perfectly willing to teach mixed classes herself. Indeed, she obtained a position in the Philosophy Department through the intercession of none other than J. Clark Murray. During her first week in residence Professor Murray, whom she described as "a much respected, liberal-minded and genial person," [31] called upon Miss Oakeley to invite her and Dr. Annie MacLean to assist in his Department. They gladly accepted and soon Oakeley was teaching Philosophy to both men and women students at McGill. So encouraged was she that she offered her services to Professor Colby of the History Department. At the very outset, these arrangements brought forth the disapproval of Dr. Alexander Johnson, Dean of Arts, who affirmed that "the ladies could not lecture at the university, he had no official knowledge of their existence" [32] —this despite the fact that "Hilda Diana Oakeley, M.A." was listed in the McGill Arts Calendar as Lecturer in the Department of Mental and Moral Philosophy!

Dean Johnson was a source of constant tension. Although his wife had once reported that Dr. Johnson enjoyed having ladies for an audience and she had "never known him to return home tired out from a lecture to the girls,"[33] he did not seem to want the women of McGill to become assertive. It had been he who had opposed the granting of regular degrees to women graduates and, though he was defeated on that issue, he continued to see every further development as an encroachment on male prerogatives by "the monstrous regiment of women." When he later discovered that Miss Oakeley had accepted second year men and women into the same class, he was furious. She had to fight him firmly but carefully lest the students suffer and not receive credit for their work. The men remained in the class, but Johnson refused to accept Oakeley's examination list which showed three or four men with first class marks. Under pressure, she altered her list and brought a couple of men down to second class. She recalled this incident with chagrin, saying regretfully, "I blush to remember my pusillanimity."

She was not always so "pusillanimous." When necessary, she exerted herself with considerable strength. For example, at the end of her fourth year, she wrote to the Principal to complain that she had found her inability to attend Faculty meetings a great drawback.[34] In those days—indeed until the 1960's—membership in a Faculty of McGill, with the right to attend and vote at Faculty meetings was a privilege of rank and not an automatic right of all full-time University teachers. Oakeley suggested that her position in relation to the women students was sufficiently strong to "overrule other grounds for disability" such as her junior standing in the teaching staff. She did not cite her sex as a ground for her having been excluded from Faculty and she did not seek special privileges. She was, in fact, "anxious that there should be no appearance of the women students requiring a special advocate." However, she found that, in practice, she had been treated as "the proper channel of communication between them and Faculty." She claimed that her attendance at Faculty would simplify administration and improve communication all round. The matter was duly considered for almost a year. Finally, in March 1904, by vote of Faculty, Hilda Oakeley was admitted to the Faculty of Arts and became the first woman to attend the meetings of that body.

In many ways such as this, Hilda Oakeley had to fight a lonely battle, one that was not always easy for her. While she appeared to some people to be aloof, she was probably shy rather than cold and she attempted to run the College in a manner that was both warm and personal. R.V.C. was to be the academic home of its inhabitants and she tried to allow it to function without laying down a formal code of rules, relying instead on co-operation and the students' sense of responsibility. When in her last year, she did develop a set of regulations called, to Dr. Peterson's amusement, "Household Order," she introduced it not as an edict from on high but in consultation with the senior students. "If I allowed more freedom than some of the University people approved," she reminisced, "I had to suffer the penalty for it in keen anxieties, as, for instance, when my residents were late in returning home from snow-shoeing or tobogganing parties, usually *à deux,* or when someone had gone out to a party omitting to leave her address. But what a happy understanding was established when they came in. . . ."[35] Miss Oakeley appeared to be remarkably liberal, more so than her successors. As the College grew in numbers and complexity, the rules increased in numbers and strictness. In other words, it is paradoxically possible that as R.V.C. moved into the twentieth century, it became more and more "Victorian."

The first Warden seems to have coped with the demands and vagaries of her position with warmth, humour and flexibility. On her first evening, she took in stride a rather unconventional visit from Dr. and Mrs. Peterson and Sir William Macdonald, when the latter climbed in through a window because nobody answered the doorbell—apparently both a porter and a bell had been installed, but the bell was out of order. During her tenure, Miss Oakeley cheerfully chaperoned mixed tobogganing parties on Mount Royal in the evening and was not too stuffy to try a few runs herself. She was not disconcerted by the boisterousness of the male students. On one memorable occasion, a great rowdy crowd of McGill men celebrating a victory in the Boer War, gathered on the R.V.C. steps, giving vent to "McGill yells" and shouting "God Save the Queen." They began to take the veil off the statue of Her Majesty. This imposing monument, which still graces the front steps, had been executed by the Princess Louise and was awaiting the official opening of the College. Discreetly covered, it was waiting to be unveiled by the Queen's representative with due ceremony and decorum. Despite the "superb" snowstorm that was raging, Hilda Oakeley went out and asked the boys to leave the statue covered as Lord Strathcona wanted it. The students greeted her cheerfully, listened to her speech, ignored her request, gave her a rousing McGill yell—"She's all right. Oh yes, you bet. Who's all right? Miss Oakeley!"—then they tore off down Union Avenue, seizing the first wagon they met, flung the veil over the horse and sped on their way to a wild confrontation with a group of Laval students who had opposing ideas about the war in South Africa. Oakeley recounted the incident with amusement. Nevertheless, she was relieved when, after a number of such unceremonious un-veilings, the official opening of the College took place and the statue of

The Draped Statue of Queen Victoria Awaits the Official Opening

Queen Victoria was finally displayed to the World.

The official opening of the Royal Victoria College in the autumn of 1900 was a gala event for all Montreal. Lord Strathcona was present and ensured that every possible honour attended the occasion. The grand edifice he had given McGill was elaborately decorated, both inside and out with the brilliance and magic of electricity. According to an eye witness: "Every gable and arch, as well as the lines of balcony and window glittered with an outline of electric lights—white and red, alternately. In the mouths of grinning stone lions they gleamed, and above their heads, high on the topmost pinnacles. Above the doorway a huge transparency of red glass showed the familiar shield and birds. Above this the Union Jack shone gloriously in lights of three colours, and higher still the crown gleamed out clear and white."[36] Within this "palace of light" Lord Strathcona, Principal Peterson, and Miss Oakeley greeted more than two thousand guests. The climax of the evening came at eleven o'clock when Lady Minto, wife of the Governor General of Canada, pulled the cord, the white draping immediately fell away and the statue of Queen Victoria was at last properly unveiled. "At the same moment new lights, forming the letters 'V.R.' flashed out on the front of the building; the rifles, who lined the street, marched up and saluted; and there arose a sound of many voices singing 'God Save the Queen.' The last touch of colour was given to the already gorgeous tableau in the beautiful bouquet of red and white roses presented by Miss Oakeley to Lady Minto." Many years later, Miss Oakeley happened to meet Lady Minto on board a ship and was dismayed to find that she who had officiated at the splendid opening of the Royal Victoria College had no recollection of the event that was so stirring for Montreal, McGill and Lord Strathcona.

Lord Strathcona revelled in the excitement of such occasions as well as the pageantry of academic life. Because he was officially in London as Canadian High Commissioner, he did not spend as much time at McGill as he might have wished, but he was certainly on hand the following year when the Duke and Duchess of York (subsequently to be King George V and Queen-Mary) visited the University. A special convocation was held at the Royal Victoria College and the Chancellor had the pleasure of bestowing LL.D.'s on the royal couple. H.R.H. the Duchess of York thus became the first woman to receive an honorary doctorate from McGill. (The degrees granted Miss Oakeley were B.A., M.A.) In all, up to the end of 1980, McGill had granted forty-one honorary degrees to women.[37] It had bestowed some eight hundred upon men.

* * *

By the time of Lord Strathcona's death in 1914, the College was functioning well under a new Warden, Miss Ethel Hurlbatt, with an enrolment of about 150 (resident and non-resident) students. However, R.V.C. still was not formally chartered. Strathcona made provision in his will for his executors to finalize arrangements for a charter he had devised. Although this matter was not as complicated as the implementation of James McGill's will, it was fraught with delays and had to have the sanction of the Governments of Canada and Quebec as well as the authorization of the Privy Council in England. Furthermore, the Board of Governors had to give its approval. While the Governors co-operated fully with Lord Strathcona's trustees, they wanted a number of changes; for example, in 1917 they insisted on being protected against any expenditure on separate education in excess of the endowment. They recognised that if women were confined to options that could only be provided in separate classes, the result would be contrary to the spirit of the charter, restricting rather than promoting higher education for women. [38] Not until 1922 [39] was the University informed that King George V had been pleased to grant a Royal Charter to the College where he had been awarded an honorary degree in 1901.

The Charter stated, *inter alia,* that "the Royal Victoria College shall be a College of McGill University, but shall retain its own corporate identity and separate administration and government, in order to conserve and develop its own resources and accomplish the intentions of the Founder on the lines indicated by him." The primary intention was identified as "to promote the higher education of women in Canada and to enable women students to obtain a collegiate education in the Faculty of Arts at McGill. . . ." The Charter also specified that the Warden and staff of the College, to be appointed by the Board of Governors, were to be responsible for maintaining educational standards comparable to those which applied at the University.

The Principal, who by that time was Sir Arthur Currie, pointed out in his Annual Report for 1922, that the Charter was significant for two major reasons: First, it clarified the position of R.V.C. which had previously been somewhat ambiguous. (The charter clearly made the College an integral part of the University, and the following year, the Board of Governors determined that the statutes of the College were to form Chapter XIV of the University Statutes.) Second, the Charter indicated that the college system of education was to be part of the McGill scheme of things. In Sir Arthur's view:

> There is no institution where esprit de corps and loyalty reach a higher point than in a college of moderate size, and the value of the Royal Victoria College to the cause of education in Canada will be

inestimable. To ensure that this value will continue to be the highest possible, it is essential that not only the staff but the undergraduates of the College shall understand and observe not only the letter but the spirit of the Charter which expresses the wishes of its founder and by which it is given its own identity and government. [40]

The college system as envisioned by Sir Arthur and others has never materialized at McGill. Royal Victoria College has remained the only institution of its kind on campus. It was, by virtue of the Charter, part of McGill, yet an independent entity. No wonder that the position of Warden of R.V.C. was considered by many as the "highest academic appointment in Canada available to a woman." The Warden's concern for scholarship, her sense of purpose and her personality were almost as important as the Charter in determining the future of the College. The successors of Hilda Oakeley proved to be a remarkable series of women and each Warden "built something of herself, something intrinsically valuable, into the invisible, the intangible, the *real* Royal Victoria College." [41]

* * *

The second Warden was Ethel Hurlbatt, who arrived in Montreal from England in January, 1907. She had crossed the Atlantic on the new "Empress of Britain," the same ship as Lord Strathcona who was making one of his periodic visits to Canada. She had already met him in his unpretentious London office the previous summer, after Principal Peterson had invited her to become Warden. She recalled that Strathcona spoke but little of the College, either in London or on the voyage out, assuming that someone who was involved with college life as she was would know what the general conditions were. She may not have received specific instructions about R.V.C., but she did gain a lasting impression of Strathcona. She said, "I was conscious that his voice revealed his personality. It was resonant and far reaching, almost hard in the way every word conveyed a sense of the power behind it. His tone was even and exact, and it was so when it was kindest and most gentle, or when other signs betrayed his amusement." [42]

Miss Hurlbatt was born at Bickley, Kent in 1866. She spent part of her childhood in South Africa, and from an early age, seems to have taken responsibility for her own education. At the age of twenty-two she went up to Oxford where she was a contemporary of Hilda Oakeley's at Somerville. She honoured in History and was remembered as "a tall, blue-eyed girl, rather clumsy in her movements, a little slow in making up her mind, but always vigorous, always to be depended upon, never

Ethel Hurlbatt

taking offence, and sometimes delightfully merry.''[43] Like Hilda
Oakeley, Ethel Hurlbatt bore something of Oxford and the college spirit
with her throughout her career. Like the other women of Oxford in the
19th century, she was denied a degree and, like many others, she
partially overcame this by getting credit for her work and a M.A. degree
from Trinity College, Dublin. In 1925, Oxford bestowed on her an
honorary M.A. At the time when she was invited to come to R.V.C., she
was Warden of Bedford College, University of London, with a distinguished reputation for scholarship and administration. She had
previously been Warden of the newly-established Aberdane Hall for
Women at the University of South Wales.

At the Royal Victoria College, Ethel Hurlbatt was Warden and a
tutor in History. Her chief concerns, as evidenced by her annual reports,
speeches, publications and letters were for scholarship and the intellectual and personal welfare of the students. She encouraged many of
them to continue their post-graduate studies abroad. Almost as
important as her interest in the College were her activities in the community, especially the Alliance Française, Serbian relief work, and the
Women's Canadian Club. She received a number of public honours and
acclaim, notably the rosette of the *Officier de l'instruction publique*
awarded by the Government of France in 1918 for ''l'effort persévérant à
la propagation de la langue Française dans l'Université'' and the Cross
of Mercy, bestowed by Crown Prince Alexander of Serbia in 1919 for her
''work and interest in the Serbian people'' and especially ''for the care
and services rendered to our wounded and sick soldiers.''

Ethel Hurlbatt's manner, as described in several published
accounts of her career, was somewhat awesome. It was said that even
Principal Peterson was afraid of her at first. However, these same
reports, even while claiming that she ''might intimidate, she might
occasionally repel, she could not be disregarded,''[44] also contain
unusually strong indications of affection and deep respect. Furthermore,
she did become firm friends with Principal William Peterson and with
his successor, Sir Arthur Currie.

Despite her rather formidable appearance, Ethel Hurlbatt suffered
with very poor health. She was ill for months during the great influenza
epidemic of 1918 and was granted a year's leave for health reasons in
1924-25. During her absence, Mrs. C.G. Garside, an able and distinguished Englishwoman who, as Miss Hardy, had once been Principal of
the Trafalgar School, acted as Warden. After a prolonged rest in Italy,
Miss Hurlbatt returned to Montreal but, early in 1928, she was stricken
once more and spent over a year in the Royal Victoria Hospital. During
that difficult time, ''the letters and flowers of students,'' she said,
''made one long unbroken chain of pleasure.''[45]

Hurlbatt's resignation was officially accepted in 1929 and the Alumnae Society presented her with a purse of $2,000 in gold "with deep gratitude" for her devotion to the wellbeing of the Royal Victoria College. The following year, in recognition of her "wise and beneficent" government of the College, McGill bestowed upon her the degree of Doctor of Laws, *honoris causa*. For her part, Ethel Hurlbatt in 1930 presented the College with the "Warden's Jewel," a pendant clip of tourmalines set in silver. Made in Ceylon as part of a chieftan's jewellery, this had been given to her by Madeleine Shaw Lefevre, Principal of Somerville College, Oxford and Hurlbatt had worn it throughout her term as Warden. As a believer in tradition, she now suggested that the Jewel be worn on special occasions by her successors.

Ethel Hurlbatt died in France in March, 1934. Her new neighbours there and her old friends in Montreal seemed to concur that, "De cette femme de coeur il ne reste qu'un doux souvenir; elle a passé au milieu de nous toujours bonne et devouée, cherchant à faire plaisir à tous."46

Though Miss Hurlbatt had a generally similar background to Miss Oakeley and shared many ideals, the College changed under her administration. She certainly was concerned for the individual student,

The Warden's Jewel

but was solidly supportive of R.V.C. as an institution, endorsing the accumulating sanction of tradition. She was said to be "incorrigibly conscientious" and "solidly reasonable" and, while not rejecting new ideas out of hand, could be exasperatingly deliberate in assessing them.

It would be unfair to suggest that Miss Hurlbatt was an autocrat. When she learned from some students in 1927 that they were "unable to guarantee the keeping of [the] rule against smoking," [47] she did not enforce it heavy handedly, but sought advice from Charles Martin, Dean of Medicine, and Ethel Cartwright, Director of Women's Physical Education. Dr. Martin said if girls under nineteen only smoked in moderation it would probably be all right, but smoking was a hard habit to control and "girls who smoke a great deal are apt to get loose in their habits otherwise;" [48] Miss Cartwright thought smoking was probably unhealthy but recommended that only senior students over twenty be permitted to use a recognized "Smoking Room." [49] Miss Hurlbatt accepted their advice and limited smoking was henceforth permitted at R.V.C.

During the twenty-odd years of her Wardenship, change was inevitable simply by virtue of the growth in numbers. By 1927-28, there were 383 women undergraduates and the total number of women at McGill, including partials, graduate and diploma students, was in the neighbourhood of seven hundred. In that year, there were sixty-three students in residence at R.V.C. Rules of conduct which had largely been tacit in the early days of very few students, now became formalized and R.V.C.'s reputation as a cloistered academy grew.

After Hilda Oakeley's pioneering efforts, Ethel Hurlbatt presided over a period of growth and consolidation. It is always difficult to be second, to follow a successful initiator. Simple comparisons are not necessarily valid when conditions are likely to be significantly different. The long Hurlbatt years not only began when the heady excitement of the establishment of R.V.C. was fading, but they covered a demanding period in Montreal and Canadian history. Though R.V.C. and McGill might have been privileged and sheltered environments, they were not immune from the impact of the events surrounding them. Hurlbatt was Warden during World War I, the Montreal conscription riots with the English-French tensions they generated, the post-war strikes and inflation.

McGill, like almost every other institution in Canada, was affected by the War. Though the University as a corporate entity was not as involved as it was to be in World War II, its work was disrupted, its staff reduced and its student body depleted. More than 3,000 McGill men were enlisted in active service between 1914-1918, many of them, like Dr. John McCrae, composer of the widely-known battle poem "In

Flanders Fields,'' did not return. The women of McGill were involved as part of the nation-wide civilian support system—raising money, staffing canteens, service libraries or convalescent homes, giving public lectures, knitting, rolling bandages—and many alumnae were active nearer the fighting—as doctors, nurses or aides in hospitals, as Red Cross workers, and as ambulance drivers.

On campus, one of the immediate effects of the War was that, for the first time, women outnumbered men in the Faculty of Arts. While in 1914 there were 138 women to 355 men (29.2% of the total), the proportion increased each year so that in 1917 there were 185 women to 182 men (50.5%). With the pressure of numbers and under wartime conditions, the old prohibitions against co-education had to give way to some extent and could not be immediately restored with the coming of peace. More women's classes were held on the main campus and there was less teaching at R.V.C. This distressed Miss Hurlbatt and, as late as 1922-23, she expressed the hope in her Annual Report that the University would soon ''return in the direction of pre-war conditions of separate classes.'' She added, in a statement that was prophetic of R.V.C. some fifty years later: ''By the sacrifice of its teaching function, the College would be reduced to a mere residential and social centre, and McGill and Canada be the poorer by the loss of a unique educational asset.''[50]

The Hurlbatt years also covered the age of agitation for, and achievement of, female suffrage in Canada. But in Quebec, the cause was still denied. Premier Louis Taschereau greeted with chilly rebuff the efforts of suffragists such as Mme Gerin-Lajoie, Idola Saint Jean (a McGill Instructor in French) and McGill graduates, Grace Ritchie, Carrie Derick, Anna Scrimger Lyman and others. Meanwhile, powerful editor, Henri Bourassa reacted to the Canadian female franchise with outright ridicule: ''La femme-électeur,'' he sneered, ''qui engendera bientôt la femme-cabaleur, la femme-télégraphie, la femme-souteneur, la femme-avocat, enfin, pour dire en un mot: la femme-*homme*, le monstre hybride et répugnant qui tuera la femme-*mère* et la femme-*femme*.''[51] The ''man-woman'' or the ''blue stocking'' or any woman who thought for herself was still likely to be considered a ''social monster'' and it took great courage for women to stand up to Bourassa-style arguments presented with such force.

''Votes for Women'' was, of course, a lively subject for undergraduate discussion. Back in 1893 McGill had won a debate against Toronto by showing that the female franchise and representation in Parliament would not be of benefit to Canada. The crafty McGill team proved its point, not by contending that Woman was unworthy to enter politics, but that politics was unworthy of Woman. However, Ethel Hurlbatt, for one, was an advocate of female enfranchisement. Not long after her arrival in 1907, she addressed the Delta Sigma Society on the subject and also spoke publicly on "The Woman Suffrage Question in England." For Delta Sigma, she reviewed the history of the suffragist movement, establishing that it was evolutionary rather than revolutionary and claiming for women the right to vote on the same basis as men. She said the reason was obvious. "If women are different from men, then what is called a representative government without them is not representative at all; if they are like men they should have a voice in the direction of the government that controls them. Representation goes with taxation, therefore those subject to laws should have a share in making them. To exclude women from having a share is to place them among infants, criminals or lunatics."[52] Hurlbatt emphasized that the problem was of vital concern to every college woman and, while she regretted the excesses of the Suffragettes, she pointed out that other social reforms had been achieved only when "demonstrative measures" had been used.

The Martlet, the undergraduate publication which had replaced the *University Gazette,* took issue with her. It quibbled over her support for votes for women on the same grounds as for men since, at that time, there was a property qualification. *The Martlet,* therefore, criticized her for denying the vote to women of the working class—something she never explicitly did. The student paper also took the opportunity to condemn the whole movement, castigating the behavior of the extreme Suffragettes, pointing out that many of them "have been brought up in the best homes or are University Graduates—witness Miss Pankhurst." It then raised the question of whether any women were fit to vote. "What good can we expect," asked *The Martlet,* "from enfranchising creatures who invade churches, who assault policemen, and who shew themselves unable to keep their heads even in the most trifling matters? Is it not courting danger to expect them to give a fair decision on national problems of war or finance?"[53] It further noted that "one of the principal dangers of Female Suffrage is the increased ignorant vote that it creates," quoting Australia as the horrible example. In conclusion, this McGill voice urged: ". . . let us agree once and for all that woman is not fitted for the ups and downs, the continual strain of national politics. Nature has fitted her for very different objects—for the care of the home and the upbringing of her children, and to insist upon her taking part in man's affairs would be simply to defy the laws of Nature."[54]

Despite the fulminations of *The Martlet* and others, women did receive the vote in Canada in 1918. This was another by-product of the War. However, it was not until 1940 that the women of Quebec, with the added energy and leadership of Thérèse Casgrain, succeeded in gaining this right. By that time, Ethel Hurlbatt was no longer Warden of R.V.C., but her term of office included the period of Prohibition in the United States, which resulted in a great influx of tourism for Montreal, the age of shorter skirts and bobbed hair, of "flappers," the Charleston and tea dances at the Windsor and Mount Royal Hotels, the first solo flight across the Atlantic, the spread of the radio, the popularity of the "talkies," the departure of the horse and the advent of the automobile. Amid all this social upsurge, the Royal Victoria College flourished in a conservative way which did not deny its students - at least in retrospect - a good deal of fun. When she left in 1929, Principal Sir Arthur Currie wrote to Miss Hurlbatt that "Under your care the Royal Victoria College has made a real advance; it has become the recognised centre for all women students at McGill, it has developed a corporate spirit, and it has contributed in no small measure to the cause of education." [55]

*　*　*

The third warden of R.V.C. was Mrs. Susan Cameron Vaughan. No stranger to McGill, as Susan Cameron she had been the original English tutor at the College and, in the 1906-07 interval between the first and second Wardens, she had been Acting-Warden. When Miss Hurlbatt assumed her duties, Susan Cameron became Vice-Warden, a position she retained until her marriage in 1918. She married Walter Vaughan, who had been the University Bursar, and they lived in England for a number of years. After his death, she returned to Montreal and, in the late 20's during the period of Miss Hurlbatt's long illness, she was again asked to serve as Acting Warden. Finally, in 1931, to the general approval of the University community, she was officially appointed as Warden of the Royal Victoria College.

Susan Cameron Vaughan was, of course, the first McGill graduate to hold the office which had such importance for all the women at McGill. Like her predecessors, she too was a scholar. At the end of her fine undergraduate career she won the Gold Medal in English Language and Literature, eliciting from Professor Charles Colby an enthusiastic note of congratulation which said in part:

> The gift of style which you possess is a gift so rare that the possessor is morally bound to make the most of it. The case is that of the talents which must be put out to usury or otherwise the steward will receive little praise at the end. Good literary style implies so many of the highest qualities—clear perceptions, simplicity, imagination—that almost anything may be expected from one who, dowered with it, castigates himself with remorseless zeal. [56]

Susan Cameron Vaughan

It could well be said that Susan Cameron did not disappoint Colby's high expectations and that she did, indeed, "put her talents out to usury" if not quite in the way he expected. Her entire professional career was spent at her *alma mater*. She wrote a good deal about McGill, leaving valuable records of the early days of women on campus, and she taught. She was not only Tutor at R.V.C. but was also listed in the Faculty of Arts English Department as Lecturer from 1902 to 1912 and as Assistant Professor until her marriage. Her students appreciated her critical acumen, her penetrating insights and more than one has affirmed that they "all sat at her feet." A. Vibert Douglas, who was to distinguish herself in Physics and as Dean of Women at Queen's, said of Cameron: "She taught us many things. She showed us the essential elements of a well balanced sentence. She expounded the art of expressing our thoughts in good, straight-forward, flowing prose. She taught us the importance of having thoughts worthy to be so expressed! We respected her judgment, we profited by her criticism—and what a wonderfully painstaking teacher she was."[57] Other R.V.C. graduates might complain about the house rules, the restricted number of leaves, and Susan Cameron Vaughan's threat to take her knitting into the common room when they were entertaining men, but few would deny that she impressed her personality on McGill and made R.V.C. a presence on campus.

Upon her retirement in 1937, the Alumnae commissioned a portrait to be painted by Kenneth Forbes and the University granted her an LL.D. During more than forty years at McGill, she had proven herself to be "a loyal and devoted servant of the University, who combined in rare measure the gifts of scholar and administrator, fulfilling her difficult and important office with an unaffected dignity, a natural understanding, a wise tolerance, a kindly sense of humour, which won the respect and affection of all who knew her."[58] She was an excellent example of McGill's education for women and a champion of the cause.

At about this time on the Canadian national scene, the famous five women from Alberta,[59] were arguing the case from the Supreme Court to the Privy Council that women were "persons" and were eligible to be members of the Senate. On the local scene, Susan Cameron Vaughan was fighting for recognition that the women of R.V.C. were genuine students of McGill. Her argument was not with *The Martlet* as Hurlbatt's had been, but with its successor, the *McGill Daily*. The problem had to do specifically with women students' relationship to the Students' Council and, by extension, their status in the University as a whole. The issue came to the fore on November 22, 1928 in a *Daily* editorial entitled "A Problem"—but the historical roots went farther back.

During the 19th century, the principal student organization at McGill was the Alma Mater Society and when women entered the University they were permitted to join it. There is no record of any particular disagreement between members of the two sexes, nor any account of efforts to oust the women. However, the Society was found to be unwieldy (there was also some whisper of trouble with the police) and a new organization was developed. This was the Students' Society of McGill University or, as it was more commonly called, the Students' Council, and its constitution, framed in 1908, stated specifically that membership should consist of "every *male* student of the University who pays the athletic fee." The Donaldas apparently did not protest strenuously when they were thus excluded and since Miss Hurlbatt had only recently become Warden of R.V.C., she was "too new to the situation to realise that it might be wise to safeguard the representation of women students" as she would have done later.[60] As a result, the women had no alternative but to establish their own organization, the R.V.C. Undergraduate Society. Before long, it became all too apparent that two parallel societies meant wasteful duplication of energy and funds. The women students then began to try to rejoin the men. Their efforts were not taken very seriously, if a report in the campus paper is any indication. In 1910, *The Martlet* noted that, "The members of R.V.C. positively insist on having votes in the Student Council matters." But then it continued, "They have a large quantity of excellent reasons in the shape of pretty frocks to support their pretensions." This totally irrelevant "pretty frocks" comment is a typical example of the subtle sexism which has pervaded the issue of equality for women in many different contexts. This is the patronizing compliment that manages both to disarm and to belittle.

By 1917, the year in which women outnumbered men in the Faculty of Arts, they had not achieved success but they at least got publicity. The Montreal *Star* reported that "A considerable amount of excitement has been aroused among the students of McGill University by the action of the student body of the Royal Victoria College in making application for membership in the Students' Society of the University. . . . The attitude of the Royal Victoria College students seems to be that they do not receive sufficient recognition as students of the University, and wish to have their status raised to a level with that of the men. If a change were made, the women students would expect either direct or indirect representation on the Students' Council. They would require that all undergraduate offices be open to them, and would require also that they be given a voice in matters affecting the whole student body of the University, including athletics, student societies, and the college paper."[61]

To satisfy the Donaldas' claims, constitutional changes would have been necessary for the Students' Society and there was just not enough support for that. So things remained unaltered through the Hurlbatt years, until the *Daily* editorial of November 22, 1928. This opinion piece began by pointing out that women had equal status with men in all student affairs yet they had distinct organizations. It said that there had been clashes in the past and predicted these would continue. It noted that each of the societies had jurisdiction over its own members only, commenting that it therefore seemed strange that there were women members, even some office holders, in affiliated clubs of the men's society. It singled out the Choral Society which had three Donaldas on its executive and which happened to have lost money that year. All this was straightforward, or at least debatable, but what Susan Cameron Vaughan found utterly wrong and infuriating was an interpretation of McGill's history to the effect that:

> As things stand, due to a ruling by a grand benefactor of McGill,— God rest his soul,—there is no place for women in McGill college. Hence they have no status as members of the University but are affiliated with it in the institution of the R.V.C. [62]

At once Susan Cameron Vaughan, then the Acting Warden of R.V.C., wrote the *Daily* a very long letter to set the record straight and leave no doubt that women had a rightful place at McGill. She acknowledged that there was no mention of them in James McGill's will, but then the Founder had no more foreseen the advent of higher education for women than he had foreseen the Students' Council. She pointed out, however, that a second great benefactor, Lord Strathcona, had thought about women's education and that the University had legally accepted women. Most important, women were students at McGill since R.V.C. was not an affiliated college, but a constituent part of the University. Each year since 1888, women had received McGill degrees.

This exchange generated considerable discussion on campus. Vaughan's letter helped clarify the situation but the issue was not yet settled. The following year, a committee of the Students' Council, set up to investigate the question of the inclusion of women, decided "the matter was not ready for settlement." The next year the issue was voted on and lost at the Students' Council elections. However, opinion was divided—one man who stood for equal rights was defeated, but so was one who opposed them; one who approved of giving women the vote without the right to hold office was elected, another was defeated. In 1930, the *Daily* in a somewhat irascible editorial headed "These Women," tried to give both sides of this recurrent issue, but seemed to conclude that nothing would be gained if women joined the men. [63]

Meanwhile, Susan Cameron Vaughan had been asked by the Alumnae Society to speak to them on "The Status of Women at McGill." It was clearly a matter of great concern, for the women graduates of McGill needed to be assured of their rights, their academic legitimacy. To make absolutely certain, Mrs. Vaughan resurrected the *Daily* articles of 1928 and collected them, together with copies of the wills of James McGill and Lord Strathcona, the Charters of McGill and the Royal Victoria College as well as the Statutes and took them all to a distinguished Montreal lawyer, W.S. Johnson, K.C. Mr. Johnson examined the legal bases of the history of women at McGill and decided that "once the purpose of education and the advancement of learning made it expedient to admit women, the Founder's will offered no substantial barrier." [64] His considered conclusion was unequivocal:

> . . . the Royal Victoria College is made and declared to be a college of McGill University, not an affiliated college. Nothing could be more clear, final and peremptory. Its students are members of the University.

The lawyer further opined that the constitution of the Students' Council made women ineligible for admission. However, since the framers of that constitution were merely a body of undergraduates of the class of 1908 or thereabouts, it could be amended at any time by a quorum of undergraduates. Corporation, which had ratified the original, might then be expected to ratify any reasonable amendment, such as the extension of membership to women. There could be no further doubt. The Acting Warden of R.V.C. had been found to be correct. Women were legally students of McGill.

So Susan Vaughan, prompted by the "These Women" editorial, wrote another long letter to the *Daily*. While reciting the whole story once more and giving Mr. Johnson's legal opinion, she refrained from suggesting that the male students amend their constitution but noted that if the women really pressed the issue, "the Students' Council will either have to modify its present attitude or fight a losing battle." [65]

In response, yet another editorial appeared. Cutely titled, "Women Are McGill Men," it noted how the issue had been simmering for years, though with little more than "curious interest" from the men and "apathy" from the women students until the Acting Warden of R.V.C. had intervened. It credited Mrs. Vaughan with leadership in bringing the matter clearly into focus, commenting dryly that "the women might even go so far this year as to want their rights." It continued in a tone that was both moderate and encouraging:

... if they ever want representation, it will be rather a hard thing to prevent them from getting it. Mrs. Vaughan has investigated enough to see that her charges have almost a case in law. Of course it is impossible that matters could come to that pass, but the fact that the girls have charters and deeds and similar documents to support them will carry weight if they ever do care to press their claims. ...

But what should be stressed is not the fact that if the women want representation they will have to be given it, but rather that if they want anything at all and only show they want it, nobody in the world, and least of all the ... Council will want to stop them.[66]

Susan Cameron Vaughan had recognised that a "baseless legend" that women were *in* McGill but not *of* it had crept from some mysterious source into the body of McGill tradition. She was determined to explode this myth and she succeeded admirably. Thanks in large measure to her efforts, women were admitted to the Students' Council in 1931. However, the lessons of history seem to keep getting lost or diminished by the force of a dominant idea, even in a university milieu. Incredible as it may seem, the anti-woman editorials continued to appear in the *Daily*. "Whither Womanhood" of November 30, 1931 decried women's efforts toward social justice claiming, with no historical justification, that "Before desirous of this equality woman was easily the superior of man" and advising women "to go back to their crochet." Another one, "The Woman in Our Midst," of March 12, 1936 noted that women at McGill seemed to be regarded as intruders, even after fifty years on campus. With liberal intentions but unfortunate phrasing it exhorted: "We should treat them more in the position of equals, come down from the lofty perch from which we have been regarding their progress with disdainful air of sufferance and realize, *before our colony revolts* [emphasis added], that their demands should meet with sympathy and respect." Susan Cameron Vaughan regretted the persistance of the myths about women and, in words borrowed from Dr. Johnson, an old "male chauvinist," urged:

"Clear your mind of cant." On this vexed question let us have done with catch words and recognize that what is wanted for women, as well as for men and for children, is better education and more of it.[67]

Meanwhile, at R.V.C. enrolment was growing steadily and more space for resident students was required. One annex had been opened in 1912 in Learmont House, a property acquired by Lord Strathcona at the corner of University and Sherbrooke Streets three years earlier; a second annex was started in 1925 and a third in 1928. In 1931, a new West Wing was added to the main building and the annexes closed—indeed, the

West Wing was constructed on the site of Learmont House. But the growing student numbers had greater impact than just the need for additional dormitory space. By 1930 there were more than seven hundred women on campus so that the College could no longer realistically be the centre for all the women of McGill. While about half were taking undergraduate courses in the Faculty of Arts and Science, there were now also women in Graduate Studies, Medicine, Law, Music, Commerce, Physical Education, Dentistry, Library Science, Nursing and Social Work. Inevitably, the pressures of enrolment were pushing women into the regular McGill classrooms with men. Furthermore, the evolving social mores, with women participating more in the world of work and social affairs, had expression on campus with women's participation in student activities, clubs and political organizations. Thus, an old problem which seemed to have been dormant for years, was found to be vigorously live and well.

Co-education was again an issue at McGill and Susan Vaughan now found herself defending her students against claims that they were lowering the standard of scholarship at the University. In 1936 she advised the women students that they would have to face such criticism and the only successful way to meet it was to apply themselves to their studies. She warned them that there were still strong critics of co-education in the University. She said, ''There are those who state that co-education is still on trial. The only way that these critics can be stilled is to show indisputably that the standard of education in our co-educational institutions of today does not compare unfavourably with the standard maintained by these same institutions before the advent of co-education.''[68]

This was sound advice from one who had personally proved how well women could succeed in academic pursuits. But it is also the kind of advice that tends to throw the onus onto women, to prove themselves better than men. It tends to lead to the kind of striving for perfection that members of minority groups typically have to cope with in order to keep their foothold in an alien environment. It is the kind of advice that Charlotte Whitton, erstwhile Mayor of Ottawa, mocked when she said, ''For a woman to get as far as a man, she must be at least twice as good as he.'' And then she added, ''Luckily, it isn't difficult!''

Susan Cameron Vaughan was all too well aware that in the McGill of the 30's, prejudice against women remained and she spoke out against it with great vigour and conviction. She was no radical, but she was assuredly a champion of women's rights, both in word and deed. She retired in 1937 after an association with McGill that had spanned forty-six years as student, tutor, Assistant Warden, Acting Warden and Warden of R.V.C. After her death in 1961, a newspaper correspondent summed up her contribution with the following tribute: "By communicating her philosophy through unconscious example, this steadfast, unworldly and well-read woman immeasurably increased the stature and enlarged the horizon of her students in the Department of English at McGill University, of the girls under her Wardenship at the Royal Victoria College and of her fortunate friends and acquaintances."[69]

* * *

Royal Victoria College's fourth Warden, and the last who had had direct contact with Lord Strathcona, was Maude Parkin Grant. She was a member of the very first R.V.C. class and, in that relatively small circle, must have seen the Founder on his visits to the College as well as on the grand occasion of the official opening. Doubtless, she also met him when he came to the meeting of the Delta Sigma Society in 1901. But more than that, she probably owed her very presence at R.V.C. to him. Her family remembers that Lord Strathcona himself persuaded her father to send Maude Parkin to his new College. Her father, Dr. (afterwards, Sir George) Parkin, was Principal of Upper Canada College and later Secretary of the Rhodes Trust. He was a friend of Lord Strathcona and years before, he had drawn the Chancellor's attention to Ethel Hurlbatt's interest in becoming Warden. Hilda Oakeley, who knew Dr. Parkin well, described him as a brilliant orator who was fired with a missionary zeal to convert his audience to his imperialist views, views very much in line with Strathcona's. Thus, though Maude Parkin Grant was a Canadian and a graduate of R.V.C., her appointment represented a link to the British tradition of McGill.[70] As the world stood on the brink of war that was to destroy the British Empire, McGill and other Canadian universities were still tied to the "Mother Country" and still sought academic respectability through their British connections. But this is not to say that the appointment was not intrinsically a good one.

Maude Parkin, whose personality according to Oakely "won her an outstanding place among the students,"[71] received her first-class B.A. degree from McGill in 1903. Two years later, when Hilda Oakeley left Montreal for Manchester, Miss Parkin agreed to go with her as Sub-Warden of the Hall of Residence. One of the first of her tasks there was to go down to the local police station and bail out the suffragette students who had been arrested for chaining themselves to civic buildings. Though Oakeley did not remain at the University of Manchester very long, Maude Parkin stayed until her marriage in 1911. One of the members of Hall council observed to Miss Oakeley that "The best thing you did for Manchester was to bring Miss Parkin here."

Maude Parkin's career had a curious circular quality. Her husband,

Dr. William Grant, succeeded her father as Principal of Upper Canada College and, after his death, she returned to Montreal and her *alma mater*. During the interval of more than thirty years between her graduation and her advent as Warden, her own daughter, Margaret, had already come to R.V.C. and had graduated. Her term as Warden was brief, only three years (1937-40), yet this was a difficult period during which there were three Principals of McGill (Arthur Eustace Morgan, 1935-37; Lewis W. Douglas, 1937-39; F. Cyril James, 1940-62—and she disliked the latter heartily). It was a time of considerable pressure for the Warden of R.V.C. and, unexpectedly, a time when a basic decision about the education of women at McGill was made.

Despite its munificent endowment, the College constantly faced financial problems. In 1930, some administrative changes had been made whereby McGill took all the tuition fees paid by R.V.C. students on the understanding that the University would pay all the teaching salaries which had previously been paid directly by the College.[72] By Mrs. Grant's era, the status of the College again seemed unclear and she believed that its autonomy was being threatened. In response to her request to Principal Cyril James, a joint committee of Board of Governors and Senate was called to examine the College, its pedagogic

Maude Parkin Grant

practices, facilities and finances. Since R.V.C.'s relationship to McGill and Lord Strathcona's intentions became part of this review, it was inevitable that the old issue of separate or co-education should again be discussed. This time agreement was unanimous so that what had begun basically as the result of fiscal difficulties, ended in a clear and official decision on a perennial issue. The committee determined that co-education was the most satisfactory arrangement for both students and faculty and that, as far as practicable, separate grade sheets, separate class sections and separate courses should all be abolished.[73] Official policy had finally caught up with the reality of common practice.

On the question of facilities, there was also general agreement that too high a proportion of the endowment income had to be spent simply on maintenance and that a further study should be made to see how the buildings might be reconstructed to make them more serviceable. Mrs. Grant suggested that it would be possible to accommodate the students in a newly constructed section, "in which case the old building, suitably reconstructed, might be used for university class rooms and for club and rest rooms for the women students as a group."[74] It is intriguing that such a suggestion came from the Warden. Nevertheless, a renovation of that kind and magnitude did not take place for another thirty years and when it happened, the decision was made entirely by male administrators, much to the chagrin of many of the women of McGill.

One of the pleasant things which occurred during Mrs. Grant's regime was the celebration in 1938 of the 50th anniversary of the graduation of the first class of Donaldas. A number of festivities were held both on and off campus. All but one[75] of the original graduates were still alive and were able to participate in one way or another. In a re-enactment of the historic occasion, Octavia Ritchie (now Dr. Grace Ritchie England) was invited to address the University convocation once again. In speaking for the class of '88, she said, "We rejoice that from such a small beginning so great a movement has grown. The little pathway to McGill made by us has since been trodden during the past fifty years by many feet into a broad highway."[76]

The Montreal newspapers as well as the campus publications made much of the occasion, reprinting the photographs of the original Donalda graduates, and retelling the tale of the admission of women to McGill in 1884. The fifty years of development were apparent in the existence of R.V.C. and in the statistics. In 1938, not eight but eighty-eight women were in the final year of Arts, while the number in the Faculty as a whole was now 385 or 58.6% of the total. In McGill as a whole, there were 616 women in various degree and diploma programmes. Even so, all Faculties were still not open to women. Grace Ritchie observed:

> Fifty years ago a plea was made for the admission of women into the Faculty of Medicine; it was not till thirty years later, that the door was opened; the architectural portal and some others are still tightly closed . . . and that august body, the Legislative Assembly of the Province of Quebec, has recently, for the thirteenth time, refused full rights of citizenship to women, in spite of their Federal qualifications, and their presence in the Senate and House of Commons. [77]

If full academic and civic equality had not yet been won, the enrolment figures did represent progress. The more than 600 women of McGill were all technically members of R.V.C. and all, to some extent, Maude Grant's responsibility.

In the summer of 1940, Mrs. Grant was to have some additional and unexpected changes. After the outbreak of World War II, R.V.C. was made a reception centre for women and children evacuated from Britain. The Warden, who had always been interested in humane causes and civil liberties, willingly took on the new responsibilities and tasks involved. Maude Parkin Grant seems to have given much in her brief time at R.V.C. In a reminiscence, her daughter Margaret said of her: ''I think perhaps an 'appetite for life' comes as close to defining her criterion of excellence as anything else, and she enjoyed saints and sinners, executive students and scholars, Communists and tories, screwballs and Establishment types.'' She added, ''I've only to remember the letters that came to the family when she died to know how many people she helped in small ways and large, and how fond of her the students and dons were.'' Her daughter, Alison, summed up Mrs. Grant as ''a marvellously intelligent woman, unsentimental but loving and supportive.''[78]

* * *

Following Mrs. Grant's retirement, the fortunes of R.V.C. were directed for more than two decades by Dr. Muriel Roscoe, another scholar, able administrator, and woman of strong personality. Muriel Roscoe was a Maritimer. She had a traditional respect for knowledge, a deep concern for orderly development and a special interest in women's education. She took her B.A. in 1918 from Acadia University, Wolfville, N.S. and then did graduate work in the United States, earning an A.M. in 1925 and a Ph.D. a year later from Radcliffe. Both her universities honoured her during her later career, Acadia with a D.Sc. in 1948 and Radcliffe with its Graduate Chapter Medal in 1949. Queen's University also bestowed upon her an LL.D. *honoris causa,* as did McGill.

Muriel Roscoe was brought to McGill in 1940 in the dual role of an

Muriel V. Roscoe

Assistant Professor of Botany and the fifth Warden of R.V.C. Her teaching and research were vital complements to her responsibilities for the welfare of women at the University. Her appointment in the Botany Department was a genuine one, not merely a formality, and her professional progress was impressive. In three years she was promoted to Associate Professor and five years later to full Professor. In 1955, she was installed as the Macdonald Professor of Botany, one of the very few women at McGill in any Department to hold an endowed chair. What is more, for the seventeen years between 1945 and 1962, Dr. Roscoe was Chairman of the Botany Department. Hers is an incredible record of ability, devotion and plain hard work.

Obviously, she did not run the College single handedly. At the beginning she had help from five assistants, a housekeeper, dietitian, nurse, librarian and secretary. In 1945, an Assistant Warden was appointed and, six years later, a second joined her. One of these Assistant Wardens then had a special responsibility for resident students, the other for non-residents. At first, these positions were held by recent graduates; later, Dr. Roscoe preferred more mature women to help relieve her of more of the weight of responsibility. These were not just housekeeping, "mothering" positions but had both counselling and academic components. Throughout her regime, Roscoe was insistent on maintaining the academic quality of all the resident staff. Indeed, some difficulties were generated in the early 40's when, as a "new broom," she chose to replace some long time resident assistants by others with stronger academic backgrounds. This brought her into conflict with at least one of the Departments in the Faculty of Arts and Science when she fired a resident assistant who held a junior position in the Department. Principal F. Cyril James, though probably embarrassed by this situation, endorsed her right as Warden to approve her staff.

In the 22 years that Muriel Roscoe was Warden, the overall enrolment of women at McGill went up appreciably—the increase in non-residents was threefold, for residents it was fourfold. Coping with the ever increasing volume put a severe strain on all of the R.V.C.'s accommodations. Some additional residence space was found by using off-campus annexes—Strathcona Hall, McLennan Hall, A.N.A. House, Donalda House, the Julia Drummond Residence and even the Y.W.C.A. However the operation of the annexes placed a burden on the staff and the finances of the College and, from the point of view of the students, annex life was not at all the same as the community of R.V.C.

Another approach was to adapt space within the main building. Gradually throughout the 40's, the old R.V.C. lecture rooms were converted to student bedrooms and other facilities. Yet another approach was to build. In 1949, a new five-storey East Wing was added to the main building. It provided accommodation for an additional 165 students as well as service and recreational facilities, bringing the total number of residents at that time to just over three hundred. But the numbers kept growing and by 1961-62, Roscoe's last year, there were almost 400 women in residence, about 80 of them still in annexes. Plans were thus developed for yet another wing to extend north along University Street. This was not opened until the fifth Warden had left, but it was named in her honour the "Muriel V. Roscoe Wing."

The question of residential space was more than a housing problem. It had serious academic implications since, at that time, all out-of-town women students were required to live in residence. Only with the Warden's permission could even mature women live elsewhere. In 1961-62, there were some 50 out-of-towners living out of residence with Dr. Roscoe's approval. Since the Warden had the authority to approve women's admission to the College, and hence to the University, her approval was all-important. By 1961-62, some 76 academically qualified women had had to be refused admission to the University because of lack of residence space. It was becoming clear that the structures governing women at McGill were no longer adequate. Either the regulations would have to be changed or more accommodation provided. For the time being, the University tried the latter approach, but the results were not entirely satisfactory.

There was another aspect to the question of admissions. It pinpointed the confusion that continued to exist about the relationship between the College and the University. Susan Cameron Vaughan's correspondence with the *Daily* in the late 20's had clarified the situation for a time, but uncertainties returned. For example, the administrative decision of 1930 that R.V.C. tuition fees should be paid directly to the University, while increasing efficiency, helped obscure the academic role of the College so that Muriel Roscoe found that the status and responsibility of the College were nebulous and that there were "both an over-all lack of knowledge and indeed misconceptions as to these among the students and staff, and possibly among some members of the Administration as well."[79] Originally, it had been simple enough—the Warden was responsible for all women in the University, but that had meant only the Faculty of Arts, and until the 1920's, all applications for academic admission were made directly to her. As women gained admission to the professional and graduate Faculties, the situation became more complex and by the 1940's, applications were made to the Registrar of the University, who made decisions in accordance with the requirements of the various Faculties. However, this proved to be very awkward, since the Warden still had to decide on residence admission and she received no information about the students from the Registrar.

In this administrative morass, and with the acute shortage of residence space, it was unhappily possible for academically qualified women to be told they were accepted by McGill, only to find later that they were rejected by R.V.C. Small wonder that they were both confused and angry, as Roscoe noted, "both academic standards and the general morale were impaired and internal working relationships became somewhat strained."[80] As a member of the University Admissions Committee, Muriel Roscoe helped devise sounder procedures whereby the activities of the Warden and the Registrar were co-ordinated—the Registrar decided on an applicant's acceptability but the final decision and the informing of the student were left to the Warden. With these arrangements, the important inter-relationship of the academic and residential functions of R.V.C. were preserved.

Meanwhile, other physical changes were taking place at R.V.C. In the early 40's, the tennis courts which had fallen into disrepair were converted to lawn; later the area behind the college was developed with shrubs and flowers. Because of the ever-present financial stringencies, the Warden herself laid out the gardens and did all the gardening from 1951 to 1958, when a full-time gardener was employed. In 1959, thanks to the generosity of Mr. Garfield Weston, whose daughters were students at R.V.C., an indoor swimming pool was added to the east end of the main building. This fine pool, of regulation length and five lanes width is dominated unexpectedly not by a diving tower, but by three great stained glass windows which incongruously cast a faintly medieval glow over a modern installation. Though they were a gift from Lady Atholston, they came indirectly from the Founder and were a direct result of the Warden's intercession. She helped rescue them from demolition or obscurity when Lord Strathcona's house on Dorchester Street was being pulled down. They had been in his dining room and, though a swimming pool might seem an unlikely second home for them, their reinstallation was an imaginative gesture that was somehow appropriate and a renewed link with the past.

As significant as the obvious additions to the College was the work done on the old main building during the Roscoe years. Extensive structural and foundational renovations and maintenance, including the cleaning of the famous statue of the Queen, assured the physical continuity of the College; transforming the old gymnasium in the basement to a cafeteria, enlarging the dining room and modernizing the kitchen meant an increase in efficiency and an improvement of services; conversion of the old lecture rooms to bedrooms, an infirmary and offices meant accommodation for more students.[81] Almost unnoticed in all this was the fact that the elimination of classroom space meant the end of the Royal Victoria College as a teaching unit of McGill.

The conversion of the classrooms took place in the 40's. This was a time when there was a general and severe housing shortage, a post-war enrolment boom, and an unquestioned faith in the University's responsibility for providing residences. The doctrine of *in loco parentis* was unchallenged and the pressures for accommodation were seen to be more urgent than the need for teaching space. Classrooms were available on the McGill campus but bedrooms were very hard to find. Furthermore, the R.V.C. teaching facilities were by then outmoded and inadequate. By 1946, there was a total of about two thousand women at McGill, distributed across many Faculties and Schools, in degree and diploma programmes, in many specialized courses. The old idea of separate instruction was simply unworkable. Indeed, separate education had never really been restored since Miss Hurlbatt's days. It had not recovered from the impact of World War I and it had never functioned in the professional Faculties. The Second World War had had even greater effects on the social fabric of McGill than the first, mixing young men and women in class and all campus activities.

When Muriel Roscoe became Warden, the only classes remaining at the College were first year English, French and Physical Education. In

An Assistant Warden, 1952: Nancy Weston

1941, classes in English were amalgamated with the regular Faculty of Arts classes and in 1946, French went too. Physical Education stayed because, at that period all Physical Education for women was taught at R.V.C. Thus, in 1946 Physical Education remained the only sex-segregated form of instruction in the Faculty of Arts.

As the decision in favour of co-education taken in Mrs. Grant's time indicated, there was no longer any advocacy for separate instruction. The actual change to co-education had taken place by gradual erosion, stimulated by the exigencies of the wars, supported by evolving social mores, and necessitated by the pressures of enrolment. It was a natural, practical response to an evolving situation. Nevertheless, the conversion of the classrooms, more than any other single event, symbolized the fact that McGill was now unequivocally a co-educational institution. No matter what the philosophical or social arguments for separate male/female instruction, the physical facilities were no longer available. This was the end of an era which passed without argument or lament. This time, there was no "hubbub."

Another physical change that affected the functioning and internal life of the College was the assigning of the Assembly Hall over to Physical Education. Originally, the Hall, which had a seating capacity of 700 and reputedly excellent acoustics, had been a splendid place which had been used for the grand opening reception, the awarding of the honorary degrees to the Duke and Duchess of York and countless University functions. It was also made available, subject always to the Warden's pleasure, for community events. However, quite early in the College's history, the basement gymnasium had proved to be inadequate and so the Assembly Hall became used more and more for physical education activities. Before the end of the Roscoe period, it was used exclusively as a gymnasium. This was not in accord with the Warden's wishes, but it was a result of the University's pressing need for space. Dr. Roscoe regretted the loss of the Hall and would have liked to have had it available for general administrative purposes, lectures, dramatics, concerts, functions for incoming students and general social activities. She considered the lack of a hall to be a "disabling factor" in the full integration of resident and non-resident students and a great disadvantage to R.V.C. and the women of McGill.[82]

These comments were included in a report when, at the end of her wardenship, Muriel Roscoe called for a thorough evaluation of the College, its needs and its suitability for the requirements of the future. When massive renovations were made to R.V.C. in the early 70's, the hall was at the heart of the change. It is ironic that, in the transformation that ultimately took place, the hall was restored as a hall—but the result was not at all what Muriel Roscoe had had in mind a decade earlier. The

Pollack Concert Hall, as it became, was no longer even part of the Royal Victoria College but of the Faculty of Music. And R.V.C. became quite a different institution. Miss Hurlbatt's prophecy was being fulfilled—but that was for the future.

For her part, Muriel Roscoe was very much aware of the history of the College and the original intent of the Founder, but she also knew that changes in the existing responsibilities of the Warden would have to be made, her staff would have to be increased, and a "new look" given to the entire administrative set-up. She foresaw a need for greater student counselling and personal contact along with a continuation of co-operation with the University, the Faculties and the student organizations. She also recommended that serious thought be given to the entire question of university education for women, including:

1. Considering ways and means of improving the quality of academics and training at the undergraduate level.
2. Providing the stimulation and encouragement of many more women at McGill to enter the field of graduate and professional study.
3. A plan and programme for academic and professional women in Canada along the lines of the Radcliffe Institute for Independent Study.[83]

"Anything less," she said, "means non-acceptance of responsibility."

When Muriel Roscoe retired from the Wardenship in 1962, R.V.C. was flourishing, though change was in the air. She stayed on at McGill for two years in the Department of Botany, then returned to her *alma mater,* Acadia, where she was persuaded to teach a special course in Botany and also serve as Dean of Women for two years. After that, she retired to live quietly in Wolfville by the edge of the Acadia campus. In those years, she returned to McGill several times, notably in June, 1967 when the University awarded her the Doctor of Laws. Professor H.N. Fieldhouse, in his introduction on that occasion said, "Muriel Roscoe was always—as was proper—the courteous but tenacious champion of the interests of the women students of McGill."

* * *

It was not easy to follow Muriel Roscoe as Warden of R.V.C. She had become a dominant personality at McGill—extremely capable, committed, confident, indisputably head of the College, hostess to important visitors, chairman of her Department, only woman on Senate —and she stayed on campus. No matter how discreet she might have been, her very presence would almost inevitably haunt her successor.

But there were other, more practical problems to be faced. The College's physical facilities were again taxed to capacity, the educational structures were straining under the pressure of changing needs, and social values everywhere were being reassessed. At R.V.C., the momentum of Lord Strathcona was dying and the original ideas about the education of women at McGill were played out. Coinciding with this situation were two great social upheavals of the 1960's, the student revolution and the women's liberation movement. Though neither manifested itself violently at R.V.C. both had a profound impact. Any new Warden who treasured the image of the past and attempted to maintain the *status quo* would find herself as caretaker, merely a link between the original concept of the Royal Victoria College and a new institution whose shape could not yet be discerned; any new Warden who acknowledged the tenor of the times would need vision, energy and leadership in helping to create an R.V.C. that would be truly "relevant" for the second half of the 20th century.

Helen Reynolds became the sixth Warden of R.V.C. in September, 1962. She, too, was a Maritimer, born in the Musquodobit Valley and a graduate in Science and Mathematics from Dalhousie University, Halifax, N.S. Her professional experience included the principalship of the Protestant Boys' High School at Antigonish, four years as teacher of science at Halifax Ladies' College, head of the Department of Science at Havergal College, Toronto and, for the seven years immediately before her appointment to McGill, the first Dean of Women at Dalhousie. In an interview shortly after her arrival in Montreal, Miss Reynolds recognised the demanding nature of her new assignment: "We are at the crossroads now," she said.[84] Even so, she cannot have known that her experience would be significantly different from that of the previous Wardens of R.V.C. or that she, indeed, was the last of that line.

One of the first changes Helen Reynolds made was in the residence policy, gaining Senate approval for senior women to live where they chose. Shortly afterwards, this right was extended to younger women, provided they had a letter of permission from their parents. (This proviso was repealed at the end of 1969.) Many students took advantage of the regulations but even with the opening of the new Roscoe Wing enrolments kept increasing so the college was still crowded. As late as 1965, tentative provision was made for the building of another women's residence, to be completed around 1972 and to accommodate a further two or three hundred students.[85] However, these plans were not to be fulfilled. A sudden shift in student living patterns in the early 70's meant that many young women preferred to have their own "pads" and, as a result, R.V.C. was left with an embarrassment of empty beds. The repercussions of this unexpected situation were extraordinary and are considered later in this chapter.

Helen Reynolds

One of Helen Reynolds' declared goals was to be accessible to students for counselling on academic and other matters, another was to help bridge the gap between resident and non-resident students. It was physically impossible for her to meet every female undergraduate, but she attempted to see that they were all interviewed at least once by a member of her academic staff. She also tried to encourage the women of McGill to undertake professional training, favouring those areas where women had proven competences and would "probably do better work" and be "more acceptable than men." She identified as appropriate, fields such as nursing, social work, and psychology—traditional female areas. Helen Reynolds admitted that she was not an ardent supporter of the Women's Movement—she said she did not go along with it "one iota," but she believed in justice.

The sixth Warden of R.V.C. followed the tradition set by her predecessors and had teaching as well as administrative duties. She was a Lecturer in Chemistry and one of her contributions to her Department's academic programme was the development of a curriculum for students in Medicine, Dentistry and Nursing. This became the course she taught. Her other contacts with the University included ex-officio membership on Senate and a number of committees. The Disciplinary Committee proved to be one of the most demanding of her time and energy for, in the turbulent mid-60's, student activism made the McGill campus a field of contention. The "McGill Français" march, the "*McGill Daily* Affair," and the "Stanley Gray Affair" were among the most publicized of the manifestations of student power at McGill.[86] The movement peaked around 1967-69 when student demands for representation on university committees and in departments, their outrage over the banning of their newspaper, outside political influences, incitements from within, and a variety of grievances, long-term or recent, led to demonstrations, sit-ins and even an invasion of Principal Rocke Robertson's office. McGill students, like those the world over, suddenly seemed to shed their docility and spontaneously reject the values of the "Establishment." Among their demands was a call for a reassessment of the role of the University as they tossed aside the traditional concept of *in loco parentis*. As the University attempted to maintain order in the face of what seemed at times complete anarchy, the Senate Student Disciplinary Committee found itself dealing with a very heavy work load. In looking back on those unruly days, Helen Reynolds recalled some "ghastly times," especially in encounters with the avowed Maoists, whom she considered "really difficult and impossible people" with whom there was no communication.[87] She found herself frequently attacked in campus publications by radicals for her conservative views but at the College, she found a reassuring measure of support.

Another of the Senate Committees on which Miss Reynolds served was the one established in 1969 to conduct an inquiry into "Discrimination as to Sex in the University." She thought that she herself had never suffered from discrimination at McGill, though she considered there were some men on campus who resented the degree of autonomy and the power of the Warden of R.V.C. In connection with the "Discrimination" Committee she attempted to champion the non-academic women at McGill because she believed that there were a number of them fulfilling administrative functions but classified and paid as secretaries, while some men, who were less competent and less devoted, worked less for more recognition. She hoped these women would come forward to the Committee and state their case. She was very disappointed when none did.

In reviewing her experience as Warden of the Royal Victoria College, Helen Reynolds declared that she especially valued her contacts with the "girls," she enjoyed participating in the building and furnishing of the Roscoe Wing, developing a collection of Canadian art, and working with Principal H. Rocke Robertson and Chancellor Howard Ross. "Despite the trouble and tenseness of it," she said, "my eight years at McGill proved to be a very, very rewarding end to my professional career." In gratitude for her untiring efforts on behalf of the women of McGill and the College, the House Committee requested that the East Wing be renamed the "Reynolds Wing." This gesture was approved by the Board of Governors in March 1970, a few months before the sixth Warden retired.

*   *   *

By the end of Helen Reynolds' term of office, it was clear that the tasks expected of the Warden of R.V.C. were impossible. No one person could teach at a university, keep up with her research, administer a residence, serve *ex officio* on numerous committees, and monitor the welfare of all the women at McGill. There were now more than 6,000 women on campus in all programmes—undergraduate, diploma and graduate. Their interests and outlooks were changing radically and the notion of the "lady," the dilettante scholar, had vanished and even seekers of the 'MRS' degree were not so obvious. The newer vision was of a young women who expected to work upon graduation and who had hopes of a satisfying career before, and probably after, marriage. As in earlier eras, independence and self-reliance were valued but now there was a greater demand for opportunities to exercise these qualities. Many of the women of McGill became concerned with the quest for identity, seeking self-actualization and rejecting stereotyped female roles. Against this background, the 1970's were to see R.V.C. undergo a metamorphosis.

The reasons for this were complex but one of the obvious aspects was the continuing financial strain on the College. During the 60's, R.V.C. regularly operated at a deficit which the University, just as regularly, covered. In 1969/70, Miss Reynolds' last year, the difference between income (derived from the endowment and residence fees) and expenditure was almost $80,000. The Warden considered it impossible to attempt to balance the budget. Part of the reason for this was the demands placed on College facilities by the non-resident women students through their use of the library, the gymnasium, the pool, the infirmary, lounges and counselling services. However, Reynolds' suggestion that a general student service fee be transferred to the College went unheeded.

While the financial problem was serious, contrary to general belief, it was not at that time caused by vacancies. Throughout the 60's, the College operated at capacity. The sudden drop in student applications for residence occurred in the 1970/71 academic year when there were suddenly about a hundred vacancies at R.V.C. and two hundred in the University as a whole. Ominously, it was predicted that by 1974/75, the number of redundant residential places at McGill would be five hundred, roughly equal to the number of places at R.V.C. The decline in residential students was partly attributable to the re-organization of the education system in the Province of Quebec, following the Royal Commission of Inquiry early in the 60's. The introduction of the *collèges d'enseignment général et professionel* (CEGEP's), which added one year to pre-university schooling, raised the age of university entry, temporally dislocated the normal flow of students at McGill, and resulted in some overall decrease in university applications. Inevitably there was a drop in residence applications. Although there was a CEGEP programme established at McGill, it did not offset this loss because it tended to attract students from the Montreal area, that is, students who were less likely to want to live in residence. Another reason for the decline in the residence population was the result of changes in student life styles. An increasing number of both women and men seemed to have forsaken institutional living in favour of apartments, co-operatives or other outside accommodation where they were not subject to University supervision or discipline and which they found a good deal cheaper. This switch in student preferences was seen as a basic sociological phenomenon, a lasting characteristic of the modern generation.

There was another important social factor in the McGill equation. This was the lowering in Quebec, and elsewhere, of the legal age of individual responsibility from twenty-one to eighteen.[88] As a result of the administrative and legal changes—the raising of the age of university entry and the lowering of the age of responsibility—most university students of the 1970's were no longer minors but legal adults. Thus, the University's legal obligations were drastically altered and its role as surrogate parent virtually terminated.

In view of all these factors, strong voices were raised for changes to the *modus operandi* of McGill's entire residence system to make it more economically viable and more compatible with contemporary student requirements. A Senate Sub-Committee on Residence Policy, established in 1969, recommended some sweeping reforms, including the conversion of the men's halls to co-educational residences. A Budget Task Force, meeting in the summer of 1970, considered *inter alia* proposals to close McConnell Hall, one of the men's residences, and convert it to other academic uses. A protest from the students and staff of the residence may have been instrumental in saving McConnell, but the building's unsuitability for the suggested alternative use probably helped more.

What McGill desperately needed just then was a home for the Faculty of Music. For years it had functioned with makeshift premises and had waited patiently for promises to be fulfilled. In 1970 it occupied seven or eight scattered buildings and used Redpath Hall for its performances. To some of McGill's administrators, the idea of converting McConnell Hall to a Faculty of Music was a neat solution to two pressing problems. The numerous bedrooms could easily be turned into practice rooms and offices, while the larger rooms could become teaching areas. However, the prospect did not appeal to Helmut Blume, Dean of Music.

Dean Blume rejected the choice of McConnell, a relatively new building, because of the small size of the rooms, their low ceilings, the enormous cost of sound-proofing, the inconvenient location and the incompatibility of function with the surrounding buildings, all residences. He much preferred R.V.C.—the grand old original building with its large rooms, high ceilings, solid construction, its auditorium, and its accessible location. What irony that the very solidity and grandeur of Lord Strathcona's gift should ultimately have been instrumental in its diversion from the women of McGill and conversion to the Faculty of Music! Apart from the architectural arguments which, in their way were valid enough, another much more sensitive justification was advanced. It was claimed that, since Lord Strathcona was a patron of Music and had brought Miss Lichtenstein, the first Music instructor, to McGill, the conversion of the Royal Victoria College to the Strathcona Music Building was quite appropriate. It was also pointed out that R.V.C. was intended as a teaching college for women but it no longer appeared to fill that function, having become only a residence. Thus the Founder's original intentions were not being fulfilled—indeed, there was no longer need for a woman's teaching college so that new uses could be found for the building.

No one asked the women of McGill what they thought. There was no suggestion that the alumnae of R.V.C. come to the financial aid of the College. The discussions were confined to the University administrators and took place during a double inter-regnum: the retirements of both Principal Robertson and Warden Reynolds took effect in the fall of 1970; their successors were too new to champion the traditions of R.V.C. Thus, plans were drawn up to allocate the main building and the newly named Reynolds' Wing to the Faculty of Music and to limit the women's residence to the Roscoe Wing. Negotiations were begun immediately with Lord Strathcona's heirs to arrange the legal matters pertaining to the R.V.C. Charter and the endowment so that, by May 3, 1971, the Board of Governors gave approval for detailed planning to proceed. It was expected that the work would essentially be finished that summer. This was a remarkably short time for such a major and complicated change—just one year after the idea first occurred to Vice Principal (Administration) Robert Shaw, an engineer who had joined the McGill administration from a top executive position with the highly successful Expo '67. In contrast to the protracted dealings that were always involved in the development of facilities for the women at McGill, the rape of R.V.C. was incredibly swift.

The conversion was an administrative solution, apparently practical, quite unsentimental. The arrangements were made, not in secret, but with minimal publicity or public discussion. Thus, almost before the McGill community or the Alumnae even seemed aware of what was happening, work had begun on the renovations. Perhaps one reason why this went largely unnoticed was that it was lost in the great events that were taking place in Montreal just then. The talk of the change had begun in the summer and fall of 1970—that was the year of the F.L.Q. terrorist activities, the year of the "October Crisis" when British Trade Commissioner, James Cross, was kidnapped and Quebec Cabinet Minister Pierre Laporte was abducted and murdered, when Prime Minister Pierre Trudeau invoked the War Measures Act, when liberals and Quebec nationalists vehemently protested the P.M.'s action, when soldiers with rifles and fixed bayonets for a time guarded the entrances to the Montreal metro stations and the houses of the mighty. Amid such drama, the reorganization of R.V.C. paled in importance. Yet, whether the McGill community recognized it or not, the extensive renovation of R.V.C. marked the end of an era—the rather special college was reduced in size and modified in tone.

*　*　*

Meanwhile, in accordance with a practice that had become standard procedure for filling important administrative posts at McGill, a committee had been established to select the seventh Warden of R.V.C. This was much more elaborate than the group of two (Principal Peterson and Lord Strathcona) which had chosen the first Warden. It was chaired by Principal Rocke Robertson and was composed of three members from each of the Board of Governors, the Senate, the Graduates Society and the McGill Association of University Teachers as well as five student representatives. Diverse though it was, the composition drew fire from some of the women of McGill who pointed out that, since two of the Student Society appointees were male, there were only three members out of eighteen on the committee representing the people most immediately affected—the women students.[89] Undeterred by charges of male chauvinism, the committee proceeded with its work and by April 1970 had produced some innovative recommendations.

It suggested that the post of Warden of Royal Victoria College be divided between the Warden, who was to be responsible for R.V.C. itself and the welfare of its residents, and another Administrator, possibly a Dean of Women or Associate Dean of Students, who would be responsible for non-resident students. It further recommended that the counselling offered by the offices of the Warden and the Dean of Students should not duplicate services given elsewhere in the University, that the number of statutory committees on which the Warden was required to serve should be reduced, and that the new administrator should replace the Warden on some committees.

When the Senate and the Board of Governors accepted the committee's report, they did not lock the new administrator into a subordinate position. It was proposed that there should be two academic persons in administrative posts in the Dean of Students' office—one who was basically, but not exclusively, responsible for male students; the other, basically but not exclusively, responsible for female students. One was to be the Dean of Students, the other the Associate Dean.[90] It was not to be assumed that the Associate Dean would always be the woman; rather, it was hoped that there would be an alternation between male and female appointments to the senior position.

On the recommendation of the Principal, the Governors approved the appointment of Dr. Elizabeth Rowlinson, Assistant Professor in the Department of Mathematics, as the first Associate Dean of Students and Mrs. Mary Robertson, Assistant Professor and Assistant to the Chairman in the Department of Pharmacology and Therapeutics as seventh Warden of R.V.C. Both appointments were on a part-time basis as the appointees were expected to continue their work in their Departments, and both became effective on September 1, 1970. The question of the

210

Mary C. Robertson

Associate Dean of Students will be considered in Chapter 9, but the seventh Warden is the concern of the present chapter.

Mary Robertson was born in Atlanta, Georgia and thus was the first "American" Warden of R.V.C. She was a 1944 graduate of Agnes Scott College, Decatur, Georgia and held two master's degrees—the first, an M.S. awarded in 1946 by Emory University, Atlanta in Biochemistry and the second, an M.P.H. in cancer research awarded by Yale in 1970. She came to McGill in 1967 to a position involving both teaching and administration and, according to the Chairman, Professor Mark Nickerson, "she ran the Department of Pharmacology." She was also a part-time instructor at Dawson College in Montreal. Mary Robertson was divorced and had two sons, one of whom took up residence in R.V.C. with her when she became Warden.

Professor Robertson was well aware that the Wardenship was ready for change. It did not disturb her that the Warden no longer attended Senate and certain academic committees. She believed that R.V.C. was in many respects "a little 19th century enclave in a modern institution" and that it was becoming increasingly unpopular with the students it was intended to serve. She considered that the previous administrations of the College had been strictly authoritarian and she wished to implement a pattern in which the women in residence played a strong role in the management of their own affairs. She also believed that there should be no such thing as "women's education," but only sound education for all who are capable of receiving it. All that one need ask for is opportunity for the individual and the wisest choice of environment—large institutions or small ones, co-educational or not—offering privacy and freedom from regulations. Mary Robertson recognised that her approach represented a break with the past and was sensitive to the fact that "during any period of change, the people most directly involved can and do feel threatened mostly because it is very human to associate change with loss, loss of advantage, privilege and authority." [91]

Robertson's term of office as Warden of R.V.C. was the shortest to date. She resigned in 1971 after a year of very demanding effort or, as she put it, "when my Pharmacology day was done, I put in a full-time Warden's day in the evening, with time-and-a-half on weekends." At the end of that year, the reorganization of the College had been effected and she returned to her Department full-time. Professor Robertson remained at McGill until 1973 when she remarried and returned to Atlanta with her husband, a Professor of Biochemistry at Emory University. She later accepted a full-time position at Emory as a Research Associate in Biochemistry.

The R.V.C. annual report for 1970-71 chronicled the changes that transformed the College during that pivotal year when Mary Robertson was Warden. The stage was set for a redefinition of the role of Warden. The administrative duties most directly concerned with the operation of R.V.C. as a residence—clerical services, business operations, housekeeping and food services—were to be handled by an Assistant Warden who would be a member of the non-academic staff so that the duties of the Warden could be restricted to the areas of student counselling and student affairs. A new full-time non-resident Assistant Wardenship was established and the position of resident Assistant Warden changed to part-time with evening and weekend duty only. The resident Assistant Wardens were given the authority to make decisions of an emergency nature in the absence of and in place of the Warden when necessary. The number of Resident Assistants was cut from twelve to six though their duties were much the same as in previous years. They were, however, given more responsibility for making decisions and handling problems involving students.

Because of the high rate of vacancies that year, a number of rooms were set aside as guest quarters and the housekeeping staff was reduced; as part of a general plan to co-ordinate University services, the clinic was moved to the newly centralized University Health Service on Pine Avenue, the library was to be absorbed into other McGill libraries, and plans were made for the offices of the Women's Athletic Department to move to the pool area; as a result of a survey which indicated that the majority of students interviewed preferred cafeteria style to formal dining-room meal service, proposals were put forward for the elimination of the latter and the development of the former. The outgoing Warden concluded her lone annual report with the hope that her successor would find the smaller residence easier to operate and more suited to the needs of its residents. She also trusted that the students who entered the following autumn would find R.V.C. a more pleasant place in which to live.

It is possible that these hopes of Mary Robertson might have been realized but it is certain that the people returning to R.V.C. in the autumn of 1971 would find a College that was scarcely recognizable. They would enter, not by passing the imposing statue of Queen Victoria and through the stately portals on Sherbrooke Street, but via the more modest entrance on University Street. They would learn that the Faculty of Music was definitely to be installed in Lord Strathcona's grand gift to the women of McGill and that it would henceforth be known as the Strathcona Music Building. As the seventh Warden departed, it was clear that the splendour and luxury of 1899 had gone forever.

* * *

The eighth Warden of R.V.C. was Donna Runnalls and she took up her appointment in January, 1972. There had been a gap of one semester in which a Resident Manager, Dorothy Brookes, had held the fort. It was also a gap in which the basic administrative changes begun under Mary Robertson became established and when a major part of the building renovations were completed.

Dr. Runnalls was the first Western Canadian to hold the position but she was no stranger to McGill. She was born in Vancouver and took her B.A. in English and History from the University of British Columbia in 1956. Upon graduation, she was employed by the United Church of Canada to teach English at the Ewha Women's University in Soeul, Korea. After three years in the Orient, she returned to Canada and came to McGill as the Associate General Secretary of the Student Christian Movement. Then she became a Resident Assistant at R.V.C. while she studied for the McGill Bachelor of Divinity degree. This experience at R.V.C. came at the end of Dr. Roscoe's Wardenship and enabled Donna Runnalls to know at first hand how the College had functioned traditionally.

In 1964 Runnalls received her B.D. with first class honours in Old Testament and then she became the Senior Don at Victoria College, Toronto while working for her Ph.D. in the University of Toronto's Department of Near Eastern Studies. Her major field was Hebrew Language and Literature with minors in Hellenistic Greek Language and Literature and Arabic Language and Literature. Upon receiving her Ph.D. in 1971, Dr. Runnalls was appointed Lecturer in Old Testament and Hebrew Language in McGill's Faculty of Religious Studies. The following year, she was promoted to Assistant Professor and also became Warden of R.V.C. She was again promoted in 1975, this time to Associate Professor. In 1979 she resigned from her post as Warden in order to spend a sabbatical year of research in the Middle East, after which she returned to full-time teaching.

The seven years that Donna Runnalls spent as Warden of R.V.C. saw the fading of the radical student revolution and a return to more settled ways. They also witnessed a revival of interest in College living so that in 1979 there were some 256 women in residence and no vacancies. The Runnalls years, however, did not witness a return to the old pattern of life at R.V.C.—both the physical changes and the value shifts had made that impossible.

Donna Runnalls had no illusions about her role. She knew that she presided over a residence rather than a college and she thought the change to have been almost inevitable. She believed that the old R.V.C. had become an anachronism. In the 60's when she first knew it as a Resident Assistant, the College had seemed not so much a vital living

Donna Runnalls

tradition as a mere reflection of times past. In the 70's, truly a decade of transition, the College was truncated but it was still operating at a deficit which was being met by endowment funds that would sooner or later run out. The future of the College did not seem firm nor had its final form yet evolved. Unfortunately, the reduced size had not proved economically viable and, ironically, Donna Runnalls believed the whole college could probably be filled if the former space were still available and if the life-style were adjusted to suit contemporary students. Yet she conceded that in a residence of 500 or so, it would be very difficult to maintain a desirable ambiance, a community spirit.

Meanwhile, R.V.C. remained a place where student welfare was of importance. The Warden's relationship with the residents was at a more informal level. She no longer presided ceremoniously over luncheon and dinner, but she did make particular efforts to meet the students during meals in the cafeteria. She specifically rejected the responsibility of parent surrogate, believing that students were mature adults respon-sible for their own behavior. Much of the day-to-day counselling was done by the Assistant Warden (Ida Chow, a Ph.D. candidate in Physiol-ogy) and eight resident Assistants, or "dons." The Assistant Warden was in charge of admissions and room assignments as well as other administrative matters. She implemented the College policy of admit-ting all qualified Quebec applicants while maintaining a balanced residence population of 50% Canadian, 30% U.S. and 20% Overseas students. As always, the foreign students contributed a great deal to the special flavour of R.V.C.

The dons played an important role in welcoming new students and in discussing personal and academic problems of the residents. They held regular semi-formal "teas" or talk sessions in their rooms and also helped organize functions such as the Hallowe'en, Christmas and Spring parties or the professor-student dinners which were still part of the R.V.C. scene. As before, the Warden was responsible for the overall management of the College, but she had a good deal of specialist help from the Residence Manager, the Cafeteria Supervisor, the Building Superintendent and other officials concerned with the various aspects of housekeeping, building maintenance and budget preparation.

Like all the Wardens before her, Donna Runnalls believed that R.V.C. should be a congenial place to live, a substitute for home, as well as an environment that encouraged study. For seventy years, this ideal had persisted at the College, but the interpretation of it had varied. Under Dr. Runnalls, the administration of the College was generally open, relaxed, low-key with "rules made only to assure as much harmony as possible among the people living there."[92] The eighth

Warden believed that if regulations were codified, they offered a challenge for someone to break them; she thought explanation and peer pressure were more effective than rules from on high. She felt that if residents were not restrained they would not create problems. This kind of attitude was a reflection, she thought, of her Western Canadian origins. Dr. Runnalls believed that the difference between Dr. Roscoe and Miss Reynolds on the one hand and herself on the other was not so much a generation gap as a cultural gap—the difference between the formality of the Maritimers and the informality of the Westerner.[93]

As Donna Runnalls withdrew from the Wardenship at the end of the 70's, it seemd that R.V.C. was still in a process of change. It was ready to be transformed into an institution appropriate to the 1980's. In 1979, a study of all McGill residences had resulted in a new consolidated policy aimed at greater efficiency through large-scale purchasing of supplies and equipment as well as centralized management of staff and resource allocation. A new post of Director of Student Housing and Residences was created and the Warden of the Royal Victoria College as well as the Directors of the other four McGill residences would report to him. This appeared to mean a loss of status for the Warden and, despite the Charter defining it as an independent college of McGill University, there was a danger that R.V.C. would lose its traditional degree of autonomy. Thus, at the annual meeting of the Alumnae Society in May, 1979, Donna Runnalls warned the women graduates of McGill that once again significant changes in the University's residential policy were taking place during a double inter-regnum—when both she and Principal Robert Bell were stepping down. Once again there would be a crucial period when there was no official to champion the women of McGill. Once again financial pressures were dictating their fate, leaving the ninth Warden when she was appointed the particularly difficult task of maintaining an individual ambiance for the Royal Victoria College in a centralized, computer-controlled context.

* * *

In the summer of 1979 to fill the gap left by Dr. Runnall's resignation, Mrs. Florence Tracy was appointed Acting Warden. Mrs. Tracy, a native of Gaspé, Quebec, with a B.A. in Applied Social Science from Concordia and a Registered Nurse Diploma from Queen Elizabeth Hospital, Montreal, had been nurse-in-charge of the R.V.C. infirmary from 1967 to 1969. When she was appointed Acting Warden, she was Nursing Co-ordinator of the McGill Student Health Service and agreed

Florence Tracy

to stay in that position while taking on the new interim responsibilities at the College. Her temporary appointment was to prove one of those happy accidents that produce lasting benefits. In a remarkably short time "Flo," as she was affectionately called around campus, had endeared herself to students and staff at R.V.C. She had also demonstrated to the McGill administration that she could effectively deal with more than one job. It therefore came as no great surprise that, in June 1980, she was formally appointed not only as Warden of R.V.C. but also as Director of Student Housing and Residences. After the worries of the previous spring concerning the perceived threat to the Warden's status and the independence of R.V.C., it now seemed ironic that the move to co-ordinate student housing had resulted in the Warden's becoming tzar.

This turn of events had resulted from a perceptive appreciation of Mrs. Tracy's individual ability. It also indicated the University's openness to appoint a woman to a responsible administrative position with authority over both male and female members of the community.

Flo Tracy was very much aware of the history of R.V.C. and considered that one of the functions of the Warden in the 80's was to preserve the traditions that made the College distinctive. She also saw her role as that of resource person, a co-ordinator of activities, a referral agency with a broad base of information about a lot of things. Here, it seemed, a little knowledge was not a dangerous thing, but something very reassuring to "the girls." In Tracy's view, it was important that the Warden be seen as a friend, a confidante, "someone who is like a mother, yet not a mother, someone you tell things you wouldn't tell your mother."[94] Other Wardens had projected the ideal of R.V.C. as a "home" for its students but it is doubtful whether any of Tracy's predecessors actually viewed themselves as mother figures. In a world that is frequently characterized as dehumanized, it is surprising—and refreshing—that the ninth Warden should adopt such a role.

From her experience with living with the students, Flo Tracy considered that, despite the recent societal changes and the apparent sophistication of contemporary young people, the need for *in loco parentis* has not really disappeared. Once described as "McGill's Nonstop Mom,"[95] the unflagging Mrs. Tracy discovered that students "need someone to tell them to put on their boots or their scarves or give them a pat on the back when they get a good mark or give them a hug when they're feeling insecure."[96] She knew that they liked to be remembered by name and to receive "a caring comment." She wisely saw that, while students do need a parent surrogate, they do not accept maternalistic help all the time. "They want you when they want you," she noted, and at other times they are perfectly independent. She believed that her medical background had been a great asset for it made her approachable. She recognised that "one can couch other needs in physical problems. A stomach ache or a sore throat is an acceptable complaint to start with and then you get to the real problem." Her door was always open, she was always ready to listen to any of the 260 residents of R.V.C. in her care.

Flo Tracy's administration was characterized by sympathy, dedication and affection. She was the first Warden to be known everywhere, all the time by her first name. In her capacity as Director of Student Housing and Residences she attempted to be equally open and friendly, to improve communications and to explode myths. She recognized that some students in the co-ed residences tended to think of the young women of R.V.C. as "spoiled brats" while some R.V.C. students thought of the other residences as "animal farm." Under Flo Tracy's effective and affective rule, such stereotypes would not be allowed to pass unchallenged.

While it was recognized that the R.V.C. of the 80's was primarily a residence, appreciation of its academic potential had not been lost. Active efforts on the part of the Warden and the dons were made to restore its vitality as a learning centre, even though attendance at College seminars was initially weak. It was obvious that the students of the so-called "Me Generation" would need to revive the college spirit diminished by the value shifts of the 60's, the reorganization of R.V.C. in the 70's and the general rejection of institutions by the young. As the 80's appeared to be developing into an uncertain era of economic stress and unemployment, it was possible that students might sublimate their insecurities into corporate allegiances once more. Neither the pressures of present-day living nor nostalgia for "the good old days" could restore the lost grandeur of the College, but the caring, personal approach of Flo Tracy, ninth Warden of R.V.C., showed great promise of healing the rifts.

*   *   *

From the glass cases in R.V.C.'s "History Corridor" and from their vantage places on the walls of the College, the original Donaldas and the early Wardens look out earnestly at the contemporary young women in blue jeans rushing to the cafeteria or talking casually with their men friends in the lounge. Perhaps they do not approve of what they see. They may be puzzled or saddened or angry but Hilda Oakeley, for one, might understand the necessity for change. Probably they would discern threads of continuity amid all the transformation but no doubt they would all wonder, "What would Lord Strathcona think?"

Chapter SIX

Student Life

As the previous chapters sought to demonstrate, ideas about Woman and theories of education, charters and rules, Founders and Wardens have all contributed significantly to the history of women at McGill. However, the day-to-day experience of the students has been affected by other factors as well, notably by their peers and the ordinary professors, and by their participation in college activities. Accordingly, this chapter attempts to recall some of the people, to describe the extra-curricular activities and to recapture some of the flavour of McGill since the founding of R.V.C. It will be noted that an examination of the women of McGill during the 20th century does not result in an account of a steady development from the old-fashioned girls at the turn of the century to the modern liberated women of the 1980's. It is clear that there have always been modern, "liberated women" at McGill and, conversely, it is possible that there are still some "old-fashioned girls" on campus. Some of the women of McGill have accepted the status quo, whatever it happened to be when they were on campus. Others both exemplified and fought for women's right to intellectual identity, challenged the double standard and rejected patronizing or paternalistic administrators or professors. There appear to have been relatively few who angrily denounced "the system." More appeared to look back on their R.V.C. experience with a measure of affection. Memory may romanticize, but even the distortions of nostalgia cannot obscure the fact that R.V.C.'s first 80 years have produced some intriguing personalities and lively student activities.

* * *

In the early days of R.V.C., the Warden may have set the tone, but the residential staff, both academic and non-academic, gave the College much of its special character. Some of the people who helped Hilda Oakeley to launch the great new venture did not stay long. Harriet Brooks, B.A. '98, tutor in Mathematics, left after only a year. She resumed her studies in Physics, earned an M.A. in 1901 under the direction of Ernest Rutherford and was credited with the discovery of the recoil of the radio-active atom. She continued her research at the Cavendish Laboratory in Cambridge under Joseph Thompson and at the Sorbonne in the laboratory of Marie Curie. Despite this brilliant background, Harriet Brooks gave up scientific work after her marriage to Frank Pitcher in 1907. She did, however, maintain a lifelong interest in the Alumnae Society and was acknowledged as one of McGill's truly distinguished graduates.

Other members of the original staff of the College stayed many years and practically became institutions in their own right. Three who made a real difference to the lives of the women of McGill were Clara Lichtenstein, Marie-Louise Milhau, and Ethel Cartwright.

Clara Lichtenstein brought music to McGill. Though she came from a talented Hungarian family, she was working in Scotland as a performer, accompanist and teacher when Lord Strathcona and Principal Peterson persuaded her to come to Montreal to organize the music department at the new Royal Victoria College. She had graduated from the Royal Academy of Music in Budapest when Franz Liszt was its Director and her recommendations came from such musical luminaires as Paderewski and Sir Charles Hallé. With such credentials, she not only became the first Resident Tutor in Music at R.V.C. but the first person to teach Music at the University. She threw herself into the task with enormous zest, giving piano or singing lessons, arranging talks on music and its appreciation, encouraging concert-going and preparing the Donaldas beforehand for the music and the performers. Her students recalled that she managed to give a sense of what music could mean, its pleasures and joys as well as its technicalities. It could have been no surprise when the men of McGill began to seek her out, asking for piano or organ lessons, or for her help in organizing a choir, or her permission to use the R.V.C. pianos. Partly because of the interest Clara Lichtenstein helped generate, the R.V.C. Music Department expanded, to become the Conservatory in 1904 and then the Faculty of Music in 1920.[1] She was Vice-Director of the Conservatory and became an Associate Professor in the Faculty. Her career at McGill spanned thirty years, during which, R.V.C. was her home while music, McGill and her students were her life.

"Klari" (as she was known to her friends) Lichtenstein, was at the height of her powers when she came to McGill. She was full of vigour, humour and enthusiasm, gladly participating in student presentations, giving informal recitals at Lord Strathcona's residence, or providing the music programme for official functions like the opening of R.V.C.. According to her colleague, Susan Cameron, "her somewhat massive build, together with her extensive knowledge of the world suggested length of life and experience."[2] She had a special talent for encouraging promising young musicians and took great pleasure in the success of her students, such as Ellen Ballon, Pauline Livingstone Donalda and Edmund Burke, who later achieved world-wide renown. (Both Miss Ballon and Madame Donalda received honorary doctorates in Music from McGill in 1954 — Ballon for her all-round musicianship and brilliant career as a pianist, Donalda for her great performances in opera.) It is said that Sir William Macdonald would often stop by the College in the

Clara Lichtenstein

evening to listen to Ellen Ballon's singing and "Klari" Lichtenstein's accompaniment. During World War I, Lichtenstein devoted much time and energy to a special rehabilitation programme designed to teach music to disabled soldiers. She counted this among the saddest but the most rewarding of her experiences at the Conservatorium.

As the years and the pressures of work took their toll, "Klari" Lichtenstein inevitably lost her gaiety. She tended to withdraw into a small circle of friends, but developed into a legendary story teller. Her voice was said to be most unusual, with a rich English vocabulary in which a faint Scottish burr blended with a distinct Middle European accent. In her special silky tones she recounted improbable tales that delighted her hearers.

Clara Lichtenstein left in 1929 after thirty years of service. Her resignation came at the same time as those of Ethel Hurlbatt and Carrie Derick, giving a Montreal newspaper an opportunity to headline "Eminent Women Leaving McGill" and to describe their three distinguished careers as pioneers in feminine education. Miss Lichtenstein spent the last part of her life in Dorset, England and news of her death in 1946 elicited regrets from generations of R.V.C. students. In a sad little coda to a long and generous performance, many alumnae attended a meeting at the University Women's Club where some of Lichtenstein's personal possessions, things which had been left in Montreal, were sold at auction. Her metronome, her china, her books were thus scattered around Montreal, like memories of the woman who had seemed to be a fixture at R.V.C. and who had brought to it the joy of music.[3]

Another memorable woman of the early days, one who infused life into the residence and verve into learning, was Mlle Marie-Louise Milhau. When Susan Cameron-Vaughan was asked, in honour of the sixtieth anniversary of the admission of women to McGill, to write about the outstanding women she had known in the Faculty of Arts, she chose to concentrate upon Mlle Milhau, the Frenchwoman who had joined the R.V.C. staff in 1900.

Marie-Louise Milhau made French at McGill an attractive and vital subject. Like Klari Lichtenstein, she was originally engaged to teach the women of R.V.C. but was soon sought out by the male students. Mlle Milhau was particularly popular with Law Students. She was said to have been an admirable and imaginative teacher who managed to bring something of the spirit of France into her classroom. But her personal charm probably had more to do with her popularity than had her pedagogic techniques. She was vivacious and elegant, with tall slender figure, bright dark eyes and she wore her Parisian clothes with a certain flair. She had friends throughout the University and in both the French and English sectors of Montreal, but she was never too busy for her students. She joined them in their activities, whether they were dances, skating parties, sleigh rides, or snow-shoe excursions. Much to the delight of all, after a trip across the continent, she appeared at an R.V.C. masquerade dance beautifully bedecked as an Indian chief, complete with war paint, feather head-dress and stone axe. Who said R.V.C. was stuffy in the old days?

After eight years, Mlle Milhau returned to France to marry M. Jules-Louis Puech but that did not mean that her connection with McGill was severed. The Puech apartment in Paris became known to dozens of Canadian students as a centre of hospitality, interesting conversation and French culture. During the first World War, she earned deep gratitude by finding over seven hundred refugee children and caring for them in "La Sauvegarde des Enfants" near her home.

Mme Puech returned to Montreal on several occasions and was always as heartily welcomed as were McGillians in Paris. She had a special place in their affections—as one of them wrote, ". . . how good it must be to meet such a good friend as Madame Puech. She was loved by all and since she went away, her old students and I have often talked about Madame Puech but they, like myself, always address her as Mlle Milhau."[4]

The third of the unforgettable pioneer teachers of R.V.C. hailed from Britain. Ethel Mary Cartwright was a graduate and member of staff of the Chelsea College of Physical Education, England before coming to Canada in 1906. She did much to help develop formal instruction in Physical Education as well as remedial and recreational activities. In 1909 she initiated after-school classes for the training of Physical Education and was instrumental in the establishment, three years later, of the McGill School of Physical Education. Miss Cartwright became Director of Physical Education for Women and, from 1919 until 1927, Assistant Director of the School. From that time, her responsibilities were divided between formal classes at the School (which was under the direction of Dr. A.S. Lamb) and women's athletics.

"Carty," as she was affectionately known to the students, was said to be strongly opposed to the widely-used term "physical culture." She emphasized that she was concerned with "physical training," not "physical straining." She assured the women of McGill that they could still be graceful and feminine even though they played hockey, climbed ropes and vaulted over apparatus. The threat to femininity had been a controversial theme at the American Physical Education Association's meeting held at R.V.C. in 1912 but the diminutive Miss Cartwright in her own person presented a convincing argument in favour of women's athletics. She delighted in putting on demonstrations in the gym. One

226

Top: Mixed Honours English, Class of '97: Marjorie Holden, Annie Grant, Professor Moyse, Dr. Colby, Andrew McMaster, S.G. Archibald
Bottom: Philosophy Class With Esther Ryan, B.A. '06, at Dr. Caldwell's Knee

memorable evening performance involved marching, rhythmic dancing and, *pièce de résistance,* the twirling of electrically illuminated Indian clubs. It was Carty who coached the first R.V.C. winning basketball team of 1919, in circumstances of high drama. Two days before the historic meet, she was stricken with appendicitis and rushed to hospital for an emergency operation. Just ten minutes before the game, she was wheeled into the gym by a medical orderly—and taken back to hospital for ten days after it. She buoyantly exemplified skill, determination and the importance of women's sport.

Miss Cartwright was also active off-campus, helping found the Women's Amateur Athletic Federation of Canada and becoming the first President of the Canadian Massage Association. When she left McGill in 1927, she was showered with praise and gifts, including a gold purse and —rather inappropriately—an arm chair.

Lichtenstein, Milhau and Cartwright, each in her different way, made a distinctive contribution to the ambiance of the college. Few who followed had such originality or stayed so long as Clara Lichtenstein, though Iveagh Munro, a graduate of the School of Physical Education, was Director of Physical Education for Women from 1939 to 1966. Mlle Toureen (later Mme Furness) was resident French tutor for many years and Mary Mackenzie taught English for fourteen. Miss Mackenzie, who retired in 1941, was the last to hold the title of "tutor" with a joint teaching appointment in R.V.C. and the Faculty of Arts. In place of tutors, Resident Assistants were appointed. These were senior students, generally in the Faculty of Graduate Studies or in the professional faculties, so that their terms were relatively short-lived. Their responsibilities involved working with the student government, operating the leaves system, being present at meals, and generally "maintaining a pleasantly disciplined and coherent residence group."[5] Later generations of women instructors at McGill were more closely associated with the academic Departments than with R.V.C.

It may be well to note that the first woman to hold an academic appointment at McGill was former Donalda, Carrie Derick, B.A. '90. The year after her graduation, she was appointed to assist Dr. Penhallow as a Demonstrator in the Department of Botany. She became a lecturer in 1895 and Assistant Professor in 1904. In 1912, Derick was made Professor of Comparative Botany, thus becoming the first woman full Professor in Canada.[6] It might also be noted that Derick was one of a number of distinguished Donaldas whose field was one of the sciences rather than the more stereotypical "feminine" humanities.

Meanwhile, some of the non-academic staff had played important roles in the lives of R.V.C. students. Of course there was Helen

Gairdner, the original chaperone, who was not at all like the stern humourless duenna of caricature, but an invaluable friend and confidante. Later, one of the basic people at the College was Mrs. Gladys Woodlands Murray who was secretary to the Warden from 1922 to 1957. She not only served the four Wardens of that thirty-five-year period — Miss Hurlbatt, Mrs. Vaughan, Mrs. Grant and Dr. Roscoe — she served all at R.V.C. She was interested in everything about the College and helpful to both staff and students. One of the students during Mrs. Vaughan's regime noted that in those days they "depended on Miss Mackenzie for cosy chats about our love life and on Mrs. Murray for practical details of life."[7] Everyone seemed to appreciate Gladys Murray. In 1955, the Women's Union presented her with an award for her outstanding service; on her retirement two years later, the residents of R.V.C. gave her a silver rose bowl; and after her death in September, 1957, the McGill Alumnae Society established a bursary in her memory. Even the Montreal newspapers honoured her. In a paean of praise, unusual for someone whose life's work had been at the non-professional level, the *Montreal Star* wrote: "Mrs. Murray was much more than a secretary. Anything that was to be known about McGill or R.V.C. was at

"Carty" (*top left*) and her Winning Team

her fingertips. Indeed, 'Ask Mrs. Murray' was the operative phrase during her long and useful tenure of office. . . . In a very real sense, hers was a life of service in a great cause.''8

* * *

Regardless of the help given by staff and administration, much of the fun of student life and much of the real learning has come from students themselves, from their informal contacts and particularly from their student organizations. Some of the clubs were academic, religious, political or philanthropic; some were athletic or recreational; some were gloriously frivolous. As was noted in previous chapters, the Delta Sigma Society, founded in 1885 by the earliest Donaldas, was a very lively organization. With the establishment of R.V.C, this debating and literary group now had a premanent home for its meetings. It revised its constitution and changed its name to the Delta Sigma Society of R.V.C. but it continued to provide the same kind of link between the classroom, the campus and the great world outside. Over the years it sponsored many amusing and contentious discussions (often on the status of

R.V.C.'s Tennis Team, 1917

women in society or their depiction in literature), held public speaking contests, and promoted inter-class and inter-collegiate debates. Its guest speakers ranged from Lord Strathcona and Lady Drummond to Stephen Leacock.

It is not surprising to find that at least one Leacock address to Delta Sigma took place "amid uproar." According to a *McGill Daily* report of 1928, the humorist Professor of Economics purported to defend attacks made on women in the press. He read extracts from newspapers stating that the American girl was without manners, that no American girl knew how to enter a room correctly, much less how to leave it. This short-coming was said to be due to her constant chewing of tobacco! The English girl also had her problems. She was wholly without grace, her movements were inferior to those of a horse, she moved like an alligator and could not sit down. The alleged reason for this was her continual drinking of gin. Perhaps it is fortunate that the account does not elaborate on Leacock and the Canadian girl!

Notes on the Delta Sigma Society's activities continued in the R.V.C. annual report through 1933-34 and then they simply stopped. As Muriel Roscoe remarked, ". . . it is not apparent either as to when or why the Delta Sigma Society ceased to exist."[9] The last reference to it appears in *Old McGill 1936,* with an indication that there was need for reorganization but hopes for new strength in the future. These hopes must have come to naught. However, a life-span of approximately fifty years is extraordinary for student societies which tend to come and go, to emerge to fill an immediate need and fade when conditions change or when the dominant personalities behind them have left and interest flags. McGill has had scores of student clubs but few have lasted as long as Delta Sigma. One of those which has endured was modelled on Delta Sigma. This was the Mu Iota, a Literary Society, which was formed in May 1889 by the first women graduates. The Greek letters of the title stood for "mutual improvement" and the intent was to keep the members in touch with each other and with matters intellectual even though they had left McGill. The first President was Georgina Hunter, one of the eight of '88. By 1890, the group had changed its name to the Alumnae Society and the aims had broadened to include philanthropic work and the development of a university spirit. The Alumnae Society still flourishes and is a force on campus. Its activities and achievements are considered in Chapter 9.

Another of the early societies was itself short-lived, but developed into a branch of a still-viable organization. This was the Theo Dora Society. Founded in 1887, it was at first called the Ladies' Missionary Society and in 1891 became the Y.W.C.A. of McGill. (A Y.M.C.A. group had been formed at McGill in 1884). The object of the new association was "the physical, social, intellectual and spiritual improvement of young women" or, as indicated in *Old McGill 1897,* "the development of perfectly symmetrical womanhood in Christ Jesus." It held classes for Bible study, distributed relief to needy families of Montreal, and in the early 1900's, joined with other Canadian YWCA's in an annual conference at Lake Muskoka. There, mornings were occupied by Bible study, the afternoons were free for recreation and, in the evening, students attended lectures in the chapel.

The name "Theo Dora" was retained for the missionary committee of the YWCA and some idea of the nature of its meetings can be gleaned from its regular reports in the *McGill Fornightly.* One entry reads: "Miss Gault, of the class of '97, directed our thoughts to Purity." The attendance on that occasion was said to be large; however, when Miss Warren dealt with "True Wisdom" the following week, "we regret to say the meeting was not so largely attended."[10] However, many of the programmes were a good deal more exotic and attracted audiences. At one of its earliest meetings, Miss Williams, B.A. read "an instructive paper on China" and Miss Kennedy "gave an account of the life of a Chinese maiden." Later, Mrs. Bompas, wife of the Bishop of McKenzie River presented "a thrilling account of missionary life among the redmen" and Mrs. Mary Carus-Wilson talked on missionary work in India. The latter spoke at some length about the status of women in the subcontinent noting that, while men "have been touched by European influence," the "fanatic bigotry of their wives and mothers" keeps the old religions alive and the women themselves enslaved."[11] On another occasion, Miss Whiteaves discoursed on the "Claims of Foreign Missions on us as Women and as College Women." Programmes such as these serve to point up the high degree of interest taken by women in missionary work in the late 19th and early 20th centuries. Missionaries provided a socially acceptable challenge to the active and enterprising young woman, offering not only an opportunity to put lofty ideals into practice, but also a chance to step out of prescribed domestic spheres, to take initiatives, to travel, and to meet people from different social strata. It will be recalled that Octavia Ritchie attempted to appeal to the need for medical missionaries as a reason for admitting women to the study of Medicine. McGill was not very prompt in responding to her pleas, yet McGill women, through their clubs and individual activities, became involved with many "good works" at home and abroad.

One of the means by which McGill students could work for social good was the Student Christian Movement. This organization developed after 1920 when the national YMCA and YWCA withdrew from college campuses, closing their university branches. The following year, the old

McGill ''Y'' re-formed as the nucleus of the Student Christian Association, with the men meeting at Strathcona Hall, the former centre for the
YMCA, and the women at R.V.C. As part of the Canadian Student
Christian Movement, these groups continued to foster non-denominational religious values and to sponsor philanthropic and social activities.

The need for a Jewish society had long been felt by the small
minority of Jewish women at McGill. Existing societies provided them
little opportunity of studying Jewish history or discussing topics of
Jewish interest. Thus, in 1915 they formed the Menorah Society but the
first year was a difficult one because McGill refused to recognize the
organization, on the ground that the group was controlled by an outside
authoritative body, the Intercollegiate Menorah Society. Thus, the
Menorah Society was unable to meet at R.V.C. but convened at the
homes of various members. After 1916, when the Chancellor of the
Intercollegiate Menorah Society visited Montreal to investigate the
problem and explain that the Menorah was non-sectarian in its aims,
McGill was more accommodating, the Society was recognized and
meetings were then held at R.V.C. The principal question examined
during the early years was the reconstruction of Jewish life after the
War, but the Society's programme was based on a syllabus in use at the
University of London and addresses were given by the presidents of the
Menorah Societies of Columbia and Harvard.

By 1925, women were admitted to the Maccabean Circle, the
parallel men's group at McGill and one which also belonged to the Inter-
collegiate Menorah Association and studied Jewish culture and ideals.
At about this time, the Newman Society was established to foster
Catholic ideals and sponsor social activities for Catholic students. Its
membership was mixed, male and female. Despite the old separatist
philosophy, it was clear that co-educational clubs could and did
function at McGill. It was also apparent that the interests and backgrounds of the students were widening. McGill's original heavy
Protestant majority was giving way to a more diversified student body.[12]

As might have been expected, there have been many kinds of
women-only societies at McGill. These often reflected quite specific
academic or recreational interests and were thus limited in their goals
and their clientele. For example, La Société Française was formed in
1907 by Mlle Milhau in order to provide an opportunity for the students
of R.V.C. to speak French. The Partial Students' Society was organized
in 1910 to help promote college spirit among ''partials'' who always felt
a little out of the mainstream and who were often slightly scorned by
regular undergraduates, as an unkind little ditty from the *McGill Outlook* reflects:

There once was an R.V.C. Partial
Who walked with a stride that was martial
"What else did she do?"
"Why, I thought that you knew
That she was an R.V.C. Partial."

Other specialist all-women societies included the Historical Club of R.V.C. which came into existence in 1919 to give graduates and under-graduates an equal footing and a forum for the discussion of current events; the Music Club, founded in 1922 to inspire an appreciation of good music; the R.V.C. Science Club, begun in the Fall of 1935 to bring together all women in science at McGill; the Women's Rifle Club, which in 1940 challenged its male counterpart. Separate societies such as these tended to disappear in the 50's as closer relationships with the McGill Students' Society developed.

However, the pattern of male/female membership in campus organizations shows anything but a consistent linear development from segregation to integration. Change has been erratic. Women belonged to the old Alma Mater Society in the 19th century, but were excluded from the Students' Society when it was formed early in the 20th; women had their exclusive groups but, from the first, they also worked with men in some extra-curricular activities, notably on publications. In the first half of the present century, some McGill clubs specifically excluded women, some imposed certain limitations, some admitted them to both membership and executive positions. Thus, for example, the Players' Club, which was founded in 1921, was open to all members of the University but its regulations stipulated that "students of the Royal Victoria College were admitted on the same basis as men, and given the same representation upon the executive, with the exception of eligibility to the Presidency."[13] At more or less the same time, a similar organiza-tion, the McGill Choral Society, placed no restrictions on membership. On the other hand, some official directives against mixed clubs seemed still to be in force—or else were used as an excuse. In 1928 the Bridge Club decided that it should be "men only" because of "the impossibility of securing suitable accommodation for a mixed club of this nature and the many inconveniences and difficulties arising out of mixed gatherings due to certain regulations of the University."[14]

Note might also be taken of the fact that, during World War II, Senate established a special programme to ensure that, in the national interest, the women of McGill should be fit. Under this War Service Programme, which was in effect from 1941 to 1944, all women students were required to take gymnastic training for two hours a week. They also

234

Y.W.C.A. and S.C.M. Students' Conference, Silver Bay, N.Y., 1905

received instruction in first aid and were required to attend lectures on such war time problems as air raid precautions, nutrition, fire fighting, and housing. As a further outcome of this programme, many students participated in voluntary community service work with hospitals or the Red Cross and attended extra classes related to potentially useful wartime skills. Some even took extra "Keep Fit" classes.

Compulsory participation in athletic activities has never been any guarantee of the development of prowess or interest and many of the women of McGill derived a great deal more satisfaction out of less formal activities and sports.

Since World War II, and especially since the 1960's, limitations to club membership have presented no serious problems and few strenuous demands. The average young woman on campus in the 1980's might simply expect to join any society in which she were interested and might even be surprised to learn that there ever had been barriers to full participation in all extra-curricular activities. Women's names appear on membership and executive lists with reasonable frequency. Nevertheless, women do not seem to have taken as dominant a role in University-wide organizations as their male classmates. One index of this is their participation in student government.

Sharon Sholzberg, President of McGill Students' Society, 1965-66

For about a quarter of a century, women had their own separate form of student government. As previously noted, they were excluded from the McGill Students' Society when it was founded in 1908 and thus, for a while, they operated under an ad hoc arrangement whereby the president of the senior year at R.V.C. was in charge of an informal organization. She was empowered to call meetings to discuss questions of general interest and to organize campus and College activities until the R.V.C. Undergraduate Society was established. The latter was modelled on the men's Arts Undergraduate Society and it governed all student activities at the College as well as serving as the official channel for grievances. Its membership was comprised of all women undergrads in Arts and resident students in Music. It admitted non-resident women from the Faculty of Medicine in 1920 and those from Law during the following year. Its strength appeared to be expanding until a rival organization developed in 1925. This was the McGill Women Students' Society which was open to all women of the University. However, it only lasted until 1931 when it was superseded by the Women Students' Union. In 1932, to clarify the situation, the women of McGill decided to place all the women's clubs and societies except Delta Sigma under the control of the Women's Union and to abolish the R.V.C. Undergraduate Society. This move was also the result of a new relationship that was developing with the McGill Students' Society.

Thanks in part to the efforts of Susan Cameron Vaughan and her fight to prove that women were indeed students of McGill, they were finally admitted to the Society. Thus, in 1932 for the first time there were two women—the President of the McGill Women's Union (*ex-officio*) and one elected by R.V.C.—on the thirteen member executive Council. In subsequent years, there were always some women on the Students' Council. The number grew with the addition of *ex officio* representatives from groups such as the Women's Athletic Association and the School of Nursing, but it was never greater than four or five. Even as women approached 50% of the total university enrolment, they remained a minority in their student government. In the half century in which women have been eligible for membership in the McGill Students' Society, only two have been President. The first was Sharon Sholzberg, who took office in 1965. She presided during a particularly difficult year, one marked by the operation of a new constitution, the opening of the new Student Union building and growing political tensions on campus and in Quebec society generally. She acquitted herself admirably as she campaigned for a reversal of student fee increases, organized "teach-ins" against the Vietnam war, and sought McGill membership in l'Union Générale des Etudiants du Québec to form a common front with the other students of the Province. The second woman President of the Students' Society, Liz Norman, was elected to office in 1981.

These widely-spaced wins suggest that women have not become thoroughly involved in their student government. There have been some notable exceptions—for example, Mary Salemi was a dynamic two-term President of the Education Undergraduate Society (1979-81)—but generally, few women have run for campus-wide office or, if they have run, they have not been elected. This is indicative of the fact that there is no women's political caucus. It also reflects the feeling that those women who do serve as their Faculty representatives on Senate or student representatives to the Board of Governors do so as representatives of their constituencies as a whole, not just the women. The general concensus would seem to be that this state of affairs is as it should be, that the gender factor is irrelevant, that the individual is important not his/her sex. Yet a problem of fair balance will remain unless both representation and participation of men and women are approximately proportionate to their numbers. In an ideal society, that would happen naturally; in the current stage of social development, an extra effort to secure female representation is still required.

In the late 1960's, consistent with the idea that "things were getting better" for women and that separate women's organizations were at once unnecessary and ghettoizing, the Women's Union as an entity disappeared. It simply dissolved into the general body of the Students' Society.[15] This was to prove premature. After a brief dormant period, it re-emerged in the early 70's, this time with a more specifically feminist focus. Its contribution to the Women's Movement on campus is considered in Chapter 9.

* * *

Meanwhile, there were other kinds of women's groups at McGill that were neither clubs nor forms of student government. These included the honour societies, the fraternities and associations for sports and athletics.

The Red Wing Honour Society was established in 1938 as the female equivalent of the Scarlet Key Society. Its membership, representative of resident and non-resident women from all sections of the University, was limited to thirty. Members were chosen by a special committee on the basis of their academic standing and their contributions to campus life. Honorary membership included the presidents of the Women's Athletic Association, the Women's Union, R.V.C. and, if they happened to be women, the president or vice-president of the

Students' Council. The Red Wings acted as official hostesses at McGill and graced such functions as football games, alumni gatherings, receptions, concerts, plays, special lectures and elections. After completing a certain number of assignments, graduating students received their "wings"—the pin of the Red Wing Society.

In 1968, the Red Wings decided to stop working at football games "as the female capacity for bouncing over-joyous members of the crowd is questionable." [16] Perhaps that was the thin end of the wedge—or the sharp tip of the feather. Shortly afterwards the Red Wings appear to have moulted. Part of the student revolution and value shifts of the 60's was a general fear of being "ripped off" and what had once been deemed an honour was now tainted with the possibility of exploitation. Thus, in that era, voluntary organizations had a tendency to become professionalized. A new agency, "Hospitality McGill," was established by the University to serve at official receptions and the like. Students still participate in this and they are still chosen carefully for the hosting services they perform under the auspices of Hospitality McGill—but now they are paid. The Red Wing Society ceased to exist in 1970-71 but the Society Key is still awarded as an honour to both men and women.

At mid-century, there was also a residential honour group for women. This was established in 1951 when Muriel Roscoe revived the title, "Donalda." The old name for women students had gradually gone out of style, having been replaced in common McGill parlance by the American term, "co-ed," an appellation which in turn went out of style in the late 60's. However, in its rejuvenated form "Donalda" applied specifically to a small group of senior resident students. Selected for their high academic standing and their conspicuous contribution to life at R.V.C., the Donaldas were expected to serve the College in much the same way that the Red Wings served the campus as a whole. They also disappeared at the beginning of the 70's when R.V.C. underwent basic restructuring.

Another kind of organization with which women had some involvement was the fraternity. Men's fraternities had been established at McGill in the 19th century but they did not meet with universal approval. The old McGill *University Gazette* denounced them as secret societies and derided their members as "a few tinselled youths." [17] The first women of McGill apparently shared these views. In a letter to the *McGill Outlook* of 1906, "A Donalda of the Nineties" wrote that the question of whether or not to have "girls' fraternities" had kept recurring. [18] She said it was rejected by her generation because the numbers of women were so small it would be unwise to divide them; as for the next generation, they had no need of fraternities because they had R.V.C. as a meeting ground with opportunities for all kinds of activities. She, too, disapproved of the invidious social distinctions implied in select groups such as fraternities. She also noted that, for women, they might more properly be called ''sororities,'' but one of the Donaldas had objected because that word always suggested stuttering.

Nevertheless, these groups, which generally aimed at good fellowship with a dash of social service and academic interest, began to grow on the edge of campus. They were without official McGill sanction and the record of their existence is incomplete. It is certain that there was a sorority, Delta Phi Epsilon, in the 20's and it hosted the first college sorority convention ever held in Montreal.[19] In 1930, Alpha Gamma Delta appeared and Kappa Alpha Theta two years later. Whether to avoid the elocution problem and the risk of stuttering or whether to emphasize an ideal of student kinship, both were called ''fraternities.'' Others have come and gone in an erratic course depending on the support of their clientele. During the 40's efforts were made to coordinate them. In 1941 two Jewish sororities (Sigma Delta Tau and Delta Phi Epsilon) prepared a report for Principal Cyril James, showing how they had contributed to friendship, developed leadership, stimulated co-

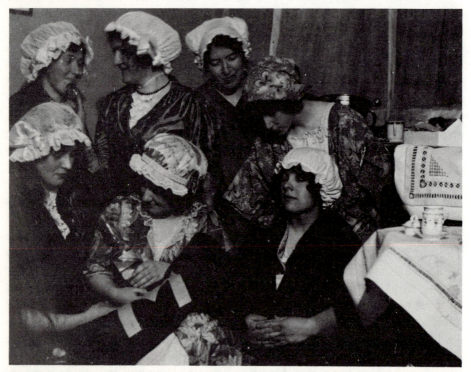

Tea Time at R.V.C.? (c. 1914)

operation, fostered University *esprit-de-corps,* contributed to war work, and encouraged scholastic achievements among their members. They recommended that the University formally recognize sororities and fraternities and use them "for the purposes of promoting whatever lies close to the heart of the University proper."[20] However, McGill did not take them under its wing just then and in 1945, Dr. Muriel Roscoe sounded rather chilly when she said that they did not have the approval of the University or R.V.C.[21] A decade later, the University did officially recognize fraternities and began to exercise some direct control over the thirty male and eight female organizations then in existence. One of the tangible outcomes of the administration's intervention was the development of a code of conduct governing such causes of citizen complaint as drinking, noise, hazing, and bizarre "initiation" rites.

There certainly have been critics enough of fraternities and frat houses but also some praise and gratitude. One R.V.C. resident of the early 30's recalled how "the shy, lonely Toronto girl who came to McGill will never cease to be amazed and grateful that she was asked to be a Kappa. What happy times and what silly times we had in the cheap rented rooms that were all that women could afford. How much we learnt of other people and, to be pretentious, what a lot we learnt about taking part in whatever society we belong to."[22]

* * *

The women of McGill have always been involved with sports and physical activities of various kinds. In her famous valedictory, Octavia Ritchie pointed out that the tennis club was the first of the Donalda's formal organizations. As early as 1889 voluntary classes in gymnastics were organized under the direction of Helen O. Barnjum and, with the completion of the R.V.C., physical education became an integral part of college life for women. Attendance at physical education classes was made compulsory in 1905. First-year students were then required to do two hours a week; by 1911, the requirement was extended to second- and third-year students; by 1914, the rules were again changed to include fourth year, so that 144 hours of physical education were required of all women before graduation regardless of their field of study. Mandatory physical education remained in force for McGill women until 1945. The requirement then relaxed, was revived during the 50's, but in 1960 the programme again became voluntary. Since then the number of participants increased each year to the point where it was impossible to accommodate them all because of limited facilities.[23]

One of the earliest sports at R.V.C. was basketball, a game invented by a one-time McGill instructor in gymnastics, James A. Naismith.

R.V.C

Athletic·Association

R.V.C. played teams from Vassar and Wellesley in 1901. The R.V.C. Athletic Association (R.V.C.A.A.) was formed that year and inter-class teams in tennis, hockey and fencing were developed under the guidance of the Physical Director. At this time, "fancy skating" was popular with R.V.C. students and, according to a contemporary report, they skated on the campus rink "on many a wintry evening to the accompaniment of a hurdy gurdy." The first swimming meet was held in 1919 but, before R.V.C. had its own pool, instruction was given off campus, including at the Montreal Amateur Athletic Association's "tank." Another important occurrence of 1919 was the visit of Queen's basketball team. Described by *Old McGill 1920* as "an epoch-making event in the history of Canadian sport," this produced the first intercollegiate game played by Canadian women—and R.V.C. won. In 1921, three women's university teams—McGill (R.V.C.), Queen's and "Varsity" (Toronto)—met for competition. The Intercollegiate League thus formed awarded winners the "Bronze Baby" trophy which was said to be an astonishingly deformed, but much coveted, bit of statuary.

The early 1920's was a period of considerable activity as the R.V.C.A.A. revived projects which World War I and the infamous influenza epidemic had curtailed. The Association sponsored competitions between R.V.C. and Macdonald College as well as the interclass games and it held annual sports days with a series of events such as high jump, broad jump, window jump, walking, relay race, obstacle race, faculty race, old girls' race and tug-of-war. After these events a *thé dansant* might be held at the College in order to raise money to finance inter-collegiate basketball games. In 1927, the McGill Women Students' Athletic Association (M.W.S.A.A.) was formed by the fusion of the R.V.C.A.A. and the Physical Education Department. It provided a very broad range of activities. Archery, badminton, field hockey, golf and skiing became part of the recreational possibilities, while weekend ski trips to the Laurentians were among the highlights of the winter term. Partial students were permitted to join in the activities of the Association but they could not hold office, play on College teams or win awards. The awards included trophies, large "R.V.C.'s" and small "R.V.C.'s," as well as badges and Strathcona cash prizes. The latter dated back to 1902.

There were quite precise rules covering the awards and activities, just as there were regulations governing dress. Every student was required to wear the costume "recommended" by the Physical Education Department. In the earliest days of R.V.C. (1899 to c. 1910), the gym costume was an outfit of navy blue serge bloomers that came fully to the knee, a matching blouse with a military collar trimmed with white braid and black stockings; the hockey uniform of that period was a full-length skirt worn with a white sweater and a wool cap; tennis players also wore skirts that touched the ground, as was the general mode. Around 1910, the blue serge blouse with the military collar of the gym uniform was changed for a white middy blouse and soon afterwards, the bloomers gave way to a blue serge tunic and black stockings. By 1920, it was possible for the hockey player to show that she had legs and she wore a short skirt, a sweater and padded gloves—though apparently, not much other padding. In the following decade, the regulation gym costume became red shorts (bulky and long by today's standards but, nevertheless, shorts), a white blouse and socks. Since the 30's, dress has become progressively freer but at the same time more protective and practical; since the 60's, it has become almost entirely individualized except for inter-collegiate play where team uniforms are provided.

Clothing styles such as these are not just superficial fashions, they are symbolic. As long as women as a class were fettered by long skirts, bustles, corsets, stays, high heels, tight bras and all the rest, their athletic prowess had to be limited. No matter how enthusiastic the participants might have been, their performances would inevitably be hampered by binding clothes and inhibiting customs. The evolution of

ENTRIES WITH NUMBERS

SENIORS

1	M. Bedford-Jones	5	W. Griffin
2	E. Cousman	6	F. Levikoff
3	M. Dougall	7	M. Ratner
4	R. Dunton	8	F. Stocking

JUNIORS

9	G. Cameron	15	A. MacKinnon
10	M. Ferguson	16	R. Murray
11	F. Louis	17	D. M. Roberts
12	B. Lyman	18	I. Scriver
13	H. Mulligan	19	A. Turner
14	M. Martin	20	R. Turley

SOPHOMORES

21	D. Bloomfield	28	N. McMartin
22	E. Brooks	29	K. Morrison
23	B. Carter	30	J. Olesker
24	J. Eve	31	M. D. Ross
25	R. Heartz	32	E. Wardleworth
26	V. Hulin	33	J. Wyers
27	F. Klineberg	34	J. Worden

FRESHIES

35	N. Barry	44	F. MacGachen
36	O. Basken	45	E. MacLean
37	J. Bennett	46	E. Peters
38	J. Davidson	47	G. Roberts
39	B. Fuller	48	M. Smith
40	B. Gilmour	49	J. Snyder
41	J. Howard	50	G. Sharp
42	E. Johnson	51	J. Wilson
43	A. Morton	52	R. Whitley
		53	O. Winters

PARTIAL

54	E. Ziff

W. H. Eaton & Son, Printers, 69 Milton Street, Montreal

Royal Victoria College

Annual Sports

SATURDAY

October 24th, 1925

McGILL STADIUM

AT 10.30 A.M.

OFFICERS
of the Athletic Association

Hon. Pres.	Miss Lichenstein
Hon. Advisor	Miss Cartwright
President	Miss R. Dunton
Sec.-Treasurer	Miss G. Cameron
Tennis Manager	Miss E. Cochrane
Sports Manager	Miss D. M. Roberts
Basketball Manager	Miss F. Secord
Hockey Manager	Miss M. Gilman

increasingly functional athletic garb for McGill women symbolized programme development and the growth of more flexible attitudes toward women as athletes.

There has been a long and close relationship between R.V.C. and women's physical education. The College provided many facilities, not only for athletics and recreational activities, but also for the Department of Physical Education. From the latter's establishment in 1917, R.V.C. provided office space until 1971, the Gymnasium until 1946 (when it was converted to a cafeteria), the Assembly Hall for use as a gymnasium and locker rooms to 1955, then limited use of the Hall until 1971, a class-room until 1971, and the Weston Pool. R.V.C.'s facilities were not adequate for an expanding instructional programme and there had been plans for Physical Education to move to the Currie Gymnasium when it was built in 1939. The old problem of insufficient funds necessitated curtailing these plans so that there was space for only limited women's activities there. Thus the six women members of the Physical Education Department and the Women's Athletic Association remained at R.V.C. The result of this was the growth of a myth that the Currie Gym was essentially a men's building. Women were accepted on sufferance and were given "last priority" in the assignment of space—for after all, the women had the R.V.C. facilities as well.[24] It was simply taken for granted that R.V.C. would continue to house Physical Education, though it was a Department of McGill rather than R.V.C., and the College was not compensated for the use of its space and services.

During the 1970's, important administrative and physical changes took place. When part of R.V.C. was converted to the Faculty of Music and the Currie Gym was expanded, women's Physical Education removed to the Currie Gym entirely (with the exception of the use and administration of the Weston Pool). Men's and women's athletics were also centered at Currie and the two programmes combined. Theoretically, the move should have assured the women of McGill more and better facilities, but not all the people concerned with women's athletics viewed amalgamation with men as an improvement. They saw the danger—perhaps one that Dawson had seen as he insisted on separate education—of women's activities being given second billing to men's. In view of the presumed importance of the men's Redmen hockey, basketball and football teams and the general tradition that men's sports are more interesting than women's, more conducive to crowds and more

McGill School of Physical Education Hockey Team, 1920-21 (Iveagh Munro on the floor)

inducive of benefactions, it was almost inevitable that a man was appointed as overall McGill Director of Athletics and that the Director of Women's Athletics became his assistant.

After seventy years of independence, this change was a significant one for the Director of Women's Athletics. The loss of independence could be counter-balanced by such positive factors as the improved opportunities for the integration of men's and women's sporting activities, the sharing of the best facilities and coaching, the co-ordination of competitions, economies and the like. However, a serious risk remained of women's athletics being eclipsed. Since amalgamation, both women students and staff members protested that adequate safeguards were not taken to ensure equal distribution between the men and women of McGill of the budget, space, staffing appointments, coaching, facilities, and publicity.[25]

The integration of male and female athletics illustrates the complexity of the co-education issue. Whereas co-education has generally been viewed as a modern improvement, an essential for women's liberation, it is not necessarily an unmitigated good. Observers of a number of U.S. women's colleges which went ''co-ed'' in the 60's detect a tendency

Gym Class, 1922-23

for women students to decline to engage in competition against men. As a result, all female executive jobs in student organizations tend to become male-dominated and women lose their opportunity for leadership. Without basic experience, they hesitate to exert leadership later and the syndrome becomes self-perpetuating. The explanation for women's opting out of responsibility and competition is to be found in the old Nature vs. Nurture argument—it is seen variously as the result of the socialization of women or part of their generic make up. The great theoretical issue may still be subject for debate, but it is clear that as long as men are given the advantage of money and superior facilities, women will not be able to catch up in the field of athletics, their performance will be poorer, their drawing power feeble, their confidence weak and so their performance will be poorer, they will receive less money and on and on. . . . The syndrome is self-perpetuating, self-fulfilling.

One solution to the problem would be for the women to retreat behind the old lady-like image, pretend that it does not matter and that physical activities are inappropriate for them. Another approach would be to break the vicious circle with a programme of affirmative action,

Dr. Gladys Bean, Director of Women's Athletics

thus encouraging the women to function near the level of their full human potential, giving women's athletics status on campus. In 1980, Dean of Students, Michael Herschorn, took a step in this direction by including in his budget a contingency fund that would make emergency money available for women's activities. That was a start but, notwithstanding the brilliant performance of some Canadian female athletes like Nancy Greene, Bev Boys and Abbie Hoffman, there is still a long way to go before the McGill community and society at large consider women's athletic prowess as interesting or as important as men's.

* * *

One of the significant aspects of student life for the women of McGill has been the residence experience at R.V.C. From the days of Lord Strathcona and Hilda Oakeley, the ideal had been advanced that the College should be a kind of academic home where a congenial family atmosphere and pleasant surroundings were deemed as important as the formal instruction. With the constant expansion this became harder and harder to achieve but, in the early days, if R.V.C. was not "a home away from home," it at least acquired a reputation as being "the best down town club in Montreal." Students had their rooms cared for, their beds made; they were called in the morning by maids, who also closed their windows; they were served their meals in the dining room and waitresses brought them coffee after dinner, as well as milk with biscuits in the evening and tea in the afternoon; they could have trays in their rooms at a charge of twenty-five cents. Over the years, the Wardens and staff attempted to retain the gracious, rather "old world" atmosphere.

Dr. Muriel Roscoe described in some detail what life in R.V.C. was like at mid-century. She pointed out that an underlying respect for authority was maintained, and there was "liberty but not licence" and a "quiet discipline that was as real as it was unobtrusive." There was a pattern to life, and a degree of ceremony. In her words:

> Dignity with respect to meals featured the every-day life, and certain traditions were soon built up. These included for dinner a lining-up by classes in the main hall, having grace (said on week nights in Latin by the Warden, on Saturdays in English by Seniors, and sung on Sundays), and having guests. There were also language tables (French, Italian, Spanish and German).
>
> Coffee hour at night and on Sunday afternoons was a very special time. After-dinner coffee was served and cleared away by the Freshies in the Drawing Room and as from 1949 in the East Lounge

as well. The Warden and Assistant Wardens were rarely absent, guests were presented to them, and conversation with students sitting all over the floor as well as on chairs and chesterfields, was animated. Ordinarily the Coffee Period terminated by eight o'clock, but frequently lasted much longer.

Music was a regular feature of the Sunday coffee hour with first-class concerts given by the students themselves. For a period of years there was an R.V.C. choir, whose theme song was ''Bless This House.''

Altogether the coffee hours resulted in a subtle amalgamation of the group, the development of an esprit de corps, the maturing of the students socially, and stimulating them mentally. They never failed to impress faculty members who were invited for ''Professors' Dinners.''

There was a constant emphasis on dress. Students were expected to be neatly dressed for dinner. At no time were they allowed to appear on the ground floor or in public rooms in slacks or shorts.

Such courtesies as standing up at the entrance of the Warden or for older people were automatic and part of the general code of behavior.

Dr. Roscoe and Students With After-Dinner Coffee (c. 1960)

The function of the Resident Assistants was clear in coffee hour discussions and also on their floors, where they very frequently had tea at 10 p.m. for their own group.

Much use was made of the common and drawing rooms in terms of debates within the House and for music, apart from group meetings and parties.

Apart from the more formal parties (annual House Dance, entertaining at Sunday teas, etc., teas at McLennan Hall and the Annex), there were many informal parties on the floors and in the Common Rooms, Freshman and Senior skits, splash parties (after the building of the Swimming Pool),—pyjama parties, and international parties were regular features of living.

In all this the Seniors gave leadership and their place in the group was a special one, with the Senior Members of the House Committee and the "Donaldas" setting the tone. Integration of overseas students was part and parcel of all the effort.

The outstanding formal event was the House Dance. One must always remember that residence life meant making provision for entertaining men—not only at parties, but at Sunday lunch, dinner, etc. This was no convent atmosphere and Sunday lunch invariably saw many men as guests.

Then there were the welcoming functions for incoming students in the fall. There were the second, third and fourth year banquets (given by the Women's Union but involving all the College and its facilities).

There was, too, the Big Sister program in the Residence for both Freshies and Freshie Sophs.

There was too, as Christmas approached, the omnipresent carolling, with the touching ceremony of Freshies singing carols through the residence in the early morning, and ending their procession and carols in the Warden's apartment.

Important to the students themselves was a less glamorous "phone duty" where this was taken care of by students on the floors.

Certainly without glamour were the monthly fire drills, as important as they were unwelcome in the middle of the night.

For the Warden, the major annual social functions given by her were the receptions for new students and their parents, the Christmas dinner (and before 1950 when the group became too large, the Christmas tea for students and guests), and her dinner near the end of term for the House Committee, Donaldas and Staff. . . .

Looking back, the all-over impression is of a happy residence life where some of the hopes of the Founder were realized in enriching students' lives and amplifying their class-room education. [26]

* * *

The traditional pattern was preserved in its essentials by Warden Helen Reynolds up to the end of the 1960's. By then, the much discussed "generation gap" was rending the foundations of R.V.C. What had long been perceived by the McGill authorities as a gracious and appropriate form of student living was now seen by the students as paternalistic, restrictive and irrelevant. In the unsettled days after the student revolution, the women of McGill rebelled, not with violence but *in absentia*— that is, they chose not to live at the College. They rejected its "fuddy duddy" image, taking up residence instead in their own "pads," effectively half-emptying R.V.C. and making it an economic liability to the University. Almost overnight, it seemed, R.V.C. became a luxury McGill thought it could not afford. The University thus had the options of hanging on to this "white elephant" while it waited for the fashion in student housing to swing back, or changing the life-style within the College to suit the "Now Generation," or changing the College itself, giving it over to some other more economically viable educational purpose. As indicated in the previous chapter, the decision was taken to modify the Royal Victoria College structure and to assign the original building to the Faculty of Music. The centre block and the Reynolds Wing were redesignated the "Strathcona Music Building" and officially blessed by the Founders' heirs, Lord and Lady Strathcona, in October, 1971.[27]

Thus, the women's college was literally relegated to the wings, the residential accommodation reduced by more than half, the grand old hall where the first Lord Strathcona had presided over the illustrious opening ceremonies became the Pollack Concert Hall, the dining room disappeared and the remodelled cafeteria in the basement became the only large communal space in the College and the only eating facility. When the dust of the renovations had settled, what was left was not the same R.V.C. merely reduced in size. It had now become what Miss Hurlbatt had feared long ago, essentially a residence rather than a college.

The change in structure was accompanied by a change of tone which could be detected in the contrast between the official "handouts" of the College. In the "old days" of Dr. Roscoe, the "General Announcement and Residence Rules" was a twenty-six page printed book which contained the following formal statement:

YOUR RESPONSIBILITY AS A
ROYAL VICTORIA COLLEGE STUDENT

From the time of your enrolment in the first year until graduation, you as a student of the Royal Victoria College enjoy marked privileges. You also accept certain responsibilities. These responsibilities include honest and consistent application to your academic work, the observance of all College and Student Government regulations, and the maintenance of high standards of personal conduct so as to uphold both your own good name and that of the College. [28]

Included in the rules and information that followed were details such as a prohibition against the wearing of shorts or slacks in the public rooms of the College and rules for gentlemen visitors who were asked to leave their coats in the Men's Cloakroom, to wear jackets and ties in the dining room, and who could not be invited to breakfast. About three pages, plus a detachable ''weekend permission slip'' to be signed by parents, were devoted to the highly structured regulations on ''permissions and leaves.'' The administration of these required almost the full-time services of one of the Assistant Wardens, aided by the Student Leaves Committee.

The considerable difference in the approach to students in the early 1960's and in the late 1970's can be seen in the seven-page mimeographed ''Information for Residents of Royal Victoria College,'' which began with the statement:

Flo Tracy (*right*) and Students (c. 1980)

Royal Victoria College is run for the convenience and advantage of the students living in it. What "rules and regulations" do exist are mainly decided upon and administered by the students themselves. Basically, living together in any community requires just a single rule: respect for the rights of others. This mutual respect, however, forces in turn a measure of adaptation and compromises on the part of the individual in the interests of the larger residence community. Without this flexibility, residence is best avoided altogether; with it, residence life can be your most rewarding university experience. 29

Just six basic rules were laid down—fire alarms must be obeyed; guests must be signed in and out and accompanied at all times; no illegal drugs are allowed; no animals or pets are allowed; cafeteria cards must be shown at each meal; cooking in the rooms is not allowed. There was no longer a Leaves Committee because the College was open virtually twenty-four hours a day, even though the main entrance was locked at 1 a.m. The information sheet made no mention of men but they were understood to be included in the provision that all guests must be signed in and accompanied and residents were responsible for the behaviour of their guests; otherwise, there were no official restrictions on male visitors.

The change in the style of R.V.C., like the change in social mores generally, can be seen very clearly in male/female relationships. By 1969, as co-ed dorms were being contemplated at McGill, an "open house" rule was established at R.V.C. allowing for male visitation to students' rooms at specified hours, three times a week. This was introduced as a result of student pressure in the form of complaints and petitions, followed by a favourable referendum. However, it was not put into practice until after Helen Reynolds, who was then in her last year as Warden, had advised all parents by letter. When Dr. Donna Runnalls took over as Warden in 1972, she was confronted by requests for further liberalization of the house rules. To the surprise of the students, even the most radical, she granted on a trial basis all their demands, even the switch to a fully "open house" residence policy. There was no real confrontation, no fuss. The change was made quietly and produced no untoward results, no outraged objections. The women of McGill had come a very long way since the days of Principal Dawson and the chaperoning of Helen Gairdner.

The changes in the house rules at R.V.C. were based on the fundamental recognition of and respect for the maturity of the women of McGill. They implied a definition of Woman as Person rather than Daughter or Lady or future Wife and Mother. J. Clark Murray might not have approved of them entirely, but they were a logical fulfilment of the view of Woman he had espoused a hundred years earlier. These rules, together with the gradual conversion of the four men's residences into co-educational establishments clearly put the responsibility for personal conduct on the students themselves. Both male and female students were accorded their rights as young adults to determine their own life-styles within the University's intellectual and social framework. In the 1970's the women of McGill had a wider range of residence options than at any time in the University's history. They could choose to live off-campus, either at home or elsewhere; or they could live in Molson, Douglas, Gardner or McConnell Halls, the co-ed residences; or they could live in R.V.C., the women's residence. The opening of these four all-male residences to women emerged from the student activism of the late 60's. The men of McGill were also restless with what they perceived as remote and complex residence administration—benevolent paternalism at best, rigid regimentation at worst. The conversion to "co-ed" was achieved without great fanfare and with little expectation of revolutionary changes in daily life. Indeed, one commentator remarked, "Next September [1971], Douglas Hall will admit women for the first

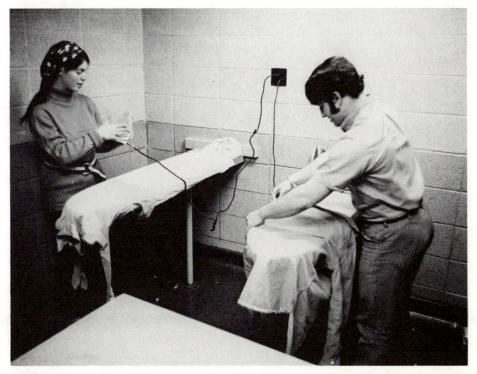

Co-ed Residence Life (c. 1975)

time. This development seems to have been received with studied indifference; however, the sports teams may find an attractive new style to their play, and social events should become more lively if less 'beery.' ''30

Little formal investigation has been undertaken of women's residence preferences now that they have a wide choice at McGill. Obviously, finances and convenience are important determinants, but why some women prefer co-ed quarters to R.V.C. and vice versa is not really known. However, it is apparent that a significant number of women do prefer separate—if not completely segregated—living arrangements. At the end of the 70's, the residence space of R.V.C. was again full, albeit, to its reduced capacity of 260. What in the late 60's had seemed to be a permanent trend toward independent, off-campus living turned out to be a temporary phenomenon so that, within a decade, there were again no empty beds at R.V.C. Apparently, students had not abandoned their independence, but they discovered there was something to be said for the comfort, security and companionship of residential life.

With a significant resurgence of interest in R.V.C., it might be argued that the University had acted precipitously in truncating the College. It was a difficult decision to make in the 60's, though an easy one to criticize with the hindsight of the 70's. In the 80's, new social factors will come to bear upon the situation—the overall decline in McGill enrolments due to the falling birthrate, the uncertainties of the political climate in the Province of Quebec, and world-wide economic difficulties. These forces, which will have direct bearing on the number of applications, together with the evolving view of Woman and her role in society, will affect the kind of accommodation the University will provide for the women of McGill in the future. Whether the kind of change that was made to R.V.C. was wise or not, it seems absolutely certain that there will be no possibility of ever restoring the R.V.C. that Dr. Roscoe knew.

* * *

It is hardly surprising to find that many alumnae profoundly regret the demise of the old R.V.C., even though most would concede that some change was inevitable. The "good old days" are gone, only to be revived (or perhaps, created) in the nostalgia of "Homecoming Weekend," the pages of publications like *Old McGill* or the memories of those who were there. By drawing on the reminiscences of some of the women who were at McGill, the remainder of this chapter attempts to evoke the spirit of the McGill experience since the establishment of R.V.C. Though the anecdotal approach to history is not sufficient in itself, it indisputably adds colour and life to any human record; and while it is difficult to condense and capture the temper of the times in a few paragraphs and though none of the writers would lay claim to being the exclusive representative of her generation, yet the following accounts of student life manage to reflect something of the special character of each of the decades in the present century as they were encountered by the women of McGill.

In the first decade of the 20th century, the women of McGill seemed to have been serious and eager for learning, much as the original Donaldas had been, but they had the great advantage of the College with its relative luxury, fun and friendship. Some record of the interest and activities, some notion of what life was like for the first inhabitants of R.V.C. emerges from a bundle in the McGill Archives marked, "Papers of Katherine and Jane Wisdom."[31] The Wisdoms were sisters who participated very fully in all McGill had to offer. Katherine graduated in '03, Jennie in '07 and during their undergraduate days, they wrote home to New Brunswick regularly, touching on many aspects of a world they found to be rich and exciting. Katherine wrote:

On Studies: "Don't ever, as you value your earthly happiness, take a course simply because you imagine it to be useful. There are some girls in the third year who are taking Latin just because they can get some kind of teacher's diploma that way, while they are just pining for biology or chemistry or English. If I were taking an ordinary course I know, oh so well, what I would take! It should be History, English, Geology, Philosophy, French and German—Doesn't that make your mouth fairly water." (Jan. 24, 1903).

". . . The next excitement will be the Strathcona Horse, without the horse though, I'm afraid. They are to arrive Monday and we are to have no lectures in the afternoon. It's something alarming, the way patriotism interferes with our last precious lectures." (n.d., c. 1901).

On Separate Classes: "Such a funny thing happened in Physics the other day. There was a practical class of men away upstairs while we were having our lecture. In the floor of the room upstairs there is a little trap door which looks down into our lecture theatre. I happened to look and see this begin to open, so I fixed my stern gaze on it till a fair head appeared. He evidently didn't expect to find anyone watching for him, for the door shut silently but speedily. Miss Cox was telling me as a great joke this morning, how when her father went upstairs, he found *four Honour men* flat on the floor, eagerly gazing after the departing Donaldas."

On Social Activities: "Been practising at our play all afternoon. It comes off two weeks from today. The Arts-Science Dance is to be a week from Wednesday. Monday is that blessed debate, and Tuesday I hold forth before the German Club. Oh, it's a strenuous life!

"Had a good time last night—went tobogganing with Mr. Mitchell. Perfectly glorious moonlight night. That was my fun for this week. By the way, though I grumble like this about the work, I never felt better in my life. . . ." (February 7, 1903)

On Professor-Student Relations: ". . . that reminds me of Dr. Walter. A girl had failed in her preparation, and he looked at her grimly and remarked, 'Sackcloth and ashes are much too good for you, much too good. I shall go to Scroggies and ask them if they have anything left over from the January sales.'

"That same facetious gentleman played a trick on me. You know I had to read my essay before the German Club. Well, he gave me a word of his own make up, one that sounded quite natural to me, because it was made on the analogy of another which I knew. It was one of those words that no one but a German would know was *not* in the dictionary. Well I used it, of course, and then I was besieged with questions as to where I got that particular word. I got back at him by saying that I got almost all my vocabulary from the Herr Professor Walter. . . ." (February 14, 1903)

On Manners: "We went down to the R.V.C. about 4 o'clock to play tennis. . . . There are some new girls there, whom the others have been very hard on. We had heard fearful reports of the 'freaks' and 'creatures.' Effie asked one of them to play tennis and thought she wasn't half bad. By and by the old residents came along and made a fuss over Ef, without so much as looking at the new one. Ef got mad, and when they asked her to have tea, she said she couldn't and turned around to the new girl and said 'Miss Hallway won't you come down with Miss Lyman and me and have a soda?' Wasn't that swell? I tell you those R.V.C. girls have had a lesson." (September 17, 1902)

On Fashions: "Ef and I went down (to R.V.C.) last night, played ping-pong and stayed to a cocoa party. The two new girls who happened to be in were invited. We didn't do any lecturing but just talked athletics and Delta Sigma and so on. They have a fad down there of wearing little silk sachets inside their blouses, so I got a good sized bag of lavender around my neck and Effie tied on a small pin cushion. You should have seen Miss Oakeley's face when we asked her to smell our sachets! The girls just shrieked. Oh the responsibility of being seniors! (September 17, 1902)

And one of Jane Wisdom's favourite clippings from the *McGill Outlook* seemed to disclose that the system of separate education was not successful in keeping the McGill men and women apart:

> Said a fussiful lad of '07,
> When speaking of things up in Heaven,
> 'No Heaven for me,
> If there's no R.V.C.,
> '07 in Heaven to leaven.[32]

* * *

The second decade of the century was dominated by the Great World War. While the daily life of the young women students of McGill was not profoundly disturbed, that of their elders was. Professors' wives and alumnae devoted a great deal of time and energy to the war effort. In October, 1914 when the campus was filled with drilling boys, the Ladies' Auxiliary to the McGill Y.M.C.A. agreed that "the women of McGill should form a group for active service in support of philanthropic and other effort as the need may arise."[33] This group of wives and mothers was originally called the Women's Union—not to be confused with the later student organization of the same name—but in 1933 voted to become the still-active Women Associates of McGill.

One of the first tasks the Women's Union undertook was to provide a parcel of comforts for each McGill man going overseas and the members were gratified to receive many cards of appreciation:

> "Dear Madam:
> Please accept my thanks for the lovely cap and socks. . . ."[34]

Later, when the numbers of McGill soldiers had multiplied, they sent clothing directly to the military units where there were concentrations of McGill men. During the course of the war, the Union made 6,210 pairs of socks, 1,260 caps, 987 flannel shirts, 890 pyjamas, 660 scarfs, 500 pneumonia jackets, 178 pairs of wristlets, 150 hospital shirts, 100 "housewives."

Another of their important activities was the making of surgical dressings from sphagnum moss, which they dried and prepared in a room made available by the Faculty of Medicine. In 1917, sphagnum dressings were officially adopted by the Canadian government. The McGill Sphagnum Depot then became the model workroom where varied types of dressings were made and tested and from which the Government accepted standard dressings. Sample dressings and instructions for making them were sent out from the workrooms to all sphagnum depots in Canada and to the American Red Cross when they took up the work.[35]

The wartime activities of the women of McGill were varied and not limited to support roles in Montreal. There was a surprising number of alumnae much closer to the scenes of conflict, even though the Alumnae Society noted, "only a favoured few of our graduates have been so fortunately placed that they have been able to render personal full time service overseas. News of those lucky ones has been received with envious interest."[36] These "lucky ones" included nurses, doctors, ambulance drivers, V.A.D.'s, canteen assistants and librarians in military hospitals. Notable individual examples of the variety of contributions made by the women of McGill include Dr. Catherine H. Travis, B.A. '95, who was in charge of a children's hospital in Serbia and, for a time, was left behind enemy lines; Agnes Warner, B.A. '94, who was with a flying column of nurses on the Belgian front; Caroline Holman, B.A. '90, who published a very successful volume of inspirational poems, "In the Day of Battle;" Georgina Hunter, B.A. '88, Mary A. Hitchcock, B.A. '05, Eleanor Tatley, B.A. '92 and many others who worked for the Canadian Patriotic Fund; Isabel Brittain, B.A. '94, who was very active in Victory Loan drives; Mary P. Henderson, B.A. '90, who was purchasing agent for three provincial Red Cross Societies; Isabel McCaw, B.A. '15, who drove an ambulance in Serbia and was decorated by the Serbian government. It will be remembered that Ethel Hurlbatt was also decorated by the Serbian government for her contribution to the war effort.

Probably the most distinguished, and decorated, of all was Helen R.Y. ("Nellie") Reid, B.A. '89, who was Convenor of the Ladies' Auxiliary of the Montreal Branch of the Canadian Patriotic Fund. Of her work in organizing the Fund's multifarious activities, American sociologist Paul U. Kellog wrote:

> Hard-won experience and the bonds of courage and sacrifice would not in themselves have created filing systems nor organized seven hundred self-controlled, largely inexperienced, women into a city-wide piece of team work which has gone on evenly and competently through zero weather and summer epidemics, in the face of misunderstanding as well as public recognition, day after day, week after week, month after month—and will go on so long as the war lasts and for a year thereafter.
>
> The answer lies in the woman who brought experience and courage and sacrifice and more besides—a genius for organization and the unmistakable flame of leadership. This is Helen R.Y. Reid,

director and convenor of the Ladies' Auxiliary and Lady of Grace of St. John of Jerusalem.[37]

After the War, in appreciation of her civic activities and especially her war work, Nellie Reid received an LL.D. from McGill—the first McGill woman graduate to be so honoured. This could be taken as a signal that an era had passed and a new one begun.

* * *

The decade of the 20's lived up to its rip-roaring reputation for some of the women of McGill—"the dancing years" one old grad called them; for others it was a time of rules and conformity. Reminiscences pour from the pen of a second generation McGill woman of the 20's. Beatrice Wyatt Johnston, B.A. '27, M.A. '29, daughter of Anna Scrimger Lyman, B.A. '99, vividly recalled the Macdonald campus as well as McGill.

Old Macdonald—I didn't go to McGill due to any burning desire for education, but simply because it was taken for granted that I would do so. . . . As I finished school at sixteen and was thoroughly non-domestic, Mother decreed that I should take a course at Macdonald in what was termed "Homemaker" (of course, we called it "Home-breaker").

The only strictly McGill women at "Mac" in my day were the few enrolled in the B.H.Sc. course, who took the last two years of their training there and were looked upon as rather exalted seniors by the rest of us. Then there was a two-year diploma, "Institution Administration" course, which qualified one to be a dietician. Below that, in larger numbers, were the humble one-year "Homemakers." We were all lumped together as "Science" to distinguish us from the far larger number of recent high school graduates taking a one-year diploma course that qualified them for some level of teaching and were called "Teachers." (When I was there, one lone man was among them.) The other male students were aiming at a regular Agricultural degree and were, of course, housed in a separate build-ing and referred to as "Aggies." There was not much mixing between the "Science" and the "Teachers" and, although the girls considerably outnumbered the men, not much dating with the "Aggies"—for no particular reason that I remember. There was, however, very definite sex discrimination in discipline—the Aggies had normal student freedom, while the women's residence was run on decidedly boarding school lines, even for the B.H.Sc. girls. Among chief complaints were the uniforms—striped green and white gingham for "Science," blue and white (which we thought a shade better) for "Teachers" and of a strictly enforced pattern about fifteen years out of date and, for "Science" anyway, *boots*. An outrage in 1922! It was remarkable how often students' boots were at the cobbler's!. . . We were not supposed to keep food in our rooms, but that was not generally enforced, and my room-mate and I always contrived to have on hand a solid stock of bread, peanut butter and strawberry jam, the latter supplied by my devoted parents. . . . All institution inmates complain of food, but, for a domestic science and agricultural college, the food *was* inferior. . . . Sundays were fearfully dull; girls were not allowed outside college boundaries, and Macdonald grounds offer little diversion. We went for walks, we tried skiing, but there are no hills, we visited classmates a bit, but. . . for the most part we argued on all sorts of subjects and, when desperate, read poetry aloud—the longer the better. We were supposed to go to church, but I don't know how much this was enforced; in the evening but not in the morning, girls were permitted to go with a man. Among the rules I have forgotten to mention the compulsory and very inferior "gym" administered by an exceedingly bored instructress, who diverted herself by organizing a small class in apparatus work, which I was happy to join. She also developed a "crush" on one of the "Administration" students, who was, I'm sure, quite unaware of it (we didn't talk about such things then). . . .

McGill Class of '27—The next year I entered McGill in the class of '27. At that time the large majority of feminine undergraduates were Arts students from Montreal and other high schools, mainly protestant. Few from the private schools entered. Engineering and Architecture were not yet open to women and, of course, many present courses were non-existent. Most classes were mixed and most were held in the shabby old Arts Building. . . . I enjoyed "Stevie" Leacock's Political Science class, but as it was the year his wife was dying tragically, he missed all too many lectures, and I found his Departmental substitutes disappointing. He was an excellent teacher—funny, yes, but not too funny and he had one teaching habit more should copy. If someone asked him a question he would reply 'That's very interesting, Mr. Smith—will you look it up and give us the answer next Thursday.'' If necessary, he hinted at where you should look, but he never forgot to ask for that answer. It was excellent training (personally, it was by that method that I discovered the, to me, unsuspected existence of the Law Library and the "Statutes of the Realm''). Prof. Leacock has been well and often described, but I don't remember finding that trick mentioned.

First year students were supposed to see appointed "advisors,'' but I don't believe most saw them once, if at all, and got little advice. My advisor was Miss Hurlbatt, the Warden of R.V.C., and she gave me one bit of sound advice, after which we discussed suitable clothes for winter horseback riding! I doubt if many people knew, or would have believed, that she actually did ride occasionally (side-saddle, of course).

It was during my days at McGill that the old Arts Building was rebuilt, to everyone's great convenience, and credit is due to the planners for retaining the original external appearance, but with the old fake wooden pillars replaced with real stone ones. We still lacked, and would so gratefully have welcomed, the later tunnel to the Redpath Library. . . . There was no discrimination at the Library but . . . in other ways, however, there *was* plenty of discrimination, but for the most part, we were R.V.C. and, like Rhett Butler, "Frankly we didn't give a damn." Women were not part of the McGill Students' Society nor members of the Mock Parliament but, if anything, we rather despised both. . . . We had our own societies . . . I remember really hot discussions over the desirability of "sororities" (later called "fraternities") for women. I was in the opposition, considering such things productive of undesirable cliques. . . . Male students had nearly escaped from compulsory athletics, but women had not. Therefore, often at great inconvenience, we had to dash down from the Arts Building, change, and perform some dreary drill in the abominable R.V.C. basement gym, obstructed by pillars and provided with most unattractive locker rooms (no showers). . . . A

Co-eds Ready for Convocation, 1922

further injustice was that men could get athletic credits if they needed them by skiing to the Lookout on Mount Royal and signing there, but this was not extended to women. Tennis was available, but no instruction was offered—I think at that period it was thought not "sporting" or even "not quite nice" to have lessons in sport.

There were no particular "college fashions" for girls at that time, and I know that I dressed carelessly and atrociously. In class, it was a fading fad to wear a gown, which was compulsory if for any reason you circulated in a gym suit (short tunic and black stockings). The "Phys. Eds.," always in uniform, had to wear gowns.

In those years, Graduation exercises took place in the incongruous surroundings of the Capitol Theatre. Our last undergraduate battle of my time was over flowers. It was the custom of girl graduates to carry large bunches of flowers. Some of us argued that it was "unacademic" with gowns, and a considerable and heated discussion raged in the M.W.S.S.. I regret to say that the flower party won. But soon (perhaps the next year) a compromise reduced the flowers to more appropriate boutonnières, and not long afterwards the flowers were altogether in the past. On the afternoon of Graduation Day there was, weather permitting, a Principal's garden party on campus, and there we were full-fledged graduates! 38

One of Bea Wyatt Johnston's classmates was Phyllis Lee Peterson who, with more than a touch of nostalgia, remembered the gaiety of student life at McGill in the 20's:

The Campus of Autumn Leaves and Flaming Youth—I close my eyes and the years drop away to the roaring twenties! I walk through the new Roddick gates and enter a campus of autumn leaves and flaming youths. A Stutz Bearcat whizzes by and I quiver with excitement as assorted pinheads emerge from racoon coats to shout raucous encouragement. Ancient jalopies crawl painfully by bearing strange legends. 'Come on Peaches, here's your can!' 'Oh, you Kid!' 'Four gals to the Gal.' 'The brazen lie,' 'No doors, no hands!'. . . The Arts Building is still the same, but Bill Gentleman is there. Kind, courtly, helpful and always a knight to damsels in distress, Bill Gentleman. . . . I rush down to Murray's for five or six cups of coffee on an original ten cent investment because women are not allowed to smoke at McGill and the management of Murray's is more understanding. . . . I eat sandwiches in the stale and odoriferous locker room of old R.V.C.. I attend afternoon classes and perhaps some form of compulsory exercise which is the only way I would take it. My exposure at that time to fencing, gymnasium and aesthetic dancing soured me on anything more strenuous than opening and shutting windows for the rest of my life. . . . The McGill Red and White

McGILL
RED & WHITE REVUE OF 1927

HIS MAJESTY'S THEATRE

MARCH - 10 - 11 - 12 - MAT - 12

Revues at Her Majesty's and the performance where bags of flour descended on three rows of audience. The catcalls and lecherous class yells of Law and Medicine. The pandemonium in the dressing rooms. . . . The football game on the campus where the quarterback split his pants and was sent back in reinforced with adhesive. The dubious contents of the water bucket in the aforesaid game. . . . The clothes we wore. Beaded evening gowns, wide belts where Nature never intended a waist, cloche hats and then Empress Eugenie (wiv fevvers!). The Med dances in the old Med Building when your partner took you out at half-time to show you the various other exhibits, also pickled in alcohol. . . . The class in Evolution and Genetics. . . . The careful mating of fruit flies for Mendelian characteristics (I believe) when everyone had test tubes full of progeny and I discovered that I had mated two males. The dancing at the Mount Royal to the music of Jack Denny. . . . My mother's discovery that the Redpath Library closed at 9 p.m. when I had been getting home regularly after midnight. Professor Willy and the chameleon he wore in Zoology lectures. . . .

The shock of Depression! Apple sellers on St. Catherine Street, suicides on St. James. Students leaving college wholesale to look for jobs that were so scarce. The bright, gaudy canvas of the campus fading into sombre grey behind us. . . . 39

* * *

In the thirties, decade of the Depression, the frivolous and the serious could still be found on campus. The *McGill Daily* continued to be interested in the ''woman question'' and mocked one aspect of changing times in terse verse:

> ''The age of chivalry is dead,''
> A very modern maiden said.
> ''No more do knights in iron dress
> Rescue poor maidens in distress!
> No more do lads on bended knee
> Say, ''Darling, will you marry me?''
> To which the girl in faint surprise
> With mounting rosy blush replies,
> ''I hardly know just what to say,
> I've never thought of you that way!''
> No, men nowadays are so elusive,
> Our answers must be most conclusive.
> If undecided, you may find
> The man is apt to change his mind. 40

Women's motives for being at college were often challenged in these years. The husband hunter was said to be ranging the campus, but Helen McMaster Paulin, R.V.C. Valedictorian '38, was more concerned with social issues and reminisced as *A Serious-Minded Person:*

What we get out of any experience is often closely related to the "set" with which we approach it. I came to McGill in the autumn of 1934 already concerned about social problems and peace. These concerns had developed through my reading of such books as *All Quiet on the Western Front* by Erich Maria Remarque and *Testament of Youth* by Vera Brittain. I saw our generation as ripe for a repetition of the horrors they reported, and I was looking for ways that repetition might be prevented. And while boarding school had insulated me from any real contact with the depression, the excellent teacher who taught history and current events had stimulated a general concern with the problems of the day.

So I reached McGill a rather serious-minded person, who identified readily with all who were concerned with changing society: the early nineteenth century poets I read for Dr. McMillan's English II, the S.C.M. students in Professor King Gordon's study group, the left-wing students who spoke of Marx and the Proletariat in Dr. Whitelaw's history classes, the graduate students in sociology who researched housing conditions in Montreal. Dr. Everett Hughes of the Sociology Department was interested in studying the processes of French-English accommodation and conflict. His eye never lost its twinkle nor his mind its questioning dry wit. Dr. Eugene Forsey belaboured the details of the B.N.A. Act, but managed to make them interesting. Student activities now encompassed a Social Problems Club, a Student Peace Movement, campaigns to Aid China, Boycott Japanese Goods, Aid Republican Spain, and Fight Duplessis' Padlock Law.

We had a song in connection with the latter:

> En bas Duplessis!
> It means Democracy,
> We'll fight till we smash
> That Padlock Law.
> Come on, let's organize
> Get all who sympathize
> Together we will smash
> His machinations!
> En bas Duplessis!
> It means democracy
> We'll fight till we smash
> That Padlock Law!

In the Christmas break of 1937, McGill students along with students from many other campuses in Canada met in Winnipeg and created a National Organization called The Canadian Student Assembly. This was outside of, and was intended to be more broadly based than, the National Conference of University Students which linked student councils across the country. Resolutions called for the creation of National Scholarships to enable more people to get to university, collective security against Hitler, and aid to Republican Spain.

Later, there was a joint delegation of students from McGill, the University of Montreal and Laval to present a Peace Petition to the Dominion Government. The wording of the petition involved a great deal of negotiation, as the sentiments of the francophone students were isolationist. Opposition to conscription was the unifying factor.

There were women who were active in all the causes I have mentioned. In the campaign to boycott Japanese goods during the Sino-Japanese war, women played the most colourful part by their refusal to wear silk stockings. This was before the era of nylon, and so those who wanted no part of trading scrap metal for silk wore lisle or woollen stockings. One of the most conscientious wearers of lisle stockings was a girl whose father made his living by importing Japanese goods!

Our particular year, R.V.C. '38, had a very strong class feeling. My McGill experience was rather schizoid because at the same time I was involved in left-wing activities on the campus, I was also involved with my year—one year as Class Secretary and another as President of the Women's Union. A number of new customs were instituted during these years. The "Junior-Freshie" system, in which a Junior had a special responsibility for introducing a Freshie to campus was one innovation. We also had a "Sadie Hawkins" dance, held at R.V.C. for a nominal charge, to which girls could invite boys. This was aimed at counteracting the then current assumptions that the boy must always ask the girl, and that student dances had to be formal and expensive.

Phyllis McKenna was President of our year and Secretary of the Women's Union. She also was a star of the McGill Women's Ski Team. It is in large part due to Phyllis that at our fortieth reunion, thirty of about seventy graduates returned for the dinner. 41

* * *

The spirited student protests of the 30's were hardly enough to ensure peace and, as the next decade began, the world was once again at war. The women of McGill participated earnestly in the required War Service Programme. Though some students were put on probation because of their inadequate war service attendance,[42] most co-operated. They listened intently as Dr. A. Vibert Douglas, B.A. '20, M.A. '21, Ph.D. '26 (McGill), quondam Lecturer in Astrophysics at her *alma mater* and later Dean of Women and Professor of Astronomy at Queen's, addressed them on the subject of:

The Challenge of War Time to University Women—The challenge to University Women to play a part in these stirring days is a very urgent challenge which no one of us has any right to ignore. To most of you there is no need to emphasize this point. You feel the challenge of the times and you hear the trumpet call to service and sacrifice. Your problem is to select the form of service for which you are most needed. You can play a worthy part in the united effort required of our country in these anxious years whether you be in uniform or out of it, so long as you carry to your tasks the enthusiasm of a burning desire to contribute the best that is in you. Skill, patience, understanding, great honesty and hard work—we must give all these, and we must think and think and keep on thinking if we are to help in the attainment of victory and in the building of a better tomorrow.

The enlisted services are calling for women with various skills and with no particular skill, but, above all, they are calling for women with qualities of leadership. There are over 22,000 women in the King's uniform today in the Canadian Navy, Army and Air Force. Some of our finest university graduates and undergraduates are giving leadership in these units. Their influence is being exerted to help keep the whole tone and standard of the women's units high and dignified. . . .

The government has laid down very explicit regulations regarding men and how far they may legitimately go with their studies. Thus far, women have been left to decide for themselves where duty lies.

Are you justified in remaining at college another year? That question you must ask yourself. No one can decide for you, though many people may advise you one way or the other. Whether you be an undergraduate or a post-graduate student you must ask yourself that question. To return and train yourself further for a specific form of national service may be the obvious path of duty and wisdom. To get right out into a job which you are now fitted to do may be the only course which in the years to come may seem to you to have been justified. There are women today who were young adults in 1914-18 but who were asleep, never realizing that they could share in the service, and, to some small extent, the sacrifice of those years. They missed an opportunity of being active participants in a great experience. Do not make the same mistake. [43]

* * *

A. Vibert Douglas, M.B.E., O.C., B.A. '20, M.A. '21, Ph.D. '26, LL.D. '60

Dr. Douglas' sincere exhortation to the women of McGill with its evocation of commitment and unquestioning patriotism, could only have been delivered in the 40's. It epitomizes the first half of that decade. In the second half, things were rather different. After the War, the proportion (though not the absolute numbers) of women at McGill declined. During the 30's, women averaged about 30% of the total student body; during the early 40's, they were about 35% of the University's population; for the first three post-war years (1945-48), the percentage of women fell to about 25%; then it began to rise slowly, regaining 30% only in 1958. The late 40's, when the proportional decline began, was the period when young women students just out of high school felt swamped by the great numbers of returning mature, male veterans. This was the era of the "New Look," with its emphasis on "femininity," the general retreat to domestication, the growth of the suburbs, the foundations of the "Baby Boom." "Rosie the Riveter," who had been a wartime heroine was fired. She was no longer a desirable social model now that, in this period of regeneration and reconstruction, society had subtly decided that, after all, women's place was in the home. Many young women who were out in the world of work were there to help meet the expenses of living while their husbands pursued their war-interrupted education. The women may have sacrificed their own education, but they frequently proudly claimed title to the degree of P.H.T. — "Putting Hubbie Through."

* * *

The late 40's were catch-up years, prelude to the next decade when the students were known, at least in retrospect, as "The Quiet Generation." Students of the 50's were characterized as people who worked and played solidly, minded their own business and, by and large, followed the rules. "Student apathy" was one of the main complaints of campus leaders. The Secretary of the Women's Union lamented in print that "women were uninterested."[44] A new column, "CO-EDiting," was written by women for the *Daily* but when it first appeared in November 1953 and called for comments, suggestion, involvement from the women of McGill, it received no immediate response from the local population, just articles from leading American "women's" magazines!

Dr. Anne Lancaster, now Professor of English at University College, University of Toronto, was a student at McGill in the late 50's. She recalls *Those Quiescent Years:*

Professor Joyce Hemlow in the Old Burney Room

I was not aware of any essential differences in the academic treatment of men and women; I found the majority of students in Arts and Science, of both sexes, to be disappointingly uninterested in intellectual matters (and the girls interested above all in getting engaged and married). I worked hard—was in large classes for the first year, smaller ones the second, smaller ones still (in part) the third and fourth; I had intended to go on eventually to a career in Journalism or the foreign service, but was encouraged by Dr. Joyce Hemlow to think about graduate work in English first—and once started on that path (at Harvard) I ended up as an English professor. I would probably never have thought about graduate school in general or about Harvard in particular if Dr. Hemlow had not cornered me one day and talked to me about both; and it is certainly true that no other professor ever mentioned the subject to me (I had only one other female professor; all the rest were male). I also ended up a specialist in the Renaissance period because I had been taught so well in that period by Dr. Hemlow (in two half-courses, one—the killer course of the 15th and 16th centuries, the other in Spenser). I was never discriminated against because of my sex (or for any other reason); I took part in a number of campus activities (Choral Society, McGill Annual, one year on the *McGill Daily,* a woman's fraternity, Red Wing Society, women's ice hockey team, etc.; I enjoyed the activities, and my courses in general, but did not on the whole enjoy McGill—I had expected to come out of high school into a charged intellectual environment, and was quickly disillusioned. I finally found that kind of environment when I went on to graduate study at Harvard.

I am still in touch with a variety of female classmates; in the late 50's and very early 60's one tended not to be simple friends with male classmates (things are much better today in university). They are doing a wide variety of things: from being wives and mothers to working as lawyers and business executives (and like me, often combining this with being wives and mothers).

I was a native Montrealer and so was not in residence at McGill; and I rather envied the residence girls in that they were involved in the university in a way in which it seemed mere commuters could never be; they were on hand for all events, all occasions. . . .

Some other good professors (especially good) that I had while at McGill: Archie Malloch, Michael Herschorn—for my compulsory first-year maths (I dropped maths as soon as I possibly could!), Alec Lucas. Hugh MacLennan was also stimulating. I also took a course in aesthetics (from the Philosophy Department) that has stood me in good stead ever since. 45

* * *

As the solid 50's slid into the rebellious 60's, there were probably few people at McGill or other institutions of higher learning who would have predicted or even believed the kinds of changes the next decade would bring. Even at the end of the 60's, R.V.C. was still sheltered from the storms that raged around many campuses. As Faith Wallis, who entered College in 1967, wrote, "Though we stood on the threshold of the great student revolution of 1968, few of us dreamed of the utter disappearance of that cozy, confining world."[46] She observed that, "There was an explicit code of regulations and practices, and an implicit canon of behaviour. These were handed down to us from above, but they were accepted by the generality of students. We made fun of, or complained about, the old-fashioned manners and anxious rules, but we lived happily with them. If one profoundly objected to any of these, one had two choices: work through the House Council to patiently negotiate changes, or move out." Her account continues:

> *Life on the Threshold:* The Warden of Royal Victoria College claimed supervision over all female students, whether living in college or no. Miss Reynolds, the Warden in my day, saw herself *in loco parentis,* and took her responsibilities to offer welcome, protection, and personal counsel to the students quite seriously. We chafed, of course, and thought her keen sense of the dangers of being a young woman living in the centre of a big city mere ludicrous timidity. . . . For Miss Reynolds, Montreal had a sort of moral geography, and R.V.C. stood on a distinct physical and spiritual frontier. "East of R.V.C." was a shady and dangerous realm. . . . The major instrument of the College's concern for our safety was the leaves system. . . .
>
> The College's official line on the leaves system was that it was intended to protect us by informing the College of our whereabouts and our intended time of return. Even those of us who accepted this rationale as sincere were irritated at the lack of trust and officious restriction that the existence of such a system seemed to imply. It was by no means lost on us that our counterparts in the men's residences had no such supervision, and the old arguments that our sex made us prey to social dangers men did not know were rapidly failing in force. We were aware as well that R.V.C.'s position as a chartered college within McGill University meant that our expulsion from residence for disobedience or any other crime was, in fact, expulsion from the university. In practice, even the worst offenders were unofficially persuaded to move out rather than be expelled. The administration made it clear, however, that this ultimate weapon was at its disposal.
>
> Another point upon which our life differed from that of male students in residence was that we were not permitted to entertain members of the opposite sex in our rooms. In the men's residence, it

was "Open House" from 4 p.m. until midnight. In my second year at R.V.C., our House Council managed to persuade the Warden to permit us to hold "Open House" one Sunday afternoon, between 2 and 5 p.m. Gentlemen were allowed in our rooms—but the door had to remain open. The logistics of supervising this modest encounter between R.V.C. students and the male sex must have utterly exhausted the staff, for the President of the House announced at the next meeting that the "Open House" had come off successfully, but that we would not be having another!

What bewildered Miss Reynolds most about us girls must have been our unconcern about being protected. Many of us felt that "danger" was largely imaginary and that we were capable of a good deal more self-protection and common sense than R.V.C. gave us credit for. Our definition of danger was so remote from Miss Reynolds' that she frequently misread our curiosity as foolhardiness —or worse. During the days immediately before the McGill Français march, she behaved as if R.V.C. were a convent besieged by bloodthirsty and rapacious Visigoths. Between grace and dinner she would announce the security precautions, describe the numbers and positions of the police in the building, and issue orders to girls whose rooms faced the street. Since we were clearly expected to spend that evening quaking beneath our beds in darkened rooms, it is little wonder that Miss Reynolds almost had a stroke when I innocently, if unadvisedly, asked permission to go up on the roof to watch the demonstration. I was refused, of course, so we crowded into the corner rooms on Sherbrooke and University where we had a good view and where the bay windows permitted the exchange of jokes and slogans with the marchers below.

Actually, there was only one man who ever frightened me when I was in R.V.C., and he was no wild-eyed radical or dissolute playboy, but a member of the staff. We called him "King Leer," and he cleaned the hall floors very late on Sunday nights, at about the time when I returned from a tryst with my future husband in Gardner Hall. As I came down the hall, King Leer would pause at his work and follow me with his eyes all the way to my room. I always locked my door on Sunday nights.

To be fair, all that care and protection we got at R.V.C. was sometimes very welcome. We had a proper infirmary with a full-time nurse and regular visits from the doctor, for instance. Moreover, Miss Reynolds' concern with our academic work was direct and sincere. She talked to every freshman resident about her programme and insisted that her schedule leave room for a few, but not too many, extracurricular activities. She very sternly talked me out of taking two new languages in my first year—an interference I resented at the time, but whose wisdom I soon acknowledged. Her accurate memory of our achievements astonished us as much as her pride in them abashed us. . . . Her awareness of us as individuals is amazing when one considers that she had about 500 girls in her immediate charge. Her little private dinners for eight or so girls may have done much to keep her *à l'heure* with our progress, but her old-fashioned devotion and sense of duty probably accomplished much, much more. . . .[47]

* * *

For a few days during the 70's, bold black graffiti on the wall of the Roscoe Wing spelled out "R.V.C.—Royal Virginity College." The institution has changed even with the "Open House" rules, but the cloistered cachet lingers. In a conversation in the casual cafeteria which replaces the formal dining room, Diana Einterz, Science '80 majoring in Math and Computer Science, acknowledged that R.V.C. does have a conservative image, but the women who stay there are there to study, not to party. For that reason, she thought some girls might find it embarrassing to acknowledge that they were R.V.C. Not all. Julie Sullivan, Arts '82 was not ashamed to confess, "I like it here; I like to be protected. This is home. It's a good place, it serves its purpose. My friends are here. I can relax and feel comfortable."

So student life goes on. . . .

Part III

THE PROFESSIONAL
FACULTIES

Chapter SEVEN

"What Are Facts Against a Theory?"

After their admission to Arts in 1884, the women of McGill gradually gained entry to all the Faculties of the University. In some cases they met with stiff resistence, in others they found warm welcomes. They were accepted without question by Science and Management, Faculties which were established as Faculties in relatively recent years when the fights to admit women as students appeared to be over. Predictably, women encountered the greatest difficulties in the Faculties representing traditional "male" professions. Time and again, the myths associated with masculinity and feminity were invoked to show how inappropriate and impossible it would be for women to become physicians, surgeons, lawyers, dentists, or engineers.

Happily, not all the men of McGill were deceived by the stereotypes nor impressed by the pompous arguments of some of the most eminent professionals. In 1889, when the *University Gazette* reported that a congress of naturalists at Cologne had discussed the question of whether or not women could be physicians, it laced its story with sarcasm.[1] This McGill publication thought the whole exercise absurd. It did not accept the argument seriously put forward at the congress that women's more delicate nature prompted them to hesitate in crises and this would cause them to lose time in any operation when only quick action could save life. The *University Gazette*, obviously approving of women in medicine, countered with the flat statement that, "We have some very successful women surgeons in America." Then it asked a nice rhetorical question that probed the problem of fixed ideas and that applied to much of the controversy concerning women in the professions. It asked rather helplessly, "What are the facts against a theory?"

With this question the *University Gazette* recognized the power of generalized prejudice to obliterate specific evidence. It illustrated the irrationality of stereotyped thinking by claiming that a congress of women might as well decide on *a priori* grounds that men were too heavy-handed, slow and clumsy to succeed in anything requiring so much dexterity and delicacy of touch as a surgical operation. For a long time, the force of this objection seemed to escape many people at McGill

279

—and elsewhere. Women seeking entry into the senior professional schools had to fight and re-fight essentially the same battles as those who had sought admission to higher education in the first place.

* * *

Medicine was the first professional Faculty of McGill University to which women aspired. However, thirty years were to pass between the time of Octavia Ritchie's daring valedictory pleas for admission and the opening of the doors of Medicine. The reasons for this delay had to do with conservatism and the traditional "Lady" concept of Woman, with a general prejudice against women in prestigious or power positions, with opposition from the medical profession, and with apparently obvious practical difficulties such as financing. None of these obstructions was unique to McGill but they seemed especially entrenched at this University. While barriers were crumbling elsewhere, they held up at McGill against the vigorous efforts of some very enterprising and determined young women and their sympathetic friends. Despite McGill's pre-eminent reputation in Medicine, it was slow to accept the innovation of the female physician and lagged behind medical institutions in the United States, Europe and even Ontario. Nowhere did women doctors have an easy time of it and, in order to see the problem of the medical education of women at McGill in perspective, it may be well to review briefly some of the developments elsewhere.

The earliest institutions regularly organized for the medical education of women were the New England Female Medical College founded in Boston in 1848, the Philadelphia Women's Medical College in 1850 and the New York Infirmary for Women and Children in 1853. Well before those mid-19th century efforts, there were women who had attempted to gain admission to the regular (male) medical schools and the history of women's medical education is a remarkable saga of individual courage. Among the most extraordinary records is that of the first medical woman in Canada, Dr. James Miranda Stuart Barry.[2] Because it was impossible for her to study Medicine as a female, she disguised herself long enough and successfully enough to graduate from the University of Edinburgh in 1812, to become a military medical officer and to be appointed in 1857 as Inspector-General of Hospitals for Upper and Lower Canada. Astoundingly, her disguise was not penetrated until after her death and then, of course, the scandal was kept as quiet as possible. And scandal it was—not only the thought of a woman masquerading as a man all those years,—it was scandalous for a "nice" young lady even to want to be a doctor. The pioneers were virtually pariahs.

Elizabeth Blackwell, M.D. 1849, was the first acknowledged woman to graduate in Medicine in North America. She had to suffer rejection by fourteen medical schools before Geneva Medical College, a small institution in upstate New York, agreed to take her. Her acceptance was actually a joke on the part of the male students who voted on the issue and the surprised faculty had to follow through.[3] Once admitted, Blackwell had to endure loneliness, ostracism and innuendo. She faced overt opposition throughout much of her career with the remarkable perseverance of all the pioneer women in this field. Sophia Jex-Blake, another woman determined to be a doctor, struggled to qualify for a medical degree at the University of Edinburgh in 1869, only to find that the University authorities then declared that they had no power to grant degrees to women. She had the unexpected fortitude to sue the University and win, but she lost on appeal. So she had to begin her studies all over again. She finally received her M.D. from Berne in 1877. Emily Stowe, first Canadian woman licensed to practise medicine, was first a teacher, then the wife of a dentist and mother of three children before she determined to study medicine. She earned her M.D. from the New York Medical College for Women in the year of Canadian Confederation, but to be licensed to practise she had to attend lectures given in Toronto by the Council of Physicians and Surgeons. With Jennie Trout, she was given permission to take the lectures provided ''they made no fuss.'' Thus they were forced to put up with innumerable petty humiliations such as booby-traps placed on their seats, so much graffiti that the walls had to be whitewashed four times in the session, and bawdy stories from some of the instructors. ''It was so unbearable on one occasion that one of the ladies went to the lecturer afterwards and asked him to desist from that sort of persecution or she would go and tell his wife exactly what he had said.''[4]

Dr. Stowe's daughter became the first woman to receive a medical degree from a Canadian institution. Augusta Stowe-Gullen's M.D. was awarded by Victoria College, Cobourg (affiliated with the Toronto Medical School) in 1883. That was one year before McGill admitted women to the Faculty of Arts and thirty-nine years before it graduated any women M.D.'s. However, the fact that women could study medicine in Ontario was to be important to a number of McGill's Donaldas. The connection with Queen's was particularly valuable.

Despite arguments that they ''could never breast the snows'' going to class, women were accepted in 1880 by the Royal Medical College (affiliated with Queen's University, Kingston). Again the pioneers did not have an easy time of it. During their second year they were subjected to such a flow of graffiti, such an antagonistic atmosphere, such objectionable leers, inflections and comments from one of the lecturers, that one of them wrote in her diary: "No one knows or can know what a furnace we are passing through these days at College. We suffer torment, we shrink inwardly, we are hurt cruelly. . . ."[5] Finally, the women protested to the Registrar. The offending lecturer counter-attacked by complaining that the presence of women forced him to "garble" his lectures. The male students supported him and threatened to migrate to Toronto. As a result, it was decided that the women would be given separate lecturers and after they had graduated, no more females would be accepted. As it happened, it was the women who left. They continued their studies at the Kingston Women's Medical College, a new institution also affiliated with Queen's. Later this college joined with a similar one associated with the University of Toronto to form the Ontario Medical College for Women. There, women were able to study in an environment free of hostility, yet upon graduation they still had to overcome the scepticism of the community at large, resistance from patients, and rejection by male colleagues.

Some of the most distinguished members of the medical profession, some of the most gracious and charming of gentlemen, were either vigorously opposed to female physicians or were coldly unencouraging. McGill's famous Sir William Osler, for example, said in his presidential address to the Canadian Medical Association in 1885: "It is useless manufacturing articles for which there is no market and in Canada the people have not yet reached the condition in which the lady doctor finds a suitable environment; in fact, Quebec and Montreal have none, and in smaller towns and villages of this country she would starve."[6] This kind of oracular opposition was discouraging for all but the most determined.

Brief and scattered though these historic notes may be, they should make it clear that in 1888 when Octavia Ritchie made her appeal to McGill for the admission of women to Medicine, female physicians might not have been generally accepted but they were certainly not unknown. A Montreal newspaper of the time wrote, "Women's medical colleges are now common, and if this part of Canada is to have one, it is natural that it should be in connection with McGill, the fame of whose medical school is known throughout the world."[7] Clearly, Ritchie was not asking for something utterly innovative or outlandish. Indeed, she was essentially seeking an opportunity for women to do good. The motivation of many of the early women doctors seems to have been missionary-related and deeply humanitarian; their concerns were partic-ularly for the health and welfare of other women and of children. To the degree that it existed, public support for the idea of women doctors also sprang from the belief that medicine would represent a proper outlet for their nurturing instincts, an extension of their traditional roles as nurses and midwives, a wider application of their meliorating influences in the home. There was also some expectation that women would help improve the profession of medicine itself. They could deal with female complaints that men could know nothing about, reassure modest female patients who were embarrassed by male physicians, and soothe sick children frightened by an aggressive male bedside manner. The would-be women doctors, accepting these responsibilities, not only sought careers for themselves but also wanted a chance to help the world.[8] They needed all their idealism to give them the persistence to stay in the fight.

Save for Principal Sir William Dawson's comment that the medical education of women was a matter of supply and demand, Octavia Ritchie's appeal produced no immediate results. It was followed in February 1889 by a letter to the Faculty of Medicine from another Donalda, Maude Elizabeth Seymour Abbott, then in her third year of Arts. This letter had been prompted by some Montreal ladies, such as "Nellie" Reid's mother and Mrs. W.H. Drummond, who held "rather advanced views." On hearing that Maude Abbott wanted to study Medicine, they offered to support her and go with her to call upon some of the leading doctors to find out their opinions. During the 19th century in Canada, the United States and elsewhere, there was a reciprocal relationship between women physicians and the women's rights movement.[9] The "strong-minded" women who stood up for women's rights recognized the need for a female presence in medicine and they gave their time, money and personal support to the cause; on the other hand, the early medical women, like Emily and Augusta Stowe, were stalwarts of the contemporary feminist movement. The encouragement of socially prominent women, members of "good" families, was a crucial antidote to the poisonous assumption that "nice" girls would not want to go into medicine. Certainly the support of some of Montreal's middle-class ladies helped spur Maude Abbott on. She requested admission to Medicine at McGill, saying that necessity compelled her to stay in Montreal and Principal Dawson's statement about supply and demand gave her hope that her *alma mater* would accept her. However the answer from the Registrar was firm and simple:

> I am sorry to inform you that the Faculty of Medicine can hold out no
> hope of being able to comply with your request.

Maude Abbott was not one to accept such a verdict meekly. She and her friends decided that if money were the problem, as it seemed to be, then the money would be raised. A number of Donaldas began canvassing the support of the McGill Governors and professors. They set up "a

Maude E. Abbott, B.A. '90, C.M., M.D. '94 (Bishop's), M.D., C.M. (*honoris causa*) '10, LL.D. '36, F.R.C.P. (C.), F.R.S.M.

cyclo-style'' in the East Wing, turning out letters to the leading women of Montreal, telling them of the growing movement for women's medical education and asking their co-operation. In March, Maude Abbott and Helen Day wrote to the Board of Governors requesting an estimate of the cost of starting medical education for women. They also wanted a commitment that if the money could be raised, it would be accepted. The Governors referred the matter to the Corporation, the Corporation referred it back to the Faculty of Medicine, the Faculty of Medicine said it would consider it only after it had been dealt with by Corporation. Even this dizzying procedure did not deter the petitioners.

Indeed, they were optimistic. The Governors and all but one of the professors appeared to be supportive. Furthermore, an influential public committee was to be formed, there was to be a large public meeting, the scheme "was to be thoroughly ventilated in the press," and according to the *University Gazette,* the movement was "a popular one supported by men of money and position." A goal of $250,000 had been set and it seemed attainable. The *University Gazette* even went so far as to state: "The medical education of women in connection with McGill University is, we believe, an accomplished fact and we have nothing but admiration for the energy and enthusiastic persistency with which the young ladies who are concerned have set about their task, and the Faculty and the University who have so liberally offered to do everything in their power for the success of the movement."[10] In the great excitement, Maude Abbott wrote to Octavia Ritchie, who was then in Kingston:

April 10, 1889

Dearest Tavie:

You will get a telegram tomorrow telling you that we need you here. It is no longer a little thing. Rosie McLea and I have just seen Cousin John [Sir John Abbott]. He says it is going to be a grand educational movement, the most important there ever has been here. He says that we must organize at once (though we have acted without a false step so far). We are to get all the people together who are interested, to meet at some person's house (like Mrs. W.H. Drummond) and then elect a committee. Then agitate, etc., etc., have a big public meeting, and have influential people like Mr. Hugh McLennan, etc. to speak at it. "Get the public at your back," he says.

We are to have a conference with the Medical Faculty before their meeting, with Mr. McLennan as spokesman, and Mrs. Drummond as leader. You *must* be home for that before Thursday.

Rosie McLea raised $6,600 yesterday, and $12,000 since Monday altogether. The success is due to her. We are going to have a conference at her house tonight. You *must* come home. It is the most cruel thing that my exams are coming on. It nearly drives me wild. The only thing I am afraid of is that I will be ill. Helen Day went out yesterday afternoon with Rosie McLea, and I made a futile attempt to study at home. I saw four doctors with her yesterday. The rest of the time she went round to rich ladies.

Cousin John says that we have acted splendidly, without doing *anything* wrong.

Dr. Howard is very ill indeed. All the rest of the Faculty excepting Drs. Mills and Cameron we have both seen. Miss McLea is going to write: she seems to be inspired. Dr. Roddick is helping us altogether, and Mr. McLennan and cousin John. Sir Billy aghast!

"Sir Billy" [Sir William Dawson] might indeed have been perturbed at these developments. He had probably not expected the demand to come so soon nor with so much public support. On the other hand, he might have known that this same kind of public interest in women's medical education had occurred in other places, for example, in Kingston and Toronto, Ontario, in 1883. In both of these cases, the public meetings succeeded in their purposes and resulted in the establishment of separate medical colleges for women.

The eagerly awaited Montreal meeting was held at the Fraser Institute Hall and resulted in the formation of the Association for the Promotion of the Professional Education of Women (A.P.P.E.W.). Supporters included some of the most prominent citizens of Montreal as well as people from the McGill community. Octavia Ritchie, who had responded to Maude Abbott's request and returned to Montreal, became the Secretary of the A.P.P.E.W. It was Ritchie who signed a formal petition drawn up by the Association to be forwarded to the McGill Corporation. This document called upon the Faculty of Medicine to approve the medical education of women in principle and to appoint a committee to discuss the practical problems with the A.P.P.E.W. It indicated that this women's education should be equal to men's in all respects, but it suggested three possible forms:

(1) Co-education throughout, under which the sexes should meet in the same classes;

(2) Separate education, under which the teaching of the sexes should be given at different hours;

(3) Mixed education, under which alternatives (1) and (2) would be combined as far as practicable.[11]

The Association favoured the third option and pledged to do all in its power to get the proposal into operation for the next academic year.

At the end of April, Helen R.Y. Reid in her valedictory address on behalf of the second graduating class of Donaldas, hoped that "if there was a desire on the part of any to enter upon such a deep study as medicine, their Alma Mater would not oblige its own offspring to seek instruction at other inferior schools." Such a sad prospect did not seem likely, that hopeful spring.

However, not everyone who had attended the meeting of the Association for the Promotion of the Professional Education of Women was favourably inclined and when the newspapers canvassed the opinion of prominent medical people, some stubborn opposition came to light. The general arguments against women in medicine were advanced once more: the undesirable hardening effect that the study of anatomy is calculated to produce upon the emotions; the impossibility for any girl or woman to pursue the thorough and prolonged course in dissecting necessary for the M.D. degree without losing the maidenly modesty and true womanliness which are her essential charms; the unsuitability of women for a public life; their health is uncertain, their powers of endurance are limited, their nerves are weak; home is their sphere; their part is that of the sympathetic companion, the careful housewife, and the tender mother. Let our women be women in the true sense of the word and not unsex themselves by quitting their own sphere for that of men.[12] There were also some specific, local variations of the arguments against female medical education: Sir William Dawson said McGill was already short of funds and so his hands were tied; Dr. J.C. Cameron wondered if the time were right and Montreal the place; Professor Fenwick threatened to resign if women were admitted to the Faculty of Medicine; Dr. F.W. Campbell of Bishop's acknowledged that women "may be useful in some departments of medicine but," he opined sarcastically, "in difficult work, in surgery, for instance, they would not have the nerve. And can you think of a patient in a critical case, waiting for half an hour while the medical lady fixes her bonnet or adjusts her bustle?"[13]

These old arguments still carried clout. The hopeful situation began to deteriorate. It became unhappily reminiscent of the 1870 "Wilkes' resolution" when support for the admission of women to Arts had seemed so strong but had somehow evaporated. At the end of July 1889, the Faculty of Medicine advised Corporation that "with reference to the petition of the Association for the Promotion of the Professional Education of Women it cannot see its way clear to undertaking their medical education in connection with the Faculty." It added that the most feasible solution would be "the establishment of an incorporated medical school for women, which when fully arranged and in successful operation might be affiliated with the University." This resolution was both disappointing and evasive. The question of principle was not really engaged, the matter of cost was avoided, and the burden of women's medical education was left to others.

The momentum was halted. The A.P.P.E.W. was helpless without the co-operation of the Faculty and it seems to have dissolved without further trace; the University had little choice but to accept the Faculty's decision and so the women of McGill who wanted to study Medicine had no option but to go elsewhere.

Octavia Ritchie had already done just that. Since it was impossible for her to become a doctor in Montreal, she had gone to Kingston in the autumn of 1888. Yet, as her participation in the A.P.P.E.W. indicated, she wanted to stay at home and would have returned to Montreal if she could. Then at the end of her second year, an astounding thing happened. She received permission to continue her training in Montreal—not at McGill, but rather at Bishop's. Since 1871, Bishop's College of Lennoxville, Quebec had had a Faculty of Medicine in Montreal. There was a good deal of tension and rivalry between the Bishop's Faculty and McGill's so that the offer to admit women was probably a political ploy as much as a gesture toward equality or the furtherance of medical education. This is all the more likely because Bishop's Dean of Medicine was none other than Dr. F.W. Campbell, he who had scorned the medical ladies and their bustles. For whatever reason, he must have had a change of heart and he is reported to have said that the movement for the medical education of women had started and could not be stopped. Furthermore, one of his colleagues, who was scornful of McGill's insistence on separate education, declared that "the difficulties which are supposed to be inseparable in mixed classes" were only "phantoms conjured in the underdeveloped minds of pessimists."

So in the fall of 1890, Octavia Ritchie transferred for her final year. She was back in Montreal, registered at Bishop's and, ironically, doing her clinical work at the Montreal General, the McGill teaching hospital. She graduated C.M., M.D. from Bishop's in 1891 and, obviously, was the first Donalda to become a doctor. After several months of postgraduate study in Glasgow, Vienna and Paris, she returned to Montreal to become a demonstrator in Anatomy at Bishop's and Assistant Gynaecologist at the Western Hospital. She married Dr. F.R. England and continued working in her private clinic. In due course, her daughter, Esther, graduated in Arts and became an instructor in English at McGill. Meanwhile, Dr. Ritchie-England had established a respected reputation for her social and political work, especially her contribution to groups such as the Red Cross, the Patriotic Fund, the Montreal Council of Women, the Montreal Suffrage Association and the Montreal Women's Liberal Club.[14] All her life she kept up the struggle for justice and equality with the energy and determination that had helped women originally gain admission to McGill.

In the meantime, her friend, Maude Abbott, had received an invitation to enroll in Medicine at Bishop's. It arrived in the summer of 1890, just after she had graduated as the valedictorian of the third class of Donaldas. Though she, too, wanted to stay at her *alma mater,* she had little choice but to accept the Bishop's offer. In an autobiographical sketch, she described her first lonely year.[15] It was "a dreary round" as she found herself "no longer within the walls of . . . beloved McGill" but among "rough students," many of whom seemed to have lower standards than those to which she was accustomed. However, she thought the Professors of Anatomy and Pathology were "great teachers and bright lights" and, besides, there was the exciting prospect the following year of clinical work at the Montreal General Hospital. Octavia Ritchie, having tested the atmosphere at the M.G.H., warned her to apply at once for her student's perpetual ticket of admission to the wards and to pay her $20 fee immediately. Maude Abbott did as she was advised. She then received a receipt but no ticket because the Hospital Board of Management, having already admitted Ritchie and having received other applications from women at Queen's, were afraid "that they had taken a step that might open the floodgates for an ill-considered innovation."[16] The ticket was withheld until, as Abbott put it, "the newspaper storm broke" and public pressure with threats to cancel subscriptions to the hospital forced the administration to relent. However, the M.G.H. Governors resolved that no more tickets would be issued to women. [17] The resolution passed by only one vote but it meant no more clinical work for women at the hospital after Abbott. Fortunately, it did not mean that Abbott's connection with McGill and its teaching hospitals was terminated.

In 1894 Maude Abbott obtained her degree in Medicine from Bishop's, winning the Senior Anatomy Prize and the Chancellor's Prize in the final examinations. Like Ritchie, she went to Europe for postgraduate work and, upon her return to Montreal in 1897, she became particularly interested in the study of pathology. A stimulus to this aspect of her career was given by Dr. Charles Martin of the McGill Faculty of Medicine when he invited her to do some work at the new Royal Victoria Hospital. As a result, she produced a statistical study on "Functional Heart Murmurs" and her paper on this subject was presented to the Medico-Chirurgical Society. It had to be read on her behalf by Dr. Francis Shepherd because she was not a member since the Society did not admit women. However, the success of her paper was instrumental in changing that restriction and she was elected the first female member. More successful research and papers followed. Maude Abbott was gradually becoming famous, especially for her work on congenital heart disease. Ultimately, she was to be considered a very highly-respected authority, one of the best known Canadian medical researchers and internationally honoured.

Dr. Abbott was also making a career at McGill. Her inconsistent *alma mater* still would not admit women to study Medicine, but it did allow her to work.[18] She was appointed Assistant Curator of the Medical Museum in 1898 and Curator in 1901; later she became Governors' Fellow in Pathology, then Lecturer in Pathology in 1910. That same year, the University conferred an unusual honour. It granted Maude Abbott, *honoris causa,* the M.D., C.M.—the degree it had not let her earn.

In another expression of confidence in her, the Faculty of Medicine sent Dr. Abbott to London, England to be in charge of a section of the 1913 Congress of the International Association of Medical Museums. This was an organization she helped to found. When a very favourable report on her display appeared in the *Times,* she sent a copy of it to Lord Strathcona who was still living in London as High Commissioner. She asked if he would support the Association which had originated through the efforts of McGill and one of his own Donaldas. She hoped for a donation of $1,000. Lord Strathcona sent her $5,000.

After Dr. Abbott had been offered at least two senior positions in the United States, McGill made her an Assistant Professor of Medical Research (1925) and Curator of the Medical History Museum (1932). She was rather bitter that she was never promoted to Associate Professor and that she was not better paid. However, she loved McGill and, apart from a two-year "on loan" appointment as Professor of Pathology and Bacteriology at the Women's Medical College of Pennsylvania, she stayed on. Maude Abbott's reputation was based on her teaching, research and writing. She used the museum as a dynamic tool for instruction in pathology so that her classes, which were voluntary in the beginning, became part of the required curriculum. She felt greatly honoured when Sir William Osler invited her to write the chapter on congenital heart disease for his multi-volume text, *A System of Medicine* (1907-10); she was enormously proud when he praised her monograph as "quite the best ever written on the subject." This woman of boundless energy also wrote a biography of Florence Nightingale, histories of nursing, of McGill's Medical Faculty, of Medicine in Quebec, and even of McGill (*McGill's Heroic Past*). She published numerous research studies and edited the *Bulletin* of the International Association of Medical Museums for more than thirty years. Her output was astounding.

Upon Dr. Abbott's retirement in 1936, McGill took another unusual step by awarding her yet another honorary degree—she is the only person to be doubly honoured in this way. On the second occasion, McGill awarded her the LL.D. in recognition of her pioneering work in medical museums, her valuable contribution to the history of medicine and, in the words of the citation, "above all as a stimulating teacher, an indefatigable investigator and a champion of higher education for women."

Maude Abbott died in September, 1940, but she had lived to see the day when McGill admitted women to its Faculty of Medicine. The example of her own brilliance should have helped the cause for, "it is doubtful if any one person did more in their generation, to make the name of McGill known throughout the medical world than did Maude Elizabeth Seymour Abbott."[19] But the Faculty of Medicine was hard to convince—for "what were facts against a theory?"—and progress was extremely slow.

* * *

After the flurry of activity around 1889, the issue of the acceptance of females for medical training was quiescent. Scattered individual applications appeared from time to time. Miss Hurlbatt, who as Warden of R.V.C. took part in the administration of admissions, kept a record which showed a total of fifteen inquiries between 1907 and 1917 from women wanting to study Medicine. In 1913 there seemed to be a possibility that a motion would be introduced favouring their acceptance but the Registrar advised Miss Hurlbatt that the Faculty had decided to take no action until the Montreal General and the Royal Victoria Hospitals had decided what stand they would take.[20] Hurlbatt prompted him into contacting the hospitals. Both quibbled—R.V.H. responded in April, 1914 that even though a petition had also been received from the Montreal Local Council of Women, the Governors would do nothing since the matter had not been brought up officially; M.G.H. replied two months later by asking if females were admitted to the clinics, would the University "be prepared and willing to give them the necessary education in connection therewith?" Here was another of those frustrating vicious circles that generated no action except that in July, 1914 the Registrar sent a questionnaire to a number of medical schools in Canada and the United States. He asked whether women were admitted, if so, on what terms, and what kind of records they had compiled. Seven responded positively—including the University of Toronto which said, "The women are treated exactly the same as the men, there is no special or extra provision made for them in connection with classes, lectures or clinics"; Harvard and Columbia said they did not accept women; Tulane said it admitted them to post-graduate work but had not yet produced any women M.D.'s of its own. But none of this information produced changes at McGill.

The continuing delay and undisguised reluctance to accept women was not the only aspect of the Faculty of Medicine's policies which, to modern eyes, seems discriminatory. In July 1916, following a resolution from the Montreal Maternity Hospital concerning "the undesirability of the presence of negro students in the hospital," the Faculty agreed to advise future black applicants "that owing to the difficulty in providing material in the hospitals for the study of Obstetrics and Gynaecology, it would be impossible to graduate them."[21] The problem apparently arose from a reluctance to having black men attend white women. The black students, who mainly came from the West Indies, protested so that the Faculty later suggested that they be admitted if their courses in Obstetrics were taken elsewhere than Montreal.[22] There was no attempt to hide the discriminating treatment. The value system of the period called for little institutional embarrassment about either overt racism or sexism.

Meanwhile, World War I had begun and the need for medical personnel became greater as the apparently interminable conflict went on. In other places this need was being met by the training of women, but still McGill took no positive action. Miss Hurlbatt was therefore still forced to refer her next inquiry to Toronto, while several of McGill's female graduates had already gone elsewhere to study Medicine. The war intensified the desire of a number of women to become doctors. Ultimately, eight of the twenty-six female Arts graduates of 1915 received their M.D.'s but, for the time being, like a besieged battalion, the Faculty of Medicine held out. It even braved the assaults of the "monstrous regiment" of the Montreal Local Council for Women. In February 1917, the Council sent the following resolution:

> In view of the increased demand for the services of duly qualified women physicians and surgeons at home and at the front, and the acknowledged necessity for women to become self-supporting during and after the war, be it resolved that The Montreal Local Council of Women do petition the authorities of McGill University to open all classes to women, and to grant them degrees in every faculty, upon the same terms as men.[23]

This caused very little excitement when it was considered at the March meeting of Faculty and "after a short discussion it was decided to allow this communication to lie on the table."[24]

However, the Faculty did not get away without another skirmish. The Council of Women had sent the same resolution to the Board of Governors, which passed it along to the Faculty of Medicine, which was thus constrained to consider it again in April. After this second encounter, the Faculty resolved that it "could not at the present moment under existing war conditions see its way to take action on the lines of the recommendation sent forward."[25] It has often been assumed that wartime pressures undermined the Faculty's corporate resistance to the admission of women, but it seems clear from these decisions that that was not the case. Quite the contrary. The Faculty actually used the war as an excuse for keeping women out rather than a reason for letting them in.

However, the idea of women doctors had infiltrated through the ranks and there were some individuals with the courage to make sorties on their own. In 1916, Dr. Robert Ruttan, Professor of Chemistry in the Faculty of Medicine, had coached Anne Purdy (B.A. '15) and Doris Murray (B.A. '15) before they went off to Johns Hopkins to study for their M.D.'s. The following spring four more Arts graduates of 1915—Mary Childs, Lilian Irwin, Eleanor Percival and Jessie Boyd—sought his help. He arranged some work for them, suggested readings, encouraged Jessie Boyd and Mary Childs to take a summer course in Chemistry at Harvard, and made tentative plans for special courses at McGill in the fall.

During the summer of 1917, Mary Childs and Lilian Irwin wrote formally to the Registrar of the Faculty applying for permission to take the regular first-year medical course in 1917-18 so that they could proceed to the second year of study at Toronto in 1918-19. Their letter was apparently important for it prompted further discussion and a decision from the Faculty of Medicine "that with the exception of the course in Anatomy, these women be admitted to all classes of the first year and that, provided proper arrangements could later be made for dissection, Anatomy be included in their course."[26] All four of Dr. Ruttan's protégées were thus able to take the regular first-year medical course in the fall of 1917. However, since the question of the admission of women had still not been decided in principle (and even though they paid full fees), they were considered "partials" and were initially registered in the B.Sc. programme. The Faculty wanted to make sure that no false hopes would be raised. It affirmed in October that in taking the action it had, it was "not thereby settling the question of admission

Eleanor Percival, B.A. '15, M.D., C.M. '22, F.R.C.P. (C.)

of women to the study of medicine but only offering such facilities as the University can provide to enable these individual women, without prejudice to the general question, to get their training in certain subjects of the first year curriculum.'' Again in December, after the Department of Anatomy reported that the first year course might be given ''without inconvenience,'' the Faculty insisted that ''this recommendation in favour of certain special students does not constitute any precedent that would bind the Faculty either to the general principle of the admission of women to the regular curriculum for degrees in Medicine or the method and policy of joint or separate education that may be adopted when that general principle comes up for settlement.''[27]

At last, the time for the discussion of the general principle seemed to be approaching. After some months, the Faculty of Medicine decided to hold a special meeting for this purpose at 8:30 p.m. on April 16, 1918.[28] As a result of that meeting, it was moved by Dr. A.D. Blackader, seconded by Dr. R.F. Ruttan and approved by Faculty that:

> ... women be admitted to the study of medicine provided they have taken a degree in Arts from a recognized University, or that they take the double course of B.A. and M.D. or M.Sc. and M.D. at McGill University and thus give evidence that they are sufficiently mature and otherwise qualified to take up the study of the professional branches.[29]

The ever-interested Montreal press hailed this development as ''a distinct advance.'' It noted, ''McGill University has always been regarded as a very conservative institution and thus the reform just inaugurated is the more impressive.''[30] What was particularly interesting, if not impressive, about the new regulation was that the admission requirement for women was higher than it was for men—a fact which the University *Annual Report* for 1918 specifically noted. The reason was said to be an attempt to ensure the maturity of the female applicants to Medicine. Dr. Ruttan had apparently not been entirely confident that Miss Hurlbatt would accept that argument and so he wrote to her on April 18, hoping for her approval.[31] She gave it. In a response addressed to Principal Peterson, the Warden of R.V.C. went on record as agreeing that women's entry qualifications should be higher than men's because this would help enhance their status as medical students throughout their careers at McGill.[32] So Miss Hurlbatt, though a champion of the women of McGill, was also a victim of the minority-group mentality that demands that they excel just to be equal.

Even after this decision, the University was not entirely sure. In May 1918, Principal Peterson sought the advice of Dr. Abraham

Jessie Boyd Scriver, B.A. '15, M.D., C.M. '22, D.Sc. '79, F.R.C.P. (C.)

Flexner, the American medical educator whose studies of medical schools and universities were justly famous. Peterson asked Flexner cautiously, "Is it your experience that it [the admission of women] can safely be done conditionally?"[33] Peterson also indicated in his convoluted prose that he personally approved of extended preliminary courses for "any young girl, who at the age of say sixteen or seventeen may take it into her head that she is going forward to professional studies before she is sufficiently mature."

Regardless of lingering doubts, women were now formally recognized in the Faculty of Medicine and the four pioneers (Mary Childs, Lilian Irwin, Eleanor Percival and Jessie Boyd) could continue their studies unimpeded. They were joined in their second year by Winifred Blampin (B.A. '17) and all five graduated in Medicine from McGill in 1922. It was a cause for great celebration. Among the festivities was a tea given at "The Ritz" in honour of the new doctors by Maude Abbott. Jessie Boyd Scriver, M.D., C.M. '22, noted wryly:

> Dr. Abbott was very proud that her beloved *alma mater* was at last bestowing the medical degree on five women undergraduates and I do not believe that she ever exhibited one of her rare congenital cardiac specimens with more enthusiasm than she displayed over her human exhibit that day.[34]

* * *

In 1922, the year that McGill graduated its first female M.D.'s, three other Canadian universities produced twenty-one more—Toronto graduated fourteen, Dalhousie five, and Manitoba two—for a total of twenty-six. The McGill five all had successful careers, both as students and as practitioners. During their training they did not appear to have had the searing experiences that many other women medical pioneers endured and because there were five of them, all old friends, they were spared the loneliness suffered by Elizabeth Blackwell, Maude Abbott and others. Dr. Jessie Boyd Scriver believed that the McGill students accepted them with "amused tolerance" and the staff exercised "a benign surveillance."[35] However, she and Dr. Mary Childs remembered the Saturday afternoon when a deputation from the Undergraduate Medical Society called upon them while they were studying together at her home and asked them to withdraw from Medicine. The women were astounded at such unwarranted officiousness and simply refused. They had no intention of withdrawing. That appears to have been the end of the matter, though Dr. Childs recalled another occasion when bloody spleens were thrown at them during anatomy class. At McGill male hostility did not seem to have reached the extreme unpleasantness shown in the early years in Ontario and elsewhere. The explanation, in Dr. Jessie's words, was because "we walked very warily . . . there was nothing militant or aggressive about us."[36] Over the years, this polite, cautious but determined approach seems to have typified many of the women at McGill. In a variety of Faculties and in diverse situations, we have walked very warily.

Another potential problem for those early "lady doctors" was the embarrassment of co-educational classes. One of Octavia Ritchie's friends from Queen's described how awkward it could be, even with friendly professors:

> We like K.N. very much but he is most beastly indecent in his operations.
> He invited us girls to go to the hospital one Saturday and see him operate on a lacerated cervix and promised us we should have it to ourselves, but when we went we found the boys all there. We were taken so much by surprise that we could not take time for consideration and so all waltzed in and took our seats on a bench by the operating table. The boys sat behind us.
> Presently the woman was brought in. She was attired in a night-dress and a pair of dreadful ragged stockings. He gathered the nighty up around her waist and proceeded with the operation. It was perfectly terrific. I was never so ashamed in my life.[37]

This extraordinary little anecdote not only says something about the surgical practice and hygiene of the period, it also illuminates the socio-personal dilemma of the female pioneers. It helps later observers to realize that efforts to provide some separate education may be interpreted as well-intentioned attempts to save the sensibilities of the young women who had probably grown up in protected environments. Though they were of a later generation, Drs. Scriver and Childs reported that they appreciated being taken aside at times—in urology, for example—and given semi-private instruction. Certain other concessions were made to decorum at McGill. The women students were always ushered into the dissecting room through the demonstrator's door, thus avoiding the anteroom-cum-lockerroom used by the male students. The women tried to be unobtrusive in this and other matters, but their gender inevitably made them conspicuous in class and their ability made them outstanding in the examination results.

They did very well throughout the course. Toward the end, Mary Childs and Jessie Boyd were elected to an honour society and, at graduation, Jessie Boyd won the Wood Gold Medal for the best examination in the Clinical Branches and placed second overall in a class of 126. Winifred Blampin won the first Senior Medical Society Prize. The Montreal press duly noted, "The worst fears of McGill medical students have been fulfilled. The first women graduates in the Faculty of Medicine have carried off two of the five prizes offered in the final year. . . . One of the chief grievances of the male students was that the women worked harder than they did, and pessimists predicted they would carry off the honours."[38] Amid all the congratulations, the new doctors received desirable hospital appointments, then went on to specialize and to practise. Almost sixty years later, two were still professionally active—Dr. Winifred Blampin in California and Dr. Jessie Boyd Scriver in Montreal. The latter was distinguished for her seminal research into sickle cell aenemia, the teaching and practice of paediatrics, and her contribution to prophylactic child care. Her history of the Montreal Children's Hospital[39] was published in 1979, the year in which she received the D.Sc. *honoris causa* from McGill.

*   *   *

People who opposed women's entry to higher education, the professions or any other arena seemed to fear that, if once the doors were opened, floods of women would come pouring in and those who were there before would be quickly drowned. This has rarely been the case. It did not occur in relation to women's medical education generally (with the possible exception of the Soviet Union) and it certainly did not happen in McGill's Faculty of Medicine. In the dialectic of social change, there is often an initial burst of pent-up interest which is usually followed by a decline and then a levelling out. Abraham Flexner noted a significant falling off in the numbers of women doctors graduating in the U.S. between 1904 and 1909;[40] at McGill, the most serious decline took place in the early 30's and was probably related to the Great Depression.

The initial intake of women (1917) represented slightly less than one percent of the total enrolment in the McGill Faculty of Medicine. Since then, there have always been some women in the Faculty and, while there were occasional spurts in the percentages, the proportion of females could hardly be considered overwhelming. Only in the 60's and 70's, following the changes in social values, the student revolution, and the Women's Movement, did the proportion of females in the McGill Faculty of Medicine exceed 10%. In the 60 years since their formal admission (1918), the decade-by-decade pattern of development has been as follows:

ENROLMENT OF WOMEN Faculty of Medicine, 1918-1978							
Year	1918	1928	1938	1948	1958	1968	1978
#	8	16	29	32	34	64	188
%	1.7	3.4	6.3	7.0	8.1	13.4	30.0

In 1977/78, the McGill female enrolment in Medicine was very close to the Canadian national average of 31.6%, a record high.

However, there was a time when quotas were imposed on the number of women admitted to the Faculty of Medicine. The number of applicants has usually exceeded the places available and during the 40's, limits were set on the intake of foreigners, coloured students, Jews and women in order to maintain "a reasonable balance."[41] Female applicants from the West Indies were in double jeopardy because, while males were told that admission to the pre-medical course in Arts did not guarantee admission to Medicine, the females received a letter from the Registrar warning them, ". . . Moreover, the number of women admitted into the faculty is always limited."[42] These restrictions no longer obtain, except that the Quebec Government watches closely the number of non-Quebeckers admitted to all medical schools in the Province. In the late 60's, the Canadian Royal Commission on the Status of Women received a brief from the Federation of Medical Women of Canada claiming that there were three universities in this country that demanded a ten percent higher academic admission requirement for female applicants. Principal Rocke Robertson was able to assure the Commission that McGill was not one of the three discriminating universities, that its policy was not to differentiate on the basis of ethnic origin or sex and that, according to recent statistics, the ratio of acceptances to applications was slightly higher for women than for men. Nevertheless, occasional complaints are still heard that women applicants are discouraged—by family, friends or university officials—on the grounds that the arduous course is not worth the effort and if the women are going to get married, they should relinquish their places to the men who really need them and intend to stay in the profession. During the 70's, regardless of this echo of ancient prejudice, the number of women in Medicine at McGill increased markedly—as the above table shows. From the records of past performances, the prospects are good that a high percentage will both complete the course and practise their profession.

From the beginning, the academic record of women medical

students at McGill has been creditable and they have won their share of scholarships, prizes and medals. The prestigious Wood Gold Medal, (the highest award) was won by a member of the first women's class and, at one point, by women two years in a row (Dr. Virginia C. Hall in 1941 and Dr. Dorothy Bentley in 1942); the Holmes Gold Medal was first won by a woman (Dr. Katherine Dawson Ketchum) in 1931. There appears to be little if any feeling of discrimination among the women medical students and it is generally held that merit not gender determines grades and awards. Curiously, a possible exception to the rule is the Maude Abbott Scholarship, which was established in 1938 by an anonymous donor as tribute to Dr. Abbott's distinguished career in order to encourage scholarship and aid students of ability. While both men and women were eligible, preference was to be given to women. In the first year, two awards were made, one to a man the other to a woman but after that, the great majority of awards went to women.

Since the days when Maude Abbott worked on the periphery of the Faculty of Medicine, the number of women on staff has increased appreciably, but not at the rate of the female students. Women could be found in all ranks from full Professor to lab technician but, at the end of the 70's, they still constituted less than ten percent of the academic staff. Like women in other Faculties and other Universities, they tended to cluster in the lower end of the appointment scale. Nonetheless, there have been many whose notable contributions to teaching and research have added to McGill's reputation in Medicine.

For example, Dr. Eleanor M.H. Venning, who first registered in Arts at McGill in 1916, went on to graduate work, earning her M.Sc. in Organic Chemistry in 1921 and her Ph.D. in Experimental Medicine some years later. In the 40's as a Research Fellow in the Department of Experimental Medicine, she "made several important contributions to the advance of knowledge, notably the discovery of pregnanediol glucuronide, the development of a method for its estimation and the demonstration that it is an excretion product of progesterone. This contribution opened up an entirely new field and has led to the publication of many papers in various laboratories all over the world".[43] Promotion through the academic ranks followed and numerous honours. In 1953, Dr. Venning was one of forty-nine distinguished scientists elected to the New York Academy of Science; two years later, she was one of three people from McGill named as Fellows of the Royal Society of Canada; in 1960 she became Professor of Experimental Medicine and in 1962, was awarded the Koch Gold Medal, the highest recognition of the U.S. Endocrine Society. One of her colleagues in the investigation of hormone function and steroids was Eleanor McGarry, M.D., C.M. '47.

Dr. McGarry also earned many distinctions including National Research Council Fellowships, the Fellowship of the Royal College of Physicians (Canada) and a full Professorship. Dr. Marion K. Birmingham of the Departments of Biochemistry and Psychiatry was another who achieved international recognition for her work in steroid biochemistry and Dr. Margaret Becklake-McGregor, Professor of Epidemiology and Health, was elected President of the Canadian Thoracic Society in 1978—an acknowledgment of her contribution to lung research.

In 1979, Dr. Brenda Milner, Professor of Psychology in the Department of Neurology and Neurosurgery, was one of the two new Fellows elected to the prestigious Royal Society of London. Dr. Milner became a teacher and researcher at McGill in 1952, the year in which she earned her Ph.D. in physiological psychology. She worked on the behavioural effects of brain lesions in humans, obtained an Sc. D. from Cambridge in 1972 and was elected a Fellow of the Royal Society of Canada four years later. Dr. Milner has a world-wide reputation for her work on the memory functions of the temporal lobes of the brain and it was this research which was cited by the Royal Society of London in announcing her election.[44] McGill women who have distinguished themselves in other medical fields include Dr. Paula H. Schopflocher in dermatology and Dr. Edith M. Mankiewicz in microbiology, especially research in respiratory diseases.

Significant contributions to the field of Paediatrics have come from a number of the women of McGill, including Dr. Mary Ellen Avery who, from 1969 to 1974 was Head of the Department and Physician-in-Chief at the Montreal Children's Hospital; Dr. Eleanor Mackenzie Harpur, M.D., C.M. '39 of the Department of Biochemistry and President of Camp Carowanis, the Quebec Diabetic Children's Camp; and Dr. Mimi Belmonte, B.Sc. '48, M.D., C.M. '52 who established a clinic for diabetic children at the Montreal Children's Hospital and was one of the founders of Camp Carowanis. While paediatrics has been considered a "woman's specialization," Dr. Belmonte did not hold that women make better paediatricians than men but considered that if women are better with children, "it is a personality trait, not a sexual one."[45]

The invisible barriers that excluded women from McGill for so long have fallen to the extent that there are many highly successful female students, teachers and practitioners who believe that no discrimination exists in the Faculty of Medicine or the profession at large. While a study published in 1976, "L'activité professionnelle des femmes médecins au Québec," indicated that differences remained in the career patterns and salaries of male and female doctors in Quebec, it considered the discriminatory differences could be changed. Reconciliation of professional and family obligations was possible and "the young female physician will be able to overcome the serious preconceptions which cause the medical profession to be considered, especially outside of large cities, exclusively as a male profession."[46] The study concluded that, given some reorganization within the profession, "there is no reason to limit the number of female students in medical schools." This is a lesson McGill seems to have learned.

*   *   *

In contrast to the long and public struggle for women's admission to the Faculty of Medicine, entry to the Faculty of Law was easy. The first serious applicant was accepted. But that was deceptively simple for there were enormous difficulties in store for the women who wanted to practise their profession once they had earned their Law degrees. They found themselves deeply involved in the fundamental arguments about Woman and her place in Society with opponents who represented the legal, political and ecclesiastical Establishment of Quebec. That was a very tough fight.

Annie MacDonald Langstaff, B.C.L. '14

The admission of a woman to the study of Law was sufficiently strange and interesting as to warrant a comment from the journalists. The *Montreal Star* of October 6, 1911 duly noted that "the singular distinction of being the first woman law student in this province falls to Mrs. A. Langstaff, originally of Prescott, Ontario, but latterly of Montreal." Annie Macdonald Langstaff was of Scottish parentage, she grew up in Ontario where she passed the senior matriculation examination at the early age of sixteen, came to Montreal in 1906 and began working in the legal firm of Jacobs, Hall and Garneau. She apparently liked the work so, in 1911 with the approval and help of her employers, she applied to the Faculty of Law for admission. The Dean's response, directed to Mr. S.W. Jacobs, K.C., the senior partner in the firm, was courteous and encouraging:

September 28, 1911

Dear Mr. Jacobs:
. . . There can be no objection to Mrs. Langstaff following lectures in law. We have, so far, had no woman candidate for the degree in law, and, until I have an opportunity of consulting my colleagues, I cannot say whether any objections would be made to this, but in any case it would be better for her to begin the lectures. They commence on Monday, October, 2nd, at four o'clock.

Yours very truly,

F.P. Walton

So, with little ado, Annie Langstaff began her course work. She was a good student, graduating in 1914 with first rank honours, an overall standing of fourth place, and a prize of $25.[47] When she began, she knew that women were not permitted to practise Law in the Province of Quebec but these barriers had fallen in the other parts of Canada. Ontario, Nova Scotia and New Brunswick all accepted women, so did France and Belgium. Mrs. Langstaff told the interviewer from the *Star* when she was admitted to Law that she was "sanguine" about having the disqualifications removed and that she hoped in a few years to be a member of the Bar of her Province. However, her application to take the Preliminary Bar Examination was refused solely on the grounds that she was a woman—one legal opinion held that pretty women lawyers might improperly sway juries. Langstaff thereupon petitioned the Superior Court for a writ of mandamus to summon the Quebec Bar to show cause why it should not be ordered to grant the application. The Bar argued that it had absolute discretion as to whom it should admit to the examination, that no right of mandamus existed against the respondents and that the petitioner had not obtained marital authority to take the action. Mr. Sam Jacobs, Langstaff's employer who argued the case on her behalf, asked if the Bar had such discretion that they could refuse a candidate because he or she had red hair! Jacobs contended that there was nothing in the Bar Act to deny women the right to practise, that the words "he," "his" and "him" were generic and not intended to exclude half the population. But the Court asked Mrs. Langstaff if she had consulted her husband when she made up her mind to enter the legal profession. The petitioner replied: "No, I did not. I did not know his address."[48] In a Province that did not grant divorce and that "protected" its women to such an extent that husbands' authorizations in writing were required before they could contract any obligations, the fact that Annie Langstaff was separated from her husband set the seal on her lost cause. In dismissing her petition, with costs, Mr. Justice St. Pierre held that:

> . . . to admit a woman, and more particularly a married woman, as a barrister—that is to say as a person who pleads cases at the Bar before judges and juries in open court and in the presence of the

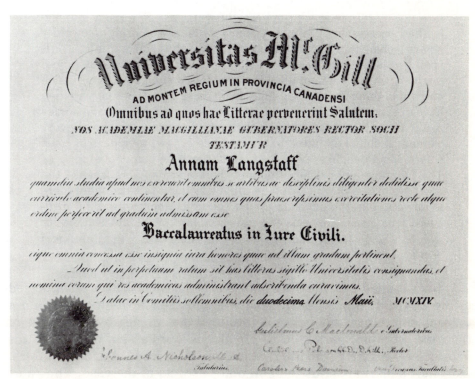

The First Professional Degree Awarded to a Woman by McGill, 1914

public, would be nothing short of a direct infringement of public order and a manifest violation of the law of good morals and public decency.[49]

Within two weeks, a mass meeting was called by the Montreal Local Council of Women to protest the decision. Many of the notable women of McGill were there: including Miss Hurlbatt, Idola Saint-Jean and Botany Professor Carrie Derick, who declared that "the professions should be open to men and women alike. It is just a question of the survival of the fittest." Mrs. Robert Reid angrily called the ruling "narrow minded" and Helen Reid, by then a prominent social worker, pointed out, "We have police matrons to look after women when they come to court, which proves that it is considered necessary that women should be dealt with as much as possible in such places. Sex should be no bar, but rather in a woman's favour."[50] Langstaff found many champions and she found herself something of a celebrity. The Equal Suffrage League offered its sympathy and Mrs. Langstaff was invited as guest of honour at the Insurance Underwriters' Dinner. She took this occasion to speak about women's role in society. She said:

It is not merely men who oppose the entrance of women into the learned professions. There are many women who are so cowardly and so lacking in true womanhood as to take the same attitude. . . . It is all very well to say that women's sole sphere should be the home, but it shows most lamentable blindness to economic conditions which one would think were potent. The plain fact . . . is that many women have to earn their living outside the home, if they are to have homes at all. There is no intention, on the part of anyone, to compel every woman, if she is admitted to the practice of law, to appear in court where some people appear to think she will be contaminated. . . . This is an age of specialization and there are many branches of the legal profession in which women could specialize to advantage; there is for example, the Juvenile Court, the adjustment of marital diffi-culties, and certain aspects of commercial law . . . all that is asked for women who desire to practise is that they shall prove [their abilities] as men have to prove them. . . .[51]

Not satisfied with the Superior Court's decision, Langstaff appealed to the Court of King's Bench. Again she lost. In November 1915, in a three to one ruling, the judges determined that women by the nature of their sex were not permitted to practise the profession of Law in this Province. During the hearing, attention was focused more on Mrs. Langstaff's marital status than on other aspects of the case. The court seemed concerned that she had not had her husband's permission to

WOULD SEE WOMAN LAWYERS IN QUEBEC

Prominent Montrealers Interested in Establishing Feminine Legal Status in the Province.

(Left) Mrs. Ethel Hurlbatt, formerly warden of the Royal Victoria College.

(Right) Mrs. Idola St. Jean, president of the Canadian Alliance for Women's Votes.

(Centre) Mrs. Pierre F. Casgrain, president of the Provincial Suffrage Committee.

(Below) Mrs. Leslie G. Bell, lawyer, and wife of Leslie G. Bell, M.P.

Mrs. A. Macdonald Langstaff, law graduate of McGill University.

Dr. Grace Ritchie England, past president of the Women's Central Liberal Club.

Fighters for Women's Legal Rights

study Law, did not live with him, had not seen him since 1906 and that she alone was responsible for the upbringing of her daughter, then aged eight. In denying her appeal, the justices claimed to be protecting her and "her more exquisite sex" from the contempt of her spouse and the "revilement" of the male sex generally. Annie Langstaff was sent home.

The judgment met with consternation and derision in liberal quarters. It prompted a great outpouring in the press, producing much ironic commentary on Mrs. Langstaff's "exquisite" nature and a listing of her disabilities:

"1. She is a woman.
2. She is under marital authority.
3. She is of irreproachable character.
4. She possesses remarkable talents."

This same writer also composed "The Lay of Mrs. Langstaff," to be sung to the tune of "The Wearing of the Green," and which went, in part:

> You are so highly exquisite
> you are not fit to jaw
> With individuals like me
> in vulgar things like law.
> So hie you to your wash-tub—
> go grasp your broom and pail!
> For broom and pail are feminine,
> but law's distinctly male.[52]

No further appeal was made to the courts but, almost immediately, Sam Jacobs tried to have changed the discriminatory legislation that had made the ruling against women possible. One of his colleagues, Lucien Cannon, drafted a bill for submission to the Quebec Legislative Assembly. McGill Principal Peterson was supportive of this attempt, saying he would personally "be very glad if the Government could see its way to promote legislation" to have Mrs. Langstaff admitted to the practice of Law, but he did not believe there was "any great movement behind her as regards this Province."[53] When the Cannon Bill came before the Legislation Committee, a delegation of three Montrealers spoke in its favour—Mr. Jacobs, Mme. Gérin-Lajoie and McGill graduate, Dr. Grace Ritchie-England. The latter recounted the fight of women to practise Medicine in the Province and asked, "Have men the moral right to refuse progress to a woman who qualifies herself in an honourable calling?"[54] Sir Lomer Gouin who chaired the Committee, apparently thought they did. He cut short the debate, called for the question and the bill was killed in committee by a vote of seven to two.

Once more, Annie Langstaff had lost but her spirit was not beaten. Though she was barred from the courts, she continued to work with her old firm—and in her spare time, she learned to fly. She worked on until 1965 when she retired at the grand age of seventy-eight. Ten years later she died, having had an interesting and busy life but without having those "sanguine hopes" of 1911 ever fulfilled.

* * *

The Langstaff experience might well have deterred other female aspirants to Law, for the prospects of a fully satisfying career seemed bleak. Indeed, in the next years there were very few women, but those who graduated were people of special ability and determination. Florence Seymour Bell, B.C.L. '20—the second woman student in the Faculty—partly solved the credentials problem in 1921 by taking the examinations and gaining admission to the Nova Scotia Bar. By virtue of reciprocity arrangements, she was then able to practise her profession in Quebec, but still could not plead a case in court. She therefore specialized in corporation law, pursuing an active career with a legal firm as well as participating in public affairs. In 1930, she was elected Vice-President for Canada of the National Association of Women Lawyers; four years later she was urged by the McGill Alumnae and the Montreal Local Council of Women to stand for a vacancy on the all-male Protestant School Board of Greater Montreal; shortly after the outbreak of World War II, she was made Senior Commandant of the Women's Volunteer Reserve Corps—but she was still ineligible for the Quebec Bar. Margaret Sim, LL.B. '23, gained admission to the New Brunswick Bar in 1926, but decided to work in Ontario rather than Quebec. Dorothy Heneker, LL.B. '24, B.C.L. '25, graduated with first class honours then worked in her father's firm. She became President of the Canadian Business and Professional Women's Clubs and, in 1931, Secretary of the International Federation of that organization with her headquarters in Geneva. She travelled, lectured, wrote a great deal about the condition of women in the world. In the early 30's, she spoke out against the Nazi regime for its attempts to put women back into the kitchen and she denounced Depression-inspired efforts to drive married women out of employment. Another of these dynamic women lawyers was Elizabeth Monk.

Elizabeth Monk, B.A. '19, graduated with first-class honours in Modern Languages and the Governor-General's Gold Medal for the highest standing in her subject. She won other distinctions, including a scholarship to Radcliffe where she obtained her M.A. and another

Elizabeth Monk, Q.C., B.A. '19, B.C.L. '23, LL.D. '75

enabling her to study abroad for one year. This award was offered by Margaret Murray's I.O.D.E. Elizabeth Monk chose to spend her year at Somerville College, Oxford. On her return to Montreal, she enrolled in Law, was extremely successful in her course work and received her B.C.L. in 1923. As a way to circumvent the Quebec restrictions, she, too, took the Nova Scotia examinations and was admitted to the Bar of that Province in 1934. In honour of this achievement, the Women's League of Voters, in which she was an active participant in the fight for the franchise, gave her a reception. Mme Thérèse Casgrain used the occasion to protest a recent speech by Montreal Mayor Camelien Houde blatantly advocating curtailment of women's right to work. Professor Carrie Derick also recalled the earlier meetings in support of Annie Langstaff's right to take the Bar examinations in Quebec.

In the intervening twenty years, little had changed for the women of this Province. However, civic pressure was gradually beginning to tell. In 1940, Adelard Godbout became Premier of Quebec. Despite formidable opposition from the Church and other conservative groups thundering against what they deemed the damnation of society and the desecration of the sanctity of womanhood, Godbout honoured his pre-election promise to give women the vote in provincial elections. That same year, Elizabeth Monk became the first woman to be admitted to the Montreal City Council. She was named by the Montreal Citizen's Committee as one of its three designated representatives. In the words of a contemporary report, this "capped with success a determined drive by a number of leading women's organizations to have their sex accorded a voice in the future government of this city."[55]

The following year, Premier Godbout again showed courage by withstanding the violent opposition of some members of the legal profession and the vilification of Maurice Duplessis when he amended the Bar Act so that women could be eligible for admission. By then, a total of four women had graduated in Law from the Université de Montréal and nineteen from McGill. Since the regulations for admission had changed over the years and now required a B.A. as well as a Law degree, not all these graduates were qualified to apply to take the Bar examinations. Annie Langstaff and Florence Seymour Bell were among those adversely affected in this way. Neither wished at that stage of their careers to return to college for a B.A. degree. Thus, Annie Langstaff was never admitted to the Bar but, in 1957, after a special oral examination, Mrs. Bell finally became a full member of the Quebec Bar.

However, as soon as it was possible for her to do so, Elizabeth Monk applied to take the regular examinations. As a result, she and Madame Suzanne Raymond-Filion became the first women admitted to the Bar of

Quebec. They were sworn in at a ceremony at the Université de Mont-réal in January, 1942. That summer, two more women (Constance Garner Short B.C.L. '36 and Marcelle Hemmond) were admitted. All four attended the opening of the Superior Court session in the fall. Chief Justice Greenshields noted the historic occasion, graciously wishing the newcomers success. Even so, he was unable to escape the stereotype in thought and language. He greeted them as "members of the gentler sex" and hoped that "their presence will soften and even sweeten the atmosphere of the courts." These kindly-meant but irrelevant expecta-tions did not deter the new barristers from acting as professionals rather than females. Certainly, Elizabeth Monk continued her distinguished career, becoming a Queen's Counsel in 1955 and practising law until her retirement in 1979. She and the other pioneers in the McGill Faculty of Law made a significant contribution to the status of women and the social fabric of Quebec. McGill awarded her the LL.D in 1975.

* * *

Until very recently, the study of Law did not seem to exert the same attraction for the women of McGill as the study of Medicine. No doubt the professional difficulties contributed to this for, even once they were eligible to plead cases before the courts, women still did not find it easy to get their first jobs or to launch their careers. Over the years, the female enrolment in the Faculty of Law was both small and fluctuating. When the barriers to the Bar fell in 1941, there was no great female influx; until 1947, there was always less than a total of ten women in the entire Faculty; some years there were none at all—for example, there was a six-year gap between Langstaff and the next women (Florence Bell and Adela Currie). By the late 60's the numbers gained strength and then, in each year of the 70's, the enrolment of women increased both absolutely and proportionally. At the end of the decade, there were well over a hundred women Law students at McGill constituting more than a third of the total Faculty enrolment. The following summary reveals the basic pattern.

ENROLMENT OF WOMEN Faculty of Law, 1918-1978							
Year	1918	1928	1938	1948	1958	1968	1978
#	6	2	2	11	18	25	117
%	11.5	2.4	3.4	5.0	7.4	9.3	34.2

Hidden amid the statistics are a number of notable individuals who have continued the work of the pioneers in the women's rights movement. Among these is Claire Kirkland Casgrain, B.A. '47, B.C.L. '50, the first woman elected to the Quebec National Assembly. Mme Casgrain practised Law for nine years and raised three children before standing for election in a Provincial riding made vacant by the death of her father. She easily won that 1961 by-election, was re-elected three years later, becoming Minister of Transport and Communication in Jean Lesage's Liberal Cabinet, and in the next government (1970) she was appointed Minister of Tourism, Fish and Game. Casgrain apparently did not face as much direct discrimination in her legal profession as in her parliamentary work. One of her "colleagues," Noel Tremblay, seemed particularly hostile to her presence, frequently insulting her under parliamentary privilege and making snide allusions to her menstrual cycle and provocative suggestions about the causes of her alleged short-temper. As Casgrain became more fully aware of the problems that women face, she pledged to work toward improving their lot. She was instrumental in the passage of a bill in 1964 guaranteeing the rights of married women to administer their own property and another in 1970 delineating the pecuniary relationship between husband and wife. These were radical reforms and Claire Kirkland Casgrain considered it a personal responsibility "to interpret these laws and their significance to the women of Quebec."[56]

Among the other notables is Ruth Hill, B.A. '42, B.C.L. '45, who had an outstanding career at McGill. She was President of R.V.C. '43, the first woman to be elected to the executive of the McGill Debating Union, President of the Women's Union, winner of a special prize for highest standing in first year Law and she graduated as a Gold Medalist and Winner of a Provincial scholarship. Other prominent Law graduates include Rosa Gualtieri, B.A. '48, B.C.L. '51, who was instrumental in the founding in 1952 of the Women's Law Association; Adela Hawthorne Pattison, M.A. (Glasgow) '23, who returned to academic study after thirty years and earned her Law degree at McGill in 1960; Kathryn Mason, B.A. '51, B.C.L. '54, who was appointed Queen's Counsel in 1976; Lillian Reinblatt, B.C.L. '61, who has practised Law and been a concerned participant in the Women's Movement. In the 70's, the women students in the Faculty of Law developed an active group called "Women in Law." This organization is a forum for the discussion of legislation—established and proposed—that affects women. It is also an agency for the airing of issues and grievances at McGill and the wider community. It has organized public meetings like equal pay legislation, the rights of Indian women, and human rights in Quebec. The status of women in the Faculty of Law and in the profession is markedly more secure than in the days of Annie Langstaff, but residual prejudice remains so that they, like Justice, must be eternally vigilant.

* * *

Women pioneers in traditional male professions have encountered the full force of sex role stereotyping, even when they have not been met with overt discrimination. Certain occupations have been deemed absolutely "unnatural" for women because they involved the performance of rough, tough work which called for physical bulk and brute strength. As members of "the gentle sex" women were simply not equipped for "men's work." Two quite different professional areas that have held out as male preserves are Dentistry and Engineering. Relatively few women have braved them, whether or not the physical requirements were real or imaginary and whether or not individual women could meet the demands.

The first woman to enter the Faculty of Dentistry at McGill possibly had little difficulty with the image of strength. In 1922, at the end of her second year in Arts, Florence A. Johnston applied to and was accepted by the Faculty of Dentistry. This caused the Montreal *Star* to headline, "Dentistry Will Soon Really Be Painless: Woman Now Invading McGill Molar Field"[57] and to observe that for a woman student to be "desirous of being initiated into the strenuous art of extracting aching molars and tantalizing canines is a novelty." The newspaper also noted that "she looks the part." Others who knew Florence Johnston concurred. One report, which may be slightly exaggerated, has it that she stood six feet tall and weighed over 200 pounds.[58] The *Star* described her as "above the usual height, of fine physique" and apparently "competent to deal with refractory teeth." Whatever her physical attributes, the Faculty accepted her with good grace, her academic record was good and she graduated B.A. '24, D.D.S. '26.

Dr. Johnston practised as a children's dentist in Montreal for several years and in a report to the Alumnae Society, she unhesitatingly recommended her profession "to any girl who aspires to earn her living in a way not only satisfying to herself but beneficial to humanity." Despite this endorsement of her calling, Dr. Johnston withdrew from Dentistry for unknown reasons and then began a successful career in real estate. Upon her retirement, she went to live in Victoria, B.C., where she died in 1970 in her 68th year. Though Florence Johnston had not been particularly active in McGill affairs while she was on campus and had not maintained close contact after graduation, she left her entire estate of $100,000 to the University. The Board of Governors assigned her bequest to dental research so that Dr. Johnston not only has the

Florence Johnston, B.A. '24, D.D.S. '26

316

distinction of being McGill's first woman dentist, she is one of its on-
going benefactors.

Johnston had broken the ice but very few women followed her
example; indeed, there was not another female student in the Faculty of
Dentistry until 1930. Throughout the 30's, 40's and half of the 50's, the
total female enrolment in the Faculty in any one year did not exceed two.
As with Medicine and Law, there was an increase in the 60's and 70's
but the numbers remained small and the proportion of women did not
take the same dramatic spurt in Dentistry as in the other two Faculties.
At the end of the 70's, approximately 10% of the graduating classes
were women. The following table shows the enrolment pattern over half
a century:

ENROLMENT OF WOMEN Faculty of Dentistry, 1928-78						
Year	1928	1938	1948	1958	1968	1978
#	0	1	1	6	8	19
%	0	1.7	0.7	4.2	5.4	11.4

These figures were more or less consistent with Canadian averages.
Women just do not seem to have been interested in the study of dentistry and there has been relatively little agitation for them to be drawn
into the profession. In March 1978, a survey of the McGill Faculty of
Dentistry was conducted by Norma Blomme, a Faculty of Education
student, to try to explore the reasons for the low female participation
rate. Questionnaires were distributed to 200 students and faculty
members; 61 replies were received. The results, which made no claim to
be conclusive, showed that the female respondents cited "tradition" as
by far the most important deterrent, with "sex discrimination" as a
secondary factor; the male respondents also ranked "tradition" as the
most important influence followed, in descending order, by "lack of
interest," "poor recruitment," "sex discrimination," and "inferior
abilities."

This last factor was assuredly belied by one of McGill's notable
students in Dentistry, Roberta P. Dundass Berster. She won a gold
medal for three consecutive years and graduated in 1947 at the head of
her class of twenty-five—all men except herself. She won the Montreal
Dental Club prize which was "awarded to the student in the final year
who stands first in the science and practice of Dentistry . . . the standing
determined not only by the written and practical examinations but by the

general work of the student during the year." The new dentist then interned at the Guggenheim Foundation in New York, later earned an M.Sc. in Pedodontics at the University of Michigan, and returned to practise dentistry with her two brothers in the Montreal area. In 1952, Dr. Dundass Berster became the first woman on the professional staff of the McGill Faculty of Dentistry. She was appointed a part-time demonstrator in Pedodontia and later a Lecturer. When she first graduated, Dr. Dundass Berster was asked whether women have enough strength in their wrists to extract teeth. She dismissed this stereotyped inquiry with "It's not at all a question of brute strength. Extractions, when performed are a matter of technique."[59]

* * *

The need for technique rather than brute force is probably just as great for engineers as it is for dentists and Engineering is another of the fields where, until recently, women professionals have remained rarities. Given our traditional social structures and value system, this has not been hard to explain. The total engineering environment has been alien to the received idea of Woman. Engineering has been public, out-of-doors, frequently concerned with massive construction projects, often associated with military ventures and its practitioners have been viewed as important, strong, powerful. All this has been the antithesis of the typical female—private, indoors, domestic, personal, small, weak. While the nature of both Engineering and of sex stereotypes is in the process of change, women who wish to enter this profession in the 1980's might still encounter a reaction met by their grandmothers who wanted to become doctors: "This is no work for a nice young woman; we have no place for you." Not surprisingly, this was precisely the attitude encountered by the first female applicants to Engineering and Architecture.

At McGill, Engineering was originally taught in the Faculty of Arts (1858-79) and then in the Faculty of Applied Science. Thus, an application received in 1909 from a woman wishing to study Architecture was referred to the Faculty of Applied Science. This body, after due deliberation, decided that it would "not be advisable" to admit women at present.[60] Four years later, the general principle was raised again when Corporation referred the following resolution to the Faculty:

May 5, 1913

MONTREAL WOMEN'S CLUB

RESOLVED,—

The Montreal Women's Club of 303 members desires to record its conviction that the time has now fully arrived, when opportunities for the highest intellectual development must be as open to women, as they are to men—and therefore calls upon the Principal and Corporation of McGill University to raise its standard to that of the seats of learning in other lands, and to that of its Sister universities in Western Canada, by throwing open all its Faculties to Women, as they are to men students, laying special stress upon the Course in Architecture, which in particular appeals to women.[61]

Again, the Faculty of Applied Science responded with a statement that "in view of the very insufficient accommodation for our present classes, they cannot recommend the admission of women to the Faculty at the present time."[62] After that decision, Principal Peterson was able to inform an American correspondent that "the only difficulty here . . . arises from our scanty accommodation," adding as if this were immutable, "Architecture is at present housed in the Applied Science Building whereas our women students use only the Faculty of Arts and the Royal Victoria College."[63]

Another individual application raised the issue once more in 1918. In that year, an application was received from Julia Dallaire, a school teacher from Moose Creek, Ontario, who wrote to explain that she had taken lessons from "a noted architect" in Moose Creek and requested to know "if it is possible to study landscape gardening, perspective, inside decoration and work in white and ink in the University. Also if it is necessary to pass examinations." She must have found the Registrar's reply quite encouraging because he noted that, although no women had yet been admitted to the course in Architecture, it was possible that "under the changed conditions consequent upon the war," an exception might be made for her. Juliana Dallaire did not have the Junior Matriculation with a pass in Senior Mathematics, the minimum entrance requirements, but she applied anyway. She was advised that her case would receive sympathetic consideration if she could meet the matriculation standard. However, in October, the Faculty was told that Miss Dallaire "did not present herself for the examinations and as there were no other women applicants, there was no need for the time being of considering the question of admitting women to the Faculty."[64]

Despite the hopeful signs in the Dallaire case, other occasional applications in the next decade made no headway—for example, a Miss Pritchard who inquired in 1920 about Chemical Engineering was advised to take the Chemistry Course leading to the B.Sc. In 1929, the Montreal

Women's Club again intervened, this time specifically on behalf of two young women who wanted to become architects. As a result of the Club's second request to Corporation, the Principal (Sir Arthur Currie) asked the Faculty of Applied Science for a report on its attitude toward the admission of women. Professor Traquaire of Architecture summarized the reasons why it was "impracticable to admit women" to his School:

1. Women are not admitted to the Faculty of Applied Science and the School of Architecture is an integral part of that Faculty.

2. There are no provisions in the Engineering Building for the accommodation of women students, and it would be an expensive matter to provide these.

3. At present the School of Architecture has a registration of forty, and there is no accommodation available for additional students.

4. Much architectural draughting is done at night, the main drawingroom being open until ten o'clock. The responsibility for the maintenance of discipline in the evening is assumed by the students themselves. If women students were admitted, it would be necessary to provide staff supervision during these evening drawing periods, and such supervision would require additional members of staff and put the School to extra expense for which it has no funds.[65]

The lack of toilet facilities was delicately disguised as the second reason. It caused an historian of the Faculty of Engineering to wonder mockingly "whether or not this problem in elementary plumbing was really insoluble by the combined intellectual effort of the entire Faculty," [66] but it, together with the awful thought of late evening co-education plus the threat of extra costs, carried the day. Thus, the Faculty voted that it did "not consider it possible to admit women to the School in Architecture." There the matter rested until 1937. Then began one of the most systematic examinations of the issue of the admission of women undertaken at McGill in the 20th century. It was reminiscent of the days of Dawson.

The campaign seems to have begun in March, 1937 with an anonymous letter to the Montreal *Star*. This communication noted how women had been turned away from Architecture for years on the grounds that "the accommodation was taxed to the utmost" but argued that, since enrolment was currently reported down from thirty-seven to twenty-seven, there must be more space and wondered "if McGill's ban against women has been removed."[67] The cry was taken up by the Alumnae Society with a letter to the Secretary of Senate (formerly Corporation) requesting that women be admitted to the School of Architecture. This matter was then referred to the Faculty of Engineering (formerly Applied Science) and a committee was struck under the chairmanship of Dean W. Brown.[68]

The committee had difficulties. Some members approved in principle the opening of the course to women, others opposed it firmly; some accepted co-education in Architecture, others thought it was "a bad thing to be recommended only on grounds of economy." And there were other complications to be dealt with such as female capabilities, additional costs, and professional acceptance of women. In order to test the experience elsewhere, letters were sent to ten universities in Canada and the United States. The replies revealed some variety of approach and a good deal of prejudice against women as architects: Harvard, Yale and Princeton accepted no women; Columbia and Pennsylvania admitted women up to ten percent of the total enrolment in Architecture; Manitoba said "women students have no trouble with the professional course and often do very well in engineering subjects"; Toronto reported that there had been seven women graduates to date but they all had difficulty getting their first job and that only one was currently practising. In summarizing, a committee member concluded that "there exists a very strong prejudice against independent women practitioners. Very few clients or corporations will employ women and give them their confidence. . . . For most people, architecture is still a man's job."[69] The responding universities found no intellectual handicap in the women students but several stressed their "physical handicap." The professor from Harvard (where women were not admitted) wrote knowledgeably about the "tremendous physical strain which in itself imposes an almost inaccessible barrier." He said, "it is quite usual for women students to be unable to carry on the work of the school in satisfactory manner, for no other reason than that they cannot physically stand long hours of draughting" (though they were standing for very long hours in the cotton mills and factories not far from Cambridge).

After weighing the evidence, the McGill committee could not reach a unanimous decision. The majority was in favour of admitting women, but the matter was referred to the Faculty for full discussion in December, 1937 when the following points were reviewed and decisions finally reached:

1. *The general principle.* There was no reason, "apart from physiological limitations, why women should not be trained as architects." In general the training of men and women should be

conducted separately, but in a small school like McGill's that would not be feasible.

2. *The question of employment.* It was recognized that there was a consensus of opinion against women working as principals, but prejudice against them as assistants was by no means general. "Women are conscientious office workers, as well fitted for draughting that involves detail." They might have difficulty fulfilling the practical experience requirement during their undergraduate training, but the university could not be responsible if its women graduates failed to obtain employment. There was no legal discrimination against women architects in Quebec.

3. *The number of women students.* The proportion of women students in Architecture in Great Britain was 12%, in the Dominions 9%, in the United States 4%. Apart from two schools in Aberdeen, McGill was the only fully recognized British school of Architecture that did not admit women.

4. *Economic considerations.* Admission would involve structural changes in the Engineering Building to provide lockers, a lavatory and a rest-room.

5. *Discipline.* "Women, if admitted to a small school such as ours, must be admitted on complete equality with men, sharing the same draughting-room and not segregated in any way. Only so can they receive full instruction."

6. *Expediency.* "As almost all schools of architecture do, in fact, admit women, it may be harmful to McGill University that she should be held up as the only, or almost the only, exception."

The Faculty of Engineering therefore resolved to approve the principle of admitting women to the School of Architecture on the same basis as men. In February 1938, Senate accepted this recommendation and forwarded it to the Board of Governors for consideration of its financial implications. As on other occasions, financial problems somehow solved themselves once the basic decision was taken and the will was there. Thus, after almost thirty years of individual and group effort and for a variety of idealistic and expedient reasons, the doors were opening to one of the last major areas of segregation at McGill.

In 1939, two young Montrealers, Arlene Scott and Catherine M. Chard, became the first women to enroll in the School of Architecture. They were the thin end of the wedge, leading the way and easily justifying the efforts made to have them admitted. At the end of her fourth year, Catherine Chard Wisnicki won the Anglin-Norcross Corp. Prize in Architectural Engineering and she had the distinction in 1943 of being the first woman to graduate from McGill in Architecture. Arlene Scott Holland, B. Arch. '44, had a fine academic career with prizes at the end of her second and third years and the Miss I. McLellan Special Prize for the highest standing in fifth year, as well as the Louis Robertson Prize for her design for a tuberculosis sanitorium. She admitted, "It was hard going at first. The boys gave me a terrific ragging for the first couple of weeks but when they found I could take it, they left me alone. The first year is definitely the stiffest and if one survives it, the rest is easy."[70]

Those who followed found the foundations well laid. Marilyn Robertson Lemieux, B. Arch. '48, for example, did not feel that she had to break entirely new ground when she decided to switch from Arts to Architecture. Though people still told her father he was wasting his money because she would only get married, her parents and professors were consistently supportive. She remembered:

"My father thought it was a great idea; he had graduated in Engineering from McGill some years earlier. My friends were also enthusiastic for me. I went to see John Bland who was Director of the School of Architecture at the time. He suggested that I stay in Arts that year and take a few courses with the architects to find out what Architecture was all about and to make sure that was what I wanted to do. It was excellent advice."[71]

After graduation, Marilyn Lemieux did not believe that she was greatly discriminated against in the job market. She said that, "People who do their jobs well can trust me to do mine well likewise." However she noted that "Men who are themselves incompetent are insufferable," and once she was told by a potential employer that she should stay home because, "There is plenty of architecture around the house."

Among the many women graduates who assuredly planned to ignore that kind of comment was Danielle Fontaine, B.Arch. '81, a specialist in industrial architecture. In her final year she became the second woman of McGill to win a prestigious Rhodes Scholarship. At Oxford she would study politics and economics as they applied to industry in the hope of returning to Canada with new interdisciplinary expertise and help make a marked difference to the industrial scene in this country.

* * *

Meanwhile, the Faculty of Engineering had received an application from a woman who wanted to enroll in Engineering rather than Achitecture. In the summer of 1942, Mary Blair Jackson wrote to the Faculty but

Mary Jackson Fowler, B.Eng. '46

the Acting Dean, while personally sympathetic, replied that "the admission of women to this Faculty is the affair of the members of Faculty," and there would not be a meeting until September. He therefore advised her, for safety's sake, to apply to Toronto as well.[72] However, this back-up was not needed. At a special meeting in September, 1942 the Faculty of Engineering voted unanimously in admit Miss Jackson.[73]

She clearly recalled that testing period of her life:

The summer of 1942 was spent writing letters, being interviewed, etc. and finally being told that I could not be accepted until a Faculty meeting had been held. This meeting would not be held until the last afternoon of the last day of general registration, so to avoid having to pay a late registration fee, it was suggested that I register in a Science course (e.g. Honours Math) and then I could transfer if I were accepted into Engineering. At about five o'clock on the afternoon before classes were to start, the Dean phoned me and said I had been accepted, told me he would personally inform Mr. Matthews, the Registrar and that I should go to the Registrar's office in the morning and transfer my registration. At that time Mr. Matthew's assistant was a middle-aged lady who was a McGill institution with a reputation among undergraduates as a bit of a dragon (probably undeserved). When I went up to the counter on that (for me) historic day and announced, shakily, that I'd come to register in Engineering, she said very firmly, "But you won't be allowed my dear." Thirty-seven years later, I still don't know how I kept from bursting into tears!! It got straightened out of course—but to add insult to injury, I was late for my first class.

The men in my class fell into predictable groups; some (not many) were actively hostile, some became very good friends and the rest ignored me. Somewhat naively, I suppose, I was surprised at the hostile reaction of many women undergraduates, most of whom did not know me. Similarly, I was shocked to find that a young man of whom I was fond and who said he loved me, was not at all pleased. I gathered that these reactions were based on my alleged "exhibitionism," as though I were going through all this simply to draw attention to myself—unbelievable!!

Faculty members reacted similarly to classmates; some (again not more than one or two) resented me, some pretended I wasn't there, most were actively helpful and encouraging, especially one or two who had daughters who also wanted to be engineers.[74]

The *McGill Daily* made much of the "advent of the first female of the species in the last stronghold of manhood" and reported a variety of reactions from the other Engineering students ranging from a stunned silence to "A female engineer, there's no such animal" to "Hey, they can't do that to us'' to ''Well, she probably won't get past her first year'' to ''It's a miracle.''[75] An editorial recognized the difficult position in which the new lone student would find herelf, noting that ''during the whole of the year all eyes, both those who supported her and those who fought her, will be upon her. . . . If she fails, it may mean that the doors of the Faculty will be closed for another decade to those women who, if few in number, may be very worthy. . . . If she succeeds . . . she might be considered one of the pioneer women of McGill and of engineering in Canada.''[76] When the *Daily* interviewed Mary Jackson and asked why she had chosen McGill, she indicated that she was ''intrigued by the prospect of striking a blow for feminine freedom as well as getting on with her career'' and when they asked her how she felt about being the only woman in a multitude of men, she simply stated that ''her reflexes were perfectly normal.''[77] Mary Jackson Fowler, B. Eng. '46, withstood all the pressures and became the first female Mechanical Engineer to be graduated from McGill.

Because women were thought to have a special flair for detailed work and a particular interest in things domestic, it was expected that the School of Architecture would attract greater numbers of women than the other Engineering Departments—Chemical, Civil, Electrical, Mechanical, Mining and Metalurgical. This did not quite prove to be the case—though the proportion of women in Architecture has been consistently higher, the numbers have not always been greater than those in Engineering as a whole. Both areas have shown some fluctuation over the years and, like Law and Medicine, strong growth in the late 70's. The following table shows the pattern over four decades.

ENROLMENT OF WOMEN Architecture and Engineering, 1939-1978															
	1939			1948			1958			1968			1978		
	Arch	Eng	Tot	Arch	Eng	Tot	Arch	Eng	Tot	Arch	Eng	Tot	Arch	Eng	Tot
#	2	0	2	6	3	9	10	13	23	21	29	50	49	110	159
%	8	0	.4	5.6	.2	.6	7.9	.9	1.4	10.4	2.3	3.4	30.1	8.4	10.8

If Architecture did not always attract more women than Engineering as a whole, it remained more popular than some of the specialized areas. Thus, it was not until spring convocation of 1978 that the first two female graduates in Mining Engineering appeared. Both were outstanding— Camille Ann Dow won the British Association Medal for achieving Great Distinction in Mining Engineering while Justyna Kuryllowicz was awarded the Charles Michael Morssen Medal which is given for high academic standing and exceptional promise in any of the Engineering Departments.

Other women in both Architecture and Engineering have compiled very creditable records, they have frequently been counted among the award winners, and they have had effective careers. Blanche Lemco Van Ginkel, B. Arch. '45, won the Lieut. Governor's Bronze Medal as well as the McLennan Prize for highest standing in each of her last two years. She later worked in Town Planning in Windsor and Regina, accepted an appointment at the University of Pennsylvania, won a Grand Prix at the International Federation of Housing and Town Planning Congress in Vienna in 1956, and became Director of the School of Architecture at the University of Toronto. Hanka H. Rosten Renehan, B. Arch., '48, won the Lieut. Governor's Silver Medal for the highest standing in the graduating year, the Louis Robertson Prize for design and the Hugh McLennan Travelling Scholarship. Henrietta L. Brants, B.Eng. '66, graduated second in her year with first class honours then received a National Research Council Fellowship to undertake her M.Eng.. A number of others have also gone on to graduate work, including McConnell Fellowship winner, Caroline S. Holland, B.Eng. (El.) '68 and M.Eng. '72, who earned a Law degree (B.C.L.) in 1976; Carol Darabaner Burnham, B.Eng. (Chem.) '61 who went on to her Ph.D. in 1967; and Captain Esther Louise Chevalier, B.Eng. '73, who became the first Canadian woman and the youngest person to graduate from the U.S. Air Force Jet Test Flying School and reportedly the only woman aerospace engineer in the Canadian defence system.

In the light of all these recent achievements, it seems ironic that a few weeks after the 1938 vote to accept women into the Faculty, the Engineering Undergraduates' Society (E.U.S.) won a debate against R.V.C. on the old motion that "A Woman's Place is in the Home." This traditional view of Woman was widely supported and McGill's women engineers often had to demonstrate that they could cope in an environment that was alien. However, by the 60's, there were reports that the Faculty was not just tolerating women but was actively seeking to recruit them.[78] Dean D.L. Mordell noted in the *Daily's* high school supplement that Engineering presented "an exciting challenge to the girl who is good at math and physics" and he said on several occasions that there were opportunities for women in this field. Also, the chances of a woman student's being treated "like one of the boys" increased as the number of women grew and the social reform ideas of recent decades gained currency. This view was supported to some extent by a survey of Canadian Engineering Faculties undertaken in the mid-70's, which suggested that while there were virtually no female professors, Engineering was no longer a shop closed against women students.[79]

However, the ''macho'' image of the ''typical'' engineer was carefully kept alive and continued to be reflected in *The Plumber's Pot*, the E.U.S. newspaper notorious for its sexist and scatological content. Silly where not prurient, sophomoric where not obscene, *The Plumber's Pot* has been obsessed with genitalia, faeces and the female body. The E.U.S. *Handbook*, an otherwise useful compendium of information about the Faculty of Engineering, usually managed to intrude irrelevant titillating material. Unlike the graffiti and innuendo aimed at the early female physicians on other campuses, the McGill Engineering publications did not seem to be specific attacks on the particular students in the Faculty. They were more generic in their vulgarity and hostility. Generally condoned with a smile (and a wink), they epitomize a ''boys will be boys'' mentality that is almost guaranteed to demand tolerance.[80] Yet over the years, *The Plumber's Pot* and the *Handbook* have been condemned by both the men and women of McGill. In 1960, Dean Mordell wrote to the President of the E.U.S. that, on various occasions, he had had to criticize *The Plumber's Pot* for its obscenity and pornography and that his predecessor, Dean Jamieson, had had the same problem; [81] correspondents to the *Daily* from time to time protest the offensiveness of the material and the ''schmucks'' who treat ''women like hunks of meat to be displayed naked in newspapers;''[82] in 1977, the Senate Committee on Women formally objected to the gratuitous sexism of the *Handbook;* and in 1978, a Foundation complained to the Chancellor about the lewdness of the *Pot*.[83] It might be noted, not as an extenuating circumstance but as an indicator of the depth of the problem, that it is by no means unique to McGill. Indeed, the publications of engineering students everywhere seem to share the same misogynist characteristics and they resiliently shake off all criticisms.[84]

The sexism in these student productions is not only at variance with espoused University policy and out of line with contemporary enlightened thought, it also presents a particularly vicious form of harassment for the women in the Faculty. These women know they are working in ''a man's world'' and they, too, walk very warily. They do not want to seem prim, prissy or puritanical and make a regular fuss about sexism. However, the desire simply to be considered as equal professionals turns into the dilemma of accepting a norm that essentially demeans their sex; the wish to show good sportsmanship or a sense of humour turns into a requirement to suffer insult. As long as they see their half of the population blatantly treated as sex objects, they will have difficulty in being taken seriously as engineers. No matter how brilliant their academic records, they will be in danger of graduating into a kind of professional "ladies auxiliary" as the makers of coffee and the secretaries of committees.

At McGill, as elsewhere, Engineering has remained a male dominated profession. One prominent engineer sees this in terms of social class and believes that this will always be the case "until upper class aversion to engineering is overcome or until lower-class women get out of the kitchen. . . . For, in a man-made world, how can women achieve the equality they seek?"[85] But getting women of any social class into Engineering is just part of the problem.

Equality will remain elusive if, in practice, women have difficulty in obtaining appropriate jobs and if they find that the stereotypes cannot even be used to help them. For example, it has been argued that women architects might not be employed in domestic design because they could have had comparatively little experience with running a home and would not necessarily produce a better kitchen than a male architect would! However, a survey of students in the McGill School of Architecture during the 1977-78 academic year suggested that Architecture may no longer be universally considered a male stereotyped profession—53% of the women surveyed and 47% of the men did not perceive Architecture in that light.[86] How much this result is a reflection of youthful idealism and confidence and how much a real attitude change is an open question. It may be worth noting that Labour Canada Statistics for the 1970's continue to show significant differences in the salaries of males and females in Architecture and Engineering, suggesting that the professions and the public still have not fully accepted women in these fields.[87] At McGill, it is obvious from the increasing numbers that "lady plumbers" are no longer rarities, it is clear that they have proved that they can do the work, it is apparent that the Faculty has recognised their worth with prizes and awards but, as long as the *Plumber's Pot* mentality remains, the women in the Faculty of Engineering and in the University as a whole cannot be satisifed that discrimination has disappeared from the campus. Sexist "theory" must give way before the facts of women's abilities and achievements if the hard-won decisions "to admit women on equal terms with men" are to be truly ratified.

* * *

The record of women's entry into the male academic domains would not be complete without some consideration of the field of Theology, one of the oldest and most venerable of the traditional professions. Rather surprisingly, there has been relatively little hassle with regard to women's studying Theology at McGill, despite the fact that the male prerogative in this area has been defended by religious sanctions of the most absolute character. Quite categorically, the maleness of the priesthood was deemed divinely ordained.

The comparatively uncontentious entry of women into the study of Theology at McGill is in large part due to the history of the discipline in the University. In the 1860's and 70's, four of the major Protestant denominations established theological colleges around the campus and these were affiliated with McGill. Their students, who were all male, took their Arts courses at the University and their theological and professional courses in the Colleges. In 1912, these four Colleges entered into a co-operative arrangement whereby a Joint Board of Affiliated Colleges administered the academic theological course while each College continued its own vocational training and recommended its own students to its own ecclesiastical authority for ordination. The Colleges began to admit women to some courses as partial students, in preparation for "church work" of auxiliary nature. In 1918, in recognition of "the splendid part that women are taking in social service, and in supplying the western fields in wartime with religious ministrations,"[88] the Joint Board resolved to adopt a more generous policy. It was prepared to accept women for registration as fulltime, regular students and as candidates for the B.D. degree. It noted that the question of ordination was one for the individual Churches to decide.

The Congregational Church opened its ministry to women before 1925 when it entered into a union with the Methodist and Presbyterian Churches to form the United Church of Canada. The United Church decided, somewhat unenthusiastically, to honour the Congregational innovation and to continue to recognise those women already in the ministry. In 1936, the General Council voted with rather more conviction to accept further women candidates for ordination. However, the continuing Presbyterian Church (formed by those who had chosen to stay outside the Union) and the Anglicans maintained the ministry as a male reserve. The number of women regularly enrolled in Theology under the Joint Board remained small, only one or two a year. It is possible that they intended to teach or simply to acquire culture rather than to enter the ordained ministry.

The subsequent story evolved differently in the separate denominational bodies and it is more the concern of their particular histories than of the history of women at McGill. But the kind of conflict that arose is well illustrated by the experience of Margaret Millen Butler. She was accepted by the United Church as a candidate for ordination and registered as a regular student in the theological courses of the Joint Board. In 1946 she graduated B.D. with the prize for highest standing in the final year, the William Brown Scholarship for highest standing over the three years of the course, and other impressive awards. Although there had apparently been a tacit understanding in the United Church that ordained women would remain celibate or resign their ministries, Margaret Millen ignored the advice of the College and, in her final year, married Melvin Butler, a fellow student. She still sought ordination. The College authorities considered that, as a wife and potential mother, a woman would not be free to make the necessary commitment to her work in the Ministry. Margaret Millen Butler protested, affirming that her interest in the Kingdom of God would be as great in wedlock as out of it. Married men were acceptable, why not married women? The faculty members of the College attempted to make it clear that they were not opposed in theory to women in the ministry but they still believed in practice that "special safeguards should be thrown around the admission of women to the candidature and especially to ordination."[89] As they surveyed their history in this matter, they recalled that the United Theological College had had two previous female candidates, both of whom they considered to be "competent and blameless girls." They also recollected that of these two, one had married and had become a mother before completing her studies, the other was ordained but married a business man within a few months and left the ministry. They declined to recommend Margaret Millen Butler for ordination at that time.

In 1948, the Joint Board of the Affiliated Colleges became the Faculty of Divinity of McGill University and naturally continued its practice of admitting women to its academic courses, leaving the Colleges and their respective communions to decide any questions relating to ordination.[90] By 1970 the Faculty, which had begun as a professional school for the training of candidates for Protestant ministries, recognized that it had evolved beyond that restriction and had become a Faculty for the study of religion in general and changed its name accordingly. As the Faculty of Religious Studies, it opened all its activities to women on the same basis as to men. The number of women registering in its courses began to grow and, by the end of the decade, there were regularly eight or nine women students with thirty or so men. The number of women students from other Faculties taking individual courses in religion was considerably greater.

Among the notable women associated with the Faculty have been Dr. Donna Runnalls, an Associate Professor of Biblical Studies, who was also eighth Warden of the Royal Victoria College; Dr. Erin Malloy-Hanley, an Assistant Professor who was also Associate Dean of Students; and Dr. Katherine Young, an Associate Professor whose research interests centered on women and religion and who introduced courses such as "Women in the Christian Tradition." One of the Faculty's distinguished graduates was Phyllis N. Smyth, B.A. '59, B.D.

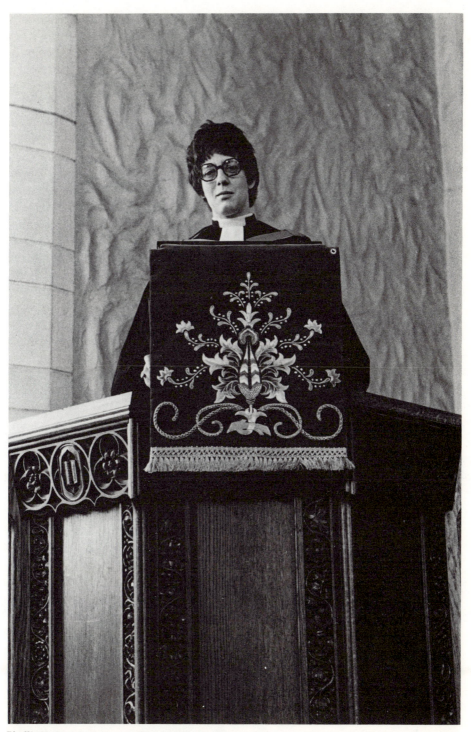

Phyllis N. Smyth, B.A. '59, B.D. '64, Ph.D. '72

'64, Ph.D. '72, who after being ordained, served as minister in several small Quebec communities before being called to Westmount's prestigious Dominion Douglas Church. After five years of exceptionally popular ministry there, Dr. Smyth returned to the academic world in 1979 when she accepted a position in the Faculty of Theology at the University of Winnipeg.

* * *

The success of women in McGill's professional Faculties—their examination results, scholarships, and prizes, their skills in practical work, their contributions to research in their fields and their competence in the work place—all add to the universally mounting pile of evidence that a woman really can do "a man's job." Here is indisputable proof that intelligence, ability, and stamina are not distributed according to sex. Here is the proof, but are there yet enough facts to demolish the theory?

Chapter EIGHT

The Other Schools

In the continuing debates about the status of women in society, it has frequently been observed that activities classified as "feminine" are not as prestigious as "masculine" concerns. The former have been deemed peripheral, the latter central; the one insubstantial, the other real. The private sphere of women simply has not commanded the authority of the public sphere of men. Though there may have been much lip service to the importance and even the nobility of activities such as mothering, teaching, or nursing, society has not rewarded these activities with manifest generosity. Women may not have accepted the devaluation of their work, but in terms of both economics and status, it is undeniable that feminine affairs occupy lowly ranks in the social hierarchy.

Similarly, formal education to prepare people to enter "women's" fields has generally suffered from low prestige. "Women's" educational fields are those that prepare people to become teachers, home economists, nurses, social workers, librarians, physical therapists and other nurturing, kindly helpers. By informal common consent, programmes in these fields have been accorded lower rank in the academic hierarchy than instruction in Arts or the "manly" professions. Women's work did not seem to need either long formal instruction or expensive training for it was assumed that women's "instinctive" abilities would almost suffice. Thus, for example, courses in Physical and Occupational Therapy, originally identified in the McGill calendar as a "profession for women," led merely to a certificate. However, the general thrust for "women's" professions has been away from such humble academic origins toward degree, post-graduate and research work. It is notable that in a number of areas this trend began or accelerated at the end of the first World War. It was, in fact, recognition of women's competent public service during a time of national emergency.

In the previous chapter, attention focused on the struggles for women's admission into some of the established male domains at McGill. The present section deals with some of the units of the University which originally had female connotations and which, therefore, were not hostile or resistant to accepting women as students. Resistance and reservations were directed more toward the programmes than at the women taking them. The apparent want of status of these fields of study may be ascribed to several factors—to their relative newness as areas of systematic inquiry, to perceived lower intellectual standards, or simply to their being associated with women and thus leading to "women's work" and to the lower end of professional salary scales. In any event, the lower status of these fields, reinforced by the fact that they prepared people for stereotypical female tasks, made them doubly unattractive to men. By the same token, they were all the more readily accessible to women.

These programmes have had similar problems in gaining academic credibility, whether their principal administrators and professors were male, for the most part, as in the case of Education, or female, as in the case of Nursing. The patterns of development of their student bodies have been almost the reverse of the other units at McGill, which began as predominantly male and gradually accepted an increasing proportion of women. The "female faculties" have been characterized by an initially high proportion of women students with a gradual and relatively recent increase in the number of men. Perversely, this increase may correlate with an improvement in their academic respectability![1]

* * *

The first of the "female" professions with which McGill had to deal was teaching. Indeed, it was in this realm that the University had its initial association with women as students, and that occurred as long ago as the middle of the 19th century. It may be recalled from Chapter 2 that the establishment in 1857 of teacher training institutions represented a step toward women's higher education in Quebec and that the appointment of J. William Dawson as Principal and Professor of Natural Science of the McGill Normal School made a connection between teacher training and the University. That connection was an administrative one but, physically and operationally, the McGill Normal School and McGill College were widely separated.

When the McGill Normal School opened on March 3, 1857, it was housed in the former Montreal High School on Belmont Street, where a Bell Telephone building now stands. The structure was adapted for its purpose with as little change as possible and was intended to accommodate 50 teachers-in-training and 200 children in the Model Schools (one for boys and one for girls) attached on either side. McGill Normal also had access to a model school for both sexes which had previously been operated by the Colonial Church and School Society. The course of study for would-be teachers was to "include all the branches of a sound english [sic] and french [sic] education, with special reference to their principles and practical application, and to the best methods of teaching them." Instruction was also to be given in "the art of teaching and the management of schools, in history, the elements of mathematics and algebra, natural philosophy, chemistry, natural history, agriculture, drawing and music."[2] Religious instruction was to be given by the professors and by ministers of the various denominations. Initially, there were to be two programmes—one year for elementary school teachers, two years for model school teachers. Later (1865), a three-year Academy Diploma was introduced, giving its holders the right to teach in "superior" schools. It was claimed that the Academy class "gave the women, as distinct from the girls from this province, their first opportunity for what we could call higher public education, . . . a third year's course of literary, classical and mathematical training."[3]

The first professors of the Normal School—three in addition to Dawson—were all male. Naturally, the head of the boys' Model School was also a man, but the head of the girls' Model School was a woman—Mary McCracken. There were also female teachers at the girls' Model School. The first pay list shows that significant salary differentials existed, but this was general practice in the schools of the time. Miss McCracken, for example, was engaged at $125 per annum while her male counterpart received $175.[4] It was not unusual to find that men's salaries were double those of women. Though there were many women teachers at the Model School—including Lucy Derick, Carrie's sister—there were relatively few at the Normal School itself. In 1884, Lilian B. Robins, daughter of the Normal School Principal, Saul Robins, was employed as a "Lady Assistant." This later gave rise to charges of nepotism when Miss Robins, who taught 14 hours per week and assisted the Principal, seemed to be receiving an unusually high salary. It was not until 1886 that a woman was appointed as an Ordinary Professor at the Normal School. She was Mme Sophie Cornu. She taught French and received the same salary as her male predecessor. Similarly, when Carrie Derick replaced Professor Penhallow as the Normal School's instructor in Botany in 1903, she did so "on the same terms." Though relatively few, the Normal School women were obviously in a higher status bracket than their Model School sisters.

The original Normal School entrance requirements specified that candidates should be fully sixteen years of age, hold certificates of character and conduct and know the rudiments of grammar, arithmetic "as far as the rule of three," and have some knowledge of geography. Though the pronouns used in the regulations were all masculine, it was obvious that the authorities expected both men and women to enroll.

The final clause of the legislation establishing normal schools (Bill 204 of 1856) reads, "The words 'Teacher' and 'Student' in the foregoing provisions shall include persons of either sex." Following this lead, the *Prospectus* of the McGill Normal School reiterated that all the regulations and privileges "shall apply to female as well as to male pupil-teachers." The entering class totalled 52, of whom 44 were young women.[5]

The regulations governing students were formidable. It was very clear that:

- Pupil-teachers guilty of drunkenness, of frequenting taverns or of entering disorderly houses or gambling houses, of keeping company with disorderly persons or of committing any act of immorality or insubordination, shall be expelled.
- There shall be no intercourse between male and female pupil-teachers while in the school, or when going to, or returning from it. Teachers in the one sex are strictly prohibited to visit those belonging to the other.
- They are on no account to be absent from their lodgings after half-past nine o'clock in the evening.
- They shall be allowed to attend such lectures and public meetings only as may be considered by the Principal conducive to their moral and mental improvement.[6]

Students were permitted to stay only in approved boarding-houses. No boarding house sanctioned for male pupil-teachers could accept females, and *vice versa.* Boarding-house keepers were required to report to the Principal any breach of the rules by any student. Professors, too, were guardians of morality and had the "power of excluding from the lectures for a time any student who may be inattentive to his studies or guilty of any minor infraction of the regulations."[7] Students were expected to be punctual and no nonsense was countenanced. The administration turned down a request written on behalf of Clara Hewton of Lachine that she be permitted to arrive in class at five past nine instead of nine o'clock because of her train schedule. Presumably she submitted to the only alternative other than withdrawal, which was to arrive two hours early. On another spectacular occasion, five young women were expelled for profanity and for circulating a certain book "of the most pernicious kind."

The degree of paternalism at the Normal School appears to have been considerably greater than it was at McGill College—though the undergraduates were not necessarily older than the Normal School students. The presence of women must explain this in part.

Normal School Graduate, 1901: Jennie Smith

While the student population at the Normal School was mixed, it can be seen from the regulations cited above, that great care was taken to keep members of the two sexes apart. Because of the relatively small number of males, mixed classes were conceded but no free and easy camaraderie was permitted. The young men were required to be seated before the women entered and they had to take their places at the front of the room where the professor could keep his eye on them.

After women were admitted to the Faculty of Arts, on the understanding that they be educated entirely separately from men, Dawson took some trouble to explain the difference in treatment of women in the two institutions bearing McGill's name. He wrote in his autobiography:

> Fault has been found with myself, and with others connected with McGill College, in that, while adopting the system of mixed education in the Normal School, we insisted on separate classes for women at McGill. But our critics forget to consider the different conditions in the two cases. In the Normal School the women constitute the large majority, and, where this is the case, the difficulties of mixed education are greatly diminished. Besides this, teachers-in-training in a Normal School are subjected to strict rules of discipline, which would be impossible in the case of college students. Notwithstanding these advantages, however, we have not been without anxieties, which . . . without any other information or experience, would deter me from advising mixed classes in an ordinary college.[8]

In fairness to Dawson, it must be remembered that the McGill Normal School came under Provincial jurisdiction and consequently many of the rules were dictated by officials with authoritarian backgrounds, and were intended also to apply to young French-Canadians who were accustomed to firm parental or Church discipline.

Yet another factor in the differential treatment of students at the Normal School and the College was their social origins. While no complete comparative analysis has been made and while there is some overlapping of the two groups, it is apparent that the students of the Normal School were generally of working-class origins and those of College were middle-class. The following letters, typical of many written on behalf of Normal School applicants, suggest how practical necessity helped recruit many students:

> . . . Her family are respectable but at present so reduced in circumstances as to render the advantages offered in connection with the Normal particularly desirable in her case. . . .[9]

. . . Her father is dead and her mother is poor and she wishes to attend the Normal School in order to qualify for the profession of a teacher. . . .[10]

. . . The 1st of September is drawing on and I am desirous to place my only daughter in the model or normal school of Montreal—to fit her for a Teacher or Governess—to enable her—when I have ceased to have connection with time—to gain her bread independent of her brothers by attending a full course of studies. . . .[11]

Without doubt, the students of the Normal School, especially those in the Elementary and Model Diploma courses, intended to join the labour force, to earn their own livings and to become working women. The Donaldas, on the other hand, were not being prepared for the professions, they were ladies and should therefore be accorded a different kind of chivalry. It was to the College students rather than the Normal School girls that Dawson's concept of Woman applied and in accordance with that concept, the "ladies" should be kept separate from the crude world of men at McGill. Again, there is a question of caste.

Overlapping of the two female populations began in 1884 when arrangements were made for women with Normal School Academy Diplomas to be admitted to classes at McGill on the same basis as members of the Montreal Ladies' Educational Association. In the following year, the Academy Diploma was recognised as the equivalent of first year Arts and students with marks above a certain level were granted free tuition.

This idea had been contained in the original *Prospectus* of the Normal School which had said in 1857 that "pupil-teachers as may be distinguished by previous education, ability and industry, shall have the . . . privilege of entering on the university course as free students." [12] Though this plan could not be implemented until women had been accepted at McGill, the very fact that it had been advanced in 1857 and that women had been specifically included in all the terms of the *Prospectus,* indicated that the possibility of women's going to the university had been publicly contemplated at that early date. This serves again to raise the question of why women's admission was delayed for so long—almost another thirty years.

The recognition of the Academy Diploma meant that a number of Normal School women could continue their studies and take degrees. However, articulation between the College and the School also went in the other direction. By 1891, it was possible for undergraduates to qualify for the Normal School Diploma by taking courses in pedagogy. The Academy classes were then transferred to McGill and given in the

340

Elizabeth Binmore, B.A. '90, M.A. '94

evening as a convenience to the students. This was a remarkably liberal innovation which was obviously appreciated. A list compiled in 1898 of the first decade of women graduates showed that 40 out of a total of 113 had taken both degrees and teaching diplomas. Sixteen had taken their Normal School Diplomas before their B.A.'s and 24 had qualified for their Diploma concurrently with or after their B.A.'s. Included in the first group were people such as Elizabeth Binmore, Carrie Derick, Georgina Hunter and Lilian Robins; among those of the second group were Maude Abbott, Isobel Brittain, Susan Cameron, Catherine Travis and Harriet Brooks—distinguished alumnae all.

That the Normal School offered a real educational opportunity for women may be seen in the example of Elizabeth Binmore. Binmore obtained her Academy Diploma in 1878, four years before women were admitted to the Faculty of Arts. This was the beginning of a lifetime of learning and professional activities. She taught for some time and then enrolled at McGill where she was active in student affairs, became Vice-President of the Donaldas in 1889 and later (1898) was to be President of the McGill Alumnae.[13] She received her B.A. from McGill in 1890 and went to the Harvard Summer School in 1893. Still not satisfied, she returned to McGill for graduate study with Professor P.D. Penhallow in Botany.[14]

In 1894, Elizabeth Binmore and another Donalda, Euphemia McLeod, were awarded the degrees of Master of Arts. Both were alumnae of the McGill Normal School and were the first women to receive graduate degrees from McGill University.

Elizabeth Binmore resumed teaching and her work was notable for its innovative emphasis. She advocated the introduction of music in the public schools and the use of ''natural'' methods of teaching French rather than formal grammar; she was also a pioneer in advancing the ''Sloyd'' method of manual instruction. Binmore was also active in professional affairs, was the first woman to be elected president of the Teachers' Association in Montreal and, in an address to the Association, showed her concern for women's rights. She said in 1893:

> This is essentially a century of change. Women are gradually declaring and proving their ability and willingness to bear the burden of their own support. It is no longer absolutely necessary that every woman in the family should be dependent upon the men—to be reduced to unknown straits and intolerable suffering on the death of the latter.[15]

She was critical of the way women teachers were being exploited, how they were initially accepted ''on sufferance'' by employers who could not pay full salaries, but noted that the women teachers of Montreal had presented a petition of protest. Producing evidence that women teachers in the United States were beginning to receive equal remuneration with men, she optimistically believed that "efficiency and success" would finally triumph and women would receive their due.[16]

The McGill Normal School was, without doubt, an educational asset for the women of the Province both before and after the opening of the Faculty of Arts to them. However, the preponderance of females in teacher preparation began to worry the educational authorities. The number of men fluctuated, but was always small — 7 men to 44 women in 1857; up to 10 to 58 five years later; down to 5 to 61 in 1866; just 9 to 96 in 1884. Around the turn of the century, the proportions slipped even lower — 6 to 116 in 1899 and, in 1903, there were but 2 men to 181 women. The feminization of teaching was considered so serious that McGill from time to time offered bursaries to encourage male students to go on to the Academy instead of the Model Diploma. When he announced these new awards at the Closing Day exercises in 1903, Principal Peterson made it clear that the object was to make the teaching profession more attractive to men by making them eligible for higher paying jobs. On that same occasion, Dr. Alex Johnson added that because salaries were so low men would not become teachers and, apparently overlooking women entirely, bemoaned that "If people do not come forward to teach, what will become of education in this Province?"[17]

The few male teachers who did emerge from the Normal School at least had the advantage of being much sought after. The women, though they commanded very small salaries, often had difficulty in finding jobs. Still they continued to enroll at the Normal School in spite of this and also in spite of increasingly crowded and uncomfortable conditions.

In 1890, the Repairs Committee had commented on the shamefully low proportion of men's water-closets to male teachers-in-training and model school pupils but added, somewhat enigmatically, "In proportion to numbers, the deficiency is even greater in the Girls' Department, but the consequences are not quite so obtrusively offensive."[18] In 1899 it was reported that two women in the Model School class were poisoned by escaping coal gas on the very morning of their first examinations. They barely escaped with their lives and were unable to write their papers.[19] A comprehensive study by Professor George Locke of the University of Chicago undertaken in 1903 revealed a situation that was "little short of criminal."[20] Locke condemned the general uncleanliness, the dreariness of the library, the lack of light especially in two rooms "which can hardly be duplicated for transgressing every rule concerning the preservation of eyesight." It must have been with tongue-in-cheek that he congratulated the model school teachers for their ingenuity in changing the classes about so that no one group would be exposed all the time to "the dungeon rooms." He also sympathized with the women students, noting that "from a cramped, cheerless room in a remote corner of a cheerless boarding house, these girls come to the Normal School and rightfully expect to find there a pleasant place to sit and read or chat with their fellow students."

The dreary quarters available to the Normal School women contrasted markedly with those provided for the Donaldas in the relative luxury of Royal Victoria College. According to Locke, there was urgent need for an agreeable dormitory for the Normal School students. "They are all young, many of them have been away from home but little, they are from families of moderate means, persons to whom every dollar means more than a corresponding amount of work. They are forced to seek boarding-houses of the cheaper sort where accomodation and food are too often not conducive to mental effort or moral well-being." Three years later, McGill's *Annual Report* repeated this plaint: "The most urgent want in connection with this part of the provincial system of education is a residential building where teachers-in-training who have left the care and protection of home may live and study under healthier and more helpful conditions." Members of the public also argued that "Much of the prejudice against professional training would disappear . . . if parents could always feel assured that their daughters had a supervised home in the city."[21] Interestingly, the Montreal Council of Women, in an open letter to the Protestant Committee of the Council of Public Instruction, discounted the dangers surrounding girls attending school in Montreal, suggesting rather that "the temptations of a village with its characteristic freedom and lack of supervision are probably greater than any likely to meet a student in the city."[22] The Council noted that "girls from the same class come willingly to the city in order to enter offices and stores, whenever the wages are large enough to be an inducement" and therefore concluded that "the lack of a residence in connection with the Normal School is not a serious difficulty."

Whatever the relative moral dangers of city and country for vulnerable young women, the Normal School was soon to pack up and move from urban Belmont Street to bucolic Ste. Anne de Bellevue. This came about through the philantropy of Sir William Macdonald. Sir William, the wealthy tobacco merchant who in the past had vied with Lord Strathcona for the honour of being the greatest of McGill's benefactors, had a long-standing interest in agricultural and manual education. With James W. Robertson, Dominion Commissioner of Agriculture and Dairying, he was responsible for the encouragement of manual training and gardening in the elementary schools. As they developed, these efforts became known as the Macdonald-Robertson movement. Macdonald also recognised both the need to train teachers to use new methods for new subjects and the importance of elevating the lives of farm women. Thus, he acquired a large tract of land at the west end of Montreal Island and constructed in sturdy red brick the college bearing his name with the three-fold purpose of providing agricultural education, instruction in household science and teacher training. Instead of starting a new teacher-education enterprise, Macdonald (somewhat reluctantly) accepted Principal Peterson's suggestion that he invite the McGill Normal School to join his venture. With little hesitation, both the Provincial and McGill authorities concerned approved this arrangement, happy at the prospect of the fine instructional facilities to be offered at the Ste. Anne de Bellevue campus, the spacious residential quarters for both men and women and the $2 million with which Sir William was prepared to endow his college.

Thus, the McGill Normal School formally ceased to exist. It re-emerged in November 1907 as the School for Teachers at Macdonald College. The College became a constituent part of McGill University and Dr. Robertson was its first Principal. George Locke, who had written the devastating report on the Normal School, became the first Head of the School for Teachers and J.A. Dale of Merton College, Oxford, was appointed as the first Professor of Education at McGill. He was a member of the Faculty of Arts and occupied a chair endowed by Sir William Macdonald.

Since that time, teacher education has edged closer to the McGill milieu. In 1955, the School for Teachers, transformed into the Institute of Education, became part of the Faculty of Arts and Science; in 1965, it evolved into a Faculty of Education in its own right; in 1970, it returned to Montreal to occupy a new building on the northern edge of the McGill campus. During these shifts, admission requirements were upgraded, new general and specialized programmes, degree courses, graduate work and research were all introduced, so that the academic offerings were significantly raised. Throughout these changes, the student population remained predominantly female, though the imbalance was no longer as pronounced as in the days of the Normal School.

During the 1970-80 decade, the era of ''Women's Liberation'' when job stereotypes were thought to be changing, the relative statistics for the Faculty of Education remained remarkably constant. On the average, 75% of the students and 35% of the faculty members were female. Ever since the appointment of ''lady assistants'' in the Normal School, there have always been some female members of staff. Apparently, this was not something to be taken for granted. As late as 1916, the Protestant Committee of the Department of Public Instruction of the Province of Quebec formally drew to the attention of the authorities at

Macdonald College Main Building

the School for Teachers the importance of having women teachers well represented on the regular staff. The Committee further expressed the hope that women applicants would receive due consideration in the filling of a current vacancy.[23] The women who did receive appointments tended to retain relatively low status but they were often the ones who helped carry the work of the institution forward. At the School for Teachers, for instance, there were stalwart individuals like Dorothy Seiveright who taught Social Studies, and Phyllis Bowers who not only taught a full complement of courses, supervised practice teaching, and advised students, but also published a text on teaching methods. Another was Francis Cook, who taught mathematics, continued her own higher education and served as Warden of Stewart Hall, the women's residence.

The first appointment of a woman as full Professor of Education was in 1965 when Marguerite F.L. Horton was promoted to rank. That was approximately 60 years after the appointment of the first male Professor of Education.[24] As will be discussed in more detail in Chapter 9, differences in male/female promotion rates and salaries have been found in many universities and McGill and its Faculty of Education are no exceptions. The reasons are complex, involving not only qualifications and competence but also opportunity. There has been relatively little direct confrontation on these issues at McGill. It is as if some words written almost a century ago by Elizabeth Binmore still apply. In 1893 she said, "Perhaps no tendency of the age is more repulsive to the general public than that of women to claim their rights too independently."[25] Perhaps the old fear of being branded "blue stocking" or "strong-minded madam" may be among the factors that have caused women in Education to refrain from pressing for change. On the other hand, administrators there as elsewhere, have claimed that women are often unwilling to take on the stresses and time-consuming demands of administrative positions. Yet some women of Education have certainly done so.

Over the years, there have been female chairpersons, co-ordinators and programme directors and, indeed, Professor Betty Jaques was head of a Department (Education in Art) for the longest term of anyone in the Faculty. However, the fact remains that in each of Education's guises— Normal School, School for Teachers, Institute of Education, and Faculty of Education—the senior administrators and most of the senior professors have been men. Thus it would appear that, though teaching has retained its image as a "female" profession, a disproportionate number of the teachers of teachers at McGill have been male and, as far as rank is concerned, Education has not really been a women's Faculty.

* * *

Another of the fields of study intimately associated with women grew up with teacher education at Macdonald College. This was Household Science. Like Education, it changed its name a number of times and, like Education, it did so as it constantly strove for academic credibility. Unlike Education, its progress has been directed mainly by women. Its inclusion with teacher training and Agriculture as one of the three main thrusts of the new college was not only because it was one of the special concerns of Sir William Macdonald, but also because formal education in Household Science was an idea whose time had come. Traditionally, of course, women had received instruction in sewing, embroidery and all manner of domestic arts. In particular, some of the convents and the Family Institutes of Quebec were famous for their work in this area, which constituted the major form of education for most French-speaking women in the Province. However, what was developed at Macdonald College had purely secular origins.

In 1891, a Professor of Chemistry at Mount Allison University (which had had the distinction in 1875 of graduating the first woman from a Canadian college) suggested the teaching of "domestic chemistry." With rather extraordinary vision, he believed that "education of this kind would raise the kitchen to the dignity of the laboratory and would add the charm of scientific interest to the housewife's tasks." [26] Though Mount Allison did not immediately take up the idea, several other Canadian institutions did so in the following decade. Most were stimulated by the need to provide some form of teacher training for new courses in domestic science that were beginning to enter the curricula of the lower schools.[27] One of the individuals who played a significant part in this movement was Adelaide Hoodless, a dynamic woman from Ontario. In 1893, in the face of ridicule and opposition, Mrs. Hoodless began to teach homemaking at the Y.W.C.A. in Hamilton and tried to persuade various women's groups to lobby for the introduction of domestic subjects into the elementary school programme. Her efforts began to achieve some tangible results when the Ontario Minister of Education[28] asked her to travel around the province championing the cause of domestic education. At her meetings, Hoodless outspokenly lectured conservative farmers on the necessity for strong, well-informed womenfolk, telling them that "The health of your wives is more important than the health of your animals."[29] In 1897, she founded the Canadian Women's Institute with its motto, "For Home and Country," and that same year Ontario introduced domestic science into the school curriculum. But Adelaide Hoodless dreamed of college education in Household Science. She was unable to interest her own Ministry of Education in this idea, but she hit upon someone who would support it. The story may be apocryphal, but it is reported that while she was in the

348

middle of cleaning her teeth, inspiration struck: the person who would certainly help would be Sir William Macdonald!

Without delay, she travelled to Montreal to recruit Sir William to her cause. She managed to overcome the major objection that he could not provide a college for women in Ontario if there were not one in Quebec simply by suggesting that he support training in that province as well.[30] And so he did. The Macdonald Institute of Home Economics was established in Guelph, Ontario in 1904, just a year before construction began on the more elaborate Macdonald College at Ste. Anne de Bellevue, Quebec.

Public opinion, which had been dubious about Adelaide Hoodless' early efforts, now seemed warmly in favour of Macdonald's endeavours. Journalists frequently reported on them with enthusiasm. One account emphasized the fact that Macdonald College, where the study of Agriculture was to be so important, would have "a woman's side," explaining that:

> In the last score of years the farmer's lot has improved wonderfully. He saves labor by a hundred contrivances, he gets more money. He has a tenfold more agreeable life. But the lot of the farmer's wife has not kept pace. She has fewer labor-saving devices, and on many a farm the windmill sends the water to the cattle while the old-fashioned pump is good enough for the housewife. Moreover, while the farmer has become incomparably more scientific in his way of doing his work, the farmer's wife has not had similar changes; in too many farm-houses the cooking is deplorable, and other departments of housework are behind the age. Suppose every farmer's wife and daughter was a thorough cook, and was a needlewoman, was a good dressmaker, knew something about millinery, was expert, in a word, in the several lines of work in which women are interested—how much better worth living in the country it would be....[31]

The initial enrolment of Macdonald, or "Mac" as it soon became known, was 215. The 28 students in Agriculture were all male, the 112 transferring from the old Normal School were mainly female, and the 62 new registrants in the School of Household Science were all women. All students were expected to live in residence; women from Quebec farms were admitted without fees; others had to pay $23 on entrance as follows:

Four weeks' board in advance.............................$13.00
Caution money deposit.......................................5.00
Laboratory fee (for cost of materials used)..................5.00

Total: $23.00 [32]

Helen A. Bainbridge

The members of staff for Household Science were all women. They, like those in Agriculture, were more practically than academically oriented. George Locke, late of the University of Chicago, tended to look down on them all as "a faculty of janitors."[33] Such a plebian sobriquet hardly seems to have fitted Helen A. Bainbridge who headed the School of Household Science in its first year. Miss Bainbridge, a vivacious young American, had been brought to Macdonald by Locke himself to teach Art in the School for Teachers but Dr. Robertson had persuaded her to take over Household Science. She knew very little about it but Robertson must have assumed that any intelligent woman would automatically know about household matters. Bainbridge convincingly proved the falsity of such an assumption during her one year (1907-08) as Head. She spent a good deal of time and money buying the furnishings and equipment for the new School. Alas, her purchases proved to be more decorative than useful and, after her departure, many of them were discreetly consigned to a storeroom until they were deemed completely obsolete and, by 1961, could decently be discarded.

Succeeding Heads of Household Science have all lasted longer than Helen Bainbridge. They were Annie B. Juniper (1908-10), Katherine Fisher (1910-1917), Anita Hill (1917-1920), Bessie M. Philp (1920-1939), Margaret McCready (1939-1949), Helen Neilson (1949-1975), Edward S. Idziak (1975-1978), Shirley Weber (1978-   ). It will be observed that the only man in this list is Professor Idziak, a microbiologist. His appointment in the 1970's may be a signal, not only that "times have changed" but also that the programme of studies has developed significantly and in a scientific direction.

In the beginning, most of the Household Science students enrolled in the three-month Short Course (which disappeared in the 1920's) or the one-year Homemaker's Course.[34] These dealt with "the selection, preparation and serving of foods in the most appetizing and economical manner; in sewing, dressmaking, and the simple forms of household art and decoration, and in the care and cleaning of rooms, fabrics etcetera— all with a view of helping the young women to conduct sanitary, comfortable and happy homes in the country."[35] These kinds of courses gradually gave way under the pressures of professionalization, increasing academic content and growing research emphases. The trend in this direction began early with a two-year diploma in Institution Administration. This produced its first graduates in 1912 and flourished during World War I when experts in Home Economics were in demand to take charge of food services in military installations and other institutions. The systematic study of dietetics began to win recognition and some of the first graduates of the Institution Administration course became prominent members of a new profession. Much of the credit for the up-grading of the courses must go to Katherine Fisher who, in her annual report for 1913, noted that ''Students would do well to recognize that the lore of the household will never be given a position of dignity equal to that accorded older departments of study without a knowledge of the sciences.'' Her words have been heeded and the scientific content of the curriculum has constantly been strengthened.

In 1919, a new course was begun which led to the awarding, in 1923, of the first four degrees of Bachelor of Household Science (B.H.S.). It has been suggested that the development of degree courses in House-hold Science at some universities was partly a device to divert women from the mainstream of higher education.[36] If that were the case at McGill, the plan failed. The School of Household Science grew academi-cally stronger over the years, became an integral part of the Faculty of Agriculture in 1934 and ten years later, changed its degree to Bachelor of Science (Home Economics). In 1963, for the first time, the School offered a Food Management option. This was of more than passing interest since it was open to men as well as to women. Men in the third year of the B.Sc. (Agriculture) could take this new programme. As Helen Neilson, then Director of the School, looked into the future, she prophe-sied that the greatest change in the field would be the increasing presence of men in the food laboratories[37] as the impact was felt of the burgeoning knowledge in those scientific disciplines which impinge upon Agriculture and Household Science. Her prediction began to be fulfilled in the early 70's after the School of Household Science had changed its name to the School of Food Science and men began to register in it. In the next decade, the full-time male enrolment in the B.Sc. (Food Science) programme showed a fluctuating but persistent pattern:

Full-Time Male Enrolment in Food Science			
1970/71	0%	1976/77	9.2%
1971/72	5.7%	1977/78	13.2%
1972/73	11.4%	1978/79	6.7%
1973/74	17.1%	1979/80	5.5%
1974/75	6.6%	1980/81	8.2%
1975/76	8.8%		

Helen R. Neilson, M.B.E., B.H.S. '39, M.Sc. (Agric.) '48

The introduction of co-education in the former Household Science raised no outcries of protest; rather it received a warm welcome, with pride. It augured well for some reduction of sex-linked job stereotyping but may also have other implications for the world of work. If Food Science should follow the model of Education, where the relatively few male graduates tend to advance quickly and to become principals in both elementary and high schools, then the female graduates of Food Science may find themselves at a competitive disadvantage in a field that was once theirs. This risk may be the price of equality. Women's best protection will not be restrictions against men, but confidence in themselves and their own expertise as well as willingness to compete and to take full advantage of their sophisticated training.

Among the people who were responsible for developing the School from an institution offering instruction in housekeeping to one with a strong emphasis on science and a focus toward business and industry was Bessie M. Philp, Director for 19 years through the 20's and 30's. She still believed in women's primary housekeeping responsibilities, yet she changed with the times, helped introduce degree courses, and recognised the potential for women's professional training in the physical and biological sciences. Other notables included Dr. Margaret S. McCready, a graduate of the University of Toronto with a Ph.D. from Aberdeen, who brought research interests and expertise in the field of nutrition to "Mac" when she succeeded Miss Philp as Director; Isobel Honey, who was particularly concerned with the education of Household Science teachers; the inimitable Francis Wren, who taught art and crafts; and Dr. Florence Farmer, a researcher and missionary in the field of human nutrition.

In recent years, the Directors have continued to supply the vision and leadership shown by Miss Fisher and Miss Philp. Professor Helen R. Neilson, a B.H.S. graduate from "Mac" who was awarded the M.B.E. for her service in the forces during World War II, became Director of the School in 1949. An acknowledged expert in food science, she served the School with distinction for twenty-six years. Her contribution was recognised by McGill in 1980 when she was accorded the status of Professor Emeritus. Professor Neilson was succeeded by Dr. Shirley M. Weber, a graduate of Manitoba with a Ph.D. from Cornell, who continues the emphasis on food research and community nutrition.

Household Science at McGill has clearly grown from practical work in sewing and cooking to specialist teaching and research in food chemistry. In the words of Professor Helen Neilson, "There is no longer any justification for separate male/female education in this sphere and, there is no need for apology for its inclusion in the university curriculum."[38]

* * *

Nursing is a third and, perhaps, the ultimate "female" profession —for who has not heard the flat, categorical aphorism: "Men are doctors, women are nurses"? This cliché sums up the stereotypical differences—men are the professionals with the high skills and intellectual background, women are helpers with the support services and practical training. At McGill, the antagonism toward women as doctors gave way just slightly before the incredulity at the idea that Nursing was a field worthy of academic preparation.

Nursing in Quebec has had a long and heroic history, beginning with Jeanne Mance and the French hospitals established in the late 17th and early 18th centuries and continuing, by grace of on-the-job learning and great devotion, through most of the 19th century. Several efforts to form a training unit at Montreal General Hospital (established 1822) failed on account of "the apparently impossible state of the hospital" and "the herculean nature of the task"[39] until the appointment as Lady Superintendent of Norah Livingstone. In 1890, Livingstone succeeded in establishing the School for Nurses which offered systematic, though practically oriented training, and was considered a fundamental reform in health care. The next step was taken toward the end of the first World War on the initiative of Grace M. Fairley, Lady Superintendent of the Alexandra Hospital, and Mabel F. Hersey, Superintendent of Nurses at the Royal Victoria Hospital, both active members in the newly formed Montreal Graduate Nurses' Association.

Miss Fairley and Miss Hersey were aware that, in the United States, nursing schools were becoming affiliated with universities. Further, they knew that some of the leaders of the Nursing Education movement in that country were Canadians[40] but that Canadian nurses who wanted professional level instruction had to go south of the border to find it—and then they often stayed there. Grace Fairley and Mabel Hersey therefore decided to approach Dr. Charles F. Martin, Secretary of McGill's Faculty of Medicine, with the revolutionary proposal that McGill follow the U.S. example. Miss Fairley recalled how they mustered their courage and went on their mission on an unpromising day in 1918.

> I remember well the day we chose to visit Dr. Martin's office on Sherbrooke Street. It was wet and cold. We both knew what we wanted but we had not a thing prepared other than to present the need verbally as we saw it, with all the urgency at our command. We walked back and forward, and once Miss Hersey said, "Let's go home and think it over." I, being more tenacious, said "No, today or not at all."[41]

In they went. Dr. Martin apparently did not know that some American universities were already providing Nursing Education, but he agreed to explore the possibilities in his Faculty—the Faculty which voted that same year to allow women to become doctors.

The idea of Nursing Education was duly taken to the Faculty; Miss Hersey was asked to prepare a curriculum; a separate department of nursing was suggested; and, finally, a committee of the McGill Corporation was struck to consider the whole matter. This Committee on the Proposed Course for Graduate Nurses was chaired by Helen R.Y. Reid— the Donalda who had distinguished herself both at College and during the War. For her conspicuous services with the Canadian Patriotic Fund she had been appointed Governors' Fellow on Corporation, so she kept her connection with McGill. She was also instrumental in the development of the Department of Social Study and Training, which grew out of her instruction of wartime volunteers and which later became the School of Social Work. She now became a primary figure in the development of Nursing Education at her *alma mater.*

By the summer of 1920, Helen Reid had successfully negotiated her way through the administrative thickets. Not only had she obtained approval of the Faculty of Medicine, the Corporation and the Board of Governors for the establishment of a separate school for nurses, but she also won a promise of financial support from the Quebec Branch of the Canadian Red Cross Society. On her recommendation, Flora Madeline Shaw, an associate of Mabel Hersey and a graduate of the Montreal General School for Nurses and Teachers College, Columbia University, was appointed Director (1920-27). This proved an excellent choice, for Miss Shaw was a dedicated professional, humane and able.

Though both Reid and Shaw hoped to provide degree programmes, they recognised the danger of trying to push too hard or too fast. Thus, the first offerings of the School for Graduate Nurses were relatively modest, drawing as far as possible on pre-existing courses in Physical Education, Education and Social Services, and leading to one-year diplomas in either Public Health Nursing or the Teaching and Supervision of Schools of Nursing. Despite very short notice, a total of 24 full-time and 18 part-time students enrolled in the autumn of 1920. They began their classes in the East Wing of the Arts Building, where the first women at McGill had taken their lectures almost forty years before.

Almost immediately upon their graduation in the spring of 1921, this first group of McGill nurses formed an Alumnae Association of their own. They elected Flora Madeline Shaw honorary president and bestowed membership upon four people they identified as "instigators of the school": Helen R.Y. Reid, Maude E. Abbott,[42] Mabel F. Hersey

Flora Madeline Shaw

and Grace M. Fairley. The latter two must have felt especially gratified that their initiative had borne such satisfactory results, that they had overcome their misgivings and had gone ahead and spoken to Dr. Martin on that cold, wet day in 1918. But the twenty-odd new alumnae could hardly have been aware of how important their new Association was to be for the future of Nursing Education at McGill.

Dr. Martin continued to help in his capacity as Dean of Medicine from 1923 to 1935. He supported proposals made by Bertha Harmer, the second Director of the School (1927-1934) for an increased academic programme that might ultimately lead to degrees in Nursing and he made funds available for fellowships.[43] But, despite his interest, regardless of the apparent good-will of Principal Sir Arthur Currie, and notwithstanding the staunch endeavours of Miss Harmer, hopes for degrees in Nursing actually receded. Even the continued existence of the Nursing programme was in jeopardy. If the School for Graduate Nurses was not quite an orphan of McGill, it was something of a stepchild.

In its first four years, major funding for it had come from the Red Cross, not McGill, but the University did provide financial support from 1924 to 1933.[44] However, under the difficult economic conditions of the Depression, this support was diminished and the School was on the point of being closed. But the nurses did not give up. For the next decade, the School for Graduate Nurses was virtually financed by its own Alumnae Association, with only limited help from McGill. Two five-year plans for fund-raising were amazingly successful—but only because of the tremendous efforts that were made by Bertha Harmer, Marion Lindeburgh (Acting Director, 1934-39, Director, 1939-51) and E. Frances Upton, who chaired the Special Finance Committee of the Alumnae Association. Alumnae and friends of nursing from all over Canada contributed, as did the students and the staff members. Economies practiced by the women of the School amounted to real sacrifices. For example, in her last year, Miss Harmer refused her salary and other people bought books and supplies from their small salaries or personal savings. That the School was able to carry on was testimony of the generosity, loyalty and devoted energy of a great many people but in such a protracted crisis, some academic stagnation was almost inevitable.

The situation was relieved by two occurrences—one a major external event, the other an important internal change. The first of these was the outbreak of World War II with its resulting shift in social priorities and an urgent need for nurses. Funds now became available from diverse sources—the Federal Government, the Kellogg Foundation, the Victorian Order of Nurses, the Canadian Red Cross and the Canadian

Nurses' Association. The School was not only able to survive, it could even expand, accept more students and increase its staff. The second occurrence was a change in the McGill Statutes. This resulted in Nursing's being placed under the Faculty of Medicine and, in 1944, Senate agreed to accept full financial responsibility for the School. Once the long economic crisis was over, attention could once again be focused on academic development.

The quest for a degree programme was resumed. Soon came Senate's approval of a two-year post-basic Bachelor of Nursing course and, in 1946, nine young women received their B.N.'s, the first ever awarded by McGill. As part of the B.N. programme a number of specialized courses in fields such as obstetrics, psychiatric and paediatric nursing were introduced. They were accompanied by an on-going reassessment of the role and responsiblity of the nurse in health care, resulting in the establishment in 1957 of a basic Nursing programme leading to the Bachelor of Science in Nursing degree. This was followed four years later by the institution of the Master of Science (Applied) and a burgeoning concern for research.[45] Nursing Education was no longer viewed narrowly as practical training but, spaciously, as professional preparation in which techniques, knowledge, and appreciation of Nursing in the total human environment were all important. In 1973, the Master's programme was revised to produce clinical nurse specialists and a formal Research Unit in Nursing and Health Care was established under Dr. Moyra Allen.

Many of these developments were set in motion by the efforts of Rae Chittick, a very distinguished Director of the School (1953-63). Rae Chittick, B.Sc., M.A., M.P.H., R.N., grew up in Alberta, received her professional education at some of the most prestigious institutions in the United States (Johns Hopkins School of Nursing, Teachers College, Columbia University, Stanford, and Harvard) and came to McGill as Director of the School for Graduate Nurses in 1953. One of her first major tasks was to revise the curriculum at the baccalaureate level and introduce the basic B.Sc. (Nursing). She hoped to enrich the general education content and to stimulate the intellectual curiosity of Nursing students. Like Edith Green, who had been Acting Director in the previous year, Rae Chittick also wanted to develop research interests — to justify Nursing as an academic field and secure its place in academe. She realized that "one reason universities objected to professional schools was that they used the resources of the universities but contributed little to it by way of new knowledge."[46] She acknowledged that it might seem unrealistic to expect basic research from Nursing, "that only recently had gained a fragile footing in the university," but this was clearly one of her goals. She succeeded, not only in introducing graduate level work for the students but actively encouraged members of faculty to upgrade their qualifications and become involved in research. Her own lively mind produced many papers which were published in nursing and medical journals; the freshness and force of her ideas made her much in demand as speaker, member of professional organizations, and consultant to health agencies, both in Canada and abroad.

In 1954, the University of Alberta bestowed upon Rae Chittick the LL.D. for her contribution to Nursing and, three years later, McGill promoted her to full Professor. She became the first occupant of the Flora Madeline Shaw Chair of Nursing. This professorship was, in large measure, the result of the unremitting efforts of the Graduate Nurses' Alumnae Association which had raised money to endow a named chair. Their extraordinary efforts not only honoured the first Director of the School for Graduate Nurses but effectively raised the status of the School.[47]

Meanwhile, there had been another interesting development. Until the 1950's, McGill had apparently assumed that Nursing was an exclusively female calling. The McGill *Announcement* even used the words "women only" apropos of the School for Graduate Nurses. However, in 1952, Elva C. Honey (the fourth Director, 1951-1952), objected to this and advised the Faculty of Medicine that the School of Nursing was prepared to accept suitably qualified male applicants. She recommended that the barrier of sex be eliminated from the admission requirements.[48] Her recommendation was approved within a matter of weeks, but it was several years before any men registered in the Nursing programme and there were no male graduates until 1960. As it happened, the first two were both Colombo Plan students, one from Ceylon, the other from Indonesia. Relatively few men have followed their lead. Until 1977, when the programme was discontinued, only one or two men received the B.N. each year. In the B.Sc. (Nursing) programme, the first man graduated in 1974 but he did not start a fashion. Up to 1980, that programme also remained basically female, with an enrolment of more than 97% women. It seemed as if there had really been no need for the "women only" restriction in the old McGill *Announcement*—role stereotyping and custom were strong enough to do the job unaided.

* * *

The School for Graduate Nurses may not yet have cast off job stereotypes, but the actions of the Alumnae Association should certainly help shatter a widely-circulated myth that women do not support each other. Similarly, the development of the School of Food Science belies the stubbornly fixed notion that women are non-scientific. And the record of Education illustrates the on-going quest for academic depth that has been pursued by ''female'' studies, once considered trivial and unworthy of a place in the academic community. There are three other areas at McGill that have been predominantly female and that have shared many of the characteristics and problems of the three dealt with above. These are Social Work, Physical and Occupational Therapy, and Library Science.

Social Work was one of the fields of study dealing with human rather than purely intellectual concerns that came to McGill around the end of the first World War. It was also another of those that owed much of its early strength to the inspiration and teaching efforts of Helen R.Y. Reid. She was not alone, however, in her recognition of the need for trained people—whether volunteers or salaried professionals—to work with the distressed and the needy. Principal Sir William Peterson, with the help of Professor of Education, J.A. Dale, formally proposed a Department of Social Study and Training in 1918 and brought J. Howard Falk from Winnipeg as its first Director. The Joint Board of the Theological Colleges affiliated with McGill supported this initiative with funds to cover the Director's salary, while the Graduates' Society and some private individuals also made financial contributions. In his first calendar description of the Department of Social Service (as it became), Howard Falk explained both the need for the new Department and its connection with the War:

> The war put a premium on man power not for a few months, as during a period of unusual prosperity, but for four long years, and the situation revealed the fact that the man power of the Mother Country had been largely reduced by bad social conditions. Mr. Lloyd George summed up the situation in one terse sentence: ''You can't have an A-1 nation with a C-3 population.'' We in the Dominion must squarely face this fact.
>
> Social agencies are mostly engaged in dealing with the C-3 part of a population. Their success depends on their ability to prevent people from sinking into the C-3 class as well as on their ability to raise people from the C-3 class; this is no mean task.[49]

No sex barrier was suggested for applicants to the new Department, but the connection with women may be seen in the qualifications Falk specified for students: ''Tact, patience, sympathy, poise, cheerfulness and that something which we may term 'religion' and which 'calls' a person into social work.'' These characteristics are not exclusively female prerogatives, but they invoke the spirit of the devoted mother

Dorothy King, O.B.E., B.A., M.A. (New York)

whose selfless service would now be extended from the home to the community.

At first the Department, which was in the Faculty of Arts, offered a one-year certificate but it soon developed a two-year diploma course. Later, fortunes began to fluctuate. Lack of funds forced it to close in 1932. The following year, with the co-operation of McGill, an independent institution, the Montreal School of Social Work, was established. This provided a two-year course for university graduates and, characteristic of female enterprises, had a staff that was largely volunteer. A little more than a decade later, it came back to the University as the McGill School of Social Work with Dorothy King as its first Director (1945-50). Thanks in great measure to the dedication of Dorothy King, an acknowledged leader in Social Work education who was awarded the O.B.E. in 1946, the School passed the test. McGill approved the degrees of B.S.W. and M.S.W. for its graduates and it became an integral part of the University within the Faculty of Arts. In the years that followed, post-graduate studies and research became increasingly important. The student body remained predominantly female, but in 1980 enrolment was 18% male, a proportion to challenge the female stereotype.

The staff has also become increasingly male and it is worthy of note that the four Directors of the McGill School of Social Work who followed Dorothy King have all been males. This replacement of women by men in administration reflects a general trend across Canada. It is not necessarily discrimination against women but it may be partly explained by the fact that, since schools of Social Work began in response to requests from social agencies, they were generally staffed by the people in the field and these people were mostly women. A change began to occur after World War II when new graduate programmes in the social sciences developed and more men than women tended to take Ph.D.'s in areas such as social policy, institutional administration, and the economics of welfare. The men thus became more eligible for appointment to directorships and better qualified to develop research programmes in their Schools. Meanwhile, the women tended to stay in the more clinical and nurturant areas of Social Work where academic recognition and promotion were more difficult to achieve. This development, coupled with some disinclination of women to take on administration, has resulted in a "feminine" field's now being largely directed by men. Awareness of this situation should be a first step toward changing it.

* * *

Physiotherapy is another of the humane and service-oriented studies in which systematic instruction was first offered at McGill at the end of the first World War. Courses for masseurs were given in the School for Physical Education at that time but it was not until 1943 that a School for Physiotherapy was developed in the Faculty of Medicine. Six years later, it became the School of Physical and Occupational Therapy. The range of its concerns grew from the rehabilitation of war veterans to involvement in a variety of community and medical fields such as neurology, orthopaedics, rheumatology, obstetrics, paediatrics and geriatrics. The instructional programmes developed from brief diploma courses to baccalaureate degrees, then graduate and research work.

Its staff members have been mainly female, though its first Director was male. Dr. Guy Fisk headed the School for thirty years (1943-73). His successors have both been women—Professor Helen M. Gault (1973-79) who had been *de facto* head for many years, and Dr. Martha Piper (1979-   ). The student body of the School remained exclusively female until the late 1960's. The first man registered in the Bachelor of Physio-therapy programme in 1967 but male registrations did not grow signifi-cantly until the mid-70's after the introduction of the B.Sc. (P.T.) and B.Sc. (O.T.) degrees. Though male registration in the latter was only 3.6% of the total in 1980, in the former it was as high as 13.3%.

The School of Physical and Occupational Therapy is currently one of the instructional units of McGill where the student body, staff, and administrators are mainly women. It does not appear to be particularly eager to change that situation but it is making a conscious effort to up-grade the academic qualifications of its faculty. Nor does it seem to consider itself peripheral and some of its members, such as Edith Aston, play a full part in the committee life of the University.

*   *   *

Library Science, yet another area of "women's work," has a rather longer history at McGill than Physical and Occupational Therapy. The McGill Library School was established in 1904 and, though shortage of funds necessitated that it offered only a summer certificate course, it had the distinction of providing the first formal library training in Canada. With predominantly female registration, it continued as a summer school for a quarter of a century but, thanks to a grant from the Carnegie Corporation of New York, it was able to offer a diploma course starting in the regular academic session of 1927.

In 1930, entrance requirements were raised and a degree pro-gramme was approved. The following year, ten women and three men graduated with B.L.S. degrees. That male/female ratio was unusually high but for 16 of the next 20 years there was at least one male student in each class. When the veterans of World War II enrolled, there were a

364

Marianne Scott, Director of McGill University Libraries

couple of years when parity between the sexes seemed possible. There were as many as 11 men to 34 women in 1947 and 17 to 22 in 1949. But that proved to be a temporary phenomenon and the old predominantly female pattern reasserted itself.

With the growing sophistication of library work, the curriculum underwent revisions to keep place with the advancements of professional practice, technological developments and communication theory. In 1956, the degree of Master of Library Science was introduced and a mixed student enrolment was clearly expected. The *Announcement* for that year indicated that the important criteria for admission included "the character of the applicant's undergraduate studies and *his, or her,* suitability for library work." [emphasis added]. By 1965, the McGill Library School had become the Graduate School of Library Science under the jurisdiction of the Faculty of Graduate Studies and Research and undergraduate work was phased out. This constant upgrading of the programme accounts in part for the fact that, by 1980, the proportion of male students was a steady 20% of the annual total.

Though the occupation "Librarian" is commonly regarded as female, until mid-20th century the McGill Librarian was always male. The University Librarianship was, and is, a senior administrative position. For 45 years, the University Librarian was also Director of the Library School. Thus, while most of the instructors were female, the first two Directors of the School were male (Charles H. Gould, 1904-20 and Gerhard Lomer, 1920-49). Suggestions that a woman be appointed were ignored. Even so, much of the leadership and innovative practices were introduced by women like Beatrice Simon who reorganized the McGill libraries, produced a classic study on medical libraries and taught in the School. Since 1949, when the position of Director was separated from that of University Librarian, all five Directors of the School have been female—Vernon Ross (1949-66), Virginia Murray (1966-70), Violet Coughlin (1970-72), Effie Astbury (1972-76), and Vivian Sessions (1976-   ). Vernon Ross, the first woman Director was known and respected in library circles across Canada for her expertise and professional commitment. She had been on the staff of the McGill libraries and the Library School since she obtained her M.A. in History and her Library School Certificate from McGill in 1926. She was finally promoted to Professor of Library Science in 1963 and was made Professor Emeritus after her retirement. Prejudice against a woman as the Director of University Libraries was overcome in 1975 when Marianne Scott was appointed to that prestigious administrative position.

* * *

The "female faculties" have all consolidated their holds on academia, not only at McGill but in North American universities generally. They have slowly ceased to be the outsiders, the "others," as they struggled for acceptance. Typically, they have strengthened and lengthened their course offerings, introduced graduate programmes and embarked upon research, they have upgraded the qualifications of their professors and removed the old gender-based admission barriers. The growing number of men is viewed as a sign of liberation from the thrall of sex-stereotypes and even as an index of the maturity and respectability of the fields of study. Paradoxically, this phenomenon is sometimes also viewed as a threat to women's professional advancement as male graduates tend to receive more rapid promotion and to reach positions of authority in the professions once dominated by women or to attain positions of prestige in professional societies actually founded by women.

At McGill, there is some sensitivity to this situation but no hint that the trend toward co-education should be discouraged or that certain professional areas should be reserved for women. The credibility of the formerly female fields would not be enhanced by the artificial reinforcing of occupational stereotypes.

Nevertheless, the fact should not go unnoticed that the female fields are the only major instructional units at McGill where women have held senior administrative positions. It would by a Pyrrhic victory for women if the admission of men and the improved status of their old fields were to result in the appointment of more males as heads of these units without female advancement elsewhere. Clearly, the desideratum is the appointment of the most suitable people, male or female, to all positions —but this must include the promotion of women in all parts of the University. Inevitably, it will involve more than pious hopes and promises; it will demand a policy of positive action.

Part IV

WOMEN OF ACTION

Chapter NINE

The Women's Movement on Campus

If the "Women's Movement" is defined as a co-operative effort on the part of women to attain rights and privileges previously reserved for men, then it is clearly no recent upstart on the McGill campus but is, in fact, about a hundred years old. The graduates of the Montreal High School for Girls who gathered at Mrs. Reid's home in 1884 to consider what to do next, the members of the little posse who called on Principal Dawson that spring, the Donaldas who helped organize the Association for the Promotion of the Professional Education of Women and worked in the unsuccessful campaign for admission to Medicine were part of it. So were the Wardens of R.V.C. who upheld the ideal of scholarship among women, the pioneers in the professional Faculties, the innovators who fought for the academic respectability of "female" studies such as Nursing. Similarly, the many defenders of women's rights to be considered "real" students of McGill, "genuine" professors, bona fide members of the University—all formed part of the Movement.

Of course, it would not be accurate to assume that all the women who have ever been to McGill have been militants or activists or even that they were particularly concerned about women's rights. For example, Mary Jackson, McGill's first female engineer said that she never thought of herself as a feminist. There have been a great many— probably the majority—who simply accepted the *status quo*, who adjusted to each new development as it came along, who applied for admission to the various Faculties after the battles had been won, who unobtrusively went about their own affairs, each one doing no more to justify her academic legitimacy than taking courses, writing examinations, preparing theses and the like. Then there were others associated with McGill who, in the Dawsonian mode of the Lady, explicitly embraced the traditional Woman's role and played it out on campus with enthusiasm. Though generally of the "ladies' auxiliary" model, they were not necessarily "languid ladies." They could be active and effective people, the souls of volunteer organizations—socializing, helping, supporting others rather than working systematically for their own professional advancement or for any feminist cause.

Included in this group have been the wives of the Principals who, beginning with Margaret Mercer Dawson, generally made real contributions to the social fabric of McGill. In recent years, the input of Roslyn Robertson was notable. Her work with the McGill Associates, an organization for wives and women faculty members, was acknowledged by the creation of the "Roslyn Robertson Herb and Scent Garden," which is a welcome oasis near the concrete massiveness of the McIntyre Medical Building. The contribution of Jeanne Atkinson Bell, B.A. '47 (Shakespeare Gold Medallist), B.L.S. '53, as "gracious First Lady" was formally recognised in the fall of 1978 when the University conferred upon her the degree of Doctor of Letters, *honoris causa*. She was the first Principal's wife to be so honoured and she felt both touched and pleased at the distinction. As her husband was signing the diploma, he noticed the Latin text, *"virum clarum et illustrem,"* that is "man (in the sense of male) bright and distinguished". The Principal made inquiries about changing the wording to encompass women, but there was not enough time before the ceremony. Thus, Jeanne Bell received an "unreformed"

McGill Women Associates

diploma but, since it was "all in the family," the Principal did not anticipate any trouble. Before the event, he wrote, ". . . my wife has not seen her diploma and has not been told anything about the text. Will she be aware of the word 'virum' when she looks at her diploma? If so, how will she react? I don't know; we've only been married for 30 years, and my ability to predict her reactions is limited."[1]

The wives of the Principals have been cast in the role of executive consort—supporter, confidant, hostess—a role that is essentially an extension of *his* office and one which has undergone little change over the years. For other women at McGill there has been more variation and it is possible to discern at least four phases of their concerns and activities. The first phase (late 19th and early 20th century) involved a wave of outstanding people who cared deeply about education, who fought for it and won against imposing odds. They were people like Octavia Grace Ritchie, Carrie Derick, Maude Abbott, Helen Reid, Annie Langstaff and Jessie Boyd. Their counterparts could be found in the universities of other countries. As sociologist, Jessie Bernard put it in reference to some members of the pioneering generation of women academics in the United States, "There were giants in those days."[2] The second phase was an overlapping continuation of the first. It included many of the same women, projecting them from the campus onto the wider social scene. There they joined with "strong-minded" club women, becoming committed workers for causes such as temperance, home and Empire, melioration of working conditions, extension of opportunities for others and votes for women.[3] The third phase (mid-20th century) was a period of artificial liberation during World War II followed by a cautious reassessment of woman's status in the home, the economy and the university.[4] In this period, Mary Jackson broke the formidable Engineering barrier, but the proportion of women at the university actually declined. The fourth phase (from the 1960's) encompasses the modern Women's Liberation Movement and is characterized by the opening of all campus activities to members of both sexes.

This pattern is, in general terms, consistent with the Women's Movement in North America generally. Its undulations have led people on several occasions to pronounce the movement dead,[5] but other observers still notice strong vital signs. This Chapter records aspects of those vital signs as they were manifest at McGill.

* * *

The very first graduates at McGill, the eight of '88, can truly be counted among the "giants." They were an enterprising group who asserted their claims to social justice and tried to effect change. As Carrie Derick more aptly said, they were "an ardent band, full of enthusiasm, deeply impressed with a sense of their responsibilities, devoted to one another and to their Alma Mater."[6] In order to maintain both social and intellectual links forged at college, they formed in 1889 the Mu Iota (or Mutual Improvement) Society, which was to be a graduate version of Delta Sigma. However, according to Derick, they found that the title lent itself to "undignified puns" and so they changed it to its present name, The Alumnae Society. These women of our great-grandmother's generation were truly alive—no fuddy duddy old ladies they. Nor was their new Society just an excuse to sit and sip tea and swap gossip—it was an activist organization dedicated to "the mutual improvement of its members in literary work and of furthering women's interests in Montreal."[7]

One of their early intellectual causes was to emphasize Canadian contributions to culture. Thus, just as Delta Sigma had done, the Alumnae sponsored discussions, debates and guest speakers with a strong emphasis on Canadian literature, history and science. The general question of Woman's role in society was also a major concern so that subjects like "The Present Course for Women at McGill," "The Advisability of Women's Working for Money" and "Women's Duty in Municipal Matters" appeared regularly on the agendas. By May 1891, the Alumnae had decided upon a programme of social action to help the working women of Montreal. At that time only thirty women had graduated from McGill—the eight of '88 plus five of '89, nine of '90 and eight of '91—but that small number was able to achieve a great deal. They sought support from their friends, then rented a house at 47 Jurors St., hired a cook and housekeeper and organized a "Girls' Club and Lunch Room." Taking turns themselves at purchasing food and managing the operation, they offered substantial meals at moderate prices to the skimpily paid female office, shop and factory workers. The "working girls" could buy tickets for meals at eight or ten cents, or they could select from the *à la carte* menu:

Vegetable soup and bread	3c.
Roast beef and potatoes	6c.
Mashed turnips	2c.
Baked beans	3c.
Apple pudding	3c.
Stewed prunes	3c.
Bread and butter	2c.
Tea, coffee or milk	2c. [8]

Carrie M. Derick, Professor of Morphological Botany

In an era when wages were very low and social services limited, this enterprising venture was both needed and appreciated. At that period, Molson's Brewery, a major Montreal employer, paid men $1.10 a day for a 10-hour day and women 60 cents a day. At that period when the legal and social rights of women in Quebec were minimal, working women were in double jeopardy because of their sex and their class status. Those in difficulties had to depend entirely on the charities of Church, temperance or other volunteer groups. Not surprisingly, the monthly reports of the Society for the Protection of Women and Children, one of the organizations specifically designed to help women in Montreal, revealed endless cases of deprivation and suffering.[9] The work of the Alumnae was typical of that done by compassionate middle-class women's groups to meliorate individual hardships.

During its first year, the Girls' Club attracted between 40 and 70 clients a day, it grew steadily, moved to larger quarters in 1894 and was responsible for serving more than 25,000 inexpensive meals a year. Other Club activities and facilities included Christmas parties and presents for poor children, dress-making classes, a fund for ill or unemployed women, a small library, a sitting room complete with piano, and four bedrooms for rent to working women. The McGill graduates were very sympathetic toward the many demands made upon women of the lower classes who frequently had the unrelieved double burden of homemaker and wage-earner. Their idealism seemed genuinely sincere as they urged each other to show "unselfish devotion to the interests not only of a narrow home-circle, but of all who are in need of help or comfort."[10] Their efforts were also enduring, so that the Lunch Room lasted for almost twenty years. Even then it did not die but modified and expanded its responsibilities in 1910 to become the University Settlement, whereupon it took on the functions of a general welfare agency and its administration passed beyond the immediate control of the Alumnae.

Another of the causes that fired the energies of the early Alumnae was the battle for the franchise. Grace Ritchie-England '88, Carrie Derick, '90, Anna Scrimger Lyman, '99 and Enid Turner-Bone, B.A. '17, M.A. '20 were among the stalwarts of the drive for women's political rights. Now that this battle has been won, it may be difficult to realize what courage it required around the turn of the century and beyond to stand publicly for votes for women. It took special determination when many women of the community were against the movement. Just as some women worked strenuously during the 1970's to defeat the Equal Rights Amendment in the United States, so some women had earlier opposed the franchise for their sex. For example, when in 1910 Delta Sigma held a debate "Resolved that women be given the franchise,"

Anna Scrimger Lyman, B.A. '99

the motion was lost; then, as a matter of interest, a standing vote of the meeting was taken to ascertain the personal views of those present. It was found that 29 were in favour of suffrage and 32 were against. Nor was the McGill Administration noticeably in favour, as could be seen the following year, when the Montreal Council of Women invited British suffragette leader extraordinaire, Mrs. Emmeline Pankhurst,[11] to come to Montreal in December 1911 to speak on the issue. Anna Scrimger Lyman, of the Council executive, asked Principal Peterson to appear on the platform with the guest speaker. Peterson replied that he was not "like the Eton boy who wrote that he detested Mrs. Pankhurst's objects but admired her methods," and that he personally did "have quite a leaning to the enfranchisement of women." Nevertheless, he declined to appear lest he seem "to endorse both the arguments and the methods with which Mrs. Pankhurst is identified."[12]

When the Federal franchise was finally granted women at the end of World War I, the vote was still denied Quebec women and thus a Quebec Women's Suffrage Association had to be formed. It was half French, half English and the first English-speaking President was the same Mrs. Anna Scrimger Lyman. She and other Alumnae were part of the indefatigable group which included Mme Gérin-Lajoie, Mme Thérèse Casgrain and Mlle. Idola Saint Jean, who taught French at McGill and published her own feminist newspaper, *La Sphère Feminine* (1933-46). Dogged and dynamic, they continued the campaign in this Province and, though they did not go to the Pankhurst extremes, they used many ingenious and unconventional devices, such as dropping leaflets from airplanes, to make their case. Success finally rewarded their efforts in 1940. Since then, prominent individual members of the Alumnae have not been so clearly associated with the political aspects of the Women's Movement. However, the Society as a whole has remained true to the spirit of its founding members and has consistently invited Canadian women politicians and public figures to participate in their conferences, workshops and other activities. Among their guests have been Agnes McPhail, the first woman member of the Canadian Parliament (who told the *McGill Daily* that women were too submissive [13]) and the Honourable Ellen Fairclough, the first woman Cabinet Minister.

Interest in women's education has been an on-going concern of the Alumnae and, from time to time when it felt a special need to assert itself, the Society became particularly active in this area. For example, in June 1937 a special meeting was held to consider the problems of a woman student who had been refused admission to Architecture. As a result, a protest was sent to the McGill Senate. This action may not have been decisive, but the extra pressure probably helped for it was the next year that the School of Architecture agreed in principle to admit women.

WOMEN WAGE CIVIL WAR, DECLARES MRS. PANKHURST.

Leader of England's militant suffragettes, snapped by a Star staff photographer as she reached Montreal. The lady to the left of the illustration is Mrs. Ritchie-England, who was at the station to welcome Mrs. Pankhurst.

Grace Ritchie England Meets Emmeline Pankhurst

Also in 1937, the Society made efforts to have representation on the McGill Board of Governors. Two years earlier the Alumnae had become a branch of the Graduates' Society whose constitution allowed three men to sit with the Governors, but no woman had yet held a seat on that august body. Thus in 1937, the Alumnae Society formally requested one of its members, Elizabeth Monk, who was then on the Graduates' Society Nominating Committee, to forward Susan Cameron Vaughan's name as a candidate for the Board of Governors. The Alumnae believed

> there has been for some time a growing feeling among the women graduates of McGill that the problems which affect women under- graduates, and even women graduates, have perhaps not received the full consideration which they merit by the Board of Governors, not indeed from any lack of interest on the part of the Governors themselves but because they are, of necessity, not familiar with these particular problems.
>
> Whether or not this feeling is justified is, of course, another matter but we believe that the appointment of a woman graduate would still any such criticism and would also serve as a great stimulus to the interest of women graduates both in the University itself and in the Graduates' Society.[14]

Unfortunately, Miss Monk had to report that "the long prevailing practice of nominating only men" for the Board of Governors prevented the other members of the Nominating Committee from accepting the Alumnae's suggestion.

While this attempt thus failed, the women graduates had at least raised the issue and in 1941 the name of one of the members, Catherine I. MacKenzie, did appear on the ballot for Graduate Society representa- tive to the Board. She was not elected and it was not until January 1970, when Claire Kerrigan took her seat, that a woman joined the Governors and it was five more years before a woman, Joan Dougherty, was elected to the Board as a Graduates' Society representative. In passing it might be noted that by 1979, a total of ten women had served on the Board— four from the community at large, one as Graduates' Society representa- tive, three as student representatives and two as non-academic staff representatives.

Other Alumnae efforts to exert influence on McGill's educational policy or practice have included supporting R.V.C.'s request that the Board of Governors acquire some property adjacent to the College (1935), recommending that the School of Social Work undertake a project on "Planning for Post Graduate Employment" (1955), success- fully petitioning the Faculty of Education to offer the Diploma in Educa-

Grace Ritchie England, Political Candidate

Idola Saint Jean

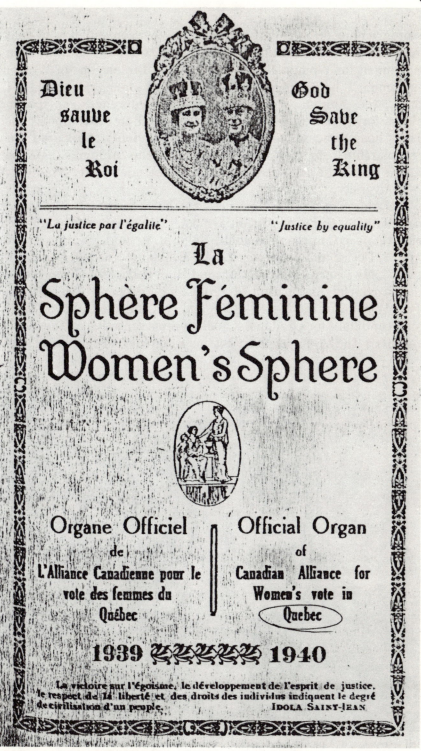

tion programme on a part-time basis for the convenience of mature women (1966) and initiating two evening courses, "Introduction to Management for Women" and "Behavioural Dimensions of Women in Management," both offered by the Faculty of Management in 1974. In addition, the Alumnae have held career conferences, co-sponsored seminars for women in management, operated an off-campus housing register, hosted receptions for new women students and raised money for scholarships. In many of these ways, the Alumnae anticipated functions later to be assumed by the Dean of Students and other officers of the University.

The Alumnae scholarships not only helped current students, but paid tribute to some of McGill's most distinguished women—Ethel Hurlbatt, Susan Cameron Vaughan, Helen R.Y. Reid, Georgina Hunter, Carrie M. Derick and Catherine I. MacKenzie. (Miss MacKenzie, B.A. '04, was Lady Principal of the Montreal High School for Girls, President of the Provincial Association of Protestant Teachers, 1937-38, Montreal's "Woman of the Year," 1938 and, as indicated above, the first woman candidate for Graduates' Society representative on the Board of Governors.) The Alumnae also set up a bursary in honour of Gladys

At the Presentation of Alumnae Scholarships, 1979: Esther England Cushing, B.A. '25, Kyre Emo Davis, B.Sc. '53, Gwendoline Fielders Buchanan, B.A. '24, Elizabeth Monk, B.C.L. '23

Murray, the long-time Secretary of R.V.C. In 1979 the Scholarship Fund received a generous contribution from the will of the late Mabel King, B.A. '07, M.A. '10, and new scholarships were established. One was named for Mabel King herself, and two others were in honour of Octavia Grace Ritchie England, the first woman valedictorian, and Hilda Oakeley, the first Warden of R.V.C. Apart from such bequests, which are all too rare, the Alumnae methods of fund-raising generally relied on such traditional ventures as bridge games in the Currie Gymnasium. By the mid-1970's, however, rising costs and increasing demands made obsolete these "ladies auxiliary" methods of a more leisured past, involving as they did so much work for relatively little return. An increasingly sophisticated Alumnae began to seek ways to raise money on a much larger scale. The first major venture was a giant auction of McGill Memorabilia, which was a very successful appeal to nostalgia and generosity organized by Arlene Gaunt, B.Sc. '53. This was followed by the McGill Book Fair, a joint effort of the Alumnae and the McGill Associates. The Book Fair has become an annual event on Campus, a time for browsers and buyers, students and professors and book lovers of all kinds to come to hunt for bargains and surprises among the thousands of items collected.

The Alumnae have also participated in women's affairs in the wider community. Their activities have included helping found the Canadian Federation of University Women (1919), sending a resolution to the Montreal School Board asking for improved salaries for elementary school teachers (1936), supporting their members for appointment to public positions such as membership on the Quebec Protestant Education Committee (1938), endorsing the idea of compulsory education in Quebec (1943), and co-operating with groups such as the Montreal Council of Women and the International Federation of University Women, for which they provided a number of office holders. In 1971, as part of McGill's Sesquicentennial celebrations, the Alumnae Society held a conference on "Issues and Opportunities for Women" and invited all interested women's groups (French and English) in Quebec to participate; from 1973, through the leadership of Lisette Marshall and Leiba Aronoff, the Society became actively involved in the Canadian Association for Adult Education programme on "Learning Opportunities for Women." All these kinds of activities testify to the fact that the Alumnae continue to seek "new ways of working together to meet the higher educational needs of women."[15]

* * *

Even though the Alumnae Society has often been in the vanguard of social ideas, it has not been able to satisfy everyone that it is a dynamic and forward-looking organization. Inevitably, with the passage of time, traditionally middle-class institutions like McGill and its Alumnae Society are almost bound to develop encrustations of gentility and new layers of conservatism. There is also a general tendency for any graduate society to attract older, nostalgic members and for younger fire-brands to think of them as reactionary "Establishment" enclaves. The development of the Young Alumni division of the McGill Graduates' Society in 1971 was an attempt to counteract this tendency. However, even that could not help everyone. Thus, three years after the establishment of the Young Alumni, one alumna who had moved to Los Angeles and had joined a women's consciousness-raising group, vehemently objected to the Graduate Society's (and the University's) custom of listing women by their husbands' names rather than their own, that is, the names by which most of them had been known when they were at McGill. Her letter of protest to the *McGill Daily* read in part:

> As you might imagine, I have long forgotten McGill, which left a slightly bitter aftertaste. No one encouraged me to explore my horizons while I was at McGill. And the McGill Society here in LA seems wedded to the old roles for women too, so I have not joined.
>
> But somewhere I have always hoped that something would happen at McGill to give women new chances, new horizons. Surely, I thought, by 1974 something MUST have changed. Canada cannot be that much of a backwater . . . or can it?
>
> But alas, today I received a letter to alumnae from Principal Bell —addressed to Mrs. Larry Saltzman. Now Larry Saltzman, my dear husband and an active feminist, has never been East of Chicago—so he has no interest whatsoever in McGill. The supposed compliment to his masculinity implied in "Mrs. Larry Saltzman" was utterly lost on him. But what of my feelings? Here is my "Alma Mater" which has utterly obliterated my identity—my name! Where was the "Buzzell," the proud Canadian name I wear? And where oh where is poor Linda? Disappeared, it seems, as far as McGill is concerned. Well, alas, so has my support for McGill. . . .[16]

This letter from the former student concluded with the hope that "some sisters" would read it and take heart for "surely it cannot be impossible to change all of those men's minds." Coincidentally, it was just about this time that the Women's Union, phoenix-like, was reappearing. This time it took on a distinctly feminist guise. As recorded in Chapter 6, the Women's Union came into being in 1932 and was the successor of a series of organizations designed to promote the general interests of women students attending the University. It was disbanded in 1969, partly through inertia and partly because the women student leaders of the day considered that separation of the sexes in campus organizations was outmoded. Noting its tearless demise, the *Daily* pronounced that "the casualties of the death of the Women's Union would be the Freshette reception and the annual book exchange,"[17] but the latter, more important function would be assumed by the University Bookstore. So it was apparently without regret on the one hand, or jubilation on the other that the women and men of McGill became equal members of the same student organization.

However, some perceptive undergraduates soon realized that the integration of the Women's Union with the Students' Society meant little more than the muffling of any voice to speak up clearly for the women of McGill. They could see there remained a need for an organization to "support, encourage and provide role models for women struggling for equality in a male-dominated society."[18] Arts students, Susan Gottheil, '75, and Basia Hellwig, '75, who were rather contemptuous of the old Women's Union as a group which perpetuated women's traditional roles through teas, bake sales, fashion shows and the like, were among those who realized that, while the W.U. had disappeared, its annual allotment —presumably by oversight—had not been removed from the Student Society's budget. Thus, they saw that a renewed organization could be established with some financial and legal base. So they began to plan. Even as they called upon the Students' Council to convene a general meeting for the revival of the W.U., they organized a successful conference on "Women and Health." Soon after the open meeting, which was held in November, 1974, and at which the Women's Union was formally revived, the women were ready with a programme and a budget. Their major projects for the first year were to develop a Women's Resource and Drop-in Centre, to hold a "Women and Arts" symposium with distinguished visiting lecturers and to support a women's paper being founded by the Women's Collective. These were ambitious, high-energy goals.

A centre, a physical focal point for the women students had long been the dream of female campus leaders. The old Women Students' Society had bemoaned in 1931 that it was "handicapped in that there is no building at McGill which might be termed a Women's Union,"[19] and it had vague plans for such a building to be erected in what was then a space between R.V.C. and the Montreal High School. But this "dream building" which was to contain among other things, a swimming pool and a gymnasium, never materialized. However, the women of McGill were not completely homeless. The Women's Union, the organization which succeeded the W.S.S., held its meetings in R.V.C. where a lounge and office space were permanently assigned and where the President had half her residence fees paid by the University so that she might live on campus. Women also had some access to the Students' Union, but their facilities were acknowledged to be unattractive and inferior—a situation that was rationalized by the fact that they paid only $1.00 student activities fees while the men paid $3.50. At the end of the 1950's, when new buildings were beginning to spring up all over campus and a new student union was contemplated, the University established a Special Committee on the Women's Union under Dr. David L. Thomson. Both that committee and a parallel group from the Women's Union agreed that there should be "lounges for women students in all teaching buildings that are extensively used by such students in considerable numbers," but that, in the new student building, women expected to have equal access to all facilities and "did not seek to have any space reserved for them, apart from powder rooms." As the Leacock Building was being constructed in the early 60's, plans for a Women-Students' Common Room and a Men-Students' Common Room were dropped in favour of rooms open to members of both sexes. However, a spirit of separation was still alive and the Building Director received a petition bearing over 80 names expressing disapproval of the disappearance of the former women's common room and asking that something be done to provide a place "where *women only* can sit and relax between classes."[20]

All these past concerns about special space for women students were similar to, yet different from, the demands of the revived Women's Union of the 70's. The early ones were more social and campus-oriented and were generally protective of women; the later ones were more aggressive and more directly related to the intellectual thrust of the Women's Movement in society at large. However, all involved something of the perennial dilemma of the historic drive for women's rights, that seeming paradox of wanting to be both special and equal, to be both distinct and in the mainstream. The women of the 70's were sensitive to this problem but they continued to see a special space for women as an essential requirement. Thus, despite the granting of what the women considered to be a "token budget," the new Women's Union's first goal, the drop-in centre, was achieved. It was opened in February 1975 on the fourth floor of the Union Building on McTavish St. and it offered a place where women from all Faculties could, if they chose and had the time or interest, meet informally "without the inhibiting presence of men," use the library which was well-stocked with up-to-date feminist literature in French and English, participate in discussions on issues such as abortion and day care, seek advice and companionship, join consciousness-raising groups and generally exchange ideas over coffee.

The centre was called, after Virginia Woolf, "A Room of One's Own."[21]

The second major goal of the new Women's Union, the "Women and Arts" symposium, was achieved in March 1975 but the third aim, support for the *Women's Collective Press,* had rough sledding. In fact, a reduced budget allocation from the Students' Society prevented the W.U. from granting the newspaper any funds at all. Nevertheless, the revived Women's Union had begun dynamically and the impetus of this strong start carried it forward. A small, but concerned, group of young women continued the effort after the moving spirits had graduated and kept the momentum alive by sponsoring or co-sponsoring events such as visits by feminist celebrity, Kate Millett.

Meanwhile, on the eve of International Women's Year, several other women's groups began to emerge on the McGill campus. Some of these, for example, the McGill Women Medical Students' Association and the McGill Association of Women in Law, had specialized interests and were intended to give support to the women students in the professional Faculties as well as to help women claim their rights in what were perceived as male dominated professions. Both the Law and the Medicine groups held regular meetings, convened special symposia and contributed papers on women to their respective professional McGill journals. In 1975, in honour of International Women's Year, the *McGill Law Journal* (a student produced publication) issued a special number devoted to Women, as did the *McGill Journal of Education* (a Faculty of Education publication).

Another kind of organization surfaced in the Women's Collective. This was a more politically oriented feminist group with a heterogeneous membership but with a generally socialist outlook. It grew out of a course on "Women's Liberation" taught by Dr. Marlene Dixon of the Sociology Department. Dr. Dixon had a reputation as a radical (she had been the centre of a student protest action at the University of Chicago) and arrived at McGill in 1969 amid a welter of publicity. Her course on Women's Liberation attracted about 200 people, mainly women, and was described by one of her students as follows:

> Unlike her staid colleagues, Marlene attacked her subject matter from all fronts, personal, political and practical, adopting the Chinese method of learning—theory perfected through practice.
>
> Before a few weeks were up the class had been divided into Consciousness Raising groups (which were held once a week outside of class) according to class background. Consciousness raising was seen as a practical way to bring women out of their personal isolation. Finally a ghetto of their own! Following this, group projects were initiated, emphasizing research, papers, struggle and whatever else might be necessary for the desired results.

Dr. Marlene Dixon

Given the style of this course, Marlene's classes were always a hub of activity. No slackers in that room as heated debate often took prominence over formal lectures and learning became a demanding and exciting process. The Women's Movement was dissected, criticized and synthesized. Women's emancipation was looked at in a new light, that of the liberation of humankind. No longer could women be seen as a species apart, oppressed in a vacuum and struggling in the same. Liberation now had a new direction, a cohesive logical path, but most important, a historically inevitable one. Thus, the women in Marlene's class were more than just gung-ho. They were not simply women's libbers or fanatics—they were not men-haters. They were women armed with a theory and equipped with the militancy necessary to bring that theory alive. They were calculating and astute and more than willing "to learn from the past to build for the future."[22]

The Women's Collective was one of the most visible and vocal of the work groups spawned by the "Women's Liberation" course. Its major project was to attempt to take on the editing of the *Free Press*, a publication sponsored by the Arts and Science Undergraduates' Society (ASUS) and made available annually to different groups to edit and publish. The ASUS did not take the proposal for an all-women's editorship seriously and awarded the *Free Press* to another bidder. This provoked a lively exchange in the correspondence columns of the *Daily*. It also prompted the Women's Collective to circulate a petition, as a result of which, the ASUS was required to hold an open meeting to determine who should edit the paper. The meeting, held late in October 1974 and variously described as "a fiasco," "bedlam," or "absolute chaos," decided in favour of the women. However, the ASUS remained reluctant to comply with the decision and, after another month of haggling, it was agreed to have two papers—one edited by the women in response to a recognized need for a women's publication, the other "regular" *Free Press* in recognition of the need for an open campus newspaper. Both were to be funded by ASUS. Thus, in December the *Women's Collective Press* finally appeared. It proclaimed a commitment to open-mindedness and insisted that its staff, though all-female, was drawn from a variety of backgrounds and represented different political persuasions. It did not, as its opponents had anticipated, refuse to accept copy written by men but it was openly sympathetic to leftist causes, adamantly supportive of suppressed groups and trenchantly critical of the *status quo*. The *Women's Collective Press* produced some literate, sophisticated and concerned writing, the equal of any campus publication of the time. It delved into issues such as U.S. policy in Vietnam as well as wages for housewives, machismo, sexism, rape and exploitation of power. It was an outspoken, unladylike publication, just as the debate over its birth had been.[23] While the members of the Collective attempted earnestly to explain in sociological terms that they wanted a woman-only editorial board because of the need for women to express themselves co-operatively as a group and to demand redress for the historic injustice meted out to their sex, they also objected violently to some of the politics and language of the ASUS, especially the incompetent and demeaning way the open meeting had been conducted, with the Chairman referring to them as "chicks" and telling at least one of them to "fuck off." On the other hand, supporters of the ASUS (both male and female) complained that the Collective members were aggressive, unpleasant, discriminatory and power hungry. But before long tempers died down and with them the fire that had energized the efforts to run a campus publication. Like many a student paper before it, the *Women's Collective Press* had difficulties in its second year, faltered and disappeared.

* * *

In the early 70's, while some women students made themselves heard in voices that were more strident than was customary at McGill, the Senate had taken an unprecedented action. In January, 1970, in response to pressure from Student Society President, Julius Grey, and others, it established a body rejoicing in the name of the Committee on Discrimination as to Sex in the University. This was just three years after a Federal Royal Commission had been appointed to inquire into the Status of Women in Canada, but several months before that Commission's report was released. This was also the era when most Canadian universities were undertaking inquiries into sexism and discrimination and some institutions, for example, the Universities of Toronto and Alberta, were beginning to consider compensatory action for the male/female discrepancies they discovered. The McGill Committee was given a mandate to examine hiring and salaries at all levels, admission policies of graduate and professional faculties, the use of facilities and participation in extra-curricular activities. It met a dozen times during the following year, called for submissions from anyone on either the McGill or Macdonald College campus, held both public and *in camera* hearings, and collected data from the Faculties and the Personnel Office. Though the final report noted that "there was not a heavy response to the Committee's request for submissions,"[24] the Committee took its task seriously and found ample evidence of sex-based differentiation in employment conditions at McGill.

It studied 979 full-time academic staff members in all ranks from Lecturer to full Professor for the three years from 1967-68 to 1969-70 and discovered that the salaries of women fell below those of men in all ranks in all years and that, though the difference never exceeded 10% in any rank, the overall average salaries of female staff were 20% below those of male staff. This reflected the fact that there was a much higher concentration of female staff in the lower ranks. While the total proportion of women on academic staff was approximately 16.5%, only about 5.5% of the full Professors, and about 13% of the Associate Professors were women but about 20% of the Assistant Professors and 40% of the Lecturers were female. The study also showed that women were promoted less rapidly than males, that things were not getting better because the new appointments at the Assistant and Associate Professorships showed a declining proportion of women, that women received lower starting salaries than men, though a larger proportion of female than male appointees held Ph.D.'s. The Committee considered that the differentials could be explained primarily on the basis of lower salaries offered at first appointment, which in turn probably reflected the weaker bargaining position of the female academic. The bargaining power of married women was thought to be less because of their lower mobility but was probably also a reflection of discriminatory attitudes in the academic community. Given a policy of fairly automatic salary increments, lower starting salaries tend to be perpetuated in subsequent salary patterns and slower promotion rates for women tend further to accentuate the salary differentials.[25] The Committee therefore recommended that a special salary award be made to female staff to close the gap between their salaries and those of their male colleagues of equal rank; that Chairmen and Deans be instructed not to take advantage of women's weaker bargaining position by offering them lower starting salaries than they would offer males of equal qualifications; that administrators be urged to encourage the recruitment of qualified female members of staff and to promote them on the basis of academic considerations only.[26]

The data concerning students were not so damning. Like others who have examined the student body of McGill, the Committee on Discrimination had some difficulty in compiling consistent statistics. However, the evidence clearly suggested that the shortage of females in the various professional areas—only 15% in Architecture and 10% in Dentistry, for example—was more a reflection of a low application rate than a restrictive admissions policy. The study also showed that, in several "male" areas, a higher proportion of female than male applicants were admitted so that the Committee blamed the paucity of women students not on the University but on the lack of female motivation and on cultural conditioning. It therefore recommended that the University publicize the fact that qualified female students were accepted on an equal basis with males and suggested that McGill should do more to encourage young women to widen their horizons. The counselling services should be expanded in an attempt to combat traditional attitudes which tended to deter women from entering professional schools.

The Committee then turned its attention to matters that were perhaps peripheral but, none the less, extremely important. It asserted that any modern university has a major responsibility to provide the climate and facilities to foster intellectual development, that McGill had not fully satisfied this obligation and that, specifically, the absence of day-care arrangements for young children resulted in *de facto* discrimination against female staff and students. The Committee countered the argument that ''the University is not in the baby-minding business'' by pointing out that the University was not in the health or the accommodation business, either, yet McGill recognized that facilities in those areas were necessary to permit and encourage the intellectually competent to pursue their academic and professional careers. So, just as it provided health services and student housing, so it should provide day-care and it should, therefore, establish a low-cost centre. McGill was also criticized for its lack of a compassionate policy on maternity leave for academic women, though there were maternity provisions for non-academic employees. Recommendations were also made that the health insurance scheme should treat men and women equitably and that an ombudsman be appointed to hear and remedy individual grievances relating to inequalities or discrimination based on sex. Overall, the Committee charged the University with the responsibility for setting an example to the community by dealing positively and constructively with lingering attitudes and structures that perpetuated both overt and covert discrimination.

Both the approach of the Committee on Discrimination as to Sex and its findings were very similar to those at other Canadian universities. Study after study and a national survey conducted by the Association of Universities and Colleges of Canada (AUCC) showed that female enrolment in professional faculties was relatively small, that fringe benefits did not favour women, that women academics tended to cluster in the lower ranks, that their promotion was slower and that there was a sizable salary differential between women and their male colleagues. [27] Perhaps if the McGill case had been unique, the University might have been shamed into taking immediate ameliorative action, but when the Committee's report was brought to Senate in March 1971 it received ''less than chivalrous treatment.'' [28] The report was introduced to Senate by Dr. Rose Johnstone, Associate Professor of Biochemistry, and seconded by Professor Frances Henry of the Department of Anthropology. In an atmosphere of somewhat bemused tension, they found themselves supported by student senators and other colleagues but also surrounded by skeptics and critics.

The strongest reaction was related to the contentious issue of salary and promotion differences. The proposal for an across-the-board upward salary adjustment for all female academics was never taken seriously but the idea drew forth an attack from Chancellor, Donald O. Hebb. Dr. Hebb, writing as psychologist rather than Chancellor, circulated a formal statement criticizing the report as being "out of touch with academic and psychological reality." He said that, ". . . the record shows that a small proportion of women are outstandingly good and must be recognized, but that women on the average are much less productive of original research. On the average, they are bound to get less promotion in a university that values research." Hebb then went on to explain that "from an early age boys are not only more active physically and more aggressive, but also less willing to follow, and in these respects they show a picture that is general in all mammalian species." None of this, according to Hebb, could be attributed to differences in the way boys and girls are brought up.

Dr. Hebb, an internationally respected psychologist and obvious authority figure at McGill, claimed that "inborn male aggressiveness" was a significant factor in research, as were male aptitudes for mathematical thinking and a greater interest in abstract problems. He appeared to justify salary differences with the argument: "Given two Ph.D.'s, male and female, equally promising as teachers, which is more likely to add to the university's reputation by doing and publishing significant research? The man is, on the record, and so he is more valuable to the university on the average. . . ."[29] Plausible though many Senators apparently found this reasoning, it dubiously ignored both the idea of individual differences and particular cases at McGill. It was, *au fond,* the conventional excuse that had been used, for example, to deny world-renowned researcher, Dr. Maude Abbott, both promotion and salary parity with her male colleagues.

Another critical reaction to the report claimed that in Arts there was no significant difference between men and women in the same professional categories, that the Discrimination Committee's findings were distorted because the picture they gave for the University as a whole might perhaps reflect the situation in a traditionally male Faculty like Engineering, but it was not true of Arts where the significant numbers of women were to be found. It was also observed that salaries differed in the various Faculties so the Committee's lumping them all together made for inaccuracies and it was pointed out that the Committee was to have investigated discrimination as to sex, but had interpreted its mandate in one direction only. Figures from the report suggested that there also existed discrimination against men at McGill.

Dr. Rose Johnstone responded to these comments by charging that the Committee had been hampered in its investigation by poor co-operation, that it had not been given access to Faculty-by-Faculty break-down of salaries and had been denied some of the other information it sought. She acknowledged that some few men in the lower ranks were at a salary disadvantage, noted that this was also undesirable, but re-emphasized that the gross discrimination at McGill was ''in one direction only,'' that is, it worked overwhelmingly against women. She also made it clear that the Committee had not intended that women should receive salary increases or promotions without regard to ability, but that their qualifications, abilities and contributions should be recognised without regard to their gender.

These fundamental issues of academic justice were strenuously argued all afternoon but gradually the McGill senators began drifting away until the quorum was challenged and the debate was closed. Subsequently, a committee of implementation was established under the chairmanship of Dean of Arts and Science, Edward Stansbury. The Committee did not develop a great deal of momentum and disbanded in 1974 without producing a report.

* * *

Yet the issue of women was not entirely dead at McGill. Members of the Women's Union were still vitally concerned and about two hundred students signed a petition calling for the establishment of Women's Studies. On the initiative of Dr. Erin Malloy, who was then Associate Dean of Students and Assistant Professor of Religious Studies, a series of open meetings was called. These attracted both students and staff members from several different Faculties, bringing together people interested in the Women's Movement but who had previously worked in isolation, unaware of each other's concerns or even existence. Very few, if any, were fiery radicals seeking direct confrontation with the Administration or the complete overthrow of the social order, but they did want change and full academic recognition for women. However, women's movements generally have been characterized by their amorphous organization, enthusiasm for many a worthy cause falls victim to apathy and, though people may want something to be done, they tend to hope someone else will do it. The McGill group

Dr. Erin Malloy-Hanley

was neither unaware of nor immune to these tendencies and appointed a Steering Committee to develop structure and programmes. From this emerged the McGill Committee on Teaching and Research on Women (MCTRW) which, among other things, made a formal proposal to Senate Academic Policies Committee concerning the establishment of a Centre for Teaching and Research on Women. The proposal was not accepted but the MCTRW then applied for and received from Principal Robert Bell a grant to assess the degree of interest in the academic study of women at McGill.

This survey [30] discovered that there were in 1975-76 nine half courses and one full course in seven departments specifically devoted to women and at least thirty courses in ten departments which included units on women or provided opportunities for research. Over the years, almost 300 theses on women had been accepted, at least forty-six scholars in twenty departments were currently doing research on women. However, women were receiving less than 5% of research funds and their status in the academic ranks had not changed significantly since the "Discrimination as to Sex" study. In 1976, just over 18% of the full-time academic staff was female and it was small comfort to know that this was 5% above the Canadian national average.[31] Salary discrepancies at McGill had remained essentially unaltered since the earlier survey. A study at a U.S. university similarly afflicted estimated that at present rates of progress, parity would be achieved in 2080. When would it happen at McGill?

Endorsing the Association of Universities and Colleges of Canada's resolution that women "with clout" be given senior posts at all institutions of higher learning,[32] the MCTRW recommended the appointment of a Vice Principal (Women) to have special advocacy for women, to encourage affirmative action and to serve as a role model. Principal Bell demurred at that suggestion but he was supportive of the idea of a Senate Committee on Women to fulfill some of these functions. Thus, by the summer of 1977 such a Committee was established with male and female membership and a mandate to explore the possibilities of establishing a Centre for Teaching and Research on Women, undertake advocacy for all women on campus, encourage more women to pursue graduate studies, and help co-ordinate research on women. It was through the work of this Committee, specifically the efforts of Dr. Irwin Gopnik, that another of the MCTRW's major recommendations became a reality. A proposal for an inter-faculty, interdisciplinary Women's Studies' Minor was approved by the Faculty of Arts and became part of the recognised McGill programme in 1979.

Meanwhile, the MCTRW kept the general question of women alive by conducting, with the help of grants from the Faculty of Graduate Studies and Research, several series of well-attended public seminars on various aspects of research on women. Though the thrust trailed off after the first year, the group continued its ad hoc, freely structured existence, producing a lively *Newsletter,* holding occasional meetings, sponsoring film festivals, discussion groups and the like. It could flourish or die at any time, depending on the impetus given by a dozen or so professors like Katherine Young and Deidre Machado and others like graduate students, Andrea Vabalis and Barbara Scales, or librarian Susie Slavin, and counsellor Rhona Steinberg who were not prepared to leave the implementation of their ideals to someone else.

One of the activities of the Senate Committee on Women during its first year was to explore an administrative manoeuvre which had effectively resulted in there being no senior woman in the Dean of Students' office. It will be recalled that when changes were made at R.V.C. in 1970 and the Warden was relieved of responsibility for the welfare of all women undergraduates, the University had decided that the newly created offices of Dean of Students and Associate Dean of Students should take on that responsibility. As noted in Chapter 5, it was made clear at the time that, though one of these officers should have special concern for women, this was not necessarily to be the Associate Dean. [33] Principal Rocke Robertson also indicated that, as far as possible, the posts of Dean and Associate Dean might be alternated between male and female appointees. Further, it was understood that the Deans should be academics in regular contact with students in the teaching/learning process as well as administrators, thus both jobs would be part-time. As it happened, the first Dean of Students was male, Dr. C.D. Solin; so was the second, Dr. E. Pedersen; so was the third, Dr. Saed Mirza. The first Associate Dean was female, Dr. Elizabeth Rowlinson, Assistant Professor of Mathematics. She held office from 1970 to 1974 and was particularly concerned about providing facilities and psychological support to encourage mature women students at the University. Dr. Rowlinson left McGill in 1978 to become Dean of Residence at St. Hilda's and Dean of Women at Trinity College, University of Toronto. Meanwhile, she had been succeeded as Associate Dean of Students by Dr. Erin Malloy, Assistant Professor of Religious Studies. Dr. Malloy-Hanley (as she later became) was indefatigable in her efforts to help individual students and to further the cause of women in the university. When she resigned in 1976, she was not replaced and at the end of Dean Mirza's term in 1978, a fourth male Dean of Students, Dr. Michael Herschorn, was appointed, but no Associate Dean. It appeared that the latter position had been quietly abolished.

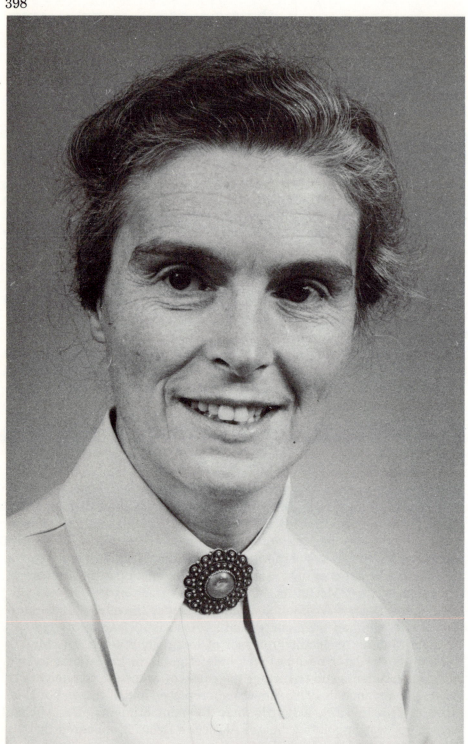

Dr. Elizabeth Rowlinson, First Associate Dean of Students

The Committee on Women brought this to the attention of Senate, pointing out that no formal decision had been made to this effect by Senate or the Board of Governors—it had just somehow happened that there would no longer be a senior academic woman in that office to serve as role model, to initiate programmes for women and to relate to the particular problems of women students. Senate endorsed the Committee's position and soon afterwards, Principal Bell established a search committee to find an Associate Dean of Students who would be a woman. However, early in the 1978-79 academic year, some student members of the Co-ordinating Committee on Student Services challenged this action. These young men claimed that the cost of an Associate Deanship, which would have to be borne from the Student Services budget, would be great and it was also unnecessary since there was a woman liaison officer in the Dean of Students office. The arguments raged in committees, Senate and the *McGill Daily*. It was reminiscent of the hassle Susan Cameron Vaughan had had with the editors of the *Daily* in the early 30's. And once again, the Warden of R.V.C. spoke out. In a letter co-signed by Barbara Scales of the M.C.T.R.W., Donna Runnalls explained the need for an academic woman in the Dean of Students' office at this time in our social history:

> The presupposition that women students have particular concerns and interests distinct from those of male students is controversial but we believe that it is valid. Certainly we are all people. But the fact of lower status for women in the university community, the persisting shortage of role models, the general sexism that still exists in the university . . . . the prospects on the job market, indicate that there are special problems of concern to women students.
>
> The point of having a Dean and an Associate and for one of the two to be a woman is not to have a figurehead in petticoats, but to have an administrator who can be an activist in the quest for solutions to these problems. . . . 34

A petition of three hundred supported the case but highly vocal male student leaders continued to argue that an academic woman was unnecessary in the Dean of Students' office. The Senate heard out the arguments on both sides and finally voted to continue the post of Associate Dean of Students. The search committee resumed its activities and in the spring of 1979 Dr. Kathleen Sibbald of the Department of Hispanic Studies was appointed the third Associate Dean of Students. The Committee on Women counted this a victory for the women of McGill.

Among the other activities of this Committee were the giving of support for a study of sexism in McGill's official publications, receiving and initiating complaints about sexism and pornography in *The Plumber's Pot* and the Engineering Students' *Handbook,* interceding in several cases of complaints of discrimination against academic and non-academic women, and considering a general question of salary discrepancies. These discrepancies were again highlighted in a study sponsored by the Féderation des Associations de Professeurs Universités du Québec (FAPUQ) in 1978.[35] This compared male and female salaries in selected departments at McGill and Laval Universities and showed that conditions for women at Laval had improved significantly and were more equitable than those at McGill. The major reason for the improvement was attributed to the fact of unionization at Laval, an interpretation which relatively few people at McGill found palatable. Meanwhile, on the initiative of Dr. Rose Johnstone, the McGill Association of University Teachers (M.A.U.T.) compared selected matched pairs in six Faculties and once again found significant differences in favour of males at McGill — some of them amounting to thousands of dollars. As a result of these findings, yet another University-wide matched peer study was authorized by Principal David Johnston in 1980.

It may be argued that the statistical techniques used in these kinds of studies are questionable; that it is virtually impossible to match pairs of persons as distinctive as academics; that differences between Faculties (for example Medicine and Arts) which, for practical reasons are related to the marketplace, are greater than differences within Faculties; that male/female differences can all be explained individually; and that there are relatively few women in administrative positions because women do not wish to accept the responsibilities. All this may be true, but the overwhelming fact of salary and promotion differences remains. It is also true that the women of McGill have not pushed vigorously for change. They have not used any of the studies cited above as tools or weapons for the improvement of their status, and when, as sometimes happens, a social scientist or a reporter from the *McGill News* or a representative of the general press asks a woman of McGill if she has personally suffered from discrimination, the answer is almost invariably ''No'' or ''No, but . . .'' The professional women of McGill seem to be reasonably content and unlikely to ''rock the boat.'' The Dawsonian vision of Woman, although modified and modernized is still alive and well at McGill. Thus, perhaps because women at this University are more absorbed in their teaching and research than concerned with their own rights, because they have adequate (if not equal) salaries, because they are temperamentally disinterested in taking on a fight that goes deep into the roots of our social structure and its definition of male and female—for all these possible reasons it does not seem likely that strenuous agitation for parity will ruffle the generally smooth adminis-

Dr. Kathleen Sibbald, Associate Dean of Students

trative waters of McGill in the near future.

That is not to say that there will not be protests by individuals and groups over perceived injustice, or that such protests have not already taken place. There have, indeed, been a number of *causes célèbres* involving female faculty members at McGill.

*   *   *

One of these was the liberation of the Faculty Club. Incredible as it now seems, there were sections of the Club reserved for male members until as recently as the late 1960's. The Faculty Club was established in 1923 but women were not admitted as members for more than a decade. Just a few months before retirement, the redoubtable Dr. Maude Abbott was admitted in March, 1936 and was the first female member of the Club. At that time, a Ladies' Committee was formed, house-rules were amended and restrictions to women's access to facilities were clearly spelled out. The new rules confined women to the main entrance hall, the main stairway, the tower room and offices on the first floor and to a separate lounge and dining room; they specified that ladies were not permitted in the main dining room, forbade them from entering the ball-room via the main lounge without special permission, restricted their use of the elevator unless accompanied by a member (i.e., male), told them not to loiter around the front door but to ascend the stairs without "unnecessary delay."[36] Despite their rampant patriarchal nature, these concessionary regulations were apparently accepted with good grace by the women faculty members. In the 30's the women themselves may not have been thoroughly convinced of their academic legitimacy, their right to belong to the collegiality to which their intellectual abilities and professional achievements entitled them. That conviction developed in the 60's. Only then were the second-class status and the restrictions challenged.

Upstairs, the main dining room, that splendid panelled room of vintage dignity, was traditionally reserved for men—except in the slow period of summer when, for financial reasons, women became accept-able. Nearby was the "ladies" dining room, smaller, more subdued, where "voices were never raised and every table had a vase of flowers on it."[37] It was a room suspected of "being especially designed to make working women feel silly."[38] Upstairs, too, was a ladies' lounge filled with "upholstered furniture covered in typically flowery chintz fabric, again presumably reflecting the taste and preferences of the very genteel ladies—mainly members of Faculty Wives Clubs and the Ladies Club—who frequented it."[39] Downstairs, in the ballroom was a lunch-time snack bar which had never seen women, except as servants. The snack bar itself was not really holy, but access to it was only possible by going through the main Lounge. The Lounge was a leathery, armchaired room where would gather around the fireplace at lunchtime in a 'Great Circle' of colleagueship and conversation, ''some of the liveliest spirits from different departments of the University''[40] —but never ever any women. At last some of the women of McGill decided that this apartheid situation was both ridiculous and unfair and that it was time for the archaic, chauvinistic traditions to be disposed of. The integration of the dining room was achieved by Dr. Virginia Douglas, Professor of Psychology and some of her colleagues; the conquest of the sandwich bar and downstairs lounge was a triumph of Dr. Frances Henry, Professor of Anthropology.

Dr. Douglas recalled how, after each summer, the female members of the Faculty Club would be relegated to the ''tea party atmosphere'' of the ladies' dining room, isolated from the informal and natural discussions that are so valuable a part of academic life. She noted that ''the arrival of male visitors to our department always underlined the ludicrousness of the arrangements. In order to avoid entertaining them amidst the chintz and velvet our colleagues were sore tempted to

Dr. Virginia Douglas, Professor of Psychology

succumb to the temptation of omitting the women members on the staff from the festivities.''[41] The breaking point was reached and, as Dr. Douglas reminisced:

> Finally, one summer, it was agreed that some of us would simply continue to frequent the main dining room. As the leaves of autumn turned to crimson, each day a few of us would nonchalantly enter the hallowed hall, usually accompanied and morally supported by our male colleagues. From time to time we would meet a pair of scandalized eyes but then the reaction seemed to subside and we began to enjoy the prospect of our 'sit-in' going down in history as a non-event. Gradually, however, the keepers of the status quo amassed a following and it was finally decided that the matter would have to be settled by a plebiscite.
>
> Although we were pleased, when the votes were counted, to learn that our cause had been victorious, it was a bit sobering to discover that something like one third of the members had voted against the change. Some confessed to us their misgivings about having to 'watch their language' in front of the ladies. One was disturbed by the prospect of having to rise when a lady joined the table.
>
> Most touching, however, was the comment of one white-haired, frail professor emeritus. A few weeks after the vote had been taken, he shuffled up to me and, placing a fatherly hand on my shoulder, he said: 'Dr. Douglas, it is such a pleasure to see you here, although I must admit I voted against having ladies in this dining room. But Dr. Douglas, I didn't mean you!''[42]

The ''gentlemen'' of the Faculty Club doubtless had no one of their colleagues in mind as they, like Ruskin at Oxford nearly a century before, ''kept the bonnets out''—it was just the ''principle'' of the thing, that plus the fact that men paid more than women. Even with the dining room liberated, the principle still held and another separate campaign was necessary in 1966 to free the downstairs male bastion. Dr. Frances Henry had to resort to almost comical tactics to integrate the lunch time facilities in the ballroom. The rules said that ladies should not enter the ballroom via the lounge without special permission. They did not say ladies should not enter the ballroom. The conundrum was how to get there without putting indecent female feet on the sacred floor of the all-male lounge. It occurred to Dr. Frances Henry that, behind one of the portals of the main dining room, there was a stairway that led directly into the ballroom. One lunch time, flanked by several male colleagues, she dramatically entered the ballroom by the back stairs, doing her best to ignore ''the looks of surprise and horror on the many bewildered male faces.''[43]

Dr. Frances Henry, Professor of Anthropology

The device of the back stairs, one which literally or metaphorically many women have used to gain their rights, was kept up until the shock effect had worn off. Then Dr. Henry and some of her female colleagues petitioned that the house rules be changed. It was indicative of the degree to which some women had internalized the patriarchal *status quo* that several refused to sign the letter of petition, saying that "they had always been well treated at McGill and couldn't do anything which might embarrass their male colleagues."[44] A poll was duly conducted by the Club executive and, though less than 10% of the members bothered to vote and though a third of those who did voted negatively,[45] the result was that finally all facilities of the Club were opened to all members on an equal basis.

No trace of the mandatory separation of the sexes can now be found in the dining facilities of the McGill Faculty Club and the "Ladies' Lounge" sign has been removed from the small room upstairs, as has another on the third floor that said, "No Ladies Beyond This Point." Downstairs, the reading room just off the lounge still manages to retain a stuffy, "Men's club" air, so that some women, especially if they happen to be young or new members, have been intimidated by the eyebrows raised over solemn journals or by the newspapers rattling like angry geese at their appearance on the threshold. Still, there is now no regulation, only lack of confidence, to deter female members of the Club from sitting beside their learned male colleagues, shaking out their own newspapers, and staring in their turn.

The liberation of the Faculty Club may now be considered complete. Differential fees based on gender have been abolished. Women now pay as much as men for, with freedom, comes responsibility and if they have equal salaries, why should they not pay the same?

* * *

Other incidents involving women and their demands for their rights have led to grievance cases against the University. In the 1970's, for example, there were four separate instances where the contracts of female faculty members were in jeopardy or were not renewed for what they believed to be grossly inadequate reasons and by processes they considered totally improper. Claire Arseneau, a Lecturer in the School of Social Work, Nancy Wolfson, an Associate Professor of Biology, Pauline Vaillancourt of the Department of Political Science, and Marlene Dixon of Sociology all formally protested the actions taken against them. Whatever the rights, wrongs and particular circumstances in each of these four separate cases, there was a common thread—a feeling on the part of the women that they had been the victims, *inter alia*, of sex discrimination. This feeling applied to the initial action and extended to a fear that they as women had hurt their causes by having the temerity to protest rather than accept. As one of them put it, ''Entrenched power dislikes any challenge to its supremacy, and when the entrenched powers are men, and one of the challengers a woman, their fury surpasses understanding. . . .''[46] In all cases, however, they found that some of their best and strongest support came from among some of the men of McGill, especially those men who served on their grievance committees in the McGill Faculty Union or the McGill Association of University Teachers.

All four cases took a heavy toll in human energy expended, time consumed, emotions drained and constructive endeavours perforce foregone. While all four received considerable attention in the public forum, that of Marlene Dixon was probably the most prominent. Dr. Dixon later produced an exceedingly bitter and scathing attack on McGill, its administration and its personnel procedures. In *Things Which Are Done in Secret,* Dixon outlined her own case and that of Pauline Vaillancourt largely by reproducing selections of letters, memoranda and minutes of meetings from the time of their appointments right through their grievance proceedings.

Dixon was by no means one to accept a complacent, Dawsonian view of her role and status at the University, nor to adopt a benign view of McGill itself. Indeed, in coming to the unhappy conclusion that ''the true essence of life and thought in our universities is hypocrisy,''[47] she castigated McGill for its ''secrecy and mystification,'' its reactionary capitalist values, its distortion of liberal ideas, and its persecution of radicals. Dixon herself was a radical who had participated actively in the student rebellion at the University of Chicago before coming to McGill in 1969 and had continued her support for Marxist-Leninist, F.L.Q. and similar causes after her appointment to McGill. She had also written a widely read, much reprinted article on ''The Rise of Women's Liberation.'' This tightly reasoned argument for women's rights and call for the end of male chauvinism was originally published in *Ramparts* in December, 1969. Her paper, ''Why Women's Liberation,'' written two years later was an even more sophisticated sociological analysis of woman's status within a context of imperialism, racism and classism. For Marlene Dixon, significant change in the social, economic and intellectual domination of women would require more than trifling cosmetic adjustments to attitudes and regulations—it demanded a supra-national political revolution so that the centuries of exploitation could be overthrown. She also challenged many of the ideas and methods, what she called the ''hollow litanies,'' of the Women's Movement.

Marlene Dixon was not a comfortable colleague. In 1971 the fight over the renewal of her contract rent the Sociology Department. With such a controversial figure, the evidence for renewal or termination was inevitably both strong and contradictory. Comments by her students were polarized—her classes were political harangues or her classes offered fresh insights; she was very responsive to her students or she was intolerant and uninterested in her students. Similarly, some reviewers of her published work considered that it added little if anything to knowledge, others praised it as a seriously worthwhile contribution; some professors considered her an intemperate trouble-maker, a meddler in politics; others thought her a courageous advocate for intellectual freedom and the right to dissent, a principled participant-observer of society.

The pros and cons were thrashed out and, finally, the decision was taken to renew Marlene Dixon's appointment. However, her career at McGill continued to be fraught with controversy and many people sighed with relief when she resigned in October, 1974. Meanwhile, Pauline Vaillancourt's case was referred to the C.A.U.T. and a decision favourable to her was reached in August, 1973.[48] By a curious coincidence, the arbitrator in her case was David L. Johnston, then of the Faculty of Law at the University of Toronto but in 1979 to become the Principal of McGill. Claire Arseneau's claim to reinstatement was also supported by an independent inquiry, but she chose not to return to the University. Nancy Wolfson's protest over her non-renewal was subject to prolonged inquiry by M.A.U.T. and C.A.U.T. She was given support by the McGill Faculty Union and an Inter-University Committee on Women with representatives from the Université de Montréal, Université du Québec à Montréal and McGill. Members of these groups considered that, after eleven years of service at McGill and promotion to Associate Professor with no indication of unsatisfactory service, a non-renewal of contract was highly unusual and hence they believed that sex discrimination was an issue in the case. However, despite the facts that no women had been appointed to the original departmental committee considering her renewal and that the Biology Department, like the other science departments at McGill, was male-dominated, the C.A.U.T.'s Committee on Academic Freedom and Tenure determined that sexism was not a real issue here. Nancy Wolfson did not agree and once bitterly remarked that she grew up in the South where an all-white jury was a hanging jury. The case was reviewed by several panels but, by late 1979 after five years of contention, it had not been completely closed. As it dragged on, C.A.U.T. representatives were scheduled to meet with Principal Johnston to achieve a final resolution of the problem. Meanwhile, Dr.

Wolfson had been given a short-term appointment as a research associate and then left the University.

It might be wondered whether or not these four much-publicized cases amounted to a conspiracy against women at McGill? Overall, such a claim would be difficult to sustain. Women have not been the only academics to have been embroiled in non-renewal and similar squabbles. There have been some well-known cases involving men just as there have been routine disputes involving women which have been resolved quietly in their favour. Such cases are usually cloaked in confidentiality. Both the participants and their advisors prefer it that way.

Yet, while the thought of any overt conspiracy can be dismissed, what still has to be reckoned with is the fact that subtle pressures of tradition have something of a conspiratorial force. The old expectations that women should be agreeable rather than assertive, together with simple condescension, may create an atmosphere more strongly conducive to conformity to the stereotype than blatant prejudice or rank injustice. Many women may actually be unaware of the subtle "put-downs" that have been widely used at McGill and other universities. These include little, apparently trivial, practices such as using social titles for female academics and professional ones for males—that is, referring to women professors as "Miss" or "Mrs." but to men as "Dr." or "Professor," even in some cases where such titles are undeserved but only assumed on the basis of gender; or "jokes" as shown by the witty Physiology Professor who said to the medical student just as she was about to take her final orals, "So you want to be a woman doctor! What is McGill coming to?"[49] ;or "gimmicks" which are meant to be amusing, such as one used by the McGill Professor of Anatomy who boasted of his teaching techniques, "I often project 35mm slides. Habitually, I will insert a picture of a naked woman in a suggestive posture in the middle of a presentation on liver disease and then blame my wife for having interfered with my filing system."[50] Even when women are sensitive to these things, not many protest them. They hardly seem worth the effort, embarrassment and risk of being branded as "paranoid" or "a humourless blue stocking." Yet cumulatively, little insults add up to a vision of woman that is less academic and more sex object. While it may be hoped that their frequency is declining, they will not completely disappear without challenge and to challenge requires some degree of anger and refusal to accept.

* * *

There can be few people of either sex who enjoy being personally involved in the nasty internecine struggles of academic politics. For women to reject the compliant "Lady" model of behaviour, to refuse to "go quietly," to realize that no one listens to the weak demands considerable courage. The risk of publicity with its potentially damaging personal and professional consequences, the chance of departmental unpopularity, the possibility of ostracism by colleagues, all these are very real. From the record, it is clear that there have been women of McGill who have been prepared to pay the price. They have amply demonstrated that docility can be shed, that they will stand up for their rights. They have shown that, short of revolution, there are many ways to do this. To bring about change, people like Virginia Douglas, Frances Henry, Rose Johnstone, and Erin Malloy-Hanley risked the ire of the community. They had to face the irritation or anger of some men and to counter the disavowal of those women who, feeling that they had been "well treated," tranquilly accepted the paternalistic status quo. The professors who had the temerity to integrate the Faculty Club, to challenge salary differentials, or to call for Women's Studies are people who show that women in the contemporary University still have something of the determination, self-respect, and spirit of the pioneers who challenged the age-old stereotypes and won for women the right to higher education. They vindicate that right.

Without question, women have come a long way since the days of Dawson and Murray, but the echoes of their debate over the nature of Woman still linger on campus and, rather incredibly, something of the genteel persona still seems to cling. In general, the women of McGill are glad to be at this University and have little thought for radical change to structures or attitudes. While some have found the socio-academic climate stifling, many others have found it sufficiently comfortable or stimulating to allow them to grow intellectually and prosper professionally. However, the several salary studies show that they have not yet reached full parity in all areas and casual observation reveals that the first woman Dean, the first woman Vice Principal and the first woman Principal have still to be appointed. At least, women have been nominated for these high administrative posts, but have not yet taken office. That is a giant leap still to be taken. Though Women's Studies have been accepted and a minor established, proposals for a Centre for Research on Woman still await development. It has been suggested that such a centre might be housed at R.V.C., thus restoring to the College the special concern for scholarship that has been eroded in recent years. The Centre is controversial and remains a question for the future, a goal still to be achieved.

Conclusion

What Have We Learned?

> . . . I saw then that you had the material to make a pretty good Dr.
> and I am sure you will if you wish. You will remember my advice not
> to spoil yourself as a woman to become a Dr. for I think you will
> always be admired as the former more than the latter. [1]

These words, written in 1890 to Octavia Grace Ritchie as she was
embarking upon her medical training, were the sentiments of a young
man just a few years her senior. They represent the sort of advice that
almost every professional or academic woman has received somewhere
along the line, but not the kind regularly given to young men. No one
says, ''Do not spoil yourself as a man to become a doctor.'' Yet, even in
the late 20th century such counsel is still proffered to women. The sentiment, ''do not spoil yourself as a woman,'' may be kindly meant, it may
be insidiously flattering, but it contains a reservation—an implication
that there is some basic incompatibility between being female and being
a professional person.

   That kind of caveat goes to the heart of the question as to whether or
not women should be taken seriously and thus fully accepted in the
world of ideas, assimilated into the world of work with all its ascending
opportunities; or whether they must remain peripheral, being kept
tentatively on the threshold of the professions; or whether, to take
another perspective, they have distinctive ''womanly'' qualities that
would significantly contribute to and enrich the arenas beyond Woman's
traditional spheres. At McGill, we have had a century of experience with
these questions but, as we know, the issues are much older than that and
definitive answers remain elusive. We may think one aspect of the
matter settled, only to discover that we are mistaken. It may have
seemed that the question of women's educability was truly conceded
when the first class of Donaldas was admitted, but then we remember
that essentially the same battles had to be fought serially in each of the
professional Faculties at McGill and that women had to prove and re-
prove their legitimacy as members of the student body. As we look back
over the record of McGill, we see that women did not turn into men, as

411

some of the critics feared they would, nor did their children grow up deformed as Dr. Edward Clarke so confidently predicted in his 1873 diatribe, *Sex in Education*. But there has assuredly been some transformation and we have learned many things.

We have learned that the Women's Movement of the 1960's and 70's is by no means the first, nor even necessarily the most outspoken, in its attempts to secure women's rights. It took enormous courage and enterprise to be academically and psychologically prepared for admission to the Faculty of Arts in 1884 and a tremendous amount of gumption to make it through the professional Faculties. Women in past generations fought determinedly for things we take for granted and perhaps do not use to full advantage. Women of the present have an obligation to the pioneers to build on their efforts and achievements. We have both the responsibility and the opportunity to shatter sexist myths, to show the inadequacies of thinking that equates cultural norms with the natural order of things. We have the advantage of the Donaldas' experience but we are still, to some extent, caught as they were in the need to prove ourselves. This may not be as extreme in the 1980's as it was in the 1880's when Carrie Derick complained that each woman had the honour of all the members of her sex at stake, but it is still there. Women in academe—like members of minority groups in society at large—have to do better to get to the top, or even the middle. We have probably reached the point where our successes may be accepted without comment, but our failures and our foibles will still be attributed to our gender.

We have learned that there has not been a constant war of the sexes at McGill, that many men have been helpful to the cause of women, and that in general, the women at this University were by no means hostile to their male colleagues. We have also learned that the non-confrontational style has achieved positive results. Yet we have learned, too, that there have been many different ways to impede our progress—procrastination, hostility, derision, reasonableness, invocation of traditional roles, tokenism, and fine, hollow rhetoric. It is clear that some of the most difficult obstacles to overcome were created by well-respected, often kindly men (Dawson, Osler, Leacock) who were not always openly antagonistic to women on campus, but may even have espoused supportive positions. They could be charming, helpful and encouraging to women they knew personally or individually, but in the last analysis, they threw their prestige and authority onto the side of tradition. It was not so much impossible as embarrassing (especially for well-mannered women of the "Lady" mode) to shatter the humbug of their apparent good will in order to disclose their basically stereotyped ideas.

As for the women, there has not been a great deal of naked anger.

Members of both sexes have generally been "reasonable" on women's issues, on the whole much more conservative than radical. It is therefore not surprising to have found that some of the most awkward obstacles were created by some women—mothers who did not want their daughters to study full-time or to take "masculine" courses, members of faculty who were humbly grateful for their lot and did not want to stir up trouble, who voted "No" in the Faculty Club referendum because they thought it was "nice" for the men to have a place of their own. Extreme cases of this type could be viewed as those in which the need for affiliation, or the addiction to approval, had led to identification with the oppressor. They believed in the received wisdom regarding sex roles as if their mental sets had become permanent waves. Just as it was more difficult to confront pleasant and apparently supportive men than outright antagonists, so it was very difficult to fight for women's rights when some of the "enemy" were women.

We have learned that there is no longer a taboo on knowledge and that women are now permitted to study in all disciplines. They are accepted in all Faculties. Since this is the case and since the overall student enrolment at McGill is now approximately 50% male and 50% female, might we not ask whether we should still compile enrolment statistics showing "male" and "female," for cannot these subcategories be subsumed by the single category of "student"? Desirable as that might seem, it is probably still too soon. We have seen from the past that waves of feminism, or periods when acceptance of women seemed certain, were followed by troughs of reaction and retreat. It is still too early to assume that women have consolidated their position sufficiently to be sure they will receive a fair proportion of appointments, promotions and opportunities of various kinds. To eliminate the subcategories would obscure many remaining issues. For while the overall student body is roughly half and half, the distribution is still very uneven —very few female students in Engineering and Dentistry, very few female professors in Engineering, Management and Law, very few male students in Nursing. Just as the women students discovered in the early 1970's that there was still a need for a distinct Women's Union if women were not to be muscled out of student affairs, so we still need separate statistics to keep a check on developments. The tendency to revert to the status quo ante is likely to be far stronger than the tendency to advance women in non-traditional areas. The goal remains to consider people as people and to have factors such as sex, ethnic origin, and religious affiliation deemed utterly irrelevant in the academic milieu. However, until the position of women is securely consolidated in all areas of the university and until sex role stereotypes (along with the attitudes which nurtured them) are dispelled, it would be premature to believe we can dispense with separate statistics. It is far too soon for complacency; there is still need for self-assertion and affirmative action.

We have learned that there seems to have been even-handedness in the awarding of grades, prizes and scholarships. This has been the case from the beginning, even when young men were dearly afraid of the humiliation of being beaten in examinations by these strange new creatures, "lady students." Some of those men had to endure a lot of "ribbing" from their fellows and even from the press when the women did outrank them. This has not entirely disappeared. Men can still find it a disgrace to be beaten by women in intellectual or physical pursuits— and the only reason for that must be the assumption that they are being beaten by inferior beings; otherwise there is nothing to be teased about.

Only in recent years has there been any suggestion of sexual harrassment—the exchange of high grades for sexual favours and the like—at McGill. Even now, it is not widely discussed and its extent is not really known. When cases are reported, they are kept confidential unless the female victims themselves choose to disclose them publicly—and that is rare indeed. With the exception of one woman in Dentistry, the older women interviewed during this study (i.e. women who graduated before about 1950) denied any untoward advances by their professors or male members of staff. The denial of any kind of discrimination was very common among both women students and faculty members. In the face of revealed differentials in numbers, salaries and promotion rates, the fact that there is no perceived problem may itself be a problem. As may the fact that some women in Engineering do not see anything wrong in the *Plumber's Pot*. They have convinced themselves that it is "all just fun." The symbolic aspects escape them now but the economic consequences of the flaunted denegration of their sex may haunt them later, especially at critical points of their careers—at entry, promotion, assignment of important contracts. Will an employer consider giving a multi-million dollar contract to someone he has always considered a centrefold?

Women students in other areas may also be in for a rude awakening when they leave the ivory tower and find themselves becoming competitors with men for jobs, or threats to their promotion. National statistics reveal unexpectedly that the salary gap between men's and women's salaries has widened in the last two decades and exists even on campus. A recent Statistics Canada survey[2] showed not only that there is a much higher proportion of men than women employed in all ranks in Canadian universities but that they receive higher salaries in almost every area— even in traditionally "feminine" fields such as Household Science and Library Science. We need to keep asking why. And we need to keep pushing for women's advancement for their own sakes and for the role models they can provide.

We have learned that areas designated as "female" fields of study have gradually gained acceptance and prestige, but remain relatively low in the hierarchy. They have admitted men and McGill has become, at least in principle, completely co-educational. Yet pockets of segregation remain. Paradoxically, it may be in women's interests that they should.

There is a realistic possibility that men might take over women's traditional domains and women may lose even their limited number of positions of administrative authority. Co-education, which was one of the hallmarks of 19th century liberalism, may require some rethinking. Even the possibility of a retreat from co-education raises the perennial dilemma of women's wanting to be defined as "regular" people, to be integrated into the mainstream, to reject special protection from kindly or authoritarian patriarchs, yet still demanding separate consideration as women. Can we have it both ways?

We can see from the record that women, their interests, needs, accomplishments, will be ignored unless a particular effort is made to correct this. Thus, we see the necessity for a transitional period of academic "catching up" and for identifiable courses in Women's Studies. Such courses do not exclude men, either as students or professors, but they do concern themselves with areas long overlooked by the traditional male academy. They do not constitute special pleading and the reader may now be in a position to judge whether this history of women at McGill was a valid scholarly enterprise, and to ruminate on the prospects of its ever having been written under purely patriarchal circumstances.

We have learned that there have been many truly remarkable women at McGill—among the students, the faculty, and the non-academic staff. We have found it impossible to include even the briefest mention of a fraction of their number. We have found that among them there were the intellectual heirs of both J. William Dawson and J. Clark Murray. We have raised some doubts about the degree of Dawson's commitment to the higher education of women and acquired some reservations about Lord Strathcona's original insistence on separate education.

We have learned that from the first Donaldas there has been a network of women supporting each other and championing wider causes. This network may not be nearly as powerful as the "old boys' network," but it has a solid base of respect, affection, and concern for matters academic. One of the questions remaining for the women of McGill—and for society in general—is how can we institutionalize the cohesive ties among women, so that despite our minority status and regardless of the traditional fragmentation of "women's work," the advances we have made will be developed and increased, so that isolated individual successes can be built upon systematically for the common good.

As we have surveyed the past, we have encountered complexities, paradoxes, and inconsistencies, but we also find we agree with a statement that looked to the future asserting that:

> ... there can be no doubt that woman has changed; she *has* been rearranged. I don't believe in "feminine freaks" if by freakishness you mean unwomanliness, but it isn't freakish to be energetic and aggressive. Of course, man has a future too. Neither of us can get along alone—not very well, that is. It is well for us to consider the signs of the times, and prepare for the future, but ought we not do it in the broader sense of humanity? not woman by herself and man by himself. Then woman's duty would be clear: to live the best she can, let go her doubts and fears, and work up quietly to the new opportunities that have come to her.[3]

This statement, strong and assertive in its call for respect for women, was penned in 1901. It could hardly be distinguished from one typed yesterday. From the perspective of its anonymous author, we are now well into the future. We have won the right to vote, we expect to work outside the home if we wish, we can demand equal pay for equivalent work, we have had a series of feminist movements—but these tend to raise clouds of dust which tend just to resettle. So we still need to make positive efforts to ensure that women are indeed included in "the broader sense of humanity" until the dust is finally swept away.

We cannot think complacently of the history of women or the history of women at McGill as a clear record of spectacular triumphs, just as we must challenge the simplistic notion of history as pure progress. Nevertheless, as the unknown writer of 1901 recorded, no one would deny that change has occurred. Through a fine blend of courage and caution, improvement of women's status and self-confidence has been built up at McGill slowly, agglutinatively, layer upon layer. And if those layers are firm enough, and if our consciousnesses are sufficiently raised, we may soon learn that the time for walking warily has passed.

Appendices

Notes and Sources

Index

Appendix A

419

1912	1st woman Full Professor: Carrie Derick (Botany—1st woman Full Professor in Canada)
1913	1st woman admitted to Agriculture
1914	1st woman B.C.L. (first professional degree to McGill woman): Annie Macdonald Langstaff
1917	1st time women outnumbered men in Faculty of Arts
	1st woman graduate appointed Board of Governors' Fellow to Corporation: Helen R.Y. Reid
1918	1st women accepted as regular students for B.D. degree
	1st women B.S.Agric.: Margaret Newton, Pearl Clayton Stanford (1st women Agriculture degrees in Canada)
1919	1st intercollegiate game played by Canadian women: Queen's vs. R.V.C. (Basketball—R.V.C. won)
1920	1st Director, School for Graduate Nurses: Flora Madeline Shaw
1921	1st woman B. Comm.: Greta Dougall
	1st McGill LL.D. awarded to McGill woman: Helen R.Y. Reid
1922	1st women M.D., C.M. degrees: Winifred Blampin, Jessie Boyd, Mary Childs, Lilian Irwin, Eleanor Percival
	1st woman admitted to Faculty of Dentistry
1923	1st B.H.S. degrees awarded
1926	1st woman D.D.S.: Florence A. Johnston
1929	1st woman Professor Emeritus: Carrie Derick
1931	1st women members of Students' Executive Council: Margaret Dodds, Doreen Harvey-Jellie
1936	1st woman member of McGill Faculty Club: Maude E. Abbott
1939	1st woman admitted to Architecture
1941	1st woman on ballot for Graduate Society representative to Board of Governors: Catherine I. Mackenzie
1942	1st women admitted to Quebec Bar: Elizabeth Monk, B.A. '19, B.C.L. '23 (and Suzanne Raymond Filion, U. de M.)
	1st woman admitted to Engineering
1943	1st woman B.Arch.—Catherine M. Chard
1945	1st Director, McGill School of Social Work: Dorothy King
1946	1st woman B.Eng. (Mech): Mary Blair Jackson
1946	1st B.N. degrees awarded
1949	1st woman Director, Graduate School of Library Science: Vernon Ross
1961	1st woman Editor, *McGill Daily*: Judi Zeisler
1965	1st woman President, Students' Society: Sharon Sholzberg
	1st woman Full Professor of Education: Marguerite F.L. Horton
1970	1st Associate Dean of Students: Elizabeth Rowlinson
	1st woman elected to Board of Governors by Graduate Society: Claire Kerrigan
1973	1st woman Director, School of Physical and Occupational Therapy: Helen M. Gault
1974	1st woman student representative to Board of Governors: Phyllis Brodie

1975	1st woman Director of Libraries: Marianne Scott
	1st woman Associate Dean, Faculty of Graduate Studies and Research: Valerie M. Pasztor
	1st woman non-academic staff representative to Board of Governors: Ida Godfrey
1977	1st Chairperson, Senate Committee on Women: Margaret Gillett
1979	1st woman of McGill to win Rhodes Scholarship: Lianne Potter, B.A. '79
1980	1st Director of Residences and Student Housing: Florence Tracy

Appendix B

CHANCELLORS OF MCGILL UNIVERSITY

1.	Charles Dewey Day	1864-1884
2.	James Ferrier	1884-1888
3.	Donald Alexander Smith, Baron Strathcona and Mount Royal	1889-1913
4.	William Christopher Macdonald	1914-1917
5.	Robert Laird Borden	1918-1920
6.	Edward Wentworth Beatty	1920-1943
7.	Morris Watson Wilson	1943-1946
8.	Orville S. Tyndale	1947-1952
9.	Bertie C. Gardner	1952-1957
10.	Ray E. Powell	1957-1964
11.	Howard I. Ross	1964-1969
12.	Donald O. Hebb	1970-1975
13.	Stuart M. Finlayson	1975
14.	Conrad F. Harrington	1976-

PRINCIPALS OF MCGILL UNIVERSITY

1.	George Jehoshaphat Mountain	1824-1835
2.	John Bethune	1835-1846
3.	Edmund Allen Meredith	1846-1853

4.	Charles Dewey Day	1853-1855
5.	John William Dawson	1855-1893
6.	William Peterson	1895-1919
7.	Auckland Campbell Geddes	1919-1920
8.	Arthur Currie	1920-1933
9.	Arthur Eustace Morgan	1935-1937
10.	Lewis W. Douglas	1937-1939
11.	F. Cyril James	1940-1962
12.	H. Rocke Robertson	1962-1970
13.	Robert E. Bell	1970-1979
14.	David Lloyd Johnston	1979-

WARDENS OF ROYAL VICTORIA COLLEGE

1.	Hilda Diana Oakeley	1899-1905
	Susan Cameron - Acting Warden	1906-1907
2.	Ethel Hurlbatt	1906-1929
	C.G. Hardy Garside - Acting Warden	1924-1925
	Susan Cameron Vaughan - Acting Warden	1929-1931
3.	Susan Cameron Vaughan	1931-1937
4.	Maude Parkin Grant	1937-1940
5.	Muriel V. Roscoe	1940-1962
6.	Helen Reynolds	1962-1970

7.	Mary Robertson	1970-1971
8.	Donna Runnalls	1972-1979
	Florence Tracy - Acting Warden	1979-1980
9.	Florence Tracy	1980-

Appendix C

WOMEN WHO HAVE RECEIVED HONORARY DEGREES FROM McGILL
1900 - 1980

Women have received approximately 5% of the honorary degrees awarded by McGill. Despite an increase during the 70's when ten were awarded, the numbers remain small. A decade-by-decade analysis shows the growth from the very first honorary degree awarded a woman in 1900 to be as follows: 2, 2, 3, 5, 4, 9, 6, 10.

The recipients may be divided into four major categories (1) distinguished McGill graduates, (2) women who have served McGill especially well, (3) women of wide renown, (4) members of royalty. These categories are not mutually exclusive—Maude Abbott, for example, fits into three of the four. It is obvious that the most numerous are the people directly associated with the University. In the list of names below, McGill graduates are marked by *, those who served McGill by •.

It is possible that the number of women honoured could increase substantially in the 80's, provided that appropriate names are put forward. In the past, McGill has not been very active in reaching out for women who have made significant contributions to scholarship and society. In the future, it may be willing to do so, but it will need help.

Year	Name	Degree
1900	Hilda Diana Oakley•	B.A., M.A.
1901	H.R.H. Duchess of Cornwall and York (later Her Majesty Queen Mary)	LL.D.
1910	Maude Elizabeth Seymour Abbott*•	M.D., C.M.
1911	H.R.H. Duchess of Connaught	LL.D.
1921	Lady Grace Julia Drummond	LL.D.
1921	Helen Richmond Young Reid* •	LL.D.
1926	Duchess of Atholl	LL.D.
1930	Ethel Hurlbatt•	LL.D.
1936	Maude Elizabeth Seymour Abbott*•	LL.D.

1937	Susan Cameron Vaughan*•	LL.D.
1938	Mabel Frances Hersey•	LL.D.
1939	Lady Tweedsmuir	LL.D.
1941	H.R.H. Princess Alice Mary of Great Britain, Countess of Athlone	LL.D.
1941	Dorothy Thompson Lewis	D. Litt.
1948	The Viscountess Alexander of Tunis	LL.D.
1949	Lillian M. Penson	LL.D.
1950	Flora McCrae Eaton	LL.D.
1953	Anna Eleanor Roosevelt	LL.D.
1954	H.R.H. Duchess of Kent	LL.D.
1954	Ellen Ballon*	D. Mus.
1954	Pauline Lightstone Donalda*	D. Mus.
1955	Gertrude D. Mudge•	M.A.
1955	H.R.H. the Princess Royal	LL.D.
1959	Irene Manton	D. Sc.
1959	Dorothy Stuart Russell	D. Sc.
1960	Allie Vibert Douglas*	LL.D.
1963	Agnes Matthews	LL.D.
1964	Dorothy Linton McMurray•	M.A.
1966	Pauline Vanier	LL.D.
1966	Lucie Touren-Furness•	LL.D.
1967	Muriel V. Roscoe•	LL.D.
1971	Anne Isobel McLeod•	LL.D.

1971	Violet Archer*	D. Mus.
1972	Sylvia Ostry*	LL.D.
1973	Marianne Newmann•	M.A.
1975	Elizabeth Monk*	LL.D.
1975	Senator Thérèse Casgrain	LL.D.
1976	Rae Chittick*•	D. Sc.
1977	Eileen Constance Flanagan*•	LL.D.
1978	Jeanne Bell*•	D. Litt.
1979	Jessie Boyd Scriver*•	D. Sc.
1980	Anne Hebert	D. Litt.

OTHER HONOURS

The first woman of McGill to receive an Emeritus Professorship was Carrie Derick who, in 1929, became Emeritus Professor of Botany. In 1980, there were 72 Emeritus Professors at McGill of whom nine were women:

Rae Chittick, Emeritus Professor of Nursing

Violet L. Coughlin, Emeritus Professor of Library Science

Isobel M. Barclay Dobell, Emeritus Curator, McCord Museum

Joyce Hemlow, Emeritus Professor of English

Gertrude Kalz, Emeritus Professor of Microbiology and Immunology

*Bertha Meyer, Emeritus Professor of German

Helen R. Neilson, Emeritus Professor of Food Science

Aileen Ross, Emeritus Professor of Sociology

Dorothy E. Swales, Emeritus Curator, McGill University Herbarium

*Now deceased

Appendix D

NOTES ON NON-ACADEMIC WOMEN

During the 1970's, women began to be appointed in unprecedented numbers to positions of authority in middle management at McGill. Thus, posts such as those of Director of Admissions, Director of Information and Liaison, Director of Public Relations, Associate Secretary of Senate, Director of the McGill Development Office, and Associate Registrar were held by Peggy Shepperd, Alta Abramowitz, Betsy Hirst, Sheila Sheldon, Betty McNab and Marjorie Paterson respectively. While appointments at these levels are relatively recent, the contribution of non-academic women to the life of the University has been both long and worthy.

Beginning from the days of Helen Gairdner, whose functions apart from chaperoning were multifarious and who stayed at McGill from 1884 to 1914, non-academic women have established a remarkable tradition of devotion and service. Scattered through archival files and McGill scrapbook clippings are records of an extraordinary collection of women who were acknowledged to be the heart of a Faculty or the soul of a Department. Some were characterized as "motherly types," others were "dragons," but their long service to the University and their knowledgeable help to students and staff have been recognized with special tributes. Unfortunately, these acknowledgements mainly seem to come when the women were leaving or retiring. The records also show many instances of patronizing attitudes toward them and ample evidence of underpayment. For many years, the "faithful tribe," as one chairman called them, were utterly dependent upon the good will of the heads of their departments who, in turn, pleaded their cases individually to the next administrative level and could usually point to the fact that salaries were very low. For example, one letter on file sought an increase for a secretary in the Faculty of Medicine who in 1940 received $30 per month on which to support herself, her mother and her younger brother. Even at 1940 prices, $30 was hardly a living wage. It is indisputable that the women of the "faithful tribe" have long subsidised the University—lovingly, willingly, or unwittingly.

Truly notable women of the support staff have been associated with all parts of McGill—R.V.C., the central administration, and virtually every Faculty. Few Principals or Deans (male) could manage without the secretaries or administrative assistants (female) who keep the establishment functioning. A sampler of some of these might include Gladys Murray of R.V.C. and her successor, Margaret Paterson, who gave the College continuity during the flux of the 1960's and 70's; Martha McCallum who was associated with the McGill libraries for 51 years (1924-75); Virginia Cameron, niece of Susan Vaughan, who knew the Registrar's Office inside-out from the 30's to the 60's; Gertrude

Mudge, who retired in 1953 after 30 years as "mother confessor" or Assistant Secretary of the Faculty of Medicine but with a total of 38 years of service to the University; Isobel Oswald who also gave 38 years of dedication to Arts and Science; Margaret Robertson who served the Graduate Society in many capacities from 1946 to 1980; Anne Ferguson and "Nellie" Williamson who both worked in the Faculty of Dentistry for well over 20 years; Kaye Clynes and Eleanor Algie, who drove a huge ten-ton bookmobile for the McLennan Travelling Libraries of McGill along the icy roads of Quebec year in, year out; Sadie Hempey, who was Acting Comptroller when she died in 1976, but mother surrogate to hundreds of students through her work with the Students' Society and who was immortalized in "Sadie's," the student refreshment spot; Rubie Napier, an acknowledged institution in the History Department; Dorothy McMurray, who accepted a temporary position in 1929 but remained for more than 30 years as secretary to four Principals—Currie, Morgan, Douglas and James—and wrote a book on the subject. (*Four Principals of McGill*, published by the Graduates' Society, 1974.)

In 1964, the University acknowledged both its debt and its admiration by awarding Dorothy McMurray the degree of Master of Arts, *honoris causa*. In his introduction of her on that occasion, Vice Principal Noel Fieldhouse recognized that:

> She worked for McGill and thought of McGill and worked for, and thought of little else; with a fierce pride in its achievement and an equally fierce eye to whatever she feared might threaten it. No one who came into contact with her could imagine the service to McGill to be an easy yoke; but, at the same time, she had a warm interest in the personal fortunes of the members of the McGill family, and she was quick with help, and generous with kindness, to members of staff who were in difficulties whether academic or personal.

The Vice Principal's words might well apply to many other non-academic women of McGill, both past and present. Though devotion to institutions may be out of fashion, it can still be found in the attitudes of many of the women of McGill. Only recently have they had the help and protection of unions or the McGill University Non-Academic Staff Association (MUNASA) and they have worked under conditions that were often far from ideal. Nevertheless, they identified strongly with the University and accepted the tribulations of McGill life as they came along. Their response to contemporary problems of energy is a case in point:

To The Shivering Secretary

> While harking to the VP's call—
> "Turn down the thermostat on the wall!"
> I rejoice to find at last
> A temperature unlike hell's blast;
> I, for one, through these past years

430

Mrs. Dorothy McMurray at Work

Would have dispensed with heat that sears.
So, while my fellow workers freeze
I, with freedom and with ease,
Type without benefit of muff or glove
While working for the McGill I love.

(D. Alison, *McGill Reporter,* November 29, 1978, p. 1.)

The kind of affection and occupational generosity suggested here are valuable and precious assets for any institution—as long as they are freely given. Some non-academic women believe, however, that emotional commitment has been more expected of them than of their male co-workers. They suspect that their fondness for McGill is sometimes exploited, that sometimes managers assume that a job is just a job for men but for women it must be a job plus devotion. If such a stereotypical difference in expectations exists, it would be patently unfair. It would also represent the kind of subtle discrimination that women so often hesitate to challenge and that, in the unsentimental reality of the world of work, can chain women to support positions.

Appendix E

NOTES ON SOME NOTABLES

There have been many notable researchers and teachers among the women of McGill and many highly successful graduates. Throughout this book, references were made to some of the prominent female professors but there have been many others including people like the late Anna McPherson (Physics) and the late Bertha Meyer (German), Dorothy Swales (Plant Sciences), Alice Johannsen (Natural Sciences and the Gault Estate), Barbara Bain (Biology), Virginia Douglas (Psychology), Gabrielle Donnay (Geology), Joan Marsden (Zoology), Joan DeVries (Dentistry), Julia Terzis (Microsurgery), Joyce Hemlow, Adele Wiseman and Bharati Blaise (English), Anne Savage (Art), Paola Valeri-Tomaszuk (Classics), Geraldine Dubrule (Athletics), Paddy Webb (Education), ...

Space obviously prevents expounding upon these and the numerous outstanding individual women students who have passed through McGill from the earliest Donaldas to the newest graduates, from Octavia Grace Ritchie England (B.A. 1888) to Danielle Fontaine (B.Arch. 1981, Rhodes Scholar). The names of successful alumnae would make a veritable "Who's Who of Canadian Women." Their exploits have been varied and their careers have reached into many spheres. Years ago, Ethel Hurlbatt made a follow-up study of women graduates from 1888 to 1923. Her results were as follows:

After Careers of 680 Graduates, 1888-1923 Inclusive*

Married	228	Journalism	7
Died	26	Law	6
Higher Degree	92		
--------------		Librarian	16
Administration	1	Medicine	12
Advertising	1	Missionary	14
Agriculture	2	Music	3
Banking	4	Nursing	13
Business	3	Phys. Ed.	8
Civil Service	10	Secretarial	9
Design	1	Social Service	10
Domestic Sc.	6	Teaching	347
Industrial Chemistry	5	Y.W.C.A.	3

*(*Royal Victoria College, Report to the Principal, 1922-23*, p. 5.)

This table is interesting, not only because it appears to make mutually exclusive categories out of being married, being dead, and having a higher degree, but also for the information it provides on career choice. It shows considerable diversity yet heavy concentration on teaching. In more recent years, there have been few attempts at systematic analysis of the career patterns of McGill alumnae and, with ever-growing numbers and increased population mobility, the task becomes more and more formidable. Perhaps some enterprising student of sociology will take it on. Meanwhile, a careful reading of the columns of *The McGill News* might provide proximate data to substantiate the hypothesis that women graduates of McGill are now tackling jobs undreamed of in Miss Hurlbatt's day.

In 1972 at the request of the Status of Women Co-ordinator in the Privy Council, the Alumnae Society drew up a list of about a hundred of its distinguished members. As well as Jessie Boyd Scriver (B.A. '15, M.D., C.M. '22), Elizabeth C. Monk (B.A. '19, B.C.L. '23), and other notables already mentioned, this list named women like Violet Archer (B.Mus. '36), composer and professor; Margaret Guaghan Brock (Dip. S.W. '36), social service director; Isabel M. Barclay Dobell (B.A. '31), museum curator; Stephanie Zuperko Dudek (B.A. '43), professor of clinical psychology; Vera Frankel (B.A. '59), writer; Teressa Rakowska (B.A. '50), executive director, U.S. League of Women Voters; Kathleen Jenkins (B.A. '26), librarian and author; Monica R. Mintz (B.Com. '68), registered stockbroker; Sylvia Ostry (B.A. '48, M.A. '50, LL.D. '72), then Director, Economic Council of Canada; Sarah Weintraub Paltiel (B.S.W. '49), now Director-General, Dawson College and member of the McGill Board of Governors; Laura Villella Sabia (B.A. '38), politician and feminist; Betty Shapiro (B.A. '38) and Dusty Vineberg (B.A. '48), journalists; Joyce Borden Reed (B.C.L. '62), business executive, ...

A more recent computerized compilation by the Media Club of Canada included 72 McGill-associated women among some 200 distinguished women from across Canada. Indeed, any list of distinguished Canadian women might be expected to include the women of McGill and names such as Greta Chambers (B.A. '47) and Doris Clark (B.A. '30, Dip. S.W. '35), media personalities; Alice Turner (B.A. '27, M.A. '28), mathematician; Clara Fritz (B.A. '14, M.A. '18) and Madelenne Fritz (B.A. '19), paleantologists; Maysie MacSporran (B.A. '27, M.A. '30) and Jean Harvie (B.A. '35, M.A. '36), independent school principals; Constance Beresford-Howe (B.A. '27, M.A. '30), Marion Engel (M.A. '57) and Joyce Marshall (B.A. '35), authors; Dorothy Ross (B.A. '30, M.A. '32, Ph.D. '39), historian and teacher; Ruth Hubbell Rose (Dip.P.E. '44), archaeologist; Susan Altschul (B.A. '63) and Sheila Arnuopolis (B.A. '61), journalists; Judith Crawley (B.A. '36) and Beverley Shaffer (B.A. '66), film directors; Catherine Hebb (Ph.D. '37), physiologist; Ann McCall (B.A. '64), artist; Madeline Parent (B.A. '40), union organizer; Catherine McLaggan (B.A. '36), Eileen Flanagan (B.A. '34, LL.D. '77), nursing educators; Mildred Eatell (M.S.W. '45), Director of Child Welfare, Saskatchewan; Esther Kerry (Dip. S.W. '30, M.A. '39), social worker; May Brown (B.Sc. (P.E.) '47), politician and sports coach; Adele Languedoc (B.A. '29), librarian; Beatrice Wyatt Johnston (B.A. '27, M.A. '29) and Sheila Abbey Firestone

(B.Sc. '47), volunteer community workers; Ethlyn Trapp (M.D., C.M. '27), radiotherapist; Margaret Chase Woodhouse (B.A. '12, M.A. '13), member U.S. House of Representatives; Marion Vaisey (M.Sc.(Agric.) '51), home economist and food expert; Rosalind Young (B.A. '96), geologist; Karen Quinton (B.Mus. '69), musician; Julia Grace Wales (B.A. '03), scholar and peace activist; Winifred M. Kydd (C.B.E., M.A. '23), educator and internationalist; Norma E. Walmsley (B.Com. '50, M.A. '54), professor of political science and founder of MATCH, an international exchange programme for women; Frances Oldham Kelsey (B.Sc. '34, M.Sc. '35), scientist and administrator, refused U.S. Drug Administration licence for thalidomide, the drug that induced grotesque birth defects. . . .

The list is random and incomplete. It could go on and on. It cannot do justice to the accomplishments of the thousands of alumnae, but perhaps it may serve to indicate something of the range of interests and achievements of the women of McGill.

Appendix F

TOTAL STUDENT AND FEMALE ENROLMENT

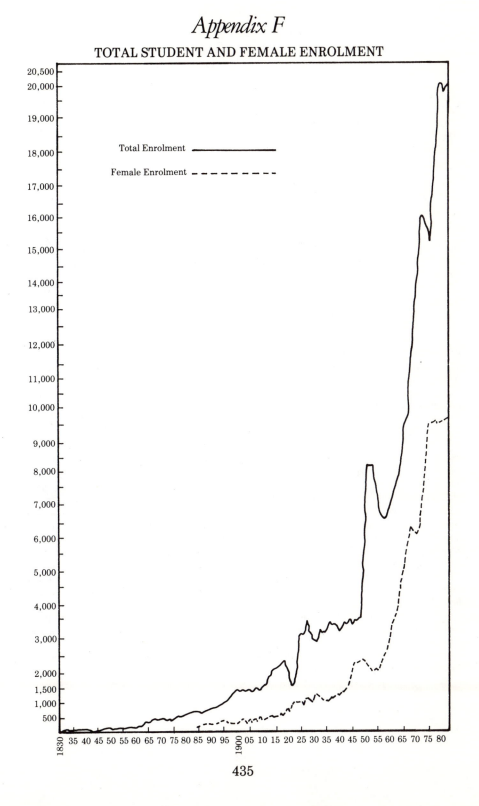

NOTES
Introduction

Abbreviations Used in Notes:
MCTRW = McGill Committee for Teaching and Research on Women
MLEA = Montreal Ladies' Educational Association
MUA = McGill University Archives
PAC = Public Archives of Canada

[1] Henry J. Morgan, *Types of Canadian Women* and of Women who are or have been connected with Canada, Vol. 1, Toronto: William Briggs, 1903, p. vi.

[2] See Vera Brittain, *The Women at Oxford*, London: George G. Harrap, 1960.

[3] Lord Curzon of Kedleston, *Principles and Methods of University Reform:* Oxford: Clarendon, 1909, p. 193.

[4] "Resident Women-Students," *The Complete Works of Lewis Carroll*, London: Nonesuch Press, 1949.

[5] In 1979, for the first time in history, the Presidents of the "Seven Sister Colleges" were women.

[6] "The Princess," Lines 142-3.

[7] "A Farewell," Stanza 3, Line 2.

[8] Raymond Clare Archibald, *Historical Notes on the Education of Women at Mt. Allison, 1854-1954*, Sackville, N.B.: Centennial Committee, Mt. Allison, 1954, p. 7.

[9] Hilda Neatby, *Queen's University, 1841-1917*, Vol. 1, Montreal: McGill-Queen's, 1978, n.29, p. 325.

[10] Robin S. Harris, *A History of Higher Education in Canada, 1663-1960*, Toronto: University of Toronto, 1976, p. 116.

[11] "A Century of Commencement Speeches," *Saturday Review*, May 12, 1979, p. 36.

[12] "The Rivals," 1.1.

[13] The origin of the term "blue stocking" is somewhat obscure but appears to be related to the French salons of the 18th century. Cf. Emily J. Climenson, *Elizabeth Montague, The Queen of the Blue-Stockings: Her Correspondence from 1720-1761*, 2 Vols. New York: E.P. Dutton, 1906, 11, p. 98—"...the Coterie of friends probably in the Rue St. Honore, where the wearing of blue stockings was the rage." Another explanation gives English social circles the dubious honour, claiming that one Benjamin Stillingfleet, who was renowned for his shabby dress, told a hostess that he could not attend her party because he had nothing appropriate to wear. To which she replied, "Don't mind dress. Come in your blue stockings." cf. Ethel R. Wheeler, *Famous Blue Stockings*, New York: John Lane, 1910, p. 22 and R. Ruchon, *Mrs. Montague, 1720-1800*, New York: E.P. Dutton, 1907, p. 273.

[14] M. Carey Thomas, "Present Tendencies in Women's College and University Education," in Judith Stacey *et al.*, eds. *And Jill Came Tumbling After—Sexism in American Education*, N.Y.: Laurel, 1974.

[15] Helene Lange, *Higher Education of Women in Europe*, N.Y. D. Appleton, 1890, p. 238.

[16] Madame Blanc. *The Condition of Women in the United States: A Traveller's Notes*, N.Y.: Arno, 1972 (reprint—original c. 1890), p. 166.

[17] A.D. Hope, "Advice to Young Ladies," *Collected Poems, 1930-1965*, Sydney: Angus Robertson, 1966, p. 207.

NOTES
Chapter 1

1 Obituary, Montreal *Gazette*, December 21, 1813.

2 Bishop Joseph Mountain, Memorandum to Lieut.-Governor Sir Robert Milnes, 1796.

3 Stanley Brice Frost, *McGill University—For the Advancement of Learning,* Vol. 1, 1801-1895. Montreal: McGill-Queen's University Press, 1980.

4 Margaret Mercer in a letter to John William Dawson dated April 1, 1843. MUA 1377/15B/15A.

5 William Dawson to Margaret Mercer, July 30, 1841. MUA 1377/15B/70.

6 J.W. Dawson to Margaret Mercer, from Pictou, September 1, 1843. MUA 1377/15B/47.

7 Identified by Dawson as a hummingbird, black capped flycatcher, yellow throat, redstart, yellow crowned warbler, purple finch mounted on a Nova Scotian maple stand.

8 William Dawson to Margaret Mercer, July 1842. MUA 1377/15B/58.

9 William Dawson to Margaret Mercer, March 31, 1843. MUA 1377/15B.

10 "The Founder's tree," so called because it was planted in James McGill's day. See J.W. Dawson, *Fifty Years of Work in Canada; Scientific and Educational,* London & Edinburgh: Hallantyne, Hanson, 1901, p. 98. The tree survived the many changes on campus until 1976 when time and the elm disease forced it to be cut down.

11 "Notes on the Trees on the Grounds of McGill University," *Canadian Record of Science,* December, 1891, pp. 407-33. Reprinted in *Educational Lectures, Addresses, Ec. 1855-1895,* Montreal: H. Ramsay, n.d.

12 S. Finley, Treasurer of the University, reported in "An Interesting Ceremony: Presentation of Sir William Dawson's Picture to McGill College," Montreal *The Witness,* April 19, 1892. Statistics of 19th century McGill are mercurial, to say the least—the Matriculation Register says there were 64 students in 1855, Finley and Dawson variously quoted 70 and 80.

13 "Educated Women," An address Delivered Before the Delta Sigma Society of McGill University, December, 1889, p. 3.

14 *Ibid.,* p. 5.

15 John William Dawson, "The Future of McGill University," p. 9.

16 "The British Association: Sir William Dawson," *Montreal Star,* August, 1884.

17 "Educated Women," p. 12.

18 *Ibid.,* p. 14.

19 *Ibid.,* p. 6.

20 *Ibid.,* p. 11.

21 The issue of women and work highlights the contradictions between the chivalrous and the realistic approach of patriarchy in the 19th and other centuries. Women have always worked, though they have not always been paid, and they have often worked longer hours, for smaller wages, under less favourable and more dangerous conditions than men. The deplorable exploitation of Victorian women has been exposed by 19th century reformers and 20th century historians. One of the most chilling contemporary accounts of a woman worker is the testimony of Betty Harris, a "Drawer," who dragged a wagon in a coal mine in places too low for the use of horses. She said, "I have a belt around my waist and a chain passing between my legs, and I go on my hands and feet. The road is very steep, and we have to hold by a rope, and when there is no rope, by anything we can catch hold of. . . . The pit is very wet where I work, and the water comes over our clogs always, and I have seen it up to my thighs: it rains in at the roof terribly; my clothes are wet through almost all day long. I never was ill in my life but when I was lying-in. My cousin looks after my children in the daytime. I am very tired when I get home at night; I fall asleep sometimes before I get washed. I am not so strong as I was, and cannot stand my work so well as I used to do. I have drawn till I have had the skin off me; the belt and chain is worse when we are in the family way. My feller has beaten me many a time for not being ready. I was not used to it at first, and he had little patience. I have known many a man to beat his drawer." Wanda Neff, *Victorian Working Women,* N.Y., Columbia University Press, 1929, p. 72.

[22] Margaret Mercer to William Dawson, August, 1842. MUA 1377/15B/61. In this letter she also acknowledged the safe arrival of the birds.

[23] Margaret Mercer to John William Dawson, March 29, 1843. MUA 1377/15B/53. Margaret Mercer's comments on the trivial and fragmented nature of women's work are strikingly similar to some of J.S. Mill's in *The Subjection of Women,* which was to be published a quarter of a century later. ''. . . . for nearly the whole of the occupations of women consist in the management of small but multitudinous details, on each of which the mind cannot dwell even for a minute, but must pass on to other things, and if anything requires longer thought, must steal time at odd moments for thinking of it.'' J.S. Mill, *The Subjection of Women,* 1869.

[24] Anna Dawson Harrington to Rankine Dawson, Nov. 21, 1898. MUA 976/29/13.

[25] Margaret Mercer to William Dawson, February 3, 1845. MUA 1377/15B/32.

NOTES
Chapter 2

1 It might be noted that Ryerson was vehemently opposed to co-education at the college level. In 1841, when the Upper Canada Academy, a flourishing secondary establishment at Cobourg, Ontario was to become Victoria College, Ryerson refused to serve as Principal until the 74 women students were dismissed. Women were excluded and remained so for 30 years. See, Nathaniel Burwash, *The History of Victoria College*, Toronto: Victoria College Press, 1972, p. 55.

2 *Prospectus of the McGill Normal School*, Montreal: 1857, p. 1.

3 For an excellent study of social class and education in Canada in 19th century, see Alison Prentice, *The School Promoters*, Toronto: McClelland & Stewart, 1977; for a perceptive historical analysis of the feminization process, see Myra H. Strober and David Tyak, "Why Do Women Teach and Men Manage? A Report on Research on Schools,"*Signs: Journal of Women in Culture and Society*, Vol. 5, No. 3 (1980), pp. 494-503.

4 Cyrus Macmillan in *McGill and Its Story, 1821-1921*, p. 249 claims that it was Miss Lyman's idea: Dawson, whose memory is not always faultless, said in *Fifty Years of Work*, p. 232, that it was his.

5 *Fifty Years of Work*, p. 232.

6 H.W. Lyman to Dr. Dawson, April 2, 1863. MUA 1431/15/4.

7 Dawson, *loc. cit.*

8 The McGill Corporation was the predecessor of Senate as the University's senior academic body. Corporation consisted of the Governors, the Principal and elected Fellows. At this time it numbered approximately forty.

9 "Memo on a Memorial to Miss Lyman," May 1871. MUA 927/23/12.

10 Board of Governors, *Minute Book*, December 2, 1871, p. 1.

11 *Trafalgar Institute*—Published by Direction of the Trustees, Montreal: Gazette Printing Co., n.d. p. 3.

12 *Ibid.*, p. 12.

13 *Ibid.*, p. 7.

14 The name was changed again in 1934 and is now the Trafalgar School for Girls. The site was changed from the "Trafalgar Property," to the present location on Simpson St., to comply with Smith's stipulation that it be within Montreal city limits.

15 Not Jane Scott, as Dawson sometimes said.

16 *The Week*, Toronto, December 14, 1888. It might be noted that the "Grace Fairley Trafalgar" Scholarship is still awarded at McGill and now has a value of $450.

17 Not 1874, as Dawson recorded in his biography. Cf. "Minute Book of the Protestant Board of School Commissioners of Montreal, Commencing January 1870," May 27, 1875, p. 302 and J.W. Dawson, *Fifty Years of Work*, p. 257.

18 "Names of Candidates for School Examinations of McGill University," MUA 927/27/326.

19 "Minute Book of the Protestant Board of School Commissioners, October 14th, 1880 to August 29th, 1888," June 10, 1884, p. 240.

20 Grace Ritchie England, B.A., M.D., "The Entrance of Women to McGill," *The McGill News*, Vol. 16, No. 1 (December, 1934) pp. 14-15.

21 Dawson, *Fifty Years of Work*, pp. 211-12.

22 C.D. Day, "Address" Delivered at the Entertainment given to Benefactors, December 20, 1870, p. 1.

23 "Meeting in Aid To McGill College,"*The Daily Witness*, Montreal, February 11, 1870, p. 2.

24 C.D. Day, *op. cit.*, p. 2.

25 *Ibid.*, p. 6. This figure does not include some late donations to the endowment drive. When Dawson referred to this matter, he usually cited a total of only $52,000, which was the amount raised by November, not at the end of the campaign. Cf. *Fifty Years of Work*, p. 234.

26 *McGill Fortnightly*, Vol. II, No. 6 (December 22, 1893), p. 146.

[27] Day, *op. cit.*, p. 6.

[28] Corporation *Minutes,* 1854-1873—Meeting of 25 January, 1871, p. 514. MUA 639/2A.

[29] "Suggestions for Classes for the Higher Education of Women," manuscript drafted either by Margaret Mercer Dawson or Anna Dawson on behalf of J.W.D. and corrected by him.

[30] *Fifty Years of Work*, p. 239.

[31] M.L.E.A. *Report,* 1871-72, pp. 9-10.

[32] M.L.E.A. *Report,* 1873-74, p. 3.

[33] M.L.E.A. *Report,* 1871-72, p. 12.

[34] "Thoughts on the Higher Education of Women," pp. 12-14. MUA 596/3.

[35] M.L.E.A. *Report,* 1882-83, pp. 7-8.

[36] M.L.E.A. *Report,* 1872-73, p. 7.

[37] *Ibid.,* p. 6.

[38] M.L.E.A. *Report,* 1873-74, p. 8.

[39] M.L.E.A. *Report,* 1876-77, p. 7.

[40] M.L.E.A. *Report,* 1871-72, pp. 4-5.

[41] M.L.E.A *Report,* 1873-74, p. 12.

[42] M.L.E.A. *Report,* 1878-79.

[43] "Long Ago," *The McGill News,* Vol. IX, No. 2 (March 1928), p. 4.

[44] M.L.E.A. *Report,* 1883-84, p. 14.

[45] "The Future of McGill University," Annual University Lecture, 1880-81, p. 11.

[46] "Recent History of McGill University," Annual University Lecture, 1882-83, p. 13.

[47] J. Clark Murray, "The Ladies' Educational Association of Montreal," *The Canadian Spectator,* May 25, 1878, p. 20.

[48] "Special Meeting of the Corporation of McGill University held to consider Dr. Murray's motion for the admission of women and to receive the Report of the Committee thereon," *Corporation Minute Book,* No. 3 (Jan. 24, 1883 to Oct. 24, 1888), p. 205.

[49] J.W.D. to Anna Harrington, November 14, 1883. MUA 976/31/37.

[50] Margaret Mercer Dawson to Anna Harrington, April 1884. MUA 976/31/5.

[51] "To everybody's surprise, a statute permitting their use of 'Honour Mods,' (the first two Honours examinations in Literae Humaniores) and of the Final Honours Schools of Mathematics, Natural Science, and Modern History was carried by 464 votes to 321." Vera Brittain, *The Women at Oxford: A Fragment of History,* London: George C. Harrap, 1960, p. 66.

[52] "The British Association: Sir William Dawson," *Montreal Star,* August 1884, McGill University *Scrapbook.*

[53] Helen R.Y. Reid, Letter to Miss Hurlbatt, November 5, n.d. (1925). MUA, Hurlbatt Papers, 1323/1.

[54] Georgina Hunter, Arts '88, "In the Beginning," *The McGill News,* Vol. X, No. 2 (March 1929), p. 14.

[55] Grace Ritchie England, *op. cit.,* p. 15.

[56] "The Higher Education of Women," Circular, August 1884.

[57] *Fifty Years of Work*, p. 260.

[58] *Ibid.*

[59] Board of Governors *Minute Book,* III, September 13, 1884.

[60] *Ibid.* See also, Extracts of Minutes, MUA 927/46/12.

NOTES
Chapter 3

[1] Grace Ritchie England, "The Entry of Women to McGill," *The McGill News,* Vol. 16, No. 1 (December 1934), pp. 15-16. Note that Ritchie was known to her college friends as Octavia but later used her second name, Grace.

[2] "McGill University—Higher Education of Women," newspaper advertisement, Sept. 24, 1884. *McGill University Scrapbook,* Vol. 1, p. 37.

[3] According to the "Special Course for Women—List of Students," December 1884, MUA 927/31/27-28, the seven Undergraduates were: Eliza C. Cross, Blanche B. Evans, Grace Foster, Donalda McFee, Rosalie McD. McLea, Alice Murray and Mary C. Simpson; the Partials were: Helen B. Blackader, Helen L. Jamieson, Martha Murphy, Helen R.Y. Reid, Octavia G. Ritchie, Edith Turner, Addie Van Horne. The first two "Partials" were listed as taking three and four subjects respectively, the others were registered for all subjects required of undergraduates. Obviously, the distinction between regular and partial was a fine one and/or the record keeping was erratic. It seems quite clear that Octavia Grace Ritchie considered herself a regular undergraduate from the beginning, though there is some variation in her account of the number of original students and those of other original Donaldas. The official record of the number of students in the Women's Class, January 26, 1885, MUA 927/31/29, shows nine Undergraduates, six Partials, and fourteen Occasionals—all Protestant and all but one from Montreal. This entry also cites 192 as the total number of students then at McGill.
Georgina Hunter, a member of the first class of women to graduate, recalled that there were originally twenty-four women, cf. "In the Beginning," *The McGill News,* March, 1929, p. 14. Other personal recollections and official records give variations of early enrolment figures.

[4] Carrie M. Derick, "In the 80's," *Old McGill 1927,* p. 200.

[5] Board of Governors, Minutes of Meeting of October 16, 1886, p. 212.

[6] The motion was moved by Dawson at the regular meeting of Corporation, October 22, 1884.

[7] The report was presented by Dean of Arts, Alexander Johnson, but appears to have been drafted by Dawson.

[8] In a preliminary draft of these regulations, Dawson minimized the mixed classes by suggesting reading courses without lectures as well as separate classes. MUA 927/31/36.

[9] Stanley Brice Frost, *McGill University-For the Advancement of Learning,* Vol. 1, 1801-1895. Montreal: McGill-Queen's Press, 1980, p. 253.

[10] "Higher Education of Women," *Montreal Daily Witness,* September, 1884.

[11] In those days before xerox machines, multiple copies of materials of this kind could best be obtained through the services of a printer. These printed summaries and reports to be found throughout the Dawson/Murray debates give the arguments an added air of formality and seriousness.

[12] *Report on the Higher Education of Women,* Presented to the Corporation of McGill University, October, 1884, p. 8, MUA 909A/2/11.

[13] *Ibid.,* p. 11.

[14] J. Clark Murray, "The Higher Education of Women," Letter to the Editor of the *Montreal Daily Witness,* November 24, 1884.

[15] "McGill University and the Higher Education of Women—Interviews with Members of the Corporation of McGill—Doctors Do Disagree," *Montreal Daily Star,* December 5, 1884.

[16] J. Wm. Dawson, *The Higher Education of Women in Connection with McGill University,* Montreal, December 6, 1884, p. 11.

[17] *Ibid.,* p. 8.

[18] "McGill University and the Higher Education of Women," *Montreal Daily Star,* December 20, 1884.

[19] "McGill University and the Higher Education of Women," *Montreal Daily Star,* December 6, 1884.

[20] "The Present Problem," *University Gazette:* Vol. VIII, No. 2 (December 1, 1884), p. 4.

[21] "Copy of Notarial Deed—Sir D.A. Smith, K.C.M.G., to the Royal Institution, October 16, 1886," Conditions #1 and 2.
The wording in this deed bears a remarkable resemblance to a document found in the Dawson papers, MUA 927/46/5. This is in Dawson's hand and, while it bears no date, an internal reference to the 1886-87 Announcement suggests that it was written in that academic year. It is entitled "Referring to the Conditions Stated in letter of Sept. 11, 1884 and accepted by the Board of Governors and Corporation of the University" and is obviously a working draft with a number of cross-outs and alterations. Its second paragraph says in part ". . . that such education for women shall be wholly in separate classes" and the last reads ". . . no portion of this endowment shall be applied (employed) directly or indirectly to maintain (in support of) mixed classes of the two sexes." These conditions simply do not appear in Smith's letter of September 11, 1884, but there they are in the deed of donation. The ideas seem to be Dawson's rather than Smith's.

[22] Lorne V. Sawula, "Notes on the Strathcona Trust," Canadian Journal of History of Sport and Physical Education, Vol. 5, No. 1 (May 1974), p. 56.

[23] This might have been a powerful argument in favour of separate education for anyone who could remember that funds raised in 1870 as a result of the "Wilkes' resolution" were at least partially supposed to be for women's education, but they were never applied to that end. Rather, they were lost in the general budget. Had a specific amount been set aside at that time, the admission of women to McGill might have happened fourteen years earlier than it did.

[24] "McGill University and the Higher Education of Women," Montreal Daily Star, December 5, 1884. Douglas was the father of Mina, who had earned the first certificate awarded by McGill to a woman but who did not go to college.

[25] Document on naming the degrees for women, n.d. MUA 927/2/58.

[26] Faculty of Arts Minute Book, III, January 23, 1886, p. 75.

[27] "Report of the Faculty of Arts on Arrangements for Classes for Women in the 3rd and 4th years of the Special Course in Arts," Minutes of Corporation, January 28, 1885.

[28] Carrie M. Derick, a member of the third class of women, loc. cit.

[29] Grace Ritchie England, op. cit., pp. 15-16.

[30] Ibid., p. 15.

[31] Ibid., p. 16.

[32] Elizabeth A. Irwin, "Women at McGill," The McGill News, Vol. I, No. 1 (December 1919), p. 41.

[33] "A Lady Undergraduate," "Jottings from the New World," University Gazette, Vol. VIII, No. 6 (February 1, 1885), p. 10.

[34] Madelon Stockwell, quoted in Dorothy Gies McGuigan, A Dangerous Experiment, Benton Harbour, Michigan: R.W. Patterson, 1970, p. 2.

[35] Irwin, loc. cit.

[36] Conversation with Margaret Gillett at Royal Victoria College, Homecoming Weekend, September 30, 1978.

[37] Memo. Sept. 1898. MUA 2160/1/3.

[38] "Royal Victoria College McGill Alumnae," The McGill News, Vol. 1, No. 2 (March 1920) p. 24.

[39] Carrie M. Derick, op. cit., p. 350.

[40] Blanche Evans Yates, "Through the Years," The McGill News, Vol. 15, No. 3 (Summer 1934), p. 19.

[41] Derick, op. cit., p. 200.

[42] Ibid. Derick discreetly did not identify Lady Dawson in her article, but she did so privately, e.g. to Elizabeth Monk, one of McGill's earliest law graduates.

[43] Helen R.Y. Reid, "Women's Work in McGill University," Dominion Illustrated Monthly, May 1892, p. 215.

[44] "The Delta Sigma Society," University Gazette, Vol. XI, No. 5 (January 6, 1888), p. 59.

[45] "McGill Lady Students and Co-Education," Montreal Star, April 1888. (The spelling used in 19th century Montreal newspaper and personal communications is of passing interest; e.g. in this example, "favor" is spelled 20th century "American" fashion.)

[46] Derick, op. cit., p. 350.

47 *Ibid.*

48 Sir Andrew Macphail, "The Old University," *The McGill News,* Vol. 19, No. 2 (Spring 1938), p. 28.

49 *McGill University Gazette,* Vol. XIII, No. 1. (November 15, 1884), p. 5.

50 "Letter to the Editor," *University Gazette,* Vol. VIII, No. 2 (December 1, 1884), p. 14.

51 "Ladies First," *University Gazette,* Vol. VIII, No. 4 (January 1, 1885), p. 3.

52 "A Lady Undergraduate," *loc. cit.*

53 *Ibid.,* p. 9.

54 "Unfortunate Vassar," *University Gazette,* Vol. VIII, No. 9 (March 16, 1885), p. 9.

55 "College News," *University Gazette,* Vol. XII, No. 1 (October 1888), p. 13.

56 *University Gazette,* Vol. XI, No. 7 (February 1888), p. 85.

57 "Between Lectures," *University Gazette,* Vol. VII, No. 3 (October 1887), p. 36.

58 Arthur Weir, "The Cigarette Smoker," *University Gazette,* Vol. XII, No. 1 (October 1888), p. 13.

59 *University Gazette,* Vol. VII, No. 1 (November 15, 1884), p. 5.

60 Helen R.Y. Reid, *op. cit.,* p. 214.

61 Faculty of Arts *Minute Book,* III, December, 1888, 207.

62 Over the years, these were Mabel Norton Evans, Lilian Norton Evans, Katie Campbell, B. May Hamilton and Annie Walker.

63 Annie Payson Call, "The Greatest Need of College Girls," *Atlantic Monthly,* January 1892 is quoted with reserved approval by Helen R.Y. Reid, *op. cit.*

64 Mabel Norton Evans, "To the Students of the Donalda Department," *McGill Fortnightly,* November 10, 1892, p. 16.

65 *McGill Fortnightly,* March 22, 1895, p. 211.

66 "Feathers from the East Wing," *McGill Fortnightly,* March 16, 1894, p. 305.

67 "Report on Physical Education in McGill University," Corporation *Minute Book,* IV, 1892, pp. 360-63.

68 Corporation *Minute Book,* IV, January 22, 1890, p. 102.

69 "Rosalie McDonald McLea," manuscript by Helen R.Y. Reid on the occasion of the presentation to Delta Sigma, March 14, 1935. The help of Miss Phebe McLea Prowse, Rosalie McLea's daughter, in obtaining this document is gratefully acknowledged. It might be noted that both of Rosalie's daughters, Phebe and Alice did graduate from McGill.

70 Maude Abbott in letter to "Tavie" Ritchie, April 10, 1889 quoted by H.E. MacDermot in *Maude Abbott: A Memoir,* Toronto; Macmillan, 1941, p. 39.

71 McGill University, *Brief Report for the Year Ending December 31, 1918,* p. 30.

72 Blance Evans Yates, *op. cit.,* p. 21.

73 Early in 1888, when it appeared certain that eight women were about to graduate, Dean of Arts Johnson reintroduced the idea of giving a "Baccalaureate" rather than a "Bachelor of Arts" degree. After some discussion, the proposal was rejected once more.

74 "The First Class of Lady Graduates," *Montreal Daily Witness,* May 1, 1888.

75 "The Address of the First Class of Lady Graduates and the Principal's Reply," McGill College, April 30, 1888, p. 4. MUA 1216/3.

76 "M'Gill University, First Lady Graduates," *The Gazette,* Montreal, Tuesday, May 1, 1888, p. 2.

77 F.W.E., "The Sweet Girl Graduate," *Old McGill '02,* p. 174.

NOTES
Chapter 4

¹ That was the way the Harvard "Annex," later Radcliffe College, functioned. The Annex was opened in 1880 and graduated its first class four years later, the year in which women were admitted to McGill.

[1] That was the way the Harvard "Annex," later Radcliffe College, functioned. The Annex was opened in 1880 and graduated its first class four years later, the year in which women were admitted to McGill.

[2] Report on McGill Convocations in Law and Applied Science, *Montreal Herald* and *Daily Commercial Gazette*, April 30, 1888. MUA 927/40/6.

[3] "Women at College—Strong Speeches in Favor of Their Co-education with Men," *Daily Witness*, May 1, 1888. Murray Scrapbook, MUA 611.

[4] "Non Mihi Sed Alus," "The Education of Girls," Letter to the Editor of the *Gazette*, Montreal, May 5, 1888.

[5] Report to Sir William Dawson by Helen Gairdner, December 23, 1893. MUA 909A/2/17A.

[6] McGill University, Royal Charter, Acts of Parliament Statutes, 1883, Chapter X, "Of Moral Conduct and Discipline" #1—"Every exertion shall be made by all members of the University for the maintenance of good morals, and the due observance of all Statutes and Regulations of the University."

[7] Agenda Item #1, Special Meeting of the Board of Governors, May 5, 1888, Governors' *Minute Book*, 1884-1891, MUA 681/5A, pp. 321-22.

[8] J. Clark Murray to Sir William Dawson, Montreal, May 5, 1888. MUA 909A/3/21.

[9] For insights into Murray's philosophy, I am indebted to Professor David Fate Norton, McGill Dept. of Philosophy, and his unpublished paper, "The Scottish Enlightenment Exported; John Clark Murray (1836-1917)."

[10] J. Clark Murray, "The Higher Education of Women," Lecture to the Ladies' Classes at Queen's College, 1870.

[11] "Report of Speech Delivered at the Annual Distribution of Prizes in the Paisley Grammar School," Newspaper Clipping, 1877. MUA 611.

[12] John Stuart Mill, *The Subjection of Women* (1869), London: Everyman, 1974, p. 238.

[13] Georgina Hunter, B.A. '88, recalled, "The invitations from Lady Dawson were in the nature of a royal command, and it was with a somewhat fearful joy that we approached the awe-inspiring East Wing. . . . I think most of the professors invited us to their homes, and it would be invidious to speak more of one than another, but a special occasion was an afternoon at Dr. and Mrs. Clark Murray's where the guest of honour was Lord Strathcona. . . ." "In the Beginning," *The McGill News*, Vol. 10, No. 2 (March 1929), pp. 15-16.

[14] "Foreword," *Imperial Order Daughters of the Empire and Children of the Empire* (Booklet outlining the history of the IODE, no publishing data), 1932.

[15] Claude T. Bissell, "Literary Taste in Central Canada During the Late Nineteenth Century," *Canadian History Review*, XXXI (1950), pp. 237-51. For a bibliography of material on women in *The Week*, see *Canadian Newsletter of Research on Women*, VI, No. 3 (October 1977), pp. 106-23.

[16] W.H., "Professor J. Clark Murray," *The University Magazine*, Vol. 17 (1918), pp. 561-66.

[17] J. Clark Murray, "University Co-Education," *Daily Witness*, Montreal, Saturday, February 18, 1888.

[18] Donald A. Smith in a letter to Sir William Dawson, February 20, 1888. MUA 909A/4/2.

[19] J.Wm. Dawson, "Memorandum for the Board of Governors with reference to certain recent statements respecting the McGill Classes for Women," February 22, 1888. MUA 909A/2/10.

[20] Governors' *Minute Book*, 1884-1891, Meeting of Saturday, February 25, 1888, Item #8, p. 302.

[21] J. Clark Murray to the Board of Governors of McGill College, Montreal, May 10, 1888. MUA 909A/3/17.

[22] J.W. Dawson to Chancellor Ferrier, May 12, 1888. MUA 909A/2/7.

[23] Governors' *Minute Book*, 1884-1891. Special Meeting, May 12, 1888, Item 1, pp. 327-28.

445

[24] J.Wm. Dawson to Messrs. Molson and Hague, May 18, 1888. MUA 909A/2/42.

[25] Governors' *Minute Book,* 1886-1891. Meeting of June 5, 1888, pp. 339-41.

[26] "Report of the Interview with Professor Murray," June 1, 1888. MUA 909A/2/18.

[27] "The Co-Education Difficulty: Both Sides Unwilling to Speak," *Montreal Star,* May 15, 1888. MUA 909A/2/14.

[28] Letter to the Editor of the *Montreal Star,* headed "Dr. Murray's Resolution," signed "Ad Inquirendum," May 15, 1888.

[29] "Algonquin," "Autocracy in McGill College," *The Week,* July 5, 1888, p. 507.

[30] Notes on Article in *The Week.* MUA 909A/2/22.

[31] "The Governing Body of McGill University," *The Week,* July 19, 1888, p. 541.

[32] W.H. Turner, "McGill University," Letter to the Editor, *The Week,* August 2, 1888.

[33] "Truth Seeker," "Further Developments of the McGill College Question," *The Week,* August 23, 1888.

[34] "Trouble at McGill," *Montreal Herald,* October 10, 1888.

[35] "A Donalda Student," "Methods of M'Gill," *The Week,* February 8, 1889, p. 154.

[36] William Dawson to Mr. Greenshields, January 26, 1889. MUA 909A/2/41.

[37] Governors' *Minute Book,* 1884-1891, Special Meeting of September 27, 1888, p. 359. MUA 681/5A.

[38] Wilson, it might be noted, had been offered the Principalship of McGill in 1853-4, but had declined in favour of a Professorship in History at University College, Toronto, where he later became President. Wilson was another important Canadian educator of Scottish origins and his approach to women's education was very similar to Dawson's. He was sympathetic to extramural classes, just as Dawson had been supportive of the M.L.E.A., and he had written in 1873:

> There is a kind of emotional response in a female audience when characterized by intelligence and refinement which is singularly calculated to call forth the very best efforts of the lecturer. Without any demonstrative expressions of sympathy one seems to feel himself *en rapport* with his audience very differently from that of a male assembly; partly, no doubt, because he appeals with confidence to emotions and sympathies less easily reached with the other sex. After some uphill work the Higher Education movement gives fair promise of success. (Diary entry, December 10, 1873 quoted in H.H. Langton, *Sir Daniel Wilson,* Toronto: Thomas Nelson, 1919, p. 91.)

However, all this sweetness and light seemed to have vanished a decade later after the Ontario Legislature had passed a resolution requiring the admission of women to University College on the same terms as men. Though Wilson knew he would have to confront the Government, he firmly refused to accept women, noting in his diary, "I have great faith in the power of steady passive resistance, notwithstanding a strong-minded madam's declaration today that she would force us to submit to woman's demand for her Rights." (Diary entry, September 25, 1883, quoted in Langton, p. 111.)

Like his friend Dawson, Wilson seemed to be supportive of higher education for women as long as it was manifestly limited or "different." He believed that "when the numbers increase trouble is sure to arise" and when faced with the reality of accepting women as co-equals, his high-sounding liberality faltered. He balked and, resentfully, he now saw the formerly "intelligent" and "refined ladies" as "strong-minded madams." Like Dawson, too, he favoured separate education —if higher education for women had to come. Co-education, he said, was inferior. It was cheap, "that is almost all that can be said in its favour." (Daniel Wilson to Dr. Harrington, Toronto, March 21, 1884. MUA 1377.)

There are other close parallels in the histories of the admission of women to University College and McGill. Wilson was actually at McGill in the summer of 1884 for the British Association meetings. It is possible that his presence at that crucial time and his agitation over his own co-educational problems intensified Dawson's antipathy to mixed classes. Just a few days before the Hon. Donald Smith called on Principal Dawson with his irrefusable offer of $50,000 for the higher education of women, Dr. Wilson received a letter from the Ontario Minister of Education, George W. Ross. Ross favoured co-education and indicated to Wilson that he was likely to enforce the

Legislature's resolution upon University College. Alarmed, Wilson telegraphed his reply, inviting Ross to come to Montreal, saying, "Sir Wm. Dawson has returned from England with valuable information on co-education and wishes to see you." His efforts were to no avail and he had to capitulate to an Order-in-Council of October 2, 1884 and accept women on the same terms as men. Thus, women were admitted to both University College and McGill in the very same month, both very suddenly and with very few prior preparations. However, since women had already been writing the University College examinations without attending the lectures, some of them were admitted there with advanced standing and five graduated in 1885, three years before the first Donaldas. In Toronto, as in Montreal, the issue of co-education was hotly debated in newspapers and student publications. A considerable body of public opinion was in favour in both cities, both President and Principal came in for criticism and both were accused by their critics of hypocrisy. (For further details on Toronto, see Nancy Ramsay Thompson, "The Controversy Over the Admission of Women to University College, University of Toronto," Unpublished M.A. Thesis, University of Toronto, 1974.)

[39] J. Clark Murray to Sir William Dawson, April 23, 1889. MUA 909A/2/26.

[40] J. Clark Murray to Sir William Dawson, April 26, 1889. MUA 909A.

[41] Sir William Dawson to J. Clark Murray, April 27, 1889. MUA 909/A.

[42] R.L. Church to Sir William Dawson, November 20, 1889. MUA 909A/1/13.

[43] J. William Dawson to J. Clark Murray, November 23, 1889. MUA 909A/1/14.

[44] Governors' *Minute Book*, 1884-91, Item #6 Meeting of December 20, 1889, p. 460, MUA 681/5A.

[45] "Educated Women: An Address Delivered Before the Delta Sigma Society of McGill University, December 1889." Printed for private circulation.

[46] Margaret Polson Murray to Lady Dawson, November 11, 1888, MUA 1377.

[47] MUA 909A/3/14.

[48] J.C.M. to J.W.D. from Cap à l'Aigle, July 15, 1893. MUA 909A/3/12.

[49] J.W.D. to J.C.M. from Little Métis, July 31, 1893. MUA 909A/3/11.

[50] J.C.M. to J.W.D., Montreal, September 23, 1893. MUA 909A/3/7.

[51] J.W.D. "Memo, Respecting the Occasion of the late [sic] Principal's Letter to Rev. Dr. Murray, of May 2, 1888. (Confidential to Board of Governors)," December 23, 1893. MUA 909/3/10.

[52] J.W.D. to Sir Donald Smith, Montreal, December 1893. MUA 909/3/2.

[53] Donald A. Smith to Sir William Dawson, Hudson's Bay House, Montreal, February 2, 1894.

[54] Grace Ritchie England, "The Entrance of Women to McGill," *The McGill News*, Vol. XVI, No. 1 (1934), p. 17.

NOTES
Chapter 5

1 "Lady Strathcona Succumbs After One Week's Illness," *The Times,* London, November 13, 1913.

2 Charles Tupper, letter to Lord Strathcona from Bexley Heath, November 13, 1913. PAC MG 29/45 Vol. 25.

3 T.P. O'Connor, M.P., "Lord Strathcona, A Study in Personality," *Pall Mall Magazine,* Vol. 51 (June 1915), p. 765; Dr. George Bryce, "The Real Strathcona—A Prince of Benefactors," *Canadian Magazine,* Vol. 46 (February 1916), p. 349; and William R. Stewart, "Baron Strathcona and Mount Royal," *Cosmopolitan,* Vol. 25 (June 1903), p. 216.

4 Beckles, Willson, *The Life of Lord Strathcona and Mont Royal,* London: Cassell, 1915, pp. ix-x.

5 Quoted by Willson, *Ibid.,* p. 10.

6 Lord Strathcona was constantly being asked for money and he gave relatively small amounts to many educational enterprises, for example, $1,000 "toward the fund for building an English academy at Rawdon, Quebec." (PAC MG/29/A5/Vol. 5/R11): upon his death, his executors chose to grant from the considerable sum left for "institutions of learning and benevolence" support to Mrs. J. Porteous Arnold, Principal of Roslyn Ladies College, Westmount. PAC MG/29/A5 Vol. 5/R9.

7 Dawson said in his convocation speech in 1888 that the offer "in so far as I was concerned ... was unsolicited," *The Gazette,* Montreal, May 1, 1888, p. 2. There is no reason to doubt this, for it seems likely that Dawson did not even know Donald Smith before September, 1884 since there is no correspondence between them before that date and no earlier references to Smith have been found among Dawson's papers. Later, when memory had played its tricks and generated anachronisms, Dawson said his his autobiography, ". . . my friend Sir Donald A. Smith [sic], Chancellor of the University [sic], called me out of the geological section to intimate his wish to bestow the handsome sum of $50,000 on the University in aid of separate classes [sic] for women." (*Fifty Years of Work,* p. 227.) The possibility has been advanced that "Sir William had been thinking aloud, or even praying aloud, in the hearing of those who might have the ear of the wealthy." (Stanley Frost, "Trouble with Women," *McGillianna,* No. 6, September 1978, p. 7.) No doubt the financially hard-pressed principal was always hoping for endowments, but this speculation does not adequately explain Smith's sudden generous gift.

8 *McGill Fortnightly,* Vol. II, No. 6 (December 22, 1893), p. 146.

9 Mrs. Lucy Simpson, "Valedictory Address," 30th June, 1863.

10 Mrs. C.W. Simpson, "Higher Education for Girls," A paper read at the school of Misses Symmers and Smith, 15th June, 1885. (Lande Collection, Rare Books, McLennan Library, McGill University.)

11 Mrs. F.P. Shearwood, Arts '90, "Women and the University," *The McGill News,* Vol. XXX, No. 2 (Winter 1948). p. 54.

12 J.W. Dawson, "An Ideal College for Women," An address Delivered Before the Delta Sigma Society of McGill University, December, 1894, p. 15.

13 Principal William Peterson, letter to Lord Strathcona, 4th November, 1897. MUA 641/33/58.

14 Principal Peterson, letter to Lord Strathcona, 22nd July, 1898, p. 7. MUA 641/33/6.

15 W. Peterson to Lord Strathcona, 17th February, 1898, p. 2. MUA 641/33/45.

16 Before his knighthood, he spelt his name "McDonald"; afterwards, Sir William chose to spell it "Macdonald."

17 "Rumours of a Princely Gift—Two McGill Endowments," *The Gazette,* Montreal, March 26, 1898.

18 Board of Governors, *Minutes* of Meeting of December 15, 1898.

19 *The Gazette,* Montreal, December 14, 1898.

20 Board of Governors, *Minutes* of Meeting, January 21, 1899, p. 97.

[21] "McGill University, Montreal, Royal Victoria College, Special Announcement for 1899-1900," pp. 7-8.

[22] Hilda D. Oakeley, *My Adventures in Education,* London: Williams and Norgate, 1939, p. 59.

[23] *Ibid.,* pp. 52-53.

[24] *Ibid.,* p. 8.

[25] Strathcona to Miss Oakeley, in a letter from Earlscourt, London, September 4, 1899. MUA 315/23/2.

[26] *Montreal Star,* July 6, 1899. As it turned out, the required degree of tact was not forthcoming and, after a disagreement with the Warden over jurisdiction, the Housekeeper left at the end of the first year.

[27] Carrie Derick was a Demonstrator and Lecturer in Botany before Oakeley's time, but only people with the rank of Associate Professor were members of the Faculty with the right to attend meetings.

[28] "Annual University Lecture," *The Gazette,* Montreal, January 25, 1900, *McGill Scrapbook* No. 1, p. 364.

[29] Board of Governors, *Minutes* of Meeting, December 15, 1898.

[30] Oakeley, *op. cit.,* p. 86.

[31] *Ibid.*

[32] *Ibid.,* p. 88.

[33] "Donalda Ladies' Lunch—The Graduating Class Sent on its Way Rejoicing," *The Gazette,* Montreal, May 2, 1889.

[34] Hilda D. Oakeley to Dr. Peterson from Royal Victoria College for Women, May 21, 1905. MUA 641/35/4.

[35] Oakeley, *My Adventures in Education,* p. 92.

[36] "Opening Ceremonies at the R.V.C.," *Old McGill,* 1902, p. 35.

[37] For a list of the recipients and their degrees. See Appendix C.

[38] Board of Governors, *Minutes* of Meeting, February 5, 1917, p. 255.

[39] In the final stages of the negotiations with the British Government, Winston Churchill (Conservative Colonial Secretary) was one of the officials involved.

[40] McGill University, *Annual Report,* 1922, pp. 23-24.

[41] A. Vibert Douglas, "Wardens of Royal Victoria College," *The McGill News,* Vol. 22, No. 1 (Winter 1940), p. 18.

[42] E. Hurlbatt, "Memories of Lord Strathcona," *The McGill News,* Vol. 11, No. 2. (March 1930), p. 19.

[43] Cornelia Sorabji, a friend at Somerville, as reported by Susan E. Vaughan in "Ethel Hurlbatt, LL.D.," *The McGill News,* Vol. 15, No. 3, (June 1934), p. 20.

[44] Susan E. Vaughan, "Ethel Hurlbatt, LL.D.," *The McGill News,* Vol. 15, No. 3 (June 1934), p. 20.

[45] "Miss Ethel Hurlbatt," — "Alumnae Section," *The McGill News,* Vol. 10, No. 4, (September 1929), p. 17.

[46] Vaughan, *loc. cit.*

[47] Ethel Hurlbatt, Confidential Letter to Miss E.M. Cartwright, February 7, 1927. MUA 1323/1.

[48] C.F. Martin, reply to Miss Hurlbatt, February 10, 1927. MUA 1323/1.

[49] Ethel Cartwright to Miss Hurlbatt, February 14, 1927. MUA 1323/1.

[50] The Warden, Royal Victoria College, *Report to the Principal,* 1922-23, p. 10.

[51] Henri Bourassa, *Le Devoir,* 30 mars, 1918.

[52] "Delta Sigma Society," *The Martlet,* Vol. I, No. 6 (November 27, 1908), p. 137.

[53] "The Woman Suffrage Question in England—A Reply to Miss Hurlbatt," *The Martlet,* January 8, 1909, p. 221.

[54] *Ibid.,* p. 223.

[55] Sir Arthur Currie, letter to Miss Ethel Hurlbatt, June 27, 1929. MUA 1323/1.

[56] Charles W. Colby to Susan Cameron, April 30, 1895. MUA 2160/7/2A.

[57] A. Vibert Douglas, "Within Her Dominions Supreme—A Tribute to Mrs. Walter Vaughan,

Retiring Warden of the Royal Victoria College," *The McGill News,* Vol. 18, No. 3 (Summer 1937), p. 28.

[58] Dean Woodhead in presenting Susan Vaughan for the degree of Doctor of Laws, *honoris causa,* 1937. MUA 639/13.

[59] Emily Murphy, Nellie McClung, Louise McKinney, Irene Parlby and Henrietta Edwards. On October 18, 1929 the Privy Council reversed the decision of the Canadian Supreme Court which had gone against the women. The Privy Council, the court of last appeal, firmly concluded that "the word 'person' includes members of the male and female sex, and that therefore . . . women are eligible to be summoned and become members of the Senate of Canada."

[60] Susan Vaughan in a letter to Walter L. Johnson, November 25, 1930. MUA 1323/3.

[61] "Donaldas Claim Equal Right in McGill Affairs," *Montreal Star,* February 19, 1917.

[62] "A Problem," *McGill Daily,* November 22, 1928, p. 2.

[63] "These Women," *McGill Daily,* December 9, 1930, p. 2.

[64] Walter L. Johnson, "Opinion" November 28, 1930, p. 7. MUA 1323/3.

[65] Susan E. Vaughan, letter to the Editor, "Women are McGill Students," *McGill Daily,* December 11, 1930, pp. 1 + 4. Ms. may be found MUA 2160/2/4.

[66] "Women Are McGill Men," *McGill Daily,* December 11, 1930, p. 2.

[67] Susan E. Vaughan, "Some Random Reflections on Women and Their Education," *Old McGill,* 1932, pp. 116-17.

[68] "Co-eds Challenged to Uphold Standard," *Montreal Star,* February 29, 1936.

[69] F. MacG., "Mrs. Walter Vaughan: A Tribute," unidentified clipping in Papers of Katherine and Jane Wisdom, MUA 2287/52.

[70] The imperial connection was to be maintained throughout Maude Parkin Grant's life. Her sister, Alice, married Vincent Massey, the first Canadian-born Governor-General of Canada and her daughter, Alison Grant Ignatieff, became a lady-in-waiting to Her Majesty, Queen Elizabeth II during the royal tour of Canada in 1978.

[71] Oakeley, *My Adventures in Education,* p. 79.

[72] Board of Governors, *Minutes* of Meeting, December 1, 1930, p. 526.

[73] *Minutes* of the First Meeting of the Royal Victoria College Survey Committee, February 16, 1940, p. 2. MUA 16/17.

[74] *Minutes* of a Meeting of the Royal Victoria College Survey Committee, March 1, 1940, p. 2. MUA 16/17.

[75] Eliza Cross Currie had died in 1907.

[76] Dr. Grace Ritchie England, Address to Spring Convocation, 1938, p. 1. (Personal copy, gift of Mrs. Esther Ritchie Cushing.)

[77] *Ibid.,* p. 4.

[78] Margaret Grant Andrew, "When Mrs. Grant was Warden: 1937-1940" in Edgar Andrew Collard, ed., *The McGill You Knew,* Toronto: Longman, 1976, p. 32; and Alison Grant Ignatieff, letter to Margaret Gillett, February 16, 1981.

[79] Muriel V. Roscoe, *The Royal Victoria College, 1899-1962: A Report to the Principal,* 1964, p. 139.

[80] *Ibid.,* p. 140.

[81] For details of the changes, see *Ibid.,* pp. 119-23.

[82] *Ibid.,* pp. 179-80.

[83] *Ibid.,* Appendix 5, p. 9.

[84] Janet Toole, "Miss Reynolds of R.V.C.," *The McGill News,* Vol. 44, No. 1, (Winter 1962), p. 55.

[85] G.A. Grimson to Miss Helen Reynolds, Memorandum on "Future Women Students' Residence," November 29, 1965. MUA 1117/23 "Royal Victoria College Extension" File.

[86] For an overview of the turbulence on the McGill campus, see Rocke Robertson, "Ten Years After," *McGill Journal of Education,* Vol. XV, No. 1 (Winter 1980), pp. 7-22.

[87] Helen Reynolds in an interview with Margaret Gillett, Halifax, N.S., July, 1976.

[88] Revised Statutes of Quebec: *Liquor Permit Act,* 1964, Ch. 4, Sec. 98—drinking age lowered to 20; 1971, Ch. 19, Sec. 84—drinking age lowered to 18. *Voting*—1964, Ch. 7, Sec. 47—"Quebec voters to be 18 on polling day."

[89] "Men to Choose R.V.C. Warden," *McGill Daily,* February 5, 1970; "We Protest," *McGill Daily,* March 13, 1970; "Warden's Responsibilities," *McGill Reporter,* April 10, 1970.

[90] "The Principal said that the intention here was to be non-specific as to sex regarding these posts, that either the Dean or Associate Dean might be a woman." McGill University Senate, *Minutes of Meeting,* 20th May, 1970, Minute 149, pp. 260-61.

[91] Mary Robertson-Wilhelmi, letter to Margaret Gillett, March 28, 1979.

[92] Donna Runnalls, quoted in "Portrait of a Don," *McGill Reporter,* January 24, 1979.

[93] Donna Runnalls, in conversation with Margaret Gillett, February 27, 1979 at R.V.C.

[94] Flo Tracy in conversation with Margaret Gillett, McGill University, October 14, 1980.

[95] "Flo Tracy: McGill's Non-stop Mom," *McGill Reporter,* Vol. 13, No. 1 (August 22, 1980), p. 3.

[96] Flo Tracy to Margaret Gillett.

NOTES
Chapter 6

[1] Thus, one of Lord Strathcona's hopes was fulfilled. The McGill *Annual Report* for 1898-1899 said in relation to R.V.C, ". . . it may be stated that the Chancellor has instituted a Department of Music in the College, which may well become the nucleus of a University Faculty," p. 3.

[2] Susan E. Vaughan, "Clara Lichtenstein," *The McGill News*, Vol. 27, No. 4 (Summer 1946), p. 13.

[3] Lichtenstein is still remembered on campus. As part of R.V.C.'s 80th birthday celebrations, the Faculty of Music dedicated a concert in her honour.

[4] Letter from A. Peters to Miss S. Cameron, July 27, 1916. MUA 2160/7/1C.

[5] Muriel V. Roscoe, *The Royal Victoria College, 1899-1962: A Report to the Principal*, 1964, p. 154.

[6] McGill did not consolidate that early triumph. With the exception of some of the traditionally "female" fields of study, the appointment of women to academic positions was not in proportion to the growing number of women students. Their progress through the ranks was also generally slow. By the mid-70's when the total student body was more than 45% female, only 18.4% of the McGill teaching staff were women. See, Margaret Gillett *et al.*, *A Survey of Teaching and Research on Women at McGill—A Report to the Principal*, December 1976, pp. 7-10.

[7] Margaret Grant Andrew, "When Mrs. Vaughan was RVC's Warden," in E.A. Collard, *The McGill You Knew*, Toronto: Longman, 1975, p. 29.

[8] "Editorial," *Montreal Star*, October 3, 1957.

[9] Roscoe, *op. cit.*, p. 107.

[10] "Y.W.C.A.," *McGill Fortnightly*, Vol. III, No. 10 (February 22, 1894), p. 179.

[11] "Our Obligations as Women in India," *McGill Fortnightly*, Vol. III, No. 1 (October 12, 1893), p. 44.

[12] For some detailed analysis of changes in enrolment patterns, see Stanley Frost and Sheila Rosenberg, "The McGill Student Body," *McGill Journal of Education*, Vol. XV, No. 1 (Winter 1980), pp. 35-53.

[13] "The Players Club," *James McGill: His Book—Old McGill*, 1921.

[14] "Only Men to be Members of Bridge Club," *McGill Daily*, November 28, 1928, p. 1.

[15] *Report* of the Warden, Royal Victoria College, 1968-69. MUA 1903/500/Box 11, Shelf 2407.

[16] "Red Wing Honour Society," *Old McGill, 1968*, p. 284.

[17] "Secret Societies," *McGill University Gazette*, Vol. VII, No. 8 (March 1885), p. 5.

[18] "A Donalda of the Nineties," on "Shall We Have Sororities?" *McGill Outlook* Vol. IX, No. 4 (Nov. 1, 1906) pp. 87-88.

[19] "Sorority Girls to Convene Here," *Montreal Star*, December 24, 1929.

[20] Report to F. Cyril James, Principal of McGill University on "Ways in Which Sororities May be Supervised and Co-ordinated That They May Make a Real Contribution to McGill University." MUA 16, Box 3.

[21] Muriel V. Roscoe in a letter to the Expansion Chairman, Iota Alpha Pi, March 28, 1945. MUA 16, Box 3.

[22] Margaret Grant Andrew, *op. cit.*, p. 30.

[23] Gladys Bean, "Brief Historical Report on the Development of Women's Athletics Program at McGill," *Report* to Dean of Students, October, 1975, p. 3.

[24] *Ibid.*, p. 5.

[25] See for example, Kathy Salamon, "Women Continue to Feel the Sports Shaft," *McGill Daily*, March 8, 1979, p. 15.

[26] Muriel V. Roscoe, *The Royal Victoria College*, pp. 173-78.

[27] In an address made on that occasion, Dean of Music Helmut Blume acknowledged that R.V.C. had given birth to music at McGill and considered the transformation as "a coming home." He assured R.V.C. that "The Faculty of Music will be a good neighbour and . . . we shall serenade you constantly." Faculty of Music, *McGill Music Month, April 10 to May 8, 1975* (publi-

cation celebrating the inauguration of Pollack Concert Hall and the 70th anniversary of music at McGill), p. 18.

[28] Royal Victoria College, *General Announcement and Residence Rules*, 1961-62, p. 7.

[29] "Information for Residents of Royal Victoria College," September, 1978, cover.

[30] Roger Clark, President of the Douglas Hall Residence Council, "Building a Residence Community," *McGill Reporter*, March 31, 1971.

[31] Papers of Katherine and Jane Wisdom, c.1899-1910. MUA 2287/63.

[32] "Exchanges" Column, *McGill Outlook*, Vol. VIII, No. 7 (Dec. 18, 1905), p. 180.

[33] Anne Christine Williams, "History of Women Associates of McGill," *The McGill News*, Vol. 26, No. 1 (October 1944), p. 15.

[34] "McGill Women's Union," *The McGill News*, Vol. II, No. 1 (December 1920), p. 42.

[35] *Ibid.*, p. 41.

[36] "McGill's Women's War Work," *The McGill News*, Vol. I, No. 1 (December 1919, p. 7.

[37] Paul U. Kellog, quoted in *Ibid.*, p. 8.

[38] Beatrice L. Johnston in a letter to Margaret Gillett, February 1, 1979.

[39] Phyllis Lee Peterson, "My Old McGill," *The McGill News*, Vol. 32, No. 3 (Spring 1951), pp. 8-9 (Excerpted).

[40] "All Sorts" Column, *McGill Daily*, November 17, 1930, p. 2.

[41] Helen McMaster Paulin, "My Memories of McGill in the Thirties," in a letter to Margaret Gillett, October 11, 1978.

[42] "Compulsory Training for Women in Wartime." MUA 16/117/9/3/6.

[43] A. Vibert Douglas, "The Challenge of War Time to University Women," *The McGill News*, Vol. 25, No. 1 (Autumn, 1943), pp. 17-18.

[44] Allison Douglas Knox, "Women Uninterested," *McGill Daily*, December 1, 1953, p. 2.

[45] Dr. Anne Lancaster, letter to Margaret Gillett, February 17, 1979.

[46] Faith Wallis, B.A. '71, M.A. '74 in letter to Margaret Gillett, June 1, 1978.

[47] *Ibid.*

NOTES
Chapter 7

[1] "College World," *University Gazette*, Vol. 12, No. 9 (February 1889), p. 111.

[2] See, Carlotta Hacker, *The Indomitable Lady Doctors*, Toronto: Clarke, Irwin, 1974, pp. 3-16.

[3] This was by way of a student prank which misfired, not some enlightened vision of the new generation of medical students. A parallel may be made with a relatively recent piece of U.S. civil rights legislation. The inclusion of "sex" in Title VII of the 1964 Civil Rights Act, which upholds the right to freedom from discrimination in employment, was half a joke and half an attempt on the part of a Southern congressman to ensure the defeat of the bill. It passed anyway, giving U.S. women the first legislative guarantee of civil rights since the right to vote (the 19th amendment to the Constitution, 1920).

[4] Elizabeth Smith Shortt, *Historical Sketch of Medical Education of Women, Kingston, Canada*, Ottawa: Private Printing, 1916, p. 1.

[5] *Ibid.*, p. 11.

[6] William Osler, "On the Growth of a Profession," *Canada Medical and Surgical Journal*, Vol. 14 (1885-86), pp. 129-155.

[7] "Medical Education for Women," *The Gazette*, Montreal, March 29, 1889.

[8] For an excellent analysis of this point of view, see Veronica Strong-Boag, "Canada's Women Doctors: Feminism Constrained," in Linda Kealey, ed., *A Not Unreasonable Claim: Women and Reform in Canada, 1880s-1920s*, Toronto: The Women's Press, 1979, pp. 109-29.

[9] See, Mary Roth Walsh, "The Rediscovery of the Need for a Feminist Medical Education," *Harvard Educational Review*, Vol. 49, No. 4 (November 1979), p. 542.

[10] "The Medical Question," *University Gazette*, Vol. 12, No. 11 (April 1889), p. 128.

[11] The entire petition is recorded in the Minutes of Corporation, April 24, 1889.

[12] These arguments were rehearsed and then dismissed in "The Medical Question," *University Gazette*, Vol. 12, No. 10 (March, 1889), p. 114.

[13] "Women and Medicine—A Meeting in the Interest of the Medical Education," *The Gazette*, Montreal, April, 1889.

[14] "McGill's Women Doctors," *The McGill News*, Vol. II, No. 3 (June 1921), pp. 14-15 and Maysie S. MacSporran, "Vale, Amica Carissima," *The McGill News*, Spring 1948.

[15] Maude E.S. Abbott, "Autobiographical Sketch," An address before the Women's Medical Society of McGill, March 31, 1928, p. 8. MUA 2354.

[16] *Ibid.*, p. 9.

[17] "Decided Against Ladies," *The Gazette*, Montreal, May 14, 1891, p. 2.

[18] Dr. Abbott's experience in being grudgingly employed by a university which excluded women as medical students was not unique. Rather, it reflects a very general willingness of patriarchal institutions to accept females when there are exceptional circumstances or when there is something to be gained. The limitations imposed on these exceptions have no doubt reduced the precedent-setting effect they might otherwise have had. As a case in point, Dr. Alice Hamilton, whose stature as an expert on industrial diseases was unsurpassed in the United States, in 1918 became the first woman appointed to the faculty of the Harvard School of Public Health. She was appointed because she was the leading expert in her field but she was never completely accepted. Harvard's President Lowell explicitly stipulated that the appointment was not to be construed as a precedent for admitting women to the Medical School and he imposed three ridiculous limitations: Dr. Hamilton was not allowed into the Faculty Club; she was not to participate in the academic procession at commencement; and she was not eligible for faculty tickets to the football game. Dr. Hamilton, like many other professional women in similar circumstances, having gained the major point, chose to overlook the humiliation of the trivial exceptions imposed upon her. But neither she nor Maude Abbott received the professional recognition, advancement or financial rewards a distinguished man would have had in similar circumstances.
See, Mary Roth Walsh, *Doctors Wanted: No Women Need Apply* (New Haven, Conn.: Yale Univ.

Press, 1977) and Mary Roth Walsh, "The Rediscovery of the Need for a Feminist Medical Education," *Harvard Educational Review,* Vol. 49, No. 4 (November 1979), pp. 464-65.

[19] "Women in Medicine: Maude Abbott," *McGill Medical Journal,* Vol. XVI, No. 3 (1947), p. 235.

[20] Correspondence between Dr. J.W. Scane (Registrar of the Faculty of Medicine) and Miss Ethel Hurlbatt, Montreal hospitals, and other Faculties of Medicine in the Maude Abbott Papers, MUA 38/180/415811.

[21] Faculty of Medicine *Minutes* (1913-23) July 8, 1916, p. 240.

[22] *Ibid.,* November 4, 1916, p. 249.

[23] *Ibid.,* March 3, 1917, pp. 265-66.

[24] *Ibid.,* p. 266.

[25] *Ibid.,* April 7, 1917, p. 268.

[26] *Ibid.,* August 30, 1917, p. 281.

[27] *Ibid.,* December 15, 1917, p. 294.

[28] *Ibid.,* February 6, 1918, p. 305 and April 6, 1918, p. 312.

[29] *Ibid.,* April 16, 1918, pp. 314-15 and May 4, 1918, p. 316.

[30] "A Distinct Advance," *Montreal Star,* May 11, 1918.

[31] R.F. Ruttan to Miss E. Hurlbatt, April 18, 1918. Peterson Papers, 1896-1918, MUA 2P 641/24/79.

[32] Ethel Hurlbatt to Principal Peterson, May 8, 1918. Peterson Papers, 1896-1918. MUA 2P 641/24/14.

[33] Principal Peterson, Letter to Dr. Abraham Flexner, May 6, 1918. MUA 59/2/P/4/2/31.

[34] Jessie Boyd Scriver, "McGill's First Women Medical Students," *McGill Medical Journal,* Vol. 16, No. 2 (April 1947), p. 242.

[35] Jessie Boyd Scriver, "McGill's First Women Doctors," in Edgar Andrew Collard, ed., *The McGill You Knew,* Toronto: Longman, 1975, pp. 132-33.

[36] Dr. Jessie Boyd Scriver in conversation with Dr. Mary Childs and Margaret Gillett, August 24, 1977.

[37] Mabel H., letter to Octavia Ritchie from Kingston, November 9, 1890. Courtesy Mrs. Esther England Cushing.

[38] "Women Medicos Carry off Prizes," *Montreal Star,* June 6, 1922. Earlier public reporting on their progress included "McGill Lady Student in Medicine [Jessie Boyd] Took Several Honors," *Montreal Herald,* July 3, 1919.

[39] Jessie Boyd Scriver, *The Montreal Children's Hospital: Years of Growth,* Montreal: McGill-Queen's Press, 1979.

[40] Abraham Flexner, *Medical Education in the United States and Canada,* New York: Carnegie Foundation for the Advancement of Teaching, Bulletin No. 4, 1910, pp. 178-79.

[41] Frederick Smith, Dean of Medicine in a letter to Principal F. Cyril James, June 29, 1949. MUA 16/202.

[42] T.H. Matthews, Registrar, memorandum to the Principal concerning "B.W.I. Pre-medical students," 6th October, 1943. MUA 16/85.

[43] J.S.L. Browne, Chairman of Department of Experimental Medicine, letter to Dean D.L. Thomson, Graduate Studies and Research, April 28, 1944.

[44] "Two Royal Fellows," *McGill Reporter,* Vol. 11, No. 25 (March 28, 1979) p. 2.

[45] "The Eight Faces of Eve," *The McGill News,* Vol. 52, No. 3 (May 1971), p. 18.

[46] André-Pierre Contandriopoulos avec Jean-Yves Rivard et Colette Meunier, "L'Activité professionnelle des femmes médecin au Quebec," édition spéciale, *Bulletin* of the Professional Corporation of Physicians of Québec, Vol. XVI, No. 1 (Janvier 1976), p. 41.

[47] A glance at the Annual Convocation Programme for 1914 would suggest that Annie Langstaff was one of two women to receive their degree of B.C.L. that year. However, Langstaff was the only female; Shirley Greenshields Dixon, whose name appeared on the same list, was a man.

[48] "Is Law Practice Closed to Women?" *The Gazette,* Montreal, 21st January, 1915.

[49] "Mrs. Langstaff Cannot Practice Law, is Decision," *Montreal Herald,* 13th February, 1915.

[50] "Mass Meeting of Protest by Local Women," *Montreal Star,* 16th February, 1915, "Mrs. Langstaff's Plea will Find Many Champions," *Montreal Star,* 20th February, 1915 and A. Macdonald Langstaff, "Will Quebec Call Her Portias to the Bar?" *The Home,* October, 1929, pp. 5-8.

[51] "Mrs. Langstaff at Insurance Dinner," *The Gazette,* Montreal, March 24, 1915.

[52] Frances Fenwick Williams, "The Lay of Mrs. Langstaff," *Annie Langstaff Scrapbook,* McGill Faculty of Law Library.

[53] Principal William Peterson in a letter to S.W. Jacobs, November 27th, 1915. MUA 59/2/P/4/2/27.

[54] "There Shall Be No Women at the Bar of Quebec," *Montreal Star,* 29 February, 1916.

[55] "Woman in Council for the First Time," *The Gazette,* Montreal, November 27, 1940.

[56] Claire Kirkland Casgrain, interviewed for "The Eight Faces of Eve," *The McGill News,* Vol. 52, No. 3 (May 1971), p. 16.

[57] *Montreal Star,* October 11, 1922.

[58] Marvin A. Rogers, *A History of the McGill Dental School,* Montreal: Faculty of Dentistry, McGill University, 1980.

[59] "Molar Tugging by This Dentist Should Really Be Painless, Men," *The Gazette,* Montreal, May 22, 1947.

[60] Faculty of Applied Science, *Minute Book* No. 6—September 29, 1909 to May 6, 1912, pp. 7 and 12. MUA RG 35/1/2.

[61] Faculty of Applied Science, *Minute Book* No. 7—13th May 1912 to 15th October 1915, p. 88.

[62] *Ibid.,* p. 89.

[63] Principal William Peterson, Letter to George Brown, South Nyack, N.Y., 24th February 1914. MUA 2/9/4/2/23.

[64] Faculty of Applied Science, *Minute Book,* No. 8, October 15, 1915 to May 7, 1920, p. 112.

[65] Faculty of Applied Science *Minute Book* No. 10, March 2, 1925 to October 1, 1934, pp. 122-23.

[66] Peter Collins, *Notes on the Centenary of the Faculty of Engineering of McGill University,* c.1971, p. 13.

[67] "Deborah," Letter headed "Neither Male Nor Female," *Montreal Star,* March 10, 1937.

[68] Faculty of Applied Science, *Minute Book,* No. 11, October 22, 1934 to September 24, 1940, pp. 133-34.

[69] Frank P. Chambers, Letter to Dean E. Brown concerning "Committee on Admission of Women into Architecture," October 29th, 1937.

[70] "She Believes Architecture is a 'Natural' for Women," *Montreal Star,* June 21, 1944.

[71] Marilyn Lemieux, letter to Margaret Gillett, September 1979.

[72] Letter from Acting Dean Chas. M. McKergon to Miss Mary Blair Jackson, July 20, 1942. MUA 1640/4y.

[73] Faculty of Engineering *Minute Book* No. 12, October 21, 1940 to December 17, 1946, p. 103.

[74] Mary B. Jackson Fowler, letter to Margaret Gillett, June 26, 1979.

[75] "Silence Reigns as Female Joins the Plumbers: Something New Has Been Added: Very Very Tasty," *McGill Daily,* October 5, 1942, p. 1.

[76] "A Woman in Engineering," *McGill Daily,* October 6, 1942, p. 2.

[77] "Lady Plumber of Engineering 1," *McGill Daily,* October 9, 1942, p. 1.

[78] "Opportune Time: McGill Engineering Image Changed to Encourage Girls," *Montreal Star,* June 17, 1963.

[79] Rose Johnstone, "Changing Patterns of Women in Engineering," CAUT *Bulletin,* Vol. 24, No. 6 (May 1976), pp. 9-10.

[80] The use of humour as a weapon against women's social progress was noted in the Introduction. Other commentators have made the same point, e.g. Kate Millett, "Hostility is expressed in a number of ways. One is laughter. Misogynist literature, the primary vehicle of masculine hostility, is both of hortatory and comic genre," *Sexual Politics,* N.Y., Avon, 1971, p. 45.

[81] Dean D.L. Mordell, letter to Mr. John Duckworth, 25th October, 1960. MUA 1011/3.

[82] P.A. Kirby, "Plumbers Scourged for Sexism," *McGill Daily*, February 22, 1969.

[83] Senate Committee on Women, *Annual Reports*, 1977-78 and 1978-79.

[84] E.g. "Engineers' Papers Under Fire," *McGill Daily*, March 6, 1980 described ongoing criticisms of Engineering students' papers at three other Canadian universities: McMaster, British Columbia and Toronto.

[85] Samuel C. Florman, "Engineering and the Female Mind," *Harper's Magazine*, February 1978, p. 58.

[86] Anne Drummond, "Women in the McGill School of Architecture," April 1978, unpublished class research paper.

[87] Labour Canada, *Women in the Labour Force: Facts and Figures*, Ottawa, Information Canada 1976, pp. 104-108.

[88] Daniel J. Fraser, "Women Theologues," *Montreal Daily Star*, May 13, 1918.

[89] *Minutes of Meeting*, Senate of the United Theological College, June 19, 1946, p. 7.

[90] Over the years, attitudes have slowly changed. In the United Church of Canada there is now no formal barrier to the continuance of the ministerial vocation after marriage, or to the ordination of a woman already married. In practice, there is a widespread sentiment that a woman minister married to another minister is more acceptable than one married to a layman. Even in the United Church there is a long way to go before the idea is completely accepted that a wife and mother can fully sustain the ministerial vocation. The other Churches have been even more slow to move in the matter. The Presbyterian Church approved the ordination of women in 1968; the Anglican dioceses of Montreal did so a decade later.

NOTES
Chapter 8

[1] A Considerable amount of research suggests that, even in the last quarter of the 20th century, occupational prestige and desirability may be directly proportional to the sex ratio of the persons engaged in any field. For an overview see Jean Stockard *et al., Sex Equity in Education,* New York: Academic Press, 1980, especially Chpaters 4 and 5.

[2] *Prospectus of the McGill Normal School,* Montreal: 1857, p. 1.

[3] Dr. S.P. Robins, Principal of the McGill Normal School, in his *Report to the Superintendent of Public Instruction,* June, 1888.

[4] "Pay List McGill Normal School, for the quarter ending April 1, 1857." MUA 927/3/57. There also used to be other aspects of salary differentials for teachers in the Province of Quebec. These included variations between country and city, Protestant and Catholic. According to the Montreal *Witness* of March 20, 1906, the average salary at that time for a Catholic woman lay teacher was $170 p.a. in town and $117 in the country; for women Protestant teachers it was $411 p.a. in town and $170 p.a. in the country.

[5] Figure obtained from class list, Dawson Papers, MUA 927/3/51.

[6] "Special By-Laws for the Government and Discipline of the McGill Normal School," *Prospectus,* p. 2.

[7] *Ibid.* It might be noted that the students were not completely docile, submissive or brow-beaten by the regulations. In 1858, there were 52 of them with courage to sign a petition to Principal Dawson complaining of "repeated provocations" and "ungentlemanly treatment" by one of the professors. According to them, this professor considered himself "altogether out of his sphere" in teaching such a class of vulgar, common pupils for he was "accustomed to refined society" and looked down upon them because they received "gratuitous educations." Letter to Principal Dawson, February 9, 1858. MUA 927/5/17.

[8] J. William Dawson, *Fifty Years of Work in Canada,* London and Edinburgh: Ballantyne, Hanson, 1901, p. 120.

[9] Margaret Robertson of the Sherbrooke Academy to Principal Dawson, 1857. MUA 927/4/49.

[10] The Rev. E.H. Dewart of Lachute to Principal Dawson, July 24, 1857. MUA 927/7/115.

[11] W.S. Smith to Principal Dawson, 27th August, 1960. MUA 927/13/35.

[12] *Prospectus,* p. 1.

[13] "Honours in Two Generations," *The McGill News,* Vol. 14, No. 3 (June 1933), pp. 35-6 and Henry J. Morgan, *Men and Women of the Time,* 1912.

[14] The subject of her thesis (which is not included in the *McGill Thesis Directory*) was "The Anatomy of the Fucaceae" and her examining committee was Professors Dawson, Moyse and Penhallow. Faculty of Arts *Minute Book,* 1884-1895, pp. 460 and 464. MUA 48/32/1/3.

[15] Miss Binmore, B.A., "The Financial Outlook for the Women Teachers of Montreal," *The Educational Record of the Province of Quebec,* Vol. XII, No. 3 (March 1893), pp. 70-1. In an interesting footnote, Binmore explained why she preferred to use the term "woman" rather than "lady."

[16] For an analysis of the status of women in the teaching profession in Canada at this time see Alison Prentice, "The Feminization of Teaching," in Susan Mann Trofimenkoff and Alison Prentice, *The Neglected Majority,* Toronto: McLelland and Stewart, 1977, pp. 49-65.

[17] "McGill Normal School Closing Day Exercises," *Montreal Gazette,* May 30, 1903.

[18] Normal School Committee *Minutes* of meeting, 2nd April, 1890, MUA 145.

[19] S.P. Robins to the Normal School Committee, January 11, 1899, N.S.C. *Minutes,* p. 332, MUA 145.

[20] George Locke, *Report on the McGill Normal School,* MUA RG2P/641.

[21] Letter to the Editor, *The Witness,* January 13, 1906.

[22] "Call for More Normal School Instruction in Quebec," *The Witness,* October, 1906.

[23] C.W. Parmelee, Secretary, Department of Public Instruction, Quebec in a letter to J.A. Nicholson, McGill University, March 8, 1916. MUA 2P/641/8/9.

[24] Things did speed up a little after that. The second female Professor of Education (Dr. Margaret Gillett) was promoted in 1967, the third (Dr. Franga Stinson) in 1973, and the fourth (Dr. Magdelhayne Buteau) in 1976.

[25] Binmore, *op. cit.*, p. 70.

[26] E.C. Rowles, *Home Economics in Canada*, Saskatoon: University of Saskatchewan Bookstore, quoted in Robin Harris, *A History of Higher Education in Canada*, 1663-1960, Toronto: University of Toronto Press, 1976, p. 284.

[27] For a brief history of this movement, see Robin Harris, *op. cit.*, pp. 284-87.

[28] The Minister was George Ross, the man who had enforced the Order-in-Council that admitted women to University College, Toronto. See Chapter 4, note 38.

[29] Quoted in Jean Bannerman, *Leading Ladies Canada*, Belleville, Ontario: Mika, 1977, p. 184.

[30] The part played by Adelaide Hoodless here evokes memories of Lucy Simpson and her possible role in persuading Donald Smith to support higher education for women at McGill in 1884; the part she played in the establishment of a national women's organization is reminiscent of Margaret Murray and the IODE.

[31] "The Macdonald College," *Toronto News*, November 3, 1906. Macdonald College Press Clippings, 1906-1926. MUA RG 43/125.
Despite all the changes that have taken place in domestic and agricultural education, the lot of the farm wife may remain largely unappreciated. "The Invisible Pitchfork," a study prepared for the first national conference of farm women held in Ottawa in December, 1980, complained of very poor media coverage and claimed that "because of farm women's absence from the press a general ignorance exists concerning a farm woman's role in agriculture." "Public 'begins to question' whether farm women exist," *The Gazette*, December 6, 1980, p. 92.

[32] "The University of Country Life," *The Montreal Daily Witness*, November 9, 1907.

[33] J.F. Snell, "The Colourful Story of 'Mac,' " *The McGill News*, Vol. 31, No. 4 (Summer 1950), p. 41.

[34] See reminiscences of Beatrice Wyatt Johnstone in Chapter 6.

[35] "A New Canadian College," *Weekly Globe and Canadian Farmer*, Toronto, May 29, 1907. Macdonald College Press Clippings, 1906-1926. MUA RG 43/125.

[36] Professor Helen Neilson in conversation with Margaret Gillett, May 30, 1979.

[37] "The Common Round, The Daily Task," *The McGill News*, Vol. 44, No. 3 (Summer 1963), p. 35.

[38] Helen Neilson to Margaret Gillett, May 30, 1979.

[39] Maude E. Seymour Abbott, *The History of Nursing*, McGill University Publications No. 25, 1924, p. 24. According to Dr. Abbott, "The state of the hospital at the time of Miss Livingstone's advent to it beggars description, for its reputation was unsavoury, its inmates overcrowded and poorly housed, and bad sanitation, dirt and disorder prevailed." *loc. cit.*

[40] For example, M. Adelaide Nutting of Waterloo, Ontario who, in 1907, became the world's first Professor of Nursing Education at Teachers College, Columbia University, New York. "Nursing Education Department Celebrates 80th Anniversary," *T.C. Today*, Vol. 7, No. 3 (Spring 1979), p. 4.

[41] Recollections of Grace M. Fairley, April 21, 1962, quoted by Barbara Logan Tunis, *In Caps and Gowns*, Montreal: McGill University Press, 1966, p. 7.

[42] Dr. Abbott, with her inimitable enthusiasm, had supported the whole project from the beginning and was to teach a course in the History of Nursing until she retired from McGill in 1936.

[43] One particularly happy award was made to Eileen Flanagan for research in Nursing and she continued her research activities for many years as a member of the School's staff, later as Director of Nursing at the Montreal Neurological Institute and, still later, in retirement when she continued to write and publish.

[44] "Administration and Finance of School for Graduate Nurses: 1920-43," mimeo. Papers of Rae Chittick. MUA 1928.

[45] School for Graduate Nurses, *Annual Report*, 1961-62, pp. 1-2. MUA RG 38/30/133.

[46] Rae Chittick, "Some Thoughts in Retirement," May 1979, Unpublished paper sent to Margaret Gillett, p. 2.

[47] In 1980, Joan Gilchrist, a successor of Rae Chittick as Director of the School for Graduate Nurses, was one of the two women of McGill occupying endowed Chairs. The other was Joan Marsden, Strathcona Professor of Zoology.

[48] Faculty of Medicine, *Minutes,* January 8, 1952. MUA 16/263.

[49] "Department of Social Services," McGill University, *General Announcement,* 1919-1920, p. 164.

NOTES
Chapter 9

[1] "All in the Family," *McGill Reporter,* November 15, 1978, p. 2.

[2] Jessie Bernard, *Academic Women,* New York: New American Library, 1964, pp. 5-28.

[3] For an analysis of this period, see Linda Kealey, ed., *A Not Unreasonable Claim,* Toronto: Women's Press, 1979.

[4] For statistics on the relative decline of women in Canadian universities during this period, see the *Report* of the Royal Commission on the Status of Women in Canada, Ottawa: Information Canada, 1970, p. 168; and Jill McCalla Vickers and June Adam, *But Can You Type? Canadian Universities and the Status of Women,* Toronto: Clarke Irwin and MAUT. 1977. For analyses of Women's place in the Canadian economy during World War II and since, see Pat Armstrong and Hugh Armstrong, *The Double Ghetto: Canadian Women and Segregated Work,* Toronto: McClelland and Stewart, 1978; Patricia Connelly, *Last Hired, First Fired: Women in the Canadian Work Force,* Toronto: Women's Press, 1978; and Ruth Pierson, "Women's Emancipation and the Recruitment of Women into the Labour Force in World War II," in Susan Mann Trofimenkoff and Alison Prentice, eds. *The Neglected Majority,* Toronto: McClelland and Stewart, 1977, pp. 125-45.

[5] See, for example, William L. O'Neill, *Everyone was Brave: The Rise and Fall of Feminism in America,* Chicago: Quadrangle, 1969; and Andrew Hacker, "E.R.A.—R.I.P. Women, not men, defeated the amendment for equal rights," *Harpers,* September 1980, pp. 10-14.

[6] Carrie Derick, "Report of the Delta Sigma Society," *McGill Fortnightly,* Vol. IV, No. 10 (February 19, 1896), p. 189.

[7] Constitution of the Alumnae Society.

[8] "Alumnae Work," *McGill Fortnightly,* Vol. 1, No. 1 (October 27, 1892), p. 119.

[9] "Once a month the Society for the Protection of Women and Children draws aside the curtain of silence and hidden things of darkness and cruel things more hurtful than blows and pitiful things that make the heart ache, spring to light. . . ." "Tales of Woe: A Morning with the Protectors of Women and Children," *Daily Witness,* Montreal March 20, 1894, p. 1.

[10] Carrie Derick, *op. cit.,* p. 191. One of Derick's own particular causes was women's health and birth control. She endorsed the controversial ideas of Margaret Sanger and resolutely put them forward at every opportunity. Prof. Bertha Meyer recalled that Derick once lectured Quebec Premier Sir Lomer Gouin on this subject—much to his embarrassment. Later he was heard to exclaim, "Comme elle m'a fait rougi, cette vieille fille de McGill!"

[11] Emmeline Pankhurst (1858-1928) was one of England's pre-eminent Suffragettes. Her Women's Social and Political Union aggressively campaigned for female suffrage and her visit to Montreal aroused some trepidation in local circles. The Montreal *Star* of December 2, 1911 tried to be reassuring. With a caption that read, "Militant Yet Womanly," it informed its readers that "The personality of Mrs. Pankhurst is far different from what one might be led to expect from the leader of the 'militant Suffragettes,' who has endured countless hardships, has been arrested and has suffered a prison sentence for the 'cause.' The slight, intelligent woman with the keen expression and the magnetic voice does not look militant in the least. The low tones of her voice, the slender hands and tapering fingers, the vivid and sparkling face form a physiological contrast. Then there is the strong instinct of humor. . . ."

[12] William Peterson, Letter to Mrs. Walter Lyman, 23rd November, 1911. MUA 59/2/P/4/2/18, p. 378.

[13] "Women Too Submissive to Men," *McGill Daily,* February 14, 1928, p. 1.

[14] Nora Morgan McCammon, Corresponding Secretary, Alumnae Society of McGill University, Letter to Miss Elizabeth Monk, May 10, 1937. MUA 1322.

[15] Marna Darragh, "McGill Alumnae," *McGill Journal of Education,* Vol. X, No. 1 (Spring 1975), p. 69.

[16] Linda Buzzell, Letter to the Editor, *McGill Daily,* December 12, 1974, p. 5.

[17] "Exit Women's Union?" and "Obituary Women's Union," *McGill Daily,* January 17 and 30, 1969.

[18] "Women's Union May Be Revived," *McGill Daily*, September 18, 1974, p. 1.

[19] "The Women Students' Council," *Old McGill, 1931*, p. 141.

[20] Most facilities of the McGill campus had been open to students of both sexes. In 1951 there was a short-lived prohibition against females entering the Arts Building by the main steps on the grounds of over-use and congestion. "Shall We Take Steps," *McGill Daily*, October 4, 1951.

[21] By 1978, it was reduced to about a third of its original size on the grounds that the student activities needed the space in the Union Building. The women made no significant protest.

[22] Laura Benne, "The *Women's Collective Press:* Its History and Present Situation," unpublished class paper, 1977.

[23] During October and November 1974, about thirty letters and ten reports had appeared in the *McGill Daily* on the subject of the *Women's Collective Press.* In language and tone they typified the forthright, "liberated" style of student rhetoric of the day, a style that Principal Dawson or Lord Strathcona or any of the old-time Wardens of R.V.C. could neither have understood nor appreciated. One letter began, "Call me a bourgeois, reactionary, fascist, sexist swine if you will, but I'm glad that the women's collective was denied exclusive control of the *Free Press.* " This drew an accolade from another male correspondent to the effect that the first writer "had big balls" and from a female reader of the *Daily*, regretting that it was necessary to resort to "phallic metaphors," diagnosing the second writer as suffering from "a common form of myopia—the inability to see beyond the end of his penis." She went on to complain that "it is just the sort of screwed up attitude that the Women's Collective could eradicate if given control of the ASUS. There has yet to be such a forum anywhere on the McGill campus where women haven't had to compromise themselves for the benefit of the male ego." To which the unabashed second correspondent responded, "Machismo is the building block of all great and noble civilizations, for God created man in his own image and woman as an afterthought. Woman was made from man's rib and men in my country make women every night, and they're glad we do. These McGillian women pretend to scorn the cold reality of machismo, all the while knowing that when they leave this protective university womb they will be on the ground, grovelling for a husband." (*McGill Daily*, October 17, 1974.)

[24] *Report of the Senate Committee on Discrimination as to Sex in the University*, February 24, 1971, p. 3.

[25] *Ibid.*, p. 21.

[26] *Ibid.*, p. 5.

[27] For an overview, see Jill McCalla Vickers and June Adam, *But Can You Type? Canadian Universities and the Status of Women*, Toronto; Clark, Irwin and Canadian Association of University Teachers, 1977.

[28] "Senate Tackles Discrimination Report," *McGill Reporter*, Vol. 3, No. 15 (March 31, 1971), p. 1.

[29] *Ibid.*

[30] Margaret Gillett, Janet Donald, Erin Malloy-Hanley, Andrea Vabalis, *A Survey of Teaching and Research on Women at McGill: Report to Principal Bell*, December, 1976.

[31] Statistics Canada and Association of Universities and Colleges of Canda, *Women in Canadian Universities: A Statistical Compendium*, Ottawa, 1975, p. 11.

[32] AUCC Report on "The Status of Women in Canadian Universities," *University Affairs*, December 1975.

[33] Minutes of Meeting of Senate, 20th May, 1970, pp. 260-61.

[34] Donna Runnalls and Barbara Scales, Letter to the Editor, *McGill Daily*, February 14, 1979, and reprinted in the *M.C.T.R.W. Newsletter*, No. 6 (Spring 1979), p. 1.

[35] Thierry Wies, *Etude préliminaire: L'impact du syndicalisme universitaire sur la discrimination salariale des femmes*, Montréal: FAPUQ, 1978.

[36] Faculty Club, *House Minutes*, Jan. 23, 1936, Vol. 1, p. 6. MUA 850/1.

[37] Frances Henry, "The Great Referendum," *A History of the McGill Faculty Club*, Montreal: The Club, 1975, p. 30.

[38] Virginia Douglas, "Reminiscences from an Earlier Period,"*Ibid.*, p. 34.

[39] Frances Henry, *loc. cit.*

[40] Frank Scott, "Some Memories of the Club,"*Ibid.*, p. 24.

[41] Virginia Douglas, *loc. cit.*

[42] Virginia Douglas, *op. cit.*, pp. 34-35.

[43] Frances Henry, *op. cit.*, p. 31.

[44] *Ibid.*, p. 32.

[45] *Report* of the Sub-Committee to Study Referendum Concerning Status of Female Members on the Basis of the Questionnaire dated 31 October 1966. MUA 850/1.

[46] Marlene Dixon, *Things Which Are Done in Secret,* Montreal: Black Rose Books, 1976, p. 117.

[47] *Ibid.*, p. 11.

[48] See *CAUT Bulletin,* November, 1973.

[49] Personal communication from Dr. June Cumberland, January 1, 1981.

[50] Jan W. Steiner, "Gambits and Gimmicks," in Edward F. Sheffield, ed., *Teaching in the Universities: No One Way,* Montreal & London: McGill-Queen's University Press, 1974, p. 124.

NOTES
Conclusion

[1] Dr. William Little to Grace Ritchie from Melbourne, January 23, 1890. Courtesy of Mrs. Esther England Cushing.

[2] Statistics Canada, *Teachers in Universities, 1978-79,* Ottawa: December 1980. The following data are extracted from Table 17, pp. 60-64.

SALARIES OF TEACHERS IN CANADIAN UNIVERSITIES, 1978-79 BY RANK AND DISCIPLINE

		Full Professor			Associate Professor			Assistant Professor		
		Professeur Titulaire			Professeur Agrege			Professeur Adjoint		
		M	F	T	M	F	T	M	F	T
All Disciplines	No.	8,154	397	8,551	10,353	1,401	11,754	6,125	1,651	7,776
	Med. $	39,250	37,000	39,100	29,700	28,550	29,550	23,500	22,700	23,300
Education	No.	521	61	582	999	223	1,222	654	271	925
	Med. $	38,700	37,550	38,600	30,750	29,750	30,600	25,200	23,700	24,500
Fine and Applied Arts	No.	251	24	275	457	76	533	305	107	412
	Med. $	35,950	36,025	35,950	27,000	28,225	27,100	21,600	21,650	21,625
Languages	No.	523	50	573	890	254	1,144	488	206	694
	Med. $	37,750	35,575	37,550	28,300	27,550	28,100	22,650	22,150	22,450
Total Humanities	No.	1,219	79	1,293	1,928	376	2,304	993	298	1,291
	Med. $	38,050	36,150	37,875	28,550	27,650	28,400	22,550	22,200	22,450
Law	No.	240	10	250	160	22	182	95	23	118
	Med. $	40,900	36,475	40,650	29,850	29,850	29,850	22,800	22,000	22,450
Psychology	No.	282	27	309	465	77	542	271	97	368
	Med. $	38,925	39,100	38,950	28,450	28,450	28,450	22,100	22,100	22,100
Social Work	No.	36	6	42	97	37	134	64	58	122
	Med. $	38,925	X	38,675	30,000	28,800	29,900	25,450	25,075	25,200
Social Sciences	No.	1,751	80	1,831	2,534	299	2,833	1,725	405	2,130
	Med. $	39,450	36,525	39,300	29,475	28,550	29,350	23,300	22,500	23,200
Household Science	No.	18	21	39	15	55	70	21	53	74
	Med. $	40,350	37,150	37,850	30,050	30,100	30,075	21,850	21,250	21,575
Library and Records Science	No.	14	8	22	17	17	34	10	15	25
	Med. $	40,450	X	40,450	32,600	30,750	31,050	24,400	22,850	23,650
Engineering and Applied Sci.	No.	933	2	935	851	7	858	323	8	331
	Med. $	38,850	X	38,850	30,600	X	30,600	23,950	X	23,900
Agriculture and Biol. Sci.	No.	744	58	802	686	103	789	420	100	520
	Med. $	39,275	37,500	39,050	29,725	29,700	29,700	22,900	21,900	22,600
Health Prof. and Occupations	No.	1,131	80	1,211	1,245	259	1,504	1,002	397	1,399
	Med. $	43,850	38,225	43,350	33,300	29,100	32,150	27,000	23,200	25,750
Math. and Physical Sciences	No.	1,463	10	1,473	1,587	53	1,640	666	55	721
	Med. $	38,500	34,550	38,500	29,400	28,000	29,350	22,725	22,400	22,700
Other	No.	141	3	144	66	5	71	37	10	47
	Med. $	43,800	X	43,700	30,050	X	30,100	23,050	23,025	23,050

[3] "A Woman of the Present," Letter to the Editor, *The Ladies Magazine* (Toronto), April 1901, p. 114.

SOURCES

Material for this book was drawn largely from primary sources. These were found mainly in the McGill University Archives (MUA), the Public Archives of Canada (PAC), the private papers of individuals, and the recollections of many persons associated with McGill. Direct references to primary sources are indicated in the footnotes. The bibliography given below is selected largely from published works consulted.

SELECT BIBLIOGRAPHY

Abbott, Maude E. Seymour. *Lectures on The History of Nursing.* Montreal: McGill University Publications, No. 25, 1924.

Altback, Philip C. *Comparative Perspectives on the Academic Profession.* New York: Praeger, 1977.

Angenot, Marc. *Les Champions des femmes. Examen du discours sur la supériorité des femmes, 1400-1800.* Montreal: Les Frères de l'Université du Québec, 1977.

Archibald, Raymond Clare. *Historical Notes on the Education of Women at Mt. Allison, 1854-1954.* Sackville, N.B.: Centennial Committee, Mt. Allison, 1954.

Argrave, James. "William Dawson, George Grant and the Legacy of Scottish Higher Education," *Queen's Quarterly,* Vol. 82, No. 1 (Spring 1975), pp. 77-91.

Armstrong, Pat and Hugh. *The Double Ghetto: Canadian Women and Their Segregated Work.* Toronto: McClelland-Stewart, 1978.

Baker, Liva. *I'm Radcliffe! Fly Me! The Seven Sisters and the Failure of Women's Education.* New York: Macmillan, 1976.

Bannerman, Jean. *Leading Ladies Canada.* Belleville, Ontario: Mika, 1977.

Beard, Mary R. *Woman as Force in History. A Study in Traditions and Realities.* New York: Macmillan, 1946.

Bernard, Jessie. *Academic Women.* New York: New American Library, 1964.

Blanc, Madame (Th. Bentzon). *The Conditions of Woman in the United States. A Traveller's Notes.* New York: Arno Press, 1972. (Reprint)

Borer, Mary Cathcart. *Willingly to School: A History of Women's Education.* Guilford & London: Butterworth, 1976.

Brittain, Vera. *The Women at Oxford: A Fragment of History.* London: George C. Harrap, 1960.

Broverman, Inge K., et al. "Sex Role Stereotypes: A Current Appraisal," *Journal of Social Issues.* Vol. 28, No. 2 (1972), pp. 59-77.

Buckmaster, Henrietta. *Women Who Shaped History.* London: Macmillan, 1966.

Burdett, Gillian Mary. "The High School for Girls, Montreal," Unpublished M.A. Thesis, McGill University, 1963.

Burwash, Nathaniel. *The History of Victoria College.* Toronto: Victoria College Press, 1972.

Carroll, Berenice A. *Liberating Women's History: Theoretical and Critical Essays.* Urbana: University of Illinois Press, 1976.

Casgrain, Thérèse F. *Une femme chez les hommes.* Montreal: Editions du Jour, 1971.

Clarke, Edward H. *Sex in Education.* Boston: James R. Osgood, 1873.

Cleverdon, Catherine. *The Woman Suffrage Movement in Canada.* Toronto: University of Toronto Press, 1974.

Collard, Edgar Andrew, ed. *The McGill You Knew.* Toronto: Longman, 1976.

Committee on the Status of Women in Universities. *Second Report on the Progress Made by AUCC Member Institutions Regarding the Status of Women.* Ottawa: AUCC, 1977.

Conable, Charlotte Williams. *Women at Cornell: The Myth of Equal Education.* Ithaca and London: Cornell University Press, 1977.

Connelly, Patricia. *Last Hired, First Fired: Women in the Canadian Work Force.* Toronto: Women's Press, 1978.

Conway, Jill. "Perspectives on the History of Women's Education in the United States," *History of Education Quarterly,* Vol. 14 (1974), pp. 1-12.

Cook, Gail C.A., ed. *Opportunity for Choice. A Goal for Women in Canada.* Ottawa: Statistics Canada—C.D. Howe Research Institute, 1976.

Cook, Ramsay and Wendy Mitchinson, eds. *The Proper Sphere. Woman's Place in Canadian Society.* Toronto: Oxford University Press, 1976.

Cross, Barbara M. *The Educated Woman in America.* New York: Teachers College Press, 1965.

Curzon, Lord C. of Kedleston. *Principles and Methods of University Reform.* Oxford: Clarendon, 1909.

Dawson, J. William. *Educational Lectures, Addresses, ec. 1885-1895.* Montreal: H. Ramsay, n.d.

Dawson, J. William. *Fifty Years of Work in Canada, Scientific and Educational.* Edited by Rankine Dawson. London and Edinburgh: Ballantyne, Hanson, 1901.

de Beauvoir, Simone. *The Second Sex.* Trans. H.M. Parshley. New York: Alfred A. Knopf, 1953.

Dixon, Marlene. *Things Which Are Done in Secret.* Montreal: Black Rose Books, 1976.

Farello, Eline Wilson, ed. *A History of the Education of Women in the United States.* New York: Vantage, 1970.

Firestone, Shulamith. *The Dialectic of Sex—The Case for Feminine Revolution.* New York: Bantam, 1970.

Flexner, Abraham. *Medical Education in the United States and Canada.* New York: Carnegie Foundation for the Advancement of Teaching, Bulletin No. 4, 1910.

Fox, Greer Litton. "Nice Girl: Social Control of Women Through a Value Construct," *Signs,* Vol. II, No. 4 (Summer 1977), pp. 805-17.

Frankford, Roberta. *Collegiate Women: Domesticity and Career in Turn-of-The-Century America.* New York: N.Y. University Press, 1977.

Frost, S.B. "A Transatlantic Wooing," *Dalhousie Review,* Vol. 58, No. 3 (Autumn 1978), pp. 458-70.

Frost, Stanley Brice. *McGill University: For the Advancement of Learning,* Vol. 1, 1801-1895. Montreal: McGill-Queen's University Press, 1980.

Frost, Stanley & Sheila Rosenberg. "The McGill Student Body: Past and Future Enrolment," *McGill Journal of Education,* Vol. XV, No. 1 (Winter 1980), pp. 35-53.

Gardner, W.J. *Colonial Cap and Gown.* Christchurch, N.Z.: University of Canterbury Press, 1979.

Gilder, George F. *Sexual Suicide.* New York: Quadrangle/N.Y. Times Book Co., 1973.

Gillett, Margaret. *A History of Education: Thought and Practice.* Toronto: McGraw-Hill of Canada, 1966.

Gillett, Margaret. "The Majority Minority—Women in Canadian Universities," *Canadian and International Education,* Vol. 7, No. 1 (June 1978), pp. 42-50.

Gillett, Margaret. "The Seahorse Society," *McGill Journal of Education,* Vol. X, No. 1, (Spring 1975), pp. 40-48.

Gillett, Margaret. "Sexism in Higher Education," *Atlantis,* Vol. 1, No. 1 (Autumn 1975), pp. 61-81.

Gillett, Margaret, Janet Donald, Erin Malloy and Andrea Vabalis. *A Survey of Teaching and Research on Women at McGill—A Report to the Principal.* Mimeo. December 1976.

Ginzberg, Eli, *et al. Life Styles of Educated Women.* New York: Columbia University Press, 1966.

Goodsell, Willystine. *The Education of Women. Its Social Background and its Problems.* New York: Macmillan, 1923.

Goodsell, Willystine, ed. *Pioneers of Women's Education in the United States —Emma Willard, Catherine Beecher, Mary Lyon.* New York: AMS Press, 1931.

Hacker, Carlotta. *The Indomitable Lady Doctors.* Toronto: Clarke Irwin, 1974.

Hale, Mrs. (Mary). *Women's Record or Sketches of all Distinguished Women from the Creation to A.D. 1868—*arranged in Four Eras with Selections from Authoresses from Each Era. New York: Harper & Bros., 1870 (3rd ed.).

Harris, Robin S. *A History of Higher Education in Canada, 1663-1960.* Toronto: University of Toronto Press, 1976.

Howe, Florence, ed. *Women and the Power to Change.* Essays sponsored by the Carnegie Commission on Higher Education. New York: McGraw Hill, 1975.

Innis, Mary Quayle, ed. *The Clear Spirit. Twenty Canadian Women and Their Times.* Toronto: University of Toronto Press, 1966.

Jean, Michèle, ed. *Québecoises du 20th siècle.* Montreal: Messageries du Jour, 1974.

Kealey, Linda, ed. *A Not Unreasonable Claim: Women and Reform in Canada, 1880s-1920s.* Toronto: Women's Press, 1979.

Kerry, Esther W., ed. *The Dorothy King Memorial Lectures.* Montreal: McGill University, 1971.

Kerry, Esther W., comp. *The Alumnae Book.* Montreal: McGill University School of Social Work, 1975.

Labour Canada. *Women in the Labour Force: Facts and Figures.* Ottawa: Information Canada, 1976.

Lakoff, Robin. *Language & Woman's Place.* New York: Harper Colophon, 1975.

Lange, Helene. *Higher Education of Women in Europe.* New York: D. Appleton, 1890.

Langstaff, A. Macdonald. "Will Quebec Call Her Portias to the Bar?" *The Home,* Montreal, October, 1929, pp. 5-8.

Langton, H.H. *Sir Daniel Wilson: A Memoir.* Toronto: Nelson, 1929.

Leacock, Stephen. "We are Teaching Women All Wrong," *Colliers,* 68 (Dec. 31, 1921), p. 15.

Lederer, Wolfgang. *The Fear of Women.* New York: Grune and Stratton, 1968.

Lerner, Gerda. *The Woman in American History.* Menlo Park, Calif.: Addison-Wesley, 1971.

Maass, Carol E. *The Story of the Women Associates of McGill.* Montreal: Women Associates of McGill, 1968.

MacDermot, H.E. *History of the School of Nursing of the Montreal General Hospital.* Montreal: The Alumnae Association, 1940.

MacDermot, H.E. *Maude Abbott. A Memoir.* Toronto: Macmillan, 1941.

MacMechan, Archibald. "Of Girls in Canadian College," *The Atlantic Monthly,* Vol. XCII (Sept. 1903), pp. 402-06.

Macmillan, Cyrus. *McGill and Its Story, 1821-1921.* London: John Lane, 1921.

Maddison, Isobel. *Handbook of British, Continental and Canadian Universities, with Special Mention of the Courses Open to Women.* New York: Macmillan, 1899.

Massey, Alice Vincent. *Occupations for Trained Women in Canada.* Toronto: J.M. Dent, 1920.

McGuigan, Dorothy Gies. *A Dangerous Experiment.* Benton Harbor, Mich.: R.W. Patterson, 1970.

McMurray, Dorothy. *Four Principals of McGill.* Montreal: Graduates' Society of McGill, 1974.

Media Club of Canada. *Canadian Women of Note*—Biographies on Computer. Institute of Behavioural Research, York University, 1981.

Mill, Alex., ed. "The Position of Women in Universities," *Congress of the Universities of the Empire—Report of Proceedings.* London: Hodder & Stoughton, 1912.

Mill, John Stuart. *The Subjection of Women (1869).* London: Everyman, 1974.

Miller, Carman, ed. *A History of the McGill Faculty Club.* Montreal: The Club, 1975.

Millett, Kate. *Sexual Politics*. New York: Avon, 1971.

Morgan, Henry James, ed. *The Canadian Men and Women of the Time*. Toronto: William Briggs, 1912.

Morgan, Henry J. *Sketches of Celebrated Canadians and Persons Connected with Canada from the Earliest Period in the History of the Province Down to the Present Time*. Quebec: Hunter, Ross & Co., 1862.

Morgan, Henry J. *Types of Canadian Women and of Women who are or have been connected with Canada*. Vol. 1. Toronto: William Briggs, 1903.

Munroe, David. "Teacher Education at McGill," *McGill Journal of Education*, Vol. VI, No. 1 (Spring 1971), pp. 29-40.

National Council of Women of Canada. *Women of Canada. Their Life and Work*, For distribution at the Paris International Exhibition, 1900. Reprinted 1975.

National Library of Canada. *Women in Federal Politics: A Bio-Bibliography*. Ottawa: National Library, 1975.

Neatby, Hilda—ed., Frederick W. Gilson & Roger Graham. *Queen's University*, Vol. 1, 1841-1917. Montreal: McGill-Queen's University Press, 1978.

Neff, Wanda. *Victorian Working Women*. New York: Columbia University Press, 1929.

Notman, W. and Fenning Taylor. *Portraits of British North Americans*. Montreal: Notman/Lovell, 1865.

Oakeley, Hilda D. *My Adventures in Education*. London: Williams and Norgate, 1939.

O'Neill, William L. *Everyone was Brave: The Rise and Fall of Feminism in America*. Chicago: Quadrangle Books, 1969.

Pilkington, Gwendoline. "A History of the National Conference of Canadian Universities, 1911-1961." Unpublished Ph.D. Thesis, University of Toronto, 1974.

Prentice, Alison. *The School Promoters*. Toronto: McClelland and Stewart, 1977.

Preston, William T.R. *The Life and Times of Lord Strathcona*. Toronto: McClelland, Goodchild & Stewart, 1915.

Rashdall, Hastings. *The Universities of Europe in the Middle Ages*. 2 Vols. Oxford: Clarendon, 1895.

Ronish, Donna A. "The Development of Higher Education for Women at McGill University from 1857 to 1899, with special Reference to the Role of Sir John William Dawson." Unpublished M.A. Thesis, McGill University, 1972.

Rogers, Marvin A. *A History of the McGill Dental School*. Montreal: Faculty of Dentistry, McGill University, 1980.

Roscoe, Muriel V. *The Royal Victoria College, 1899-1962: A Report to the Principal*. Mimeo., 1964.

Rossi, Alice S. *The Feminist Papers: From Adams to de Beauvoir*. New York: Columbia University Press, 1973.

Royce, Marion V. "Arguments Over the Education of Girls—Their Admission to Grammar Schools in this Province," *Ontario History,* Vol. LXVII, No. 1 (March 1975), pp. 1-13.

Saint-Jean, Idola, ed. *Morceaux à dire.* Montreal: Librarie Beauchemin, 1936.

Sawula, Lorne V. "Notes on the Strathcona Trust," *Canadian Journal of History of Sport and Physical Education,* Vol. 5, No. 1 (May 1974), pp. 56-61.

Schirmacher, Kaethe. *The Modern Woman's Rights Movement: A Historical Survey.* Translated from the German by Carl Conrad Eckhardt. New York: Macmillan, 1912.

Sheffield, Edward F. *Teaching in the University: No One Way.* Montreal: McGill-Queen's University Press, 1974.

Shortt, Elizabeth Smith. *Historical Sketch of Medical Education of Women, Kingston, Canada.* Ottawa: Private Printing, 1916.

Slack, Zerada. "The Development of Physical Education for Women at McGill University." Thesis for High Diploma of the McGill School of Physical Education, 1934.

Snell, John Ferguson. *Macdonald College of McGill University. A History from 1904-1955.* Montreal: McGill University Press, 1963.

Stacey, Judith, *et al.*, eds. *And Jill Came Tumbling After—Sexism in American Education.* New York: Laurel, 1974.

Stanton, Elizabeth Cody, Susan B. Anthony, Matilda Joslyn Gage, eds., *History of Woman Suffrage, 1848-61.* New York: 1881.

Statistics Canada. *Teachers in Universities, 1978-79.* Ottawa: Statistics Canada, 1980.

Stephenson, Marylee, ed. *Women in Canada.* Toronto: General Publishing, 1977 (rev. ed.).

Strathcona & Mount Royal, Donald Alexander Smith. *Imperialism and the Unity of the Empire.* London: McCorquodale & Co., 1901.

Stockard, Jean, *et al. Sex Equity in Education.* New York: Academic Press, 1980.

Stone, Lawrence. *The Family, Sex and Marriage in England, 1500-1800.* New York: Harper & Row, 1977.

Summers, Anne. *Damned Whores and God's Police—The Colonization of Women in Australia.* Ringwood, Victoria: Penguin, 1975.

Thompson, Nancy Ramsay. "The Controversy Over the Admission of Women to University College, University of Toronto." Unpublished M.A. Thesis, University of Toronto, 1974.

Trofimenkopf, Susan Mann and Alison Prentice, *The Neglected Majority.* Toronto: McLelland and Stewart, 1977.

Trueman, Margaret. *Women of Courage.* New York: William Morrow, 1976.

Tunis, Barbara Logan. *In Caps and Gowns. The Story of the School for Graduate Nurses, McGill University, 1920-1964.* Montreal: McGill University Press for the Flora Madeline Shaw Memorial Fund Committee and the Alumnae Association of the School for Graduate Nurses, 1966.

Vickers, Jill McCalla and June Adam. *But Can You Type? Canadian Universities and the Status of Women.* Toronto: Clarke, Irwin & Co., in association with CAUT, 1977.

Vincus, Martha, ed. *Suffer and Be Still. Women in the Victorian Age.* Bloomington & London: Indiana University Press, 1973.

Walsh, Mary Roth. *Doctors Wanted: No Women Need Apply.* New Haven, Conn.: Yale University Press, 1977.

Wheeler, Ethel R. *Famous Blue Stockings.* New York: John Lane, 1910.

Willison, Marjory (MacMurchy). *The Woman—Bless Her. Not so Amiable a Book as it Sounds.* Toronto: Gundy, 1916.

Willson, Beckles. *The Life of Lord Strathcona and Mount Royal, 1820-1914.* London and Toronto: Cassell, 1915.

Wollstonecraft, Mary. *Thoughts on the Education of Daughters with Reflections on Female Conduct in the More Important Duties of Life.* New York: Garland, 1974. (Facsimile ed.)

"Women and Education," *Harvard Educational Review,* Special Issues, Vol. 49, No. 4 (Nov. 1979) and Vol. 50, No. 1 (Feb. 1980).

Women on Campus—The Unfinished Liberation. New Rochelle, N.Y.: Change, 1975.

Woods, Letha. "Finding a Room of Their Own," *The McGill News,* Vol. 56, No. 2 (Summer 1975), pp. 8-11.

Index